MR. SMITH
GOES TO
TOKYO

Japanese

Cinema

MR. SMITH
GOES TO
TOKYO

under

the

American

Occupation,

1945–1952

Kyoko

Hirano

SMITHSONIAN INSTITUTION PRESS • WASHINGTON AND LONDON

Editor and typesetter: Peter Strupp/Princeton Editorial Associates
Production editor: Jack Kirshbaum
Designer: Linda McKnight

Library of Congress Cataloging-in-Publication Data
Hirano, Kyoko
    Mr. Smith goes to Tokyo : the Japanese cinema under the
American occupation, 1945–1952 / Kyoko Hirano.
        p.   cm.
    Includes bibliographical references (p.   ) and indexes.
    ISBN 1-56098-157-1
    1. Motion pictures—Japan—History. 2. Motion picture
industry—Japan—History. 3. Motion pictures—Censorship—
Japan.
    PN1993.5.J3H57   1992
    791.43′0952′09044—dc20   92-7033
                                            CIP

British Library Cataloging-in-Publication data available

96 95 94 93 92   5 4 3 2 1

∞ The paper used in this publication meets the minimum
requirements of the American National Standard for Permanence
of Paper for Printed Library Materials Z39.48-1984.

Jacket illustrations:
Front: The emperor's new clothes from *The Japanese
Tragedy*. Courtesy of the Library of Congress and by
permission of Nippon Eiga Shinsha.

Back: Setsuko Hara (l.) and Shuji Sano in *A Toast to the
Young Miss (Here's to the Girls)* [*Ojosan ni kampai*]
(1949), directed by Keisuke Kinoshita. Courtesy of the
Kawakita Memorial Film Institute and Shochiku Co.,
Ltd.

FOR

THE

MEMORY

OF

JAY LEYDA

CONTENTS

FOREWORD

Kyoko Hirano's magnificently researched, ground-breaking investigation of Japanese cinema under the American occupation inaugurates a new series of books at the Smithsonian Institution Press. Although this series on film and television will be centered on the United States, many of the forthcoming books—like Hirano's—will have a critical international dimension.

Fifty years ago, the U.S. government was mobilizing its American motion picture resources to help fight a war against Germany, Italy, and Japan. Frank Capra, whose *Mr. Smith Goes to Washington* (1939) had helped rekindle Americans' faith in their political traditions and essential goodness, joined the U.S. Army to make such propaganda masterpieces as *Prelude to War* (1942) and produce the unreleased *Know Your Enemy: Japan* (1944). Meanwhile, officials in the civilian Office of War Information (OWI) sought to induce Hollywood producers to project an image of the nation as democratic and egalitarian, which often meant glossing over or obscuring un-comfortable truths about American life. They typically saw the war as a revolutionary turning point in the battle for individual rights and justice, in which Americans were fighting for the Four Freedoms—freedom of speech and religion, freedom from want and fear. Although Roosevelt "New Deal-ers" sometimes found a receptive audience in Hollywood, they were fre-quently challenged by conservative Republicans such as Louis B. Mayer and Paramount chief Y. Frank Freeman. This relationship between the OWI and Hollywood, which involved both script consultation and film review by the domestic branch and censorship through export licensing by the overseas branch, did not end with the war but was reconfigured and transferred to Japan and other occupied territories. Hirano's book shows how this happened.

In Japan, former OWI officals and other occupation personnel found themselves with much stronger supervisory clout in the post–World War II Japanese industry than their wartime predecessors had ever enjoyed in Hollywood. Many of the same concerns, however, carried over. Earlier fights for democracy and women's equality and against Japanese militarism and feudalism continued, but under new conditions and on a new terrain. One can therefore situate *Mr. Smith Goes to Tokyo* in relation to two other significant works of film history: Clayton R. Koppes and Gregory D. Black's *Hollywood Goes to War,* which examines the ways in which the U.S. govern-ment, particularly the OWI, sought to bend Hollywood to its own needs and purposes; and Joseph Anderson and Donald Richie's *The Japanese Film,* which devotes a chapter and a half to the occupation period.

Both Anderson and Richie were in Japan during the occupation pe-riod and write about it from their firsthand experience. Without invalidat-ing the broad outlines of their historical narrative, Hirano quietly but forcefully engages their analysis of this period. Dates are clarified, and names, backgrounds, and political motivation are given to heretofore anonymous officials.

Focusing on the documentary *The Japanese Tragedy,* which was alter-nately fostered and then banned by occupation personnel, Hirano explores the ways in which Japanese filmmakers were sometimes caught between radical New Dealers such as David Conde and ascendant anticommunist cold warriors. Hirano is able to avoid the ideological value judgments, perhaps inescapable during the Cold War, that sometimes weaken other accounts of Japanese cinema after the war. Rather she displays a remarkable ability to offer a sympathetic understanding of individual motivations on both sides of the American-Japanese interchange. While not forsaking her critical judgment, she retains an exceptional sensitivity to the complexities of the postwar situation.

U.S. occupation forces were intent on concealing the full measure of their intrusion into Japanese life. Any discussions of censorship were themselves censored. It is only through extensive research in the archival riches left by the occupying forces that Hirano has been able to piece together the nature of U.S. supervision and control. Moreover, Hirano is one of the few historians whose research moves easily and comprehensively between English and Japanese sources. It is her ability to dig out and then synthesize information and documents in both languages, her familiarity with both cultures, that helps to make this book such a significant contribution to historical scholarship. *Mr. Smith Goes to Tokyo* is not only an outstanding example of film history, but a model for cross-cultural understanding in an era when nationalistic backlash vies with the need for transnational, global cooperation.

Charles Musser

ACKNOWLEDGMENTS

This book could not have been completed without the generous assistance of many people and organizations on both sides of the Pacific. I ask in advance for the forgiveness of those whose names I may have neglected to mention here.

For crucial financial support, I would like to thank the following organizations and individuals: the Fulbright Commission, which made possible my postgraduate study at New York University; Jay Leyda and the Chair's Fund of the Department of Cinema Studies, for helping to support my research in Japan in 1984; the Sankei-MacArthur Memorial Travel Grant, which also helped pay for this 1984 research trip to Japan; the Toyota Foundation Humanities Grant, which made possible the final year of my dissertation writing; and the Association for Asian Studies–Northeast Asia

Council Grant, which assisted my research trip to the McKeldin Library of the University of Maryland in 1989. I would also like to thank the Publication Assistance Program of the Japan Foundation for their generosity in helping to produce this book.

I owe a sincere debt of gratitude to the staff members at several institutions: Ann Harris and her staff at the Study Center of the New York University Department of Cinema Studies; Kashiko Kawakita, Akira Shimizu, and their staff at the Kawakita Memorial Film Institute; Sadamu Maruo and his staff at the National Film Center of the Museum of Modern Art, Tokyo; Noritsune Takagi and his staff at the Institute of Journalism and Mass Communication, University of Tokyo; Kenichi Hoshi and Sakae Edamatsu of the National Diet Library, Tokyo; the staff of the Japanese Association for the Study of the History of the Occupation; the employees in the Modern Military Section of the National Archives, Washington, D.C.; the staff of the National Records Center, Suitland, Maryland; the office of the MacArthur Memorial, Norfolk, Virginia; Frank Joseph Schulman and his staff at the McKeldin Library of the University of Maryland; Charles Silver of the Museum of Modern Art, New York; and the staff of the Japan Society, New York.

This study began as a doctoral dissertation at New York University, and I am most grateful to Robert Sklar, whose academic standards and generous guidance truly helped me to shape my ideas. I would also like to thank William Simon, the chairperson of the Department of Cinema Studies at New York University, and the members of my dissertation committee, who worked with me over the course of several years: Robert Sklar, Brian Winston, Charles Musser, and Antonia Lant, and Carol Gluck of Columbia University. I am especially fortunate to have been able to work with Jay Leyda, who believed in my work and supported it until his death in 1988.

In addition to those who took the time to share with me their knowledge by agreeing to be interviewed for my dissertation (their names are gratefully listed in the bibliography), the following people were of particular assistance in providing and sharing various kinds of information: Elizabeth Nichols, Rinjiro Sodei, Yuki Sato, Kazuto Ohira, Makoto Iokibe, Takao Ogasawara, Yasuhiro Kobayashi, Kazuo Mayuzumi, Hidetoshi Sotooka, Eiki Kogo, Tamaki Tachibana, Thomas Burkeman, Marlene Mayo, John Dower, Sebastian Swann, Sey Nishimura, Cheryl Silverman, Michael Yoshitsu, Susan Noble, Michiko Onaka Perry, Norman Wang, Bill and Mary Kochiyama, Ned Loader, Natsuno Nakamura, and David Desser. Glenn Stulpin, Julie Abrams

Sacks, Judy Ames, and Akira Tochigi helped in proofreading. In addition, I owe Steve Sacks special gratitude. He proofread and critiqued the entire text, and, more importantly, without his patience and encouragement over the years this book would not have been possible.

Finally, I would like to thank my editors—Charles Musser, Mark Hirsch, Ruth Spiegel, Jack Kirshbaum, and Peter Strupp—for their invaluable assistance in formalizing this book.

An earlier version of Chapter 3 appeared in Robert Sklar and Charles Musser, eds., *Resisting Images: Essays on Cinema and History* (Philadelphia: Temple University Press, 1990), 200–224, and in *Radical History Review* 41 (1988), 67–92.

Japanese names are written with given names first and family names second, following the Western order. At the first reference to a film, the Japanese title, if known, is given in parentheses after the English title used in the censorship documents; subsequent references have only the English title.

Translations are mine except direct quotations from the original materials written in English.

INTRODUCTION

As the economic and political importance of the relationship between Japan and the United States has dramatically increased in recent years, the peoples of the two countries have begun to discuss the cultural aspect of their relationship more seriously. Throughout much of this century—but especially since the end of World War II—the Japanese people have enthusiastically adopted American culture, from jazz to jeans, into their daily lives, and have followed avidly new phenomena and trends in the United States, from New York's hottest clubs to the latest beach fashions in California. Perhaps as much for the insights they give into American life as for their intrinsic entertainment value, American films have been popular in Japan almost continuously since the 1910s, except during World War II. America may import many of its cars and most of its consumer electronics from Japan, but the trade balance in the film industry is in America's favor by at least one hundred to one. American film stars have always become heroes and heroines in Japan as well—witness the year 1991, in which the most popular star among Japanese audiences was not Toshiro Mifune but Arnold Schwarzenegger.

On the other hand, Americans have only recently begun to show widespread interest in the culture of the country that has fast become the second superpower in the world economy. Although their curiosity may be motivated largely by fear, Americans are nonetheless studying the Japanese language, enjoying Japanese food, and even seeing Japanese films more than ever before.

One of the crucial periods in this bilateral relationship was the one in which many of our attitudes and policies vis à vis one another were initiated—the postwar occupation period. Beginning in August 1945, the Japanese greeted the Americans not as hated enemies but as powerful conquerors. On their side, the Americans turned from the task of destroying their former foes to that of transforming the hard-core militarism with which the Japanese had been inculcated into American-style "democracy." The current Japanese economic success, and the nation's virtually complete rehabilitation in the eyes of most nations (with the notable exception of some of the Asian countries it invaded during the war), are at least partly attributable to the success of the American occupation.

This study is an attempt to recount how, under these unique historical circumstances, the two nations met (and often locked horns) on the field of cinema, a popular cultural form that both have loved passionately. It is my hope that shedding light on this all-important era will put the current trans-Pacific tensions into perspective, and perhaps even inspire solutions for the future.

THE AMERICAN OCCUPATION OF JAPAN: HISTORICAL BACKGROUND

With the Japanese imperial government's decision to accept the Allies' Potsdam Declaration, World War II was brought to an end on August 15, 1945. The Japanese defeat meant the liberation of Korea, China, and other Asian nations from military domination and colonial rule. For the Japanese people, the war's end not only brought to a close a century of military rule, but also marked the beginning of the occupation by the Allied countries. The period of the occupation continued until the Peace Treaty came into effect on April 28, 1952. It was Japan's first experience in her two thousand–year history of subjugation by an ethnically and culturally alien occupying army.[1]

The occupation was officially carried out by the Occupation Council for Japan, consisting of the United States, the USSR, China, and Australia (on behalf of Britain). However, its direction was soon taken over for most practical purposes by the United States government, acting through the Supreme Commander, Allied Powers, (SCAP), Gen. Douglas MacArthur. (The term also refers to the occupation government as a whole.) Thus, it may be properly termed the "American Occupation." The Allied occupation's film policy was almost completely decided and implemented by the Americans, and this American influence is the exclusive focus of this work.

The occupation government's principal task was to eliminate completely from the Japanese government and society all militaristic and fascistic institutions and tendencies, which it believed to have been the essential causes of the Pacific war. Its other role was to reconstruct Japan according to its own "democratic" ideals, to prepare the conquered country for a role in the new world order. Hence, the American occupation wrought upon Japan drastic political, economic, and social changes, whose influence on Japanese cultural values is still extremely significant.

The occupation forces introduced to Japan basic democratic rights and progressive policies, such as universal suffrage, freedom of assembly and speech, agrarian reform, and unionized labor. These reforms are embodied in the Constitution of Japan (which superseded the 1889 Imperial Constitution), originally drafted by General MacArthur's staff in February 1946 and put into effect on May 3, 1947. This new constitution has remained controversial in Japan up to the present day, because conservatives have condemned it as the "MacArthur Constitution" or the "American-imposed Constitution."

One of the most unusual ideas of this new constitution is embodied in its ninth article, the renunciation of war and the instruments thereof, which earned for it the label of the "Peace Constitution" from the left wing. At the beginning of the occupation, General MacArthur's idea was to make Japan the "Switzerland of Asia"—a peaceful country completely free of aggressive military tendencies. Yet this clause was doomed to be first ignored and then betrayed by its own creators, the Americans, as the rise of the Cold War and other factors changed the international political situation. The occupation government was eventually to regret its early liberal policies, which were later seen as nourishing leftism and communism.

Thus we may distinguish the first part of the occupation period, the phase of idealistic reconstruction, from the second part, the retrogressive reorganization of Japan to conform with the ideology of the Cold War. The turning point was General MacArthur's banning of the first nationwide general strike called by labor unions, set for February 1, 1947, on the grounds that the nation's economic stability would be endangered.

Finally, less than two months after the outbreak of the Korean War on June 25, 1950, the Police Reserve Army was established at the suggestion of the American government. This force, under the Truman Doctrine, later became the still-controversial "Defense Army" in 1954. The United States wanted Japan as a faithful ally in the Far East. At the same time, to support such a policy, the occupation government began to push for a hasty recovery of the Japanese economy, despite protests from the other Asian countries that had so recently suffered under Japanese military rule. These countries feared that the economic recovery program would rekindle Japan's imperialistic ambitions.

During the initial stage, the occupation government had a strong sense that its mission was to revolutionize Japan. Many occupation staff members were young New Dealers who believed in the institution of social and economic reforms under the auspices of governmental authority. Because they were implementing their ideas abroad, and in a way that did not directly affect their own country, the Americans could experiment ambitiously without fear of provoking the voters' opposition or causing confusion.

However, as Cold War attitudes and anticommunist rhetoric came to dominate American political discourse, conservatives began to take over positions of power in the occupation government. They regarded the early policies as too radical. Their fear of communism led them to retract many of the liberal policies of the first phase so as not to risk the growth of a strong left-oriented labor movement or other such potential dangers.

OCCUPATION FILM POLICY

In determining the policies of the occupation, the Americans distinguished between the Japanese military rulers and the general public, believing that the latter could be reeducated according to the new democratic values. One might say that the occupiers' inherent optimism (and perhaps their sense of manifest destiny) led them to cross the Pacific to conduct social experiments in a foreign country that had, in their eyes, been led astray by an evil militaristic cabal. They believed that, if these experiments succeeded, the Japanese, a people traditionally inclined to collaborate with any kind of authority, would indeed become the sort of nation of which America could approve.

The occupation authorities planned to use the Japanese media to re-mold the Japanese mind. Film (along with radio, theater, and the print media) was one of the important vehicles for the occupation government's propaganda. During the war, the U.S. Army had commissioned first-rate Hollywood film directors—including Frank Capra, John Ford, and Ernst Lubitsch—to make a series of documentary films intended to mobilize the American people's support for the "war for justice and democracy." The effectiveness of using films for indoctrination was proved by studies commissioned by the U.S. government. For example, a study in 1942 on the effects of the four films from the *Why We Fight* documentary series found that these films were "far superior" to the orientation lectures given to soldiers.[2]

At the same time, the U.S. government, with the help of a group of scholars, learned of the propaganda power of the dramatic, realistic, well-made Japanese prewar and wartime feature films, which were a far cry from the crude propaganda one might have expected.[3] The occupation government would see the great potential of the use of film in democratizing Japan. The American occupiers knew that the artistic and technical standards of Japanese cinema were more than adequate for their purposes, and they set about taking advantage of their censorship powers to control the selection of films that the Japanese people would be allowed to see.

The occupation government abolished the Japanese wartime restrictions on political freedom and the secret police that had enforced them. The wartime government's totalitarian, nationalistic administration of the film industry, and the straitjacket of regulations that it had established, were similarly done away with.

However, not content with merely destroying these institutions and their policies, the occupation government almost immediately began issuing its own commands and prohibitions. As early as September 22, 1945, the Civil Information and Education Section (CIE) of the occupation government summoned representatives from each Japanese film company, and told them that the occupation government would like the Japanese film industry to pursue the principles of the Potsdam Declaration and help reconstruct

Japan positively. At the same time, this section established the three principal
aims of the occupation: complete disarmament and demilitarization of the
nation, encouragement of individual liberties and fundamental human rights,
and directing Japan to contribute to world peace and safety. To pursue these
principles, desirable subjects and directions for films were suggested by this
section.

In October 1945, CIE demanded preproduction censorship of film
projects and scripts, which had to be translated into English by the film
companies for this purpose. Completed films were also to be shown to CIE,
and censored by the Civil Censorship Detachment (CCD), which was under
the direct control of military intelligence. This double censorship officially
began in January 1946 and continued until June 1949, when the Film Ethics
Regulation Control Committee (Eirin) was established under the auspices of
the Japan Film Association (the present-day Japan Association of Film
Producers). CIE's postproduction censorship continued until the end of
the occupation in April 1952. Although it was headed by military personnel, the mission of this section, staffed primarily by civilians, was educational guidance, and it was thus considered to have conducted civil
censorship. On the other hand, CCD was mostly staffed with military
personnel and was primarily engaged in military intelligence and counterintelligence activities; it was thus considered in general to have conducted military censorship.

In November 1945, CIE announced a list of subjects with which the
Japanese film industry was forbidden to deal. At the same time, the occupation government banned 236 Japanese films made between 1931 and 1945 as
"ultra-nationalistic," "militaristic," or "propagating feudalism."

By means of these directives, prohibitions, and recommendations, the
Americans endeavored to redesign the political and ideological orientation
of Japanese film in precise detail. Inevitably, these minute directives were
sometimes applied arbitrarily, to the great annoyance of the filmmakers.

Moreover, in response to changes in the international political climate,
the American censors became increasingly antileftist and anticommunist,
and reshaped the course of Japanese cinema to reflect their newly conservative ideology. This change led to bitter struggles with the film industry labor
union movement, as exemplified by the three strikes at the Toho Studio
between 1946 and 1948, the last of which was suppressed by the Japanese
police aided by the American occupation forces. The outbreak of the Korean
War further exacerbated the anticommunist direction.

OCCUPATION SCHOLARSHIP: A REVIEW

Study of the Allied Occupation period in Japan has recently become quite popular in both Japan and the United States in the fields of history, political science, economics, and intellectual history.[4] This phenomenon has resulted partly from the declassification by both governments of more and more documents from this period.

During the past decade, two important controversies have arisen among scholars of the Allied Occupation. The first is over a theory presented by Japanese literary critic Jun Eto, who since 1978 has argued that censorship during the occupation severely repressed Japanese literature and other forms of cultural expression. He uses the documents of the agencies responsible for that censorship to support his argument that they were destroying Japanese traditionalism and national identity.[5] Eto's theory has been welcomed by Japanese conservatives, who regard the policies of the American occupation as having been imposed on an unwilling populace, and who consider the occupation years to have been a tragic period for Japanese nationalism.

On the other hand, this thesis has been criticized by Japanese and American scholars and intellectuals who believe that it ignores the Japanese people's own desire to democratize their country. The latter group also claims that Eto understates the oppressiveness of the Japanese government's prewar and wartime censorship, thus overemphasizing the impact of the occupation programs, in order to rationalize his ideological biases and to further his personal influence within conservative Japanese institutions. Furthermore, I agree with this group that, although Americans imposed new ideological limitations on Japanese literature, film, and journalism, the occupation censors simultaneously helped liberate Japan from the yoke of feudalism and from political oppression of another kind.

The second controversial theory was presented in 1980 by the American historian Peter Frost. He argues that there was no distinct "reverse course" or shift in political direction during the occupation period. Frost instead emphasizes the consistency of the American occupation's efforts to protect Japan, and ultimately American interests, from communist takeover, and ascribes any change in policy to the ideological evolution of the Japanese people themselves.[6]

On the contrary, what I find more noteworthy than the consistencies described by Frost are the struggles behind the formulation and implementation of occupation censorship policy. The officials involved came from diverse backgrounds, with widely varying agendas for the reformation of Japanese cinema. Moreover, they were human beings, and their actions reflect many of the contradictions inherent in human behavior within institutions. Ultimately, it was the dynamic interactions among the occupation officials themselves, and between them and the Japanese authorities and film people who were under their jurisdiction, that determined the course of occupation film policy. Although mine is a historical study of life during a specific period under a specific institution, it is a history of individuals as well.

The history of this film policy is full of paradoxes and apparent contradictions between the occupation's stated goals and the methods it chose to achieve them. These contradictions are largely due to the rise of anticommunist sentiment among the American censors. Far from the ideological consistency described by Frost, the "reverse course" in the area of cinema began much earlier than has been generally understood. Even before General MacArthur's banning of the general strike in February 1947, a drastic change in film policy had already occurred.

This change was symbolized by the resignation of David Conde, the first chief of the Motion Picture Unit of the Motion Picture and Theatrical Branch of CIE, in July 1946. Having participated in wartime psychological warfare operations at the Office of War Information, Conde enthusiastically pursued the liberalization of the Japanese film industry. It is widely believed that Conde was forced to resign his position because of his role in the making of Fumio Kamei's *The Japanese Tragedy* [*Nihon no higeki*], a 1946 Japanese documentary critical of capitalism and of the imperial system, which the American military censors found objectionable. There has been much speculation among Japanese and Americans as to whether or not Conde was actually a communist or communist sympathizer.[7]

Preceding Conde's departure, in late May 1946, Brig. Gen. Kermit (Ken) Dyke, the head of CIE, returned home to resume his prewar work at the National Broadcasting Company. Dyke, known for his liberal democratization policy, was succeeded by the conservative Lt. Col. D. R. Nugent, who headed this section until the end of the occupation. Journalist Mark Gayn believes that Dyke might have been maneuvered out of his position by the conservatives, who labeled him a "commie"—a typical instance of the forcing out of officials who, although not necessarily radical or even liberal, were enthusiastic reformers and open to such ideas as the unionization of labor.[8]

Although a few Japanese filmmakers have written memoirs on the subject in Japanese, to date there has been no comprehensive study of the occupation's effect on cinema, in either Japanese or English. Nonetheless, this period of cinema history is of particular interest. Noel Burch has written that the 1930s were the golden age of Japanese cinema, whereas others have argued that the real golden age began in the 1950s.[9] Although it is not my intention to claim this title for the period between 1945 and 1952, the occupation period is nonetheless highly deserving of serious and thorough investigation. This era has been the sole period in the century-long history of Japanese film during which the industry was under the direct control of a foreign country.[10] Although Japanese cinema has always been influenced by foreign ideas and styles (especially those of Hollywood), the immediate postwar period was unique in that Japanese filmmakers were force-fed American ideas.

Since Japan was opened to the West in the mid-nineteenth century, the influence of foreign ideas on indigenous Japanese values and cultures has led the Japanese people to consider the meaning of modernization. The American occupation exposed them to still more new values, which resulted in drastic sociopolitical and cultural changes in Japan. Some Japanese Marxist historians argue that these changes would have occurred without the American occupation; because the postwar period must be considered a stage in the inexorable historical tide leading from capitalism to communism, the occupation may have merely speeded them up at best.[11]

Interestingly, Japanese leftist filmmakers tend to emphasize the continuity between the prewar and postwar progressive movements by downplaying the importance of the American influence. For example, screenplay writer Yoshikata Yoda, who was active in the proletarian film movement in the early 1930s, and director-writer Kaneto Shindo claim that the Japanese labor and human rights movements were only temporarily interrupted by the repressive wartime government. According to these filmmakers, the postwar groups were merely continuing the activities of the prewar groups, although there is no doubt that the occupation helped them achieve some of their goals.[12]

GOALS AND STRUCTURE OF THIS VOLUME

One aim of my study is to explore both the continuity and the changes in cultural and social values embodied in Japanese films made during the occupation period. I hope to show that, although Japanese film may seem to have been fundamentally transformed on the surface owing to the changed political circumstances (determining the *context* of filmmaking), its essential values (represented in the *text* of the films) were not changed by the occupation. American historian John Dower argues that the purification of the populace through the purging of evil wartime militarism is one of the main themes of the occupation period Japanese cinema; similarly, the wartime Japanese cinema concentrated on the purification of the populace through the purging of Western-influenced decadent and individualistic ideas.[13] I will also argue that, despite what one might expect, occupation period films and wartime films alike were substantially apolitical. Wartime films generally avoided clear statements or representations of what the Japanese were fighting for. Some of the important postwar films—even including Akira Kurosawa's *No Regrets for Our Youth* [*Waga seishun ni kui nashi*] (1946), widely considered to be a shining example of the postwar "democratization film" genre—are similarly nebulous about what democratic values actually are.

I will discuss the transition from the wartime period to the postwar period of the Japanese film industry in chapter 1. This chapter will also clarify the structure of the American occupation's film censorship bureaucracy. Chapter 2 will examine what kinds of subjects and themes were prohibited by the Americans for being antidemocratic or otherwise objectionable. In chapter 3, I will discuss how the depiction of the Japanese emperor was censored by the Americans through a study of Kamei's film *The Japanese Tragedy*, the only film banned by the Americans during the occupation period, in order to illustrate the changing nature of the occupation's policies.

I will then examine what kinds of subjects and themes were recommended by the Americans, in chapter 4. Chapter 5 is a case study of Kurosawa's highly successful *No Regrets for Our Youth*.

Chapter 6 will recount the history of the strikes at the Toho Studio, one of the most crucial episodes in the development of the postwar Japanese film industry. The effects of Cold War politics on occupation film policy in Japan will be discussed in chapter 7. The last chapter will briefly examine how the occupation affected post–occupation period Japanese filmmakers.

I had originally hoped to see as many Japanese films as possible from the occupation period. However, achievement of this goal was limited not only by their sheer number (approximately one thousand films were made in Japan between September 1945 and April 1952), but also because prints no longer exist of many of them. I saw many wartime and postwar Japanese and American films at the Museum of Modern Art, at the Japan Society, and at commercial theaters in New York, as well as at the National Archives in Washington, D.C., and at the National Film Center and at commercial theaters in Tokyo. Especially helpful was the Japan Society's film series, *Japan at War,* consisting of twenty-seven wartime and immediate postwar films, prints for some of which were made available from the Library of Congress.[14] Furthermore, during the last few years, a number of Japanese films from the 1930s through the 1950s have become available in videocasette form from commercial distributors, and I took advantage of this new technology.

In addition to the films themselves, Japanese screenplays originally submitted to CIE and CCD, then censored and kept at the U.S. National Archives, proved to be the most interesting primary sources for this study, along with the directives, memoranda, conference records, and correspondence of the occupation government, which are also kept at the National Archives and the MacArthur Memorial in Norfolk, Virginia. CIE's documents are stored in microfiche form at the Japanese Diet Library in Tokyo, where I spent several months doing research. I also read Japanese film magazines and periodicals, including local film fan club newsletters and high school students' film magazines, submitted to and censored by the occupation government, which are kept and catalogued in the Gordon W. Prange Collection at the McKeldin Library of the University of Maryland.

I conducted interviews with Japanese directors, producers, screenplay writers, studio liaisons with the occupation government, and critics who were working during the occupation period. Although many of them did not remember the details of events that occurred over forty years ago, most were very cooperative. My attempts to reach former occupation officials on the American side were not as successful. I am deeply grateful to have been able to talk directly with some important people, both Japanese and American, who have since passed away.

My secondary sources included books, magazines, and newspapers concerning film and the occupation policy. I visited Tokyo twice to do research at the Kawakita Memorial Film Institute Library, Shochiku Studio's library, and the library at the University of Tokyo Institute of Journalism and Mass Communication.

I hope that this study will contribute to film history by illuminating a heretofore unstudied area, and will constitute a significant addition to the scholarship of Japanese film history written in English. In addition, I would like to offer my work as a testimonial to the importance of the continuing cultural relationship between the United States and Japan, two of the most important nations in today's world.

1

FROM
WAR TO
OCCUPATION

JAPANESE PREWAR AND WARTIME CENSORSHIP

The first Japanese censorship leading to the suppression of film took place early in this century, within twelve years after the introduction of the moving image exhibition from the West in 1896. The suppression was intended to protect images of the royal family from subversive ideas and children from bad influences. In February 1908, a French film called *The Reign of Louis XVI* [*Le Règne de Louis XVI*] (1905) was banned by the police because of its depiction of the people attacking the royal palace. But the film's exhibitor did not give up so easily. The film's title was changed to *The Curious Story of North America: The Cave King* [*Hokubei kidan: Gankutsuo*] and the subject became the story of a wealthy American bandit couple, who at the film's end are attacked by the people in collaboration with the police. The alterations

Zigomar (1911), directed by Victorin Jassex. Courtesy of the Kawakita Memorial Film Institute.

were smoothly and easily made, by changing the lines recited by the *katsuben* or *benshi* (narrator for silent films).[1] In November 1911, a French detective film, *Zigomar,* was released and became very popular. It was imitated during the following year by numerous Japanese filmmakers, who produced Japanese Zigomars, "new" Zigomars, and female Zigomars. Because many children were alleged to have imitated the crimes portrayed in these films, any films whose titles included the word "Zigomar" (including the French sequels to the original film) were outlawed in October 1914.[2]

The police adopted the Film Control Regulations (Eiga torishimari kisoku) in 1917.[3] Censorship was conducted by local governments through business-licensing laws until 1925, when the first Japanese national law on film censorship, Censorship Regulation of Moving Pictures or "Films" (Katsudo shashin "firumu" ken'etsu kisoku) was issued in 1925.[4] The law forbade the showing of some films to those under fifteen years old, in order "to maintain public decorum." Furthermore, it required theaters to have separate seating sections for male and female spectators, "to maintain custom," and, in order "to maintain hygiene," mandated intermissions between showings. This regulation also protected copyrights and distribution rights. As for censorship, it required film producers to submit completed films along with "explanatory scripts" for government approval. The government reserved the right to cut films or to ban their distribution altogether.[5]

This law was superseded by the more comprehensive Film Law (Eigaho), promulgated on April 5, 1939, and put into effect on October 1, 1939. It was a product of the militaristic and nationalistic political climate dating from the Sino-Japan Incident of 1937.[6] The Film Law was modeled after the Nazi Spitzenorganisation der Filmwirtschaft by the Japanese government, which had seen the propaganda role that cinema had played in Nazi Germany. The first article proclaimed that "The purpose of this law is to promote the quality of film and the sound development of the film industry so that films can contribute to the nation's cultural development."[7] According to film director and writer Nagisa Oshima, until 1939 the Japanese government's film policy had been carried out primarily by means of postproduction censorship. After 1933, the government had suggested general goals and practices for the film industry, until it assumed total control of the industry under the 1939 Film Law.[8]

As for preventive measures, the law authorized the deletion and suppression of scenes that might be harmful to public order and behavior. Impermissible scenes included

1. Those that might profane the dignity of the royal family or undermine that of the empire.
2. Those that might inspire questioning of the Imperial Constitution.
3. Those that might damage the political, military, diplomatic, economic, or other interests of the empire.
4. Those that might hamper the enlightenment and propaganda basic to the exercise of national policies.
5. Those that might disturb good decorum and/or otherwise threaten the national morality.
6. Those that might undermine the proper use of the Japanese language.
7. Those that were notably inferior in production technique.
8. Others that might obstruct the development of the national culture.

The law also encouraged the production of films "useful to the national education" and required the showing of these films. It also introduced the new terms "culture films [bunka eiga]," documentary films intended to "contribute to the nourishment of the national spirit and national intelligence," and "current films [jiji eiga]," newsreel films showing current events so that "the nation will be informed about domestic and foreign situations." Theaters were obliged to show one or more of each of these types of films along with each feature film.[9]

The Film Law authorized the government to require licensing of producers, distributors, and theater operators. By canceling or refusing licenses, the government could ban its opponents from working in the film industry.

As the war progressed, censorship became stricter. In 1940, Naimu-sho, the Ministry of Internal Affairs, issued the following regulations concerning films:

1. National movies of healthy entertainment value with themes showing persons ready to serve are hoped for;
2. Comedians and vaudeville satirists will be restricted if they overdo their comedy;
3. Slice-of-life films, films describing individual happiness, films treating the lives of the rich, scenes of women smoking, drinking in cafes, etc., the use of foreign words, and films dealing with sexual frivolity are all prohibited;
4. Films showing industrial and food production, particularly the life in farming villages, should be presented; and
5. Scripts will be censored before production and will be rewritten until they fully satisfy the Censorship Office of the Ministry of Internal Affairs.[10]

Under the 1925 law, the government had suppressed mainly explicit sexual scenes and openly subversive ideas. While nudity was of course prohibited, even kissing and hand-holding were not allowed on the screen.[11] If a foreign film included a kissing scene, the climactic moment was cut out so that it looked as if the faces of the man and woman approached each other and then quickly moved away. In response to censorship demands, companies that imported foreign films had to cut the parts at issue, insert fades, and change the Japanese subtitles deftly, in order to smooth the narrative flow in the censored films.[12] Adultery by women was also prohibited to avoid disturbing public morality (although men's adultery was not questioned), and such scenes were mercilessly cut out, often leaving the story completely confusing.[13]

As for subversive thoughts, the government was most nervous about anything reflecting negatively on the royal family. Even shots of chrysanthemums or of patterns similar to the flower were strictly censored, because the chrysanthemum is the emblem of the Japanese royal family. Director Daisuke Ito wrote that a scene of a peasant sitting near chrysanthemums was ordered cut from one of his films.[14] Wheel patterns on costumes and on the background screens in period films were also censored. Censors would count the number of petals of chrysanthemum-like flowers to be sure that it was not the same as that of the royal family's emblem.[15] As in the case of 1905's *The Reign of Louis XVI*, even foreign films about foreign monarchs were carefully screened. For example, from René Clair's *The Last Millionaire* [*Le Dernier Millionaire*] (1934, released in Japan in 1935), the censors demanded deletions including not only kissing and "immoral" love scenes but also scenes that supposedly profaned the royal family.[16]

Communist ideas were also suppressed. For example, a close-up of a communist book title was not allowed.[17] Some films espousing leftist ideas—for example, those in the "tendency films (keiko eiga)" genre—survived because, according to Masaru Shibata, the film producers had taken pains to avoid potentially problematic expressions.[18] The tendency films, seeking to "encourage, or fight against, a given social tendency" stemmed from the economic and social crisis of the 1920s. Owing to the severe repression of the proletarian movement by the government, films of this genre had disappeared by the beginning of the 1930s.[19] However, traces of their ideology may be found in later films, e.g., *Osaka Elegy* [*Naniwa erejii*] (1936), directed by Kenji Mizoguchi and written by Yoshikata Yoda. Before its release, *Osaka Elegy* was found problematic by the censors and its distribution suspended. However, after summoning the director and producer to a hearing, the Ministry of Internal Affairs allowed the film to be released without deletions.[20]

Under the 1939 law, broader interpretations of their legal prerogatives enabled the wartime authorities to consolidate further their ideological control over the film industry. They strictly imposed a standardized morality based on an austere life-style and an unquestioning sense of dedication to the war effort. The drinking scene in Kajiro Yamamoto's *Horse* [*Uma*] (1941) was ordered cut because "it was in contravention of the ban on daytime alcohol consumption."[21]

The families of soldiers leaving for the front had to be portrayed as proud, with no sadness or misgivings. This of course was contrary to reality, and filmmakers with heart tried to express more authentic human feelings. One of the best-known examples is Keisuke Kinoshita's *Army* [*Rikugun*]

Hideko Takamine (r.) in *Horse* [*Uma*] (1941), directed by Kajiro Yamamoto. Courtesy of the Kawakita Memorial Film Institute.

(1944), which includes an unobstructed long-take shot of an obviously emotional and agitated mother following her departing son on a crowded street. Because the Army believed that the audience would interpret her emotional state as anguish and sympathize with this unacceptable sentiment, it began to regard this director as dangerous. Many have praised Kinoshita as an antiwar hero for such taciturn resistance, whereas others, like director Masahiro Shinoda, have reservations. Shinoda argues that this scene is ambiguous, and could also be construed as showing the mother's enthusiastic and heroic sacrifice of her son to the war effort.[22] If the Army's interpretation had been more clearly justifiable, the censor would certainly have cut the scene. Film critic Tadao Sato believes that contemporary viewers were conditioned to recognize this scene as an expression of natural human feelings, but that every Japanese was obliged to overcome such private feelings for the more important national cause of the war effort.[23]

Although occasionally, such ambiguity survives in Japanese wartime films in which the true intention of the filmmaker is hard to determine,

Kinuyo Tanaka in *Army* [*Rikugun*] (1944), directed by Keisuke Kinoshita. Courtesy of the Kawakita Memorial Film Institute.

more explicitly subversive scenes were not permitted. Masahiro Makino has described his method of silent resistance under similar circumstances. In the scene in his musical *Miss Hanako* [*Hanako-san*] (1943) in which a newly married wife is supposed to be happy about her husband's departure, the couple put on masks of the type used in folk festivals. When her mask trembles, the audience would understand that she is crying under it. Then her husband comes to her, saying "You should not cry." She takes off her mask, tears shine, she smiles, and martial music starts on the soundtrack as the two walk away in a field of pampas grass (considered the most ordinary and least unpatriotic flower at a time when only the cherry blossom was recognized as the symbol of sacrifice). This beautifully lyrical scene naturally upset the censors and was cut.[24]

Such an obvious challenge to the government's idea of acceptable emotions could not survive censorship. However, other sources list different reasons for the suppression of this scene. According to Tadao Saito, who was a publicity representative for the film, the last scene upset the censors be-

From left to right, Reizaburo Yamamoto, Katsuhiko Haida, Hideko Takamine, and Yukiko Todoroki in *Miss Hanako* [*Hanako-san*] (1943), directed by Masahiro Makino. Courtesy of the Kawakita Memorial Film Institute.

cause it appeared that the couple donned masks to play hide-and-seek in the field. The censors thought this "too frivolous" for a scene portraying a husband about to leave for the front. Saito claimed that the censors were not even aware of the covert antiwar message of the scene; nonetheless, most of it was cut out.[25] According to film critic Rentaro Kyogoku, it was the scene of the wife dancing madly while trying to overcome her sadness under her mask that upset the censors.[26]

Actress Isuzu Yamada recalled the situation as follows:

... I had to play the role of a heroine whose lover is going to war just as they are finally to marry. I felt that it was a lie to express happiness at sending the lover off to war, suppressing the heroine's sadness, as was then demanded by the government. I could not make films that were really human and moving. I was, so to speak, forced to play a soulless human being, like a hollow grain. However, my audience seemed to be most moved by my underlying sadness while trying to portray the heroine happily sending her lover off.[27]

Susumu Fujita in *Sanshiro Sugata* [*Sugata Sanshiro*] (1943), directed by Akira Kurosawa. Courtesy of the Kawakita Memorial Film Institute.

Therefore, it seems that neither the filmmakers nor the audience was satisfied with these emotionally distorted films. The film companies were merely carrying out the government's orders and filmmakers were following their companies' requests.

The censors commonly deleted scenes that they considered "Anglo-American" (although frequently no one but the censors themselves could detect the Anglo-American influence). Kurosawa resentfully cited the examples of the birthday party scene in his wartime screenplay, *The San Puguita Flowers* [*San-puguita no hana*], and the so-called love scene in *Sanshiro Sugata* [*Sugata Sanshiro*] (1943), both of which were regarded as "Anglo-American." The former was never allowed to be filmed, owing to Kurosawa's dispute with the censor, and the latter was ordered cut by the censors.[28] Makino also remembered that several scenes from *Miss Hanako* were so labeled and therefore cut. He does not understand how a scene of a young actress appearing with a Pekinese dog, or one of the hero and heroine

Yoko Yaguchi (l.) and Ichiro Sugai in *The Most Beautiful* [*Ichiban utsukushiku*] (1944), directed by Akira Kurosawa. Courtesy of the Kawakita Memorial Film Institute.

walking together, singing with their shoulders swaying, could be "Anglo-American."[29]

Makino guessed that the wartime censors did not like scenes with Western music. However, this criterion seemed to be applied rather arbitrarily, for Kurosawa mentioned that the censors did not find the martial music of John Philip Sousa "Anglo-American" in his *The Most Beautiful* [*Ichiban utsukushiku*] (1944).[30] In many cases, it was more likely that the censors simply wanted to enjoy their power over the filmmakers, and, whenever they could not think of a legitimate reason to cut something, they would use one of the convenient labels.[31]

There were frequent incongruities in the implementation of censorship policy. For example, scenes in which Japanese Navy officers are playing bridge—a British card game—were allowed to be included in some Japanese war films, even though the Japanese were then fighting the British in Southeast Asia.[32]

Hiroshi Kikuchi, an influential writer and playwright who had become Daiei Studio's president in March 1943, complained during the war of the narrow-mindedness of film censorship policy. He criticized the censors' prohibition of undesirable characters in contemporary settings. Gangsters, leftists, and drunkards were not to appear on the screen even if they were to be shown as awakening to the importance of the national cause during the course of a film. Kikuchi claimed that it had become impossible to portray dramatic or interesting situations, owing to the lack of clear conflict between good and evil. He concluded that this problem had been created by the censors, who were too nervous about having to take responsibility for decisions that might later be condemned by their superiors.[33]

In this solemn atmosphere, the censors insisted on the "primacy of spirituality," as if to hide Japan's comparative lack of resources. They based their judgments on such abstract ideas as the "seriousness of the [film's] subject" and its "sincerity,"[34] to the dismay of filmmakers, who needed more practical and concrete guidelines.

The belief that the Pacific war was a war between Japanese "spirituality" and American "materialism" or "science" was widely propagated in Japan. It was obvious that American science and technology were more advanced than those of Japan, and Japanese filmmakers, who knew the extent to which filmmaking is based on modern technology, thus found it harder to rationalize the claims of Japan's ultimate superiority.

Tsutomu Sawamura, a screenplay writer and one of the most enthusiastic war policy propagandists of the Japanese filmmaking community, argued as follows: America's material supremacy was based on "American aggressive fighting power and spiritual inferiority." Furthermore, in contrast to the Western view of one God governing human beings on earth and saving their souls after death, every Japanese could himself become a god by "crystallizing divinity." Although Japan had progressed toward becoming a perfectly divine society, other nations had not "purified" themselves as Japan had. To defeat these people of "animalistic nature," Japan needed war-making power as well as spiritual power. Thus, Japanese films should help defeat the nation's technologically superior American enemy by emphasizing Japan's spiritual primacy, for example by promoting the *kamikaze* (meaning divine wind) suicide missions, and pointing out that their pilots were assured of becoming divine.[35] The emphasis on spiritual purity was thus connected with the fanatic patriotism, propagated by war films, that required complete submission and self-sacrifice to the emperor and the national cause.

Japanese war films preached that, in fighting the more technically advanced Americans, each Japanese must kill ten enemy Americans by a suicide mission. In order to indoctrinate the importance of Japanese spirituality into the minds of viewers, these films repetitiously portray their characters bowing in the direction of the Imperial Palace of Tokyo and to the Shinto shrine altars inside houses, headquarters, and warships. These ritualistic gestures were also mandated in everyday life during the war. The reverence for the symbolic altars sometimes becomes obsessive. For example, in *Torpedo Squadrons Move Out* [*Raigekitai shutsudo*] (1944), written and directed by Kajiro Yamamoto, the Americans attack a South Pacific island under Japanese military rule. The Japanese restaurant proprietress on the island begs a Japanese officer to let her kill a captured American pilot— not because he killed people on the island, but because she simply is infuriated that "the blue-eyed, corn-like, red-haired" American "dared to ruin the god"—while the camera shows her destroyed shrine altar.

AMERICAN PREPARATION FOR THE OCCUPATION FILM POLICY

On the other side of the Pacific, the Americans had begun to prepare for the occupation of Japan in 1943. The principal participants were governmental bodies, including the Department of War, the Department of the Navy, the Office of War Information, the State-War-Navy Coordinating Committee, and the Office of Strategic Services. The Japanese and Americans differed greatly in their attitudes toward their opponents. As soon as the war broke out, the American government began to train Japanese language officers and encourage the study of Japanese society and culture. The title of the film *Know Your Enemy: Japan* (commissioned by the Department of War, supervised by Frank Capra, written by Joris Ivens and others, and completed in 1944) sums up neatly the American concern with understanding their foe. This effort helped launch the careers of many now-prominent Japanologists, such as Donald Keene, William Theodore de Bary, and Herbert Passin.[36]

In Japan, the government made "American and British Devilish Beasts" the slogan of the era. The teaching of English was prohibited in schools; occidental customs were frowned upon; Japanese who had been brought up or educated in Western countries (except Germany and Italy) were suspected as spies. The hysteria led to the banning of the English words "play ball," "strike," and "foul" in baseball; they were replaced by awkward Japanese translations.

Of course, American films, which had always been the most popular and lucrative foreign films in Japan, had been controlled since 1935, when the government decided to impose importation restrictions and censorship on American films. In 1938, the limit of one hundred features per year and the revised restrictions on remittances were decided through negotiation; however, the Japanese government failed to fulfill its part of the agreement.[37] After Pearl Harbor, all American films were banned and confiscated, and only films from the Axis and neutral countries were allowed to be shown.

In America, too, hysterical anti-Japanese sentiment (more than anti-German or anti-Italian) obviously existed and was encouraged in the wartime American public. Japanese-Americans living on the West Coast were relocated to inland internment camps. However, the American government at least was practical enough to value the study of the enemy's culture for strategic purposes. Americans also had to learn quickly about Japan, because there had been almost no education in Japanese language or culture before the war, in contrast to the situation in Japan, where English language and literature had been taught at schools, and the Japanese had adopted elements of American culture to which popular films had exposed them.

Japan's strategy for winning the war relied on the cultural purification of the Japanese people, while the Americans sought victory through a thorough understanding of their foe. From this contrast, one may draw many conclusions regarding the differences in the two nations' histories and their reasons for being at war in the first place.

The Japanese wartime government considered using seized American films for psychological warfare operations; for example, the soundtrack of Gone With the Wind (1939) was once considered for use in a radio broadcast to American soldiers to make them homesick and demoralized.[38] However, it seems that, in contrast to the activities of the American Office of Strategic Services, there was no systematic research by the wartime Japanese government on American films as a key to American cultural and psychological patterns. The Department of War thoroughly studied Japanese films in order to collect intelligence and to understand the Japanese culture.[39] They took great interest not only in the films' subjects, but also in their themes, cinematic technique, and dramatic effect. The Research and Analysis Branch of the

Office of Strategic Services issued a report entitled "Japanese Films: A Psychological Warfare" that analyzed "the themes, psychological content, technical quality, and propaganda value of twenty recent Japanese films." This report pointed out that the most important theme of wartime Japanese feature films was "self-sacrifice." When the heroes and heroines are confronted by the choice between the pursuit of their private happiness based on family ties or romance and their obligation to the national cause, they invariably find the latter more important than the former. The process by which they reach this decision is emotionally highlighted and dramatized.[40]

Japanese war films tended not to portray hideous enemies or to rationalize the war as a struggle for democracy, justice, and civilization.[41] On the other hand, American war films carefully manipulated and juxtaposed contrasting images to portray "our side" as the heroic guardian of humanity. They took the same care to show "our enemy" as cold-blooded, treacherous, and inhuman. They thus tried to inspire their audience to fight for the good cause by destroying the enemy.[42]

However, the report concluded that the artistically and technically superior Japanese films were greatly effective as "the vehicle for nationally-controlled propaganda" owing to their dramatic and realistic power. Frank Capra, Alexander Korda, Samuel Spewack[43] and other directors then active in Hollywood saw sample films in the spring of 1943. They agreed unanimously that these films were very effective, and expressed doubts as to whether they themselves could compete with this type of film. Capra, who was producing and making war propaganda films and whose feature films the occupation forces would consider among the best representations of American ideas of "democracy,"[44] mentioned one of the films, entitled *Chocolate and Soldiers* [*Chokoreto to heitai*] (1938), directed by Takeshi Sato: "We cannot beat this kind of thing. We make a film like that maybe once in a decade. We haven't got the actors." (By that he meant actors capable "of restrained acting and emphasis by underacting.")[45]

Based on a newspaper story, *Chocolate and Soldiers* is about a family whose father at the China front collects the premiums on chocolate bar wrappers and sends them to his children at home. After the father is killed in battle, his comrades keep sending the wrappers to his children. Simple, warm-hearted stories such as this were developed with great craftsmanship, making the viewers empathize with the characters. The producer of the film, Naozane Fujimoto, wrote that Bradford Smith, then an instructor at St. Paul University in Tokyo, saw the film when it was released in 1938 and was very impressed. When Smith was stationed in Japan as an occupation official at CIE, he mentioned *Chocolate and Soldiers* as an example of a humanistic film made during the war, and it was not included in the list of films banned as undemocratic.[46]

Many Japanese spectators may have felt the ludicrousness of new brides cheerfully sending their husbands off to war. At the same time, they had been prepared by nationalistic education and media propaganda to work hard and to sacrifice for the sake of their nation in a time of crisis. Furthermore, the repressive social climate of that time made it unwise to criticize such implausible situations in public. As Gordon Daniels points out, the collaboration of Japan's best directors and actors with the propaganda effort gave it credibility and effectiveness.[47]

Thus the Americans came to see the great potential for democratizing Japan through film. The same kind of propaganda power that had been used in wartime Japan was to be used in reeducating the Japanese according to occupation policies. The American wartime preparation for occupation had led the government to decide that the elimination of the militaristic wartime ideology and the dissemination of democratic ideas would be the first priorities in the occupation's program to transform Japan. To this end, the press, publishing, and the entertainment media were all to be subjected to the American occupation forces' censorship.

The idea of reeducating the Japanese through the mass media was thus paired with the idea of reform of educational institutions, and their relationship had been firmly established at an early stage in the occupation planning process.[48] Thus, the Motion Picture and Theatrical Division was placed under CIE. After the war's end, the "psychological disarmament" and "ideological reorientation" of the Japanese people were to begin. After military victory had been achieved, the ideological conflict would continue during the occupation.[49]

JAPANESE FILM AT THE END OF THE WAR

At the war's end, the Japanese film industry was operating at less than half its capacity. Because of the wartime shortage of film stock, only 845 theaters had the required governmental licenses. Of the rest, 260 had been forced to cease operation, 166 had been converted from movie theaters to other uses, and 530 had been destroyed in the Allied air raids.[50]

As for production, only three film companies (Toho, Shochiku, and Daiei) were making fictional films, and only four documentary and newsreel companies (Nichi-ei, Asahi, Riken, and Yokohama Cinema [Dentsu]) were operating. These companies had been allowed to absorb many smaller companies in order to facilitate governmental control. The Film Distribution Corporation (Eiga Haikyu Kosha) was established in 1942 to monopolize distribution. It was reorganized as the Film Corporation (Eiga Kosha) in 1945.

At the time of the Japanese surrender to the United States, Kajiro Yamamoto, the director of several very successful war films, was on location in Tateyama City on the Pacific Ocean, shooting *Straight to the Americans* [*Amerika yosoro*]. This film was designed to promote a Japanese suicidal effort upon the anticipated American invasion, which had been considered imminent at the time the film was planned. *Straight to the Americans* was unusual among war films for its use of as many as fifteen actresses, featuring such big stars as Hideko Takamine and Takako Irie. This fact alone illustrates how important the film was considered, because by then so many actresses had been evacuated from Tokyo that it was difficult to use any.[51]

On August 12, 1945, three days before the end of the Pacific war, director Yamamoto received a secret letter written by Toho studio head Iwao Mori and delivered by a special messenger from Tokyo. In this letter, Mori gave detailed orders "in case of the 'emergency,' which might happen in a few days." In that event, Mori wrote that Yamamoto should

> stop shooting and first of all send the actresses back to Tokyo as soon as possible; second, . . . make sure that no one in the crew acts carelessly in the confusion or attempts suicidal actions; and third, [remember] that the safety of the crew is the first priority, and do not worry about the possible loss or destruction of their equipment.

Reading between the lines, Yamamoto sensed that the last day of the war was not far off.

Upon the emperor's August 15 broadcast proclaiming the end of the war, Yamamoto stopped shooting immediately. That evening, the actresses were sent back to Tokyo. The rest of the crew managed to return to the Toho studio in Tokyo the next day, despite the confused railway schedule.[52]

According to one of the stars, Hideko Takamine, Tateyama was heavily bombed by American airplanes, which frequently interrupted the shooting. Contrary to Yamamoto's account, she remembered staying in Tateyama on the night of August 15, while listening to Japanese Zero fighter planes being ditched in the sea by pilots bent on suicide.[53]

Masahiro Makino, who was the head of Shochiku's Shimogamo Studio in Kyoto, was another director who had learned about the Japanese defeat before the emperor's radio proclamation. He had been engaged in shooting *The Portrait of Karachin* [*Karachin-sho*] when the USSR joined the war against Japan on August 8, 1945. The film concerned five Japanese soldiers killed on a Manchurian battlefield during the Meiji Era (1868–1912) at a time when Russia was still a Japanese ally, before the Russo-Japanese War (1904–1905). Although the film was nearly complete, the Japanese government's Information Bureau (Johokyoku) ordered him to stop production. Makino was then assigned to produce a film titled *The Song of the Destruction of Anglo-America* [*Eibei gekimetsu no uta*], with director Yasushi Sasaki and an all-star cast. Just before the production was due to begin, the project was suddenly halted by order of the company. Thus did Makino realize that Japan's defeat was imminent.[54]

At Toho's Kinuta Studio in Tokyo, director Akira Kurosawa had been shooting *The Men Who Tread on the Tiger's Tail* [*Tora no o o fumu otokotachi*]. Originally, the director had planned a period film that was to include spectacular battle scenes. However, the many horses required for these scenes were not available because of the war, and Kurosawa had to change his plan. The revised film used only one set and one location in "the imperial forest that at that time stretched right to the back gate of the studio."[55] In addition, this film did not include a single actress.

On August 15, all of the employees were summoned to the studio to listen to the emperor's proclamation. Kurosawa had been prepared for Japan's defeat. After the emperor's broadcast, Iwao Mori told his employees: "Although the war has ended, we do not have anything to do but continue filmmaking. Let's continue our daily work without being confused."[56] So Kurosawa continued with the making of his film through August and September. The film is an adaptation of a famous Kabuki play, *Kanjin-cho* (based in turn on the Noh play *Ataka*), a dramatization of a historical anecdote from the twelfth century. It is concerned with the loyalty of a subordinate named Benkei to an ill-fated warrior, Yoshitsune, and the kindness of a customs officer named Togashi to them. The studio did not believe that the postwar authorities would consider this film offensive, and thus allowed its production to continue.

From these episodes, we can understand much about the situation of the Japanese film industry around the time of Japan's defeat. On one level,

Denjoiro Okochi (far l.) in *The Men Who Tread on the Tiger's Tail* [*Tora no o o fumu otokotachi*] (1945), directed by Akira Kurosawa. Courtesy of the Kawakita Memorial Film Institute.

the industry was bending over backwards to meet the demands of the military government to make a film intended to mobilize the whole nation to fight until the death of the last man, woman, or child. For example, Daiei Studio was holding project conferences to make "light and sound entertainment films," "national films based on Japanese ethics," and "enlightening propaganda films to promote the war effort" every day until August 14, 1945.[57] At the same time, many in the industry were levelheadedly predicting Japan's defeat. It is ironic that a studio head secretly ordered his employees to avoid suicidal behavior when they were making a film on the very subject of promoting a suicidal war effort.

Had the Japanese people been truthfully informed about the progress of the war, any reasonable Japanese might have been able to predict Japan's defeat by that time. As the Makino episode shows, filmmakers were sometimes directly susceptible to the day-to-day changes of national policy, and as such were more aware of the nation's true predicament. Yamamoto later wrote that film people are in general quick to catch the latest news and gossip, which is why the wartime military authorities and police carefully monitored them, along with "those who have lived abroad for a long time, liberals, Christian ministers, writers, and newspaper journalists." He wrote that on the morning of August 7, somebody who (illegally) heard an American short-wave broadcast informed the filmmakers that an atomic bomb had been dropped on Hiroshima the day before. News of the atomic bomb was at that point being strictly suppressed by the Japanese government, which would only say that it had been "a new type of bomb." Yamamoto continued that on August 9 a colleague who went to Army headquarters saw the officers distributing their rations among themselves and drinking, and they informed the film people that the end of the war would come soon. Yamamoto continued, however, that even the alert film people could not, in the war's immediate aftermath, figure out what would happen to the film industry under the occupation.[58]

Japanese filmmakers met their country's surrender with mixed emotions. Their strongest feeling was one of relief after the long, exhausting war experience. Long before the Japanese attack on Pearl Harbor on December 7 (in Japan, December 8), 1941, Japan had been at war with China since the Manchuria Incident of 1931.[59] Japan's military government had suppressed freedom of thought and expression through censorship, and Japanese filmmakers were soon forced to collaborate with the national war effort. Not a few film directors and producers had been resentful of the wartime censorship of films conducted by the Ministry of Internal Affairs and the Information Bureau.[60] Suddenly, they felt released from these oppressive institutions, not to mention the stifling mood that had confined their filmmaking to meeting the needs of the Japanese war effort.

Their second typical response was bewilderment at the sudden changes taking place in society. They realized that the heretofore invincible Japanese empire had actually been defeated and would be occupied by foreign forces. They knew that they would inevitably be forced to help change its political, economic, social, and ideological directions. Although they understood these changes intellectually, it was difficult to accept emotionally the trauma of defeat.

The third reaction was uneasiness and fear at the prospects for the occupation of their country. Most Japanese filmmakers had collaborated with the war effort in one way or another. They realized that they would have to change drastically the ideology expressed in their films, but they did not know exactly how and to what extent. Many of them actually began to worry about the possibility of being condemned as war criminals, as many Japanese were seriously afraid of Allied reprisals. The Japanese wartime authorities had instilled in the Japanese a fear of the dire consequences of an American victory, until the overwhelming majority of them expected anything from enslavement to annihilation.[61] There had been rumors that, when Japan was defeated, the Allied forces would castrate all Japanese men and rape all the women. The Japanese remembered the atrocities that their forces had committed in the occupied areas of China, the Philippines, and other parts of Asia, and thus may have had good reason to fear similar treatment at the hands of the Allied forces. Among the filmmakers, even the Marxist Akira Iwasaki, who had suffered much wartime oppression, was anxiously wondering what would become of his nation under the enemy occupation and how it could survive, recalling the Japanese occupation of China during the war.[62]

Until they received orders from the occupation government's General Headquarters, Japanese film people decided to continue making films as best they could. Naturally, they had the common sense to stop voluntarily making films that were obviously propagandistic. In fact, more films than they had expected were soon to be banned by the occupation government as "ultranationalistic" and "feudalistic." One of these was Kurosawa's *The Men Who Tread on the Tiger's Tail*.

Kurosawa attributed the banning of this film by the occupation government to a Japanese censor at the Ministry of Internal Affairs with whom he had argued. The censor, he maintained, deliberately omitted this title from a report on Japanese films produced since the beginning of the war submitted to the occupation authorities. Kurosawa contended that American censors saw his film three years later, liked it, and lifted the ban.[63] However, it is generally believed that the film was in fact banned because it was a period film, depicting feudal loyalty. The film was actually not released until April 24, 1952, shortly before the end of the occupation.[64] The occupation documents support this record.

On April 19, 1951, Toho Studio, along with Daiei Studio, requested that the occupation government reexamine seven films on the list of films banned for release in Japan, which included *The Men Who Tread on the Tiger's Tail* and *Sanshiro Sugata*. Toho requested that particular attention and consideration be given to the former title, because, together with another Daiei film, the two were "the only films in custody which have never been released for public exhibition."[65] The two films were approved for release in Japan the following February.[66]

The filmmakers were in most cases conscious of what they were doing. Kurosawa might not have conceived of *The Men Who Tread on the Tiger's Tail* as an attempt to promote the war effort, but the Americans later decided that its theme of feudal loyalty made it suspect. Kurosawa's earlier films—*Sanshiro Sugata, The Most Beautiful,* and *Sanshiro Sugata Part II* [*Zoku Sugata Sanshiro*] (1945)—could more easily be interpreted as collaborating with and promoting the war effort, because of their theme of sublime spirituality. *Sanshiro Sugata* is about a young man's search for the true spirit of judo; the film was awarded the first prize in the National Film Competition that had been recently established by the Information Bureau. This first film of Kurosawa's was not only technically excellent, but also highly regarded by the military regime for its underlying ideology. *The Most Beautiful* depicts, in a semidocumentary manner, a group of young women drafted and assigned to work at a lens factory. The main theme was the girls' dedication to meet the production quota. *Sanshiro Sugata Part II,* a sequel to the very successful *Sanshiro Sugata,* included evil Westerners as the enemies of the noble hero.

Other films made during the war were more obviously propagandistic, and there have been numerous accounts of how influential these films were, particularly on young people, in bending the nation's will to support the war effort, despite the skepticism of some. The smallest expression of antiwar opinion was either repressed or overwhelmed by war fever. A few leftist filmmakers, such as producer Akira Iwasaki and director Fumio Kamei, were imprisoned, but more chose to survive by continuing to make films under strict governmental control.

It is not certain whether the filmmakers of the time seriously believed in forced suicide. They may have hoped that their audience would not believe in it, but nonetheless pretended enthusiasm for this idea and for the war effort in general, for the sake of appearances. They might have disliked their assigned task of promoting the war spirit, homefront productivity, and the national defense, but they could not swim against the tide of public opinion. Although they might have been aware of the absurdity of the films that they were making on themes such as the glorification of the suicidal fighting spirit, they continued to do so. They stopped only after the old Japanese regime had been abolished, and only out of fear of provoking the new Allied regime that now was to rule over their country. The studios may have shown a genuine concern for the lives of their employees, but we must also consider their lack of concern for the lives of their audience.

THE DUAL STRUCTURE OF OCCUPATION
MEDIA POLICY

The first American occupation forces landed in Japan on August 27, 1945. On that day, General MacArthur authorized the creation of the Information Dissemination Section, United States Army Forces in the Pacific, headed by Gen. Bonner Fellers. Fellers had been working as the head of MacArthur's own Psychological Warfare Branch since its creation in 1944. The new section, for all practical purposes, succeeded the Psychological Warfare Branch, and Col. J. Woodall Greene, Fellers's executive officer for psychological warfare, continued to work under him.

As Washington's wartime planning organizations had envisioned, and as the State-War-Navy Coordinating Committee and Office of War Information guidelines made clear, the Information Dissemination Section was to be in charge of an information policy whose goal was the reeducation of the Japanese people through the media. In early September, Fellers directed Greene to retain key Office of War Information and Psychological Warfare Branch personnel, including Bradford Smith, who was chief of Central Pacific Operations for the Office of War Information, and Lt. Col. Harold Henderson, a specialist in propaganda leaflets under Fellers.[67]

On September 22, the Information Dissemination Section became the Civil Information and Education section, headed by then-Col. Kermit Dyke. Dyke had been vice-president for promotion and research at NBC Radio, and during the war, had worked for the advertising section of the Office of War Information and then for MacArthur's headquarters in the Southwest Pacific as head of the Information and Education Division.[68] CIE was "charged with expediting the establishment of freedom of religious worship, freedom of opinion, speech, press, and assembly by the dissemination of democratic ideals and principles through all media of public information." It had

> the responsibility of making clear to all levels of the Japanese public the true facts of their defeat, their war guilt, the responsibility of the militarists for present and future Japanese suffering and privation and the reason for the objectives of the military occupation of the Allied Powers. It was also responsible for keeping the Supreme Commander factually informed of public reactions to the occupation and rehabilitation program in order to ensure a dependable basis for program formulation and modification of policies and plans.[69]

With the creation of this new division in the occupation government, the notion of reeducating the Japanese people through the media crystallized into concrete policy.

The occupation government exercised control over the media by means of propaganda and censorship. Propaganda was the responsibility of the Information Dissemination Section, then CIE, whose main goal was to teach American values to the occupied nation through the Japanese media, by encouraging certain values and goals and discouraging others. The second task was given to the censorship division, whose goal was to prevent the media from conveying anything that might be unsuitable or dangerous to the occupation.

General MacArthur, who had been made completely responsible in May 1945 for preparing for civil censorship in Japan,[70] landed on August 30 and established the General Headquarters, or, formally, the General Headquarters, United States Army Forces in the Pacific, in Yokohama on the same day. Two days later, on September 1, each Japanese newspaper company received a directive from the Japanese government Information Bureau ordering the suppression of news about problems caused by American soldiers. On September 3, the Information Bureau changed its policy to allow the publication of news of the inevitable violence and other problems created by American military personnel, as long as "it does not exaggerate, and adheres to the clear facts."[71] As a result, the *Mainichi Shimbun*'s Kanagawa prefecture issue of September 8, 1945, reported a total of 931 cases of crimes committed by American soldiers (9 rapes, 3 injuries, 487 thefts of arms, 411 thefts of money and possessions, 5 burglaries, and 16 others) during the first week or so of the occupation.[72]

Kokichi Takakuwa believes that these early censorship measures were taken at the request of the General Headquarters.[73] Perhaps the policy was changed because American authorities soon realized that it would be unrealistic to expect to completely suppress such news. Even though people did not hear the news in the media, it must have been impossible not to hear the stories and rumors in the street, and thus perhaps the authorities felt it wiser to give the impression of relaxing their censorship.

The Japanese surrender was officially signed on the USS *Missouri* on September 2, and General MacArthur moved to Tokyo on September 8. During the first two weeks of the occupation, General Headquarters followed Washington's guidance and for the most part kept its hands off the Japanese media. At the same time, a separate censorship operation was established under Gen. Elliot Thorpe, who had been MacArthur's chief of counterintelligence, Army Forces in the Pacific, and Col. Donald Hoover, the theater's chief censorship officer and one of the principal contributors to all past civil censorship plans for Japan. On September 3, the CCD began operations under General Thorpe, as directed by MacArthur. This agency was to engage in censoring the Japanese media as well as mail and tele-communications.[74]

The precise date upon which CIE and CCD began censorship is not clear. On September 10, the Press, Pictorial and Broadcasting Division of CCD was set up, and on October 2, CCD was formally placed under the Civil Intelligence Division of General Headquarters, when MacArthur established the office of Supreme Commander, Allied Powers.[75] Hence, General Headquarters had a double function as General Headquarters, United States Army Forces in the Pacific, which had been moved from Yokohama to Tokyo on September 17, and General Headquarters, Supreme Commander, Allied Powers, which was to administer the occupation in Japan. MacArthur led both of these organizations, and some officials, such as Dyke and Thorpe, also held positions in both.[76] The Civil Intelligence Division was to be absorbed into the office of the Assistant Chief of Staff for Intelligence (G-2) under Brig. Gen. Charles A. Willoughby in May 1946, when General Thorpe resigned.[77]

On September 12, its first statement of official policy toward the press was released by General Headquarters through the Japanese Information Bureau. It prohibited the publication of "news that fails to adhere to the truth or disturbs public tranquility, such discussion . . . [that would have harmful] effects on Japan [as it] emerges from defeat as a new nation entitled to a place among the peace-loving nations of the world, false news about Allied troop movements, false or destructive criticism of the Allied Powers and rumors." The directive threatened suspension as the penalty for noncompliance.[78]

This statement became the model for the Press Code for Japan, which was mandated on September 21, and was the first such policy document released directly from the Public Relations Section of General Headquarters, rather than by the Japanese Information Bureau. Worded along the lines of the previous directive, this Press Code further restricted editorial opinion and propaganda. It established the fundamental framework for the control of the Japanese media. By applying clauses prohibiting any news that would "disturb the public tranquility" or constitute "destructive criticism of the

Allied Powers," the occupation authorities could suppress practically any news or description that they might find inconvenient.

FILM POLICY

For a week after August 15, 1945, all theaters were closed. In its announcement concerning the reopening of theaters on August 22, the Film Corporation prohibited the distribution of films portraying chauvinistic patriotism and including war scenes, as well as all culture films and current newsreel films; ordered the reopening of theaters that had been closed during the war; and ended the restrictions on show times.[79] It is noteworthy that the Film Corporation voluntarily prohibited the showing of films on the same war themes that it had itself imposed on Japanese filmmakers until several weeks earlier. The inevitable changes that filmmakers had predicted would follow the surrender were thus being implemented a mere week after the end of the war.

Before the industry received its first directives straight from General Headquarters, the Ministry of Internal Affairs and the Information Bureau issued on September 18 a statement to the prefectural governments: "Kogyo nado shido torishimari hoshin ni kansuru ken [Concerning the Guidance and Regulation of Performances and Exhibitions, etc.]." Essentially the same as the previous order from the Film Corporation, this document repealed more specifically the wartime emergency measures. It again urged the reopening of theaters that had been closed, gave permission to run open-air shows temporarily, set guidelines for the reconstruction of theaters, and abolished the one hundred–minute length restriction for fictional films.[80] The Japanese clearly expected that the film industry, although exhausted by long ideological suppression and great physical damage, would soon recover and prosper on a larger scale in peacetime Japan.

On September 20, all film companies received a summons from the Information Dissemination Section at General Headquarters to attend a meeting two days hence. On September 22, the same day that the agency became the Civil Information and Education Section, officials including Col. Greene, Major Michael Mitchel, Bradford Smith, and David Conde addressed, through interpreter George Ishikawa, some forty Japanese film executives, producers, directors, and wartime film bureaucrats. The American officials explained that the occupation government would like the Japanese film industry to pursue the principles of the Potsdam Declaration and help reconstruct Japan positively. By abandoning nationalistic militarism in favor of developing individual liberties and human rights, Japan would never again threaten world peace.[81]

To encourage this development, the following desirable subjects and directions for films were suggested:

1. Showing Japanese in all walks of life cooperating to build a peaceful nation.
2. Dealing with the resettlement of Japanese soldiers into civilian life.
3. Showing Japanese prisoners of war formerly in our hands being restored to favor in the community.
4. Demonstrating individual initiative and enterprise solving the post-war problems of Japan in industry, agriculture, and all phases of the national life.
5. Encouraging the peaceful and constructive organization of labor unions.
6. Developing political consciousness and responsibility among the people.
7. Approval of free discussion of political issues.
8. Encouraging respect for the rights of men as individuals.
9. Promoting tolerance and respect among all races and classes.
10. Dramatizing figures in Japanese history who stood for freedom and representative government.[82]

The Americans then brought up a problem that they believed was common to Japanese film and theater:

Kabuki theater is based on feudalistic loyalty, and sets faith in revenge. The present world does not accept this morality any more. The Japanese will never be able to understand the principles of international society insofar as things such as fraud, murders, and betrayals are justified by the principle of revenge, regardless of law.

Of course, serious crimes also occur in Western countries; however, Western morality is based on concepts of good and evil, not on feudal loyalty.

For Japan to participate in international society, the Japanese people must be made to understand the basic political ideals of law and democratic representative government, respect for the individual, respect for national sovereignty, and the spirit of self-government. The entertainment media and the press should all be used to teach these ideals.

Cooperation and autonomy in the nation, the family, and the labor union are basic concepts that must, over the long years of Japanese reconstruction, become the basis of civil life. All feature films made from now on must give proper clues to make the masses understand these concepts.

Japanese films must never inspire or approve of militarism, whether it is set in the past, present, or future.

Newsreels have a very important role to play in the present situation. They are obliged to record all the facts that will contribute to the acceptance of the Potsdam Declaration, including politicians criticizing war criminals, accounts of repatriated Japanese who tell the truth about the war abroad, and the meetings of labor, industrial, and agricultural groups discussing the various problems of the reconstruction of Japan. [Original in Japanese.][83]

The first CIE directive to the Japanese film industry was thus quite detailed and concrete in clarifying the purposes of the occupation and specifying the role of film as an educational tool. The United States and its allies had fought the war to defend democratic values and practices. Having won the war, they would now impose these values and practices on the Japanese as the models on which to base the reconstruction of their society. The occupiers found that the Japanese people had been denied every basic human right under the military regime, but assumed that democracy would lead to "tolerance and respect among all races and classes." It was America's duty to tackle the difficult job of transforming the uncivilized Japanese nation into a civilized fellow citizen of the world. Films were to become instrumental in bringing about this change.

As we have seen, the civil censorship officials felt a strong antipathy toward Kabuki theater and the traditional values of loyalty and revenge, which they considered of a piece with militarism and fascism, and thus believed should be banished from the movie screen. Significantly, labor unions and basic civil rights were considered basic ingredients in the rebuilding of Japan. The prewar Japanese government's suppression of the labor union movement was well known and considered by the early occupation officials to be one of the most serious aspects of the current Japanese situation.

On October 16, the "Memorandum Concerning Elimination of Japanese Government Control of the Motion Picture Industry" was issued, liberating the Japanese film industry from the 1939 Film Law and wartime governmental supervision. The Film Corporation would end its operations in early December, to allow each film company to pursue its own production and distribution activities.

By mid-October, General Headquarters had already issued several directives restoring freedom of the press and of speech: on September 10, regarding the dissemination of news; on September 24, regarding disassociation of the press from the government; on September 27, regarding further steps toward freedom of the press and of speech; and on October 4, regarding removal of restrictions on political, civil, and religious liberties.

However, the occupation government implemented its own system of censoring film subjects and content throughout the occupation. Its censorship of newspapers had begun on October 5, after the Information Bureau ceased to function on October 1 (it was officially abolished on December 31).[84]

CIE began its censorship of the film industry some time in early October.[85] It demanded prior censorship of film projects and scripts. These at first could be submitted in Japanese (at the beginning, a Nisei [second-generation Japanese-American] officer at CIE, Clifford Toshio Konno, was translating the documents from Japanese into English), but soon translation into English of both project descriptions and scripts was demanded of the companies themselves.[86] Each film company created a liaison section, staffed by specialists accustomed to dealing with General Headquarters. The completed films were shown to CIE for civilian censorship and then to CCD for military censorship.

In addition, both civilian and military censorship authorities required that all foreign films to be shown in Japan be cleared with them first. Not only feature films but also 16 mm films, documentaries, and educational films required such clearance. This double censorship of all films shown in Japan began officially with the "Memorandum Concerning Motion Picture Censorship" issued on January 28, 1946. It continued until June 1949, when the Film Ethics Regulation Control Committee (Eiga rinri kitei kanri iinkai or Eirin) was established. Preproduction censorship was discontinued at that time; however, CIE's clearance continued to be required for completed films until the end of the occupation on April 28, 1952, as ordered by the Civil Intelligence Division (which took over CCD in July 1949).[87]

After review by the military censors, each film was given a CCD identification number, without which it was not allowed to be screened "in the islands of Japan for public or private audiences in places of public entertainment."[88] Until a film had been assigned such a number, only those who had worked on the film could see it, and anyone else found at a studio screening was subject to arrest by the military police.[89]

THE BANNED FILMS

On November 16, a "Memorandum Concerning the Elimination of Undemocratic Motion Pictures" from General Headquarters banned 236 feature films and many culture films and current newsreel films that had been made after the 1931 Manchurian Incident. The list included several that had just been completed and were awaiting clearance. This directive condemned past Japanese films for having been utilized to propagate "nationalistic, militaristic and feudalistic concepts; i.e., conformity to a feudal code, contempt for life, creation of the 'Warrior Spirit,' the uniqueness and superiority of the 'Yamato' (Japanese race), the 'special role of Japan in Asia,' etc."[90]

The list is said to have been originally prepared by the Psychological Warfare Branch of the Office of War Information, whose staff included Don Brown, Arthur Behrstock, and David Conde. They had been questioning Japanese prisoners of war, including those who had been in the film business, and these people became their source of information concerning the Japanese film industry.[91] Toru Watanabe, who was working for the Film Corporation, remembered that, in early September 1945, when several American soldiers visited the corporation to ascertain the whereabouts of films regarded as collaborating with the Japanese government's war effort, they already had a list in English "prepared by the Psychological Warfare Branch."[92] The Psychological Warfare Branch used this information in planning the occupation film policy. Brown had lived in prewar Japan as a reporter for the *Japan Advertiser*, was fluent in Japanese, worked with the General Headquarters from the beginning, and, "while continuing on the payroll of the State Department's Office of International Information and Cultural Affairs," became the chief of the Information Division when it was created within CIE in June 1946.[93] At the Office of War Information, Behrstock was under Brown, and Conde was under Behrstock. Both Behrstock and Conde were reputed New Dealers. Behrstock, in addition, was active in the labor, agricultural, and women's movements.[94]

As the chief of the Motion Picture Unit, Conde had been directly responsible for film policy. Born in Canada, he acquired United States citizenship in California. Although his tenure at CIE lasted less than one year,

Conde impressed Japanese film people as an earnest reformer. As he was particularly eager for radical reforms, many Japanese considered him either a communist or a strong communist sympathizer.[95]

In October 1945, CIE had demanded that the Film Corporation submit a list of all feature films made after 1931. The corporation made up a list of their English titles and plot summaries, ending up with 455 films. The American censors then demanded that the Film Corporation decide which among these had helped propagate the war and should thus be banned. The Japanese hurriedly chose 227 films, probably based on their titles and the information at the Ministry of Internal Affairs and the Information Bureau.[96] Conde insisted that he did not add any to this list, merely approving the list prepared by the Film Corporation, although somehow the number increased from 227 to 236 in the November 16 directive. (Nevertheless, many sources have listed the final number of banned films as 227.)[97] Some people have criticized the excessively zealous application of this directive; however, Conde blamed it on the "self-censorship" of the Japanese themselves, who made up the list in a hurry, and probably decided to ban questionable films out of fear of provoking American authorities.[98]

All negatives and prints of the films on the list were confiscated after a thorough search on a prefecture-by-prefecture basis.[99] As a result of this search, it was discovered that many negatives and prints had been destroyed in the wartime air raids. In addition, Toho and Daiei had voluntarily burned the negatives and prints of several films on the list at the end of the war, presuming that these films "were not appropriate to be shown."[100] Toho had destroyed the negatives and prints of *Fire on That Flag* [*Ano hata o ute*] (1944), *The Big Wings* [*Ooinaru tsubasa*] (1944), and *I Believe I Am Being Followed* [*Ato ni tsuzuku o shinzu*] (1945), and Daiei had done so with *The Day England Collapses* [*Eikoku kuzururu no hi*] (1942), *The Human Bullet Volunteer Corps* [*Nikudan teishintai*] (1944), and *The All-Out Attack on Singapore* [*Shingaporu sokogeki*] (1943).[101]

In at least one instance, however, war films were successfully hidden from the occupation authorities. According to Tadao Saito, seven or eight Toho employees were selected by studio head Iwao Mori immediately after Japan's surrender to hide *The War at Sea from Hawaii to Malaya* and seven other war films. The studio anticipated that Americans would confiscate these films. The group of selected employees buried a print and a negative of each title on the grounds of Toho's "second studio," a lot that had been put into operation during the war for shooting films on restricted military subjects. These films survived the occupation period undetected by General Headquarters.[102]

After the prints and negatives were collected at the Ministry of Internal Affairs, it was decided that four prints and a negative of each film would be sent to General Headquarters, and would later be submitted to the Library of Congress in Washington, D.C., and that one negative and two prints of each film would be filed at CCD for six months for further analysis.[103] All the other negatives and prints were burned by the U.S. Eighth Army at the Yomiuri Airfield, on the banks of Tokyo's Tama River, on April 23, May 2, and May 4.[104]

In the press release concerning the directive on banned motion pictures, Conde acknowledged that some films on the list might have "some cultural or literary value" and said that he had no intention to destroy such films; however, he remarked that they "have been so distorted in their use for propaganda purposes that they cannot now be shown without continuing to foster anti-democratic attitudes." Thus, Conde contended that these films had to be banned and that the surplus prints in Japan, which "might be subject to misuse," should be destroyed.[105]

This sensitivity of the American censors, which resulted in the unprecedented action of burning films, gave the occupation forces an authoritarian image. In addition to the political risk of keeping the films, it would have been highly dangerous to store a large number of flammable prints for an indefinite period, and the burning of these films was thus largely justified as a safety measure. Yet even the extremely oppressive wartime Japanese government had not gone so far as to burn banned films.

Joseph Anderson and Donald Richie state that in the rural areas, particularly those served by traveling projection units, many wartime films continued to be shown, not as a sabotage effort, but simply because "the rural operators were completely unaware of SCAP orders and because they had no other films to show."[106] As late as December 1950, the Ministry of Education (Monbu-sho) reported to American civilian censorship authorities that "there are a great number of films of this nature being circulated throughout Japan. Because of the magnitude of this operation . . . it is difficult to keep a constant watch," and that the Ministry of Education was preparing a special memorandum on the subject, to be forwarded to superintendents of education all over Japan.[107]

Before the end of the occupation, the Japanese film industry made efforts to be allowed to release some films on the banned film list. In an April

1951 letter to civilian and military censorship authorities requesting a reexamination of seven films on the list, Toho and Daiei claimed that these films were "originally produced solely for the purpose of entertainment, from well-known Japanese folk tales and, in our consideration, are no more militaristic or ultranationalistic than such well-known Western stories of chivalry as *Robin Hood* and *The Three Musketeers* and other tales of love and romance."[108] The following November, the Motion Picture Association of Japan requested that American authorities reconsider thirty-seven films (eight from Toho, eleven from Daiei, seven from Shochiku, and eleven from Nikkatsu).[109] Finally, only two months before the end of the occupation, the occupation government gave permission to release eight films from this list.[110]

The prints of the 236 films on the list were returned by the Ministry of Education, which had been keeping them as ordered by General Headquarters, to the film companies four months after the termination of the occupation in August 1952. Furthermore, 483 prints, including some of those seized during the war and during the occupation by American authorities, were returned by the Library of Congress to the National Film Center of the Museum of Modern Art in Tokyo in December 1967.[111]

PROHIBITED SUBJECTS

In addition to banning wartime films, the occupation government defined prohibited subjects in film production at an early stage of the occupation. On November 19, 1945, CIE announced thirteen themes that would be prohibited in films produced under the occupation. Henceforth forbidden were any films deemed to be

1. infused with militarism;
2. showing revenge as a legitimate motive;
3. nationalistic;
4. chauvinistic and anti-foreign;
5. distorting historical facts;
6. favoring racial or religious discrimination;
7. portraying feudal loyalty or contempt of life as desirable and honorable;
8. approving suicide either directly or indirectly;
9. dealing with or approving the subjugation or degradation of women;

10. depicting brutality, violence or evil as triumphant;
11. anti-democratic;
12. condoning the exploitation of children; or
13. at variance with the spirit or letter of the Potsdam Declaration or any SCAP directive.[112]

This November 19 directive on the prohibited subjects was as detailed as the September 22 directive that had enumerated the subjects to be encouraged. The American censors believed that the Japanese film industry was in such deplorable condition, owing to wartime misdirection, that it had to be closely watched and guided. General MacArthur later announced that the mental level of the average adult Japanese during the occupation period had been that of a (presumably American) twelve-year-old. The occupation government film policy reflected this patriarchal attitude, which seemed to have prevailed among the occupation officials, even those who were sincerely enthusiastic in their desire to help reeducate the Japanese people.

The most important of the forbidden subjects on this list, from the viewpoint of many Japanese, was the prohibition of any criticism of the Supreme Commander or the Allied powers. Anything that the occupation government did not like could be prohibited by broadly interpreting this clause. All of the contradictions inherent in the occupation were summed up in this issue: the Allies had come to Japan to bring democracy; however, in order to disseminate and inculcate democratic ideas, they had to suppress some of the ideas that might have inhibited the growth of the new ideology.

This suppression was to be accomplished by means of censorship. Although censorship is to some extent practiced in democratic as well as authoritarian and totalitarian countries, it is hardly a model democratic institution in the same sense as universal suffrage or freedom of religion. However well intentioned censors may be, in reality, as we shall see, their judgments are often based on arbitrary interpretations, extraneous political considerations, or personal biases. The criteria of the occupation censorship authorities for allowing or prohibiting ideas to be expressed in films in fact changed significantly over the course of the occupation, corresponding to shifts in occupation policy that reflected decisions made in Washington and the overall international climate.

However, the basic policy of keeping the Japanese people ignorant of the existence of censorship was maintained throughout the occupation. Jay Rubin points out that the prewar Japanese censors, working under a military regime in a country with long-standing and strong authoritarian traditions, did not take the trouble to hide their existence. On the other hand, the occupation censors had to disguise their operations as well as they could, because they were ostensibly promoting democracy.[113] Ironically, under these conditions, an editor's note in a Japanese magazine praising the "democratic" attitude, thoughtfulness, and efficiency of American censors, compared with the wartime Japanese censors, was also suppressed by the American censors.[114] The occupation censors required Japanese film producers to rework and smooth over deletions to keep the flow of the narrative consistent, whereas the prewar Japanese censors did not care how inconsistent the film looked after being cut and patched, despite the protests of the filmmakers.

Thus, upon learning of these directives, Japanese film people realized that, although they had just been at long last relieved of the repressive Japanese wartime censors, their confinement, by a new set of censors, was to continue.

2

PROHIBITED SUBJECTS

The occupation government's film censorship, administered by the civil censor at CIE and the military censor at CCD, could be a fairly lengthy and complex process. CIE reviewed all domestic productions at the stages of synopsis, screenplay, and completed film. Although technically it had no power to prescribe or proscribe, the Japanese producers nonetheless considered the agency's "suggestions" on how to rid films of "anything detrimental to the objectives of the occupation" as orders.

The division of authority between the civilian and military censors inevitably led to disagreement and competition between the two agencies. It was the military censors who had the final authority over whether or not a film could be shown to the Japanese public. At their screening sessions, the military censors checked films for violations of the established guidelines and gathered intelligence for their own future use. After so doing, they would either pass the film as it was, pass it with deletions, or suppress it altogether.

Approved films were given identification numbers that had to be displayed upon their theatrical release. If sections were deleted, the censors cut out and confiscated the objectionable parts and returned the rest of the film to the owners, without even splicing it back together. The censors rechecked the edited versions after they were resubmitted. Suppressed films were not returned to the owners, and all prints and negatives of such films were ordered to be surrendered to the military censorship office of CCD. After this office and other occupation agencies had studied the suppressed films and deleted sections, in order to gather intelligence on Japanese geography, history, strategy, language, and culture, all but one negative and two prints of each film (which were apparently eventually sent to the U.S. Library of Congress) were destroyed. The stock of the destroyed films seems to have been recycled via a chemical process, so that this scarce commodity could be reused by Japanese film companies, under American supervision.[1] After authorizing a film for release, military censors conducted nationwide spot checks for violations. The censorship was extended to critical, introductory, and theoretical writings on film and to paid advertisements in magazines and periodicals.

The most important goal of CIE was to inculcate in the Japanese people an American-style conception of democracy through film. This was no easy task, because the Americans knew that the Japanese people had been thoroughly indoctrinated by the wartime military regime's propaganda. The role of the civilian censors was not only to evaluate films in terms of their value to the reorientation and educational efforts of the occupation,[2] but also to root out any manifestations of militarism and feudalistic attitudes. The censors at CCD were mostly concerned with security issues, eliminating subversive tendencies in general and real or perceived opposition to the occupation in particular.

This chapter will examine what kinds of subjects, ideas, and filmic techniques were found objectionable by the American censors, in order to understand just what they considered "undemocratic" and therefore undesirable. We will then see how Japanese filmmakers responded. Japanese film titles are cited if known; otherwise, only the English titles (not necessarily accurately translated but used in U.S. documents) are mentioned. The English translations of film scripts (which, as noted in the previous chapter, were prepared by the Japanese producers for the censors) as well as the notations made by the censors themselves have been cited in their original form without editing. Unfortunately, this means that they are often ungrammatical, factually inaccurate, and/or simply incomprehensible, but I feel it necessary to portray accurately the kind of language used by the censors, as well as by the Japanese producers in their translations. Misunderstandings between American censors and Japanese filmmakers were quite probably caused to a certain extent by the incompetent translations provided by the Japanese producers.

MILITARISM, WARTIME ACTIVITIES, AND WAR CRIMES

The American censors allowed no sympathetic, indeed no noncondemnatory, mention of Japanese militarism. It may be argued that they were unreasonably meticulous on this point. For example, in the dialogue of Yasujiro Ozu's *Late Spring* [*Banshun*] (1949), a line mentioning that the daughter's health had deteriorated "due to her work after being conscripted by the Navy during the war" was ordered changed to "due to the forced work during the war."[3] It is difficult to understand what the danger might have been in specifying that the work was done for the Navy.

The censors tried to prohibit the use of military personnel as film characters as much as possible, believing that showing them would arouse the audience's sympathy. Commenting on *One Night* [*Yurusareta yoru*] (1946), the censors instructed that a framed photo of a man killed in the war, sitting on a desktop, should not depict him in military uniform.[4] Occasionally, the censors suggested that the characters be changed from ex-military personnel to ones "in the field other than the military," as they did with the main character of *It's Not Hopeless* [*Nozomi naki ni arazu*] (1949).[5] They also recommended that this film's story of a character selling a war medal on the black market be changed: because the medal was a symbol of militarism and imperialism, it should be burned. If the story had been thus changed, there would have been no further plot development after the black market scene, so the film producer had to explain that selling a medal on the black market would be perceived as more insulting to the military.[6]

Predictably, military songs were prohibited. For instance, the censors ordered the elimination of a Japanese naval song from a newsreel when it was used as background music in a scene of a harbor known as a prewar naval port.[7]

From left to right, Setsuko Hara, Jun Usami, and Chishu Ryu in *Late Spring* [*Banshun*] (1949), directed by Yasujiro Ozu. Courtesy of the Kawakita Memorial Film Institute.

After the censors determined in May 1950 that the script of *The Japanese Army Was Defeated* [*Nippongun yaburetari*] had no reorientation value, Toei Studio decided not to shoot it. The points that the censors found particularly offensive included

> the prominence given the War Minister's exhortations for "the entire nation to rally in fury, 100 million men in one body," and for women and children to prepare to fight the enemy with bamboo spears. This sort of zealotry, even though it is "balanced" by indicating that the Foreign Office and Navy Ministry were good, sensible people who really didn't have their hearts in the war, does not need any encouragement.[8]

The filmmakers involved, producer Akira Iwasaki, screenplay writer Yasutaro Yagi, and director Satsuo Yamamoto, were all communists, and it is likely that they intended this film to be a critique of wartime fanaticism. Despite their good intentions, because they were prohibited from showing the Japanese military's attempts to marshal public sentiment behind the war effort, their project came to naught.

Japanese war criminals were to be depicted without sympathy, and be avoided unless they were relevant to the story.[9] The filmmakers were instructed to emphasize "how the Japanese people were blindly led into a war of aggression,"[10] and that "the guilt of war rests with the past military leaders of Japan."[11]

The occupation government ordered every newsreel to carry a sequence of testimony at the Tokyo Trial (International Military Tribunal in the Far East).[12] In addition, CIE spent over six months carefully planning the newsreel that was to be released when the verdicts of the Tribunal were handed down (the tribunal began on May 3, 1946, and ended on November 12, 1948). This section regarded this project as especially important and ordered the collaboration of the three major newsreel companies (Nichi-ei, Shin-Sekai, and Riken News) and the three major distribution companies (Toho, Shochiku, and Daiei).[13] In May 1948, the first draft outline was submitted by Nichi-ei, the only producer at that point. The second draft, written by the three companies together, was submitted on October 23, and was approved by CIE censor Harry Slott, who inserted a note saying that the "Ruling class, i.e. Tojo and his militarist clique," should be featured prominently.

Hideki Tojo, the star of the Tribunal and this film, appears most frequently; others among the accused also appear in the indictment for the Nangking massacre and the atrocities in the Philippines. In the revised script, Japanese viewers were to be constantly reminded of the attack on Pearl Harbor, emphasizing the responsibilities of Tojo and the accused at the Tribunal: "There is now also no room to doubt the deceptive attack on Pearl Harbor. With this attack as a fuse, the ambitions of the Japanese militarists for domination of the whole of Asia were bloodily begun. In order to carry out this war of aggression, Hideki Tojo and the other accused first carried out a deceptive attack on even we Japanese."[14]

The verdicts for the principal defendants were handed down on November 4, 1948, and the third draft of the script was submitted and examined on November 16, 1948. The rough cut of the film was screened on the same day. A few sections were found objectionable and deleted. The censors prohibited any commentary on the occupation or on the difficulties of postwar life, as well as any criticism of the verdicts. The growing power of the labor union movement was not to be emphasized, but an attempt was made, at the same time, not to provoke the Soviet Union by mentioning the Japanese POWs who still remained there.[15]

Another kind of concern was brought up by the military censors, who had observed during a spot check that some ultranationalistic Japanese viewers demonstrated promilitary sentiments when this newsreel was shown at an Osaka theater. Enthusiastic applause "from ten to fifteen scattered persons in the audience" broke out during the flashback scenes of the Pearl Harbor attack, a shot of a Japanese national flag on the battlefield in China, and a close-up of Tojo bowing to the court after receiving his death sentence. After this report reached the Military Intelligence Section, CCD ruled that the flashback scenes and depictions of Tojo were clearly pejorative, and thus deletions would not be necessary.[16]

After the war criminals were convicted, the occupation government was afraid of Japanese attempts to overturn the court's decisions. Thus, when the project of a film called *Sentence of Hanging* [*Koshi-kei*] charged (plausibly enough) that innocent people could be condemned by false testimony, the censors concluded that pointing this out would not "serve a constructive purpose." The film was about a condemned Japanese war criminal being proved innocent by an American attorney, and thus perhaps was not as direct a challenge to the occupation as it might have been. One could even imagine that depiction of the proving of a man's innocence in a proper legal proceeding could advance the occupation's prodemocracy campaign. Nevertheless, the American censors did not dare to allow such a subversive idea to be promulgated even in this indirect form, and the film seems never to have been made.[17]

These elements were relatively clearly related to censored militarism. However, less obvious militaristic wartime customs and practices were also banned. For example, during the war, *tonari-gumi* (neighborhood groups) had been formed to boost morale and also functioned as mutual surveillance organizations. *Kairan-ban* (circulation boards) had been created to circulate orders and information from house to house. Upon the 1948 reissue of the 1941 comedy *Kinta Becomes a Popular Man* [*Enoken no Kinta uridasu*], the censors demanded the deletion of the scenes of the circulation board because "this method was used in 1940 by order of the Home Ministry [Ministry of Internal Affairs] for the purpose of thought control." Songs promoting neighborhood groups were also deleted because censors considered such songs to have epitomized the aggressive military spirit.[18]

Mt. Fuji, a powerful symbol of Japanese nationalism, was similarly taboo. During the war, the Japanese government had tried to promulgate a

Director Masahiro Makino (c.) in 1950. Courtesy of the Kawakita Memorial Film Institute.

sacred, mystical image of the mountain. However, the occupation's link-
ing of Mt. Fuji with nationalism and militarism might seem somewhat
paranoid. Director Masahiro Makino had an argument with a Japanese-
American censor at CIE who insisted on this point, and thus forbade him to
show Mt. Fuji in his *Sophisticated Wanderer* [*Ikina furaibo*] (1946). The
director was distressed. The story was about cultivating land on the slopes of
Mt. Fuji, and avoiding shooting the mountain itself would be most difficult.
Makino replied that Mt. Fuji was not a symbol of nationalism but of the
Japanese people; however, the censor was not persuaded. Makino continued:
"If you really believe so, why didn't you drop atomic bombs on Mt. Fuji, and
not on Hiroshima and Nagasaki?" Soon thereafter, he was summoned to
appear before the occupation government, which worried him greatly. But
they attempted to placate him, even taking him out for a dinner. The American officials then admitted that he was right, but nonetheless insisted that he
not include Mt. Fuji in his film.[19] During the occupation period, Mt. Fuji
only appeared on the Japanese screen in the Shochiku Studio logo.

CRITICISM OF THE OCCUPATION

Regarding the occupation, the American censors tried not only to suppress criticism of it, but also to hide the very fact that Japan was being occupied at all and that foreign officials were closely supervising the Japanese media. Although Americans had their own history of censorship on the state and local levels, in Japan they wanted to preserve an image as uncompromising fighters for freedom. The occupation government's sensitivities on these points sometimes surprised the unwary among Japanese filmmakers.

No visual or verbal description of the devastation resulting from Allied attacks during the Pacific war was allowed. One filmmaker recalled that the line "Yakedasareta ne [We were burned out of our house, weren't we?]" was cut from a script.[20] Conversations referring to the war devastation without mentioning "the Japanese responsibility for the war" were also judged problematic.[21] An air raid scene in *The Fourth Lady* [*Yoninme no shukujo*] (1948) was ordered completely cut "unless some reference is made as to the war guilt."[22] In *Late Spring*, after one of the characters exclaims at the serenity of Kyoto City, saying "Tokyo does not have such a [wonderful] place," the following line was changed from "It [Tokyo] is full of burned sites" to "It's so dusty all over." In the same script, in a description of Kamakura City as "a quiet, wealthy residential area, which escaped the wartime air raids," the latter phrase was underlined for deletion, even though the line was not actually part of the dialogue.[23]

The censors required that the postwar social and economic confusion be explained as a consequence of Japanese militarism. They forbade criticism of food rationing, crowding on the trains, and such, suggesting that filmmakers propagate the notion that such conditions would be alleviated through "patience and work."[24]

In *Between War and Peace* [*Senso to heiwa*] (1947) directed by Fumio Kamei and Satsuo Yamamoto, a Japanese soldier was shown floating in the ocean after his ship had been destroyed by bombs. Because a Red Cross box could be seen in the background, the scene was cut.[25] Kamei has since said that he did not mean to suggest that the Allied forces attacked the Red Cross, but merely wanted to show the humanistic motivation of a hero medic.[26]

Many other scenes from this film were ordered deleted by the military censors, on the grounds that they were somehow critical of the occupation government or of the United States. It is hard to understand how some of them could be so judged, for example, a scene set in a bar, its walls full of posters of Joan Crawford, Jean Harlow, and nude foreign women, or a scene of young children selling pictures of nude foreign women.[27] A display of promiscuous kissing in a cabaret was ordered deleted because the censors thought it "suggestive that such display of public affection is due to American influence," and because "kissing was introduced by Americans, not Russians." The portrayal of a man (his face hidden) negotiating in sign language for a date with a streetwalker was cut because it "infers [sic] that allied personnel is involved."

One censor even saw an allusion to General MacArthur in a capitalist character sitting in the back seat of a limousine who paid off a jealous husband. The censor was also disturbed by the fact that the images of strikebreakers were of "Western-style" characters, not wearing Japanese-style shoes or carrying Japanese-style weapons. The scene of strikebreakers beating strikers was, in the eyes of the censor, "obviously pantomiming American 'gangster' methods" and "subtly intended criticism of U.S."

This censor criticized almost everything about the scene, in a manner that demonstrates his excessive concern over what he imagined to be covert criticism of things American. He further found that the man who "extracts money to pay off the protagonist from a wallet stuffed with yen" was an "allusion to yen-rich Americans," and that the pantomime of the "pay-off" scene was "patently conveyant of a hidden meaning: not a word of Japanese is spoken during the sequence." Furthermore, an instance of an ex-soldier who goes insane and yells "Banzai for the emperor!" was excised, not (as we might imagine) because it was considered favorable to the emperor and therefore subversive, but because it was "an attempt to belittle the [emperor] system [which the occupation government had recognized] by inferring [sic] that only ex-soldiers who have gone insane ever think of their emperor."[28]

In this atmosphere of suspicion, even the film's title became a target of the censors' concern. Another censor stated that the title (which could be also translated as War and Peace) was "apparently taken from Dostoevski's [sic] famous novel."[29] This statement manifests not only the depth of this censor's ignorance, but also his knee-jerk overreaction to anything Russian.

In a particularly startling display of illogic, a scene of demonstrating strikers carrying banners and posters, such as "Freedom of Speech" and "Let Us Who Work Eat" was deleted for being "suggestive of criticizing SCAP censorship and encouraging labor strikes."[30] The occupation government took great pains to hide its close supervision of the Japanese media: the Japanese people were not supposed to know that Americans were censoring the Japanese media and were, according to the censors, unlikely to know that free speech was actually restricted. This poorly thought-out rationalization is an obvious cover for some other objection to the scene, about the nature of which we can only speculate—perhaps its "communist" content.

Obvious allusions to forbidden subjects did not escape the eyes of censors, particularly those in the military censorship section, who were more security-conscious than their civilian counterparts. In a Japanese documentary film on the new Constitution, the military censors found objectionable a shot of "the front of the Dai-ichi Building" (housing General Headquarters, where General MacArthur worked), with the written title "The New Constitution" superimposed, and deleted the shot.[31] The censor saw the obvious allusion that the New Constitution had been promulgated at MacArthur's initiation and under his protection. This reference was problematic because MacArthur was trying to propagate the notion that the Constitution had been initiated and written by the Japanese themselves.

Cinematographer Kazuo Miyakawa remembered that it was acceptable to include the words "MP" and "PX" in dialogue, but that it was prohibited to show these letters printed on signs or on armbands.[32] Hideo Komatsu, one of Shochiku Studio's liaison people to CIE, recorded that agency censors told him not to shoot the "PX" signs intentionally, and that they would be allowed only if they were unavoidable and integral to the background of the scene.[33]

Director Kajiro Yamamoto recalled that it was very difficult to avoid completely signs in English, occupation facilities, or areas leveled by the air raids because at that time Tokyo was full of such sights.[34] American film historian Joseph L. Anderson was living in Japan during the occupation period because his father was working for the Railroad Section of the occupation government. He was amazed, upon viewing Hiroshi Shimizu's *Children of the Beehive* [*Hachi no su no kodomotachi*] (1948), how much care had been taken to "keep out traces of an occupation presence." Anderson remembered that, during that period, large railroad stations were heavily patronized by the occupation troops. Nonetheless, he found no indication of the occupation's presence in the railroad station scenes, "not even the ubiquitous 'RTO' [military Railroad Transportation Office] signs."[35]

Prohibition of the use of English words was carried to great lengths. CIE censor David Conde deleted the scenes of a toy jeep bearing the letters "USA" and the statement by a girl that she is studying English conversation from *Her Voice in the Matter* [*Kanojo no hatsugen*] (1946).[36] In another

Shunsaku Shimamura (l. rear) in *Children of the Beehive* [*Hachi no su no kodomotachi*] (1948), directed by Hiroshi Shimizu. Courtesy of the Kawakita Memorial Film Institute.

instance, CIE censor George Ishikawa called CCD, requesting the deletion of a scene in which the English letters A, B, C, . . . and the words I LOVE YOU are written on a stage backdrop in *The Almost-Stolen Music Festival* [*Nusumarekaketa ongakusai*] (1946). CCD did not believe this deletion necessary and did not order it, although Daiei Studio cut the scene anyway.[37]

Setsuo Noto and Kajiro Yamamoto, on separate occasions, remembered that the sound of airplanes flying in the background was found objectionable because the censors claimed that, since only occupation forces airplanes were allowed to fly in Japan at that time, the sound of airplanes would remind the audience that Japan was occupied by the Allies.[38] Similarly, Komatsu recalled that the line "Ah! An airplane [is flying]!" was cut from *A Boy in Asakusa* [*Asakusa no bocchan*] (1947).[39] The censors were thus willing to go to great lengths to prohibit any reference, no matter how oblique, to the occupation. It is an indication of how concerned they were about stirring up anti-American sentiment, and testifies to their high estimation of the power of film to do so.

Kyoko Kagawa (r.) and Eiji Okada (c.) in *The Tower of Lily* [*Himeyuri no to*] (1953), directed by Tadashi Imai. Courtesy of the Kawakita Memorial Film Institute.

The subjects of fraternization between occupation personnel and Japanese women, and of mixed-blood children fathered by American soldiers, were forbidden until after the end of the occupation. Hideo Sekigawa made *Mixed-Blooded Children* [*Konketsuji*] in 1956, and Tadashi Imai made *Kiku and Isamu* [*Kiku to Isamu*], on black-Japanese mixed-blooded children, in 1959. In 1953, Senkichi Taniguchi made *Red-Light District Base* [*Akasen-kichi*], depicting the Japanese living around an American base resorting to prostitution and specializing in American soldiers. Mention of crimes committed by American soldiers was also taboo. During the occupation period, written media such as newspapers and magazines had to use euphemisms when describing such crimes, for example, "The criminals were unusually tall and hairy men." In film, this type of subterfuge was obviously impossible.

Portrayals of the harsh battles on Okinawa were also proscribed. *The Tower of Lily* [*Himeyuri no to*] was examined by the civilian censors on July

5, 1950. The intention of the film was described in the following cloyingly subservient prose:

> This picture presents our cordial gratitude to the goodwill of the U.S. Army and at the same time offer our deep mourning to the many young souls which died for the spirit of Red Cross, depicting the story of the "Monument of Himeyuri—Red Star Lily," which was built in Okinawa by the cooperation of U.S. Army.[40]

Director Tadashi Imai could not film this project until 1953, after the occupation had ended. When Toei Studio released it in the same year, the film became the studio's greatest commercial hit.[41]

THE ATOMIC BOMB

The news of "a new type of bomb" dropped on Hiroshima reached Nichi-ei in early August 1945, and the company promptly sent its cameramen to Hiroshima. Two separate documentaries were made, one by Toshio Kashiwada from Nichi-ei's Osaka branch and the other by Shihei Masaki from the company's Tokyo headquarters. Although the footage for the latter was somehow lost on the way to Tokyo, the former was immediately confiscated by the Japanese Army, which feared that its devastating images would destroy the Japanese people's fighting spirit. When the Americans landed in Japan, the occupation government confiscated all of the prints and negatives of Kashiwada's documentary.

Nichi-ei producer Tadao Uriu states that other footage recording the devastation in Hiroshima was shot in 8 mm by an amateur Hiroshima cameraman. The footage was donated to the Hiroshima Memorial, but it was later discovered that the most critical scenes, including those of human corpses, were missing from it, and Uriu suspects that this was also confiscated by the Americans.[42]

Nichi-ei made a newsreel in late September 1945 on "The Atomic Bomb." On September 24, Conde recommended changing the title. He also recommended including some shots of the "great destruction of Tokyo" because he believed that the film overemphasized the destructive impact of the atomic bomb. He concluded that to emphasize the destruction was misleading, because "Japan was actually militarily beaten," and thus it was not "the atomic bomb [that] ended the war." On October 3, C. B. Reese of CCD recommended that this newsreel be suppressed and withdrawn from public circulation altogether because Conde's revisions seemed technically too difficult to make. However, CCD decided that, because the production had already been passed by "CCD personnel (not Pic[ture] Sec[tion])," it should be allowed to run. The censors also believed that the withdrawal would mean "bad publicity." It seems that this newsreel used some of the Nichi-ei's documentary footage on Hiroshima.[43]

Despite these setbacks, Japanese filmmakers felt it urgent to create a permanent record of the destruction wreaked by the atomic bombs. Nichi-ei executive Kan'ichi Negishi planned a new documentary with a crew and equipment volunteered by Toho Studio head Iwao Mori, and Minoru Yamanashi of the Film Distribution Corporation offered financial backing. In late September, after approval from the Japanese Ministry of Education, shooting was started in Hiroshima and Nagasaki, with the collaboration of nuclear and medical scientists.

In late October, a cameraman from the Nagasaki crew was arrested by an American military policeman; it was thus that the occupation government learned of the project. The Military Intelligence Section ordered Nichi-ei to stop filming immediately. After Nichi-ei protested, it was eventually allowed to continue, probably because it wanted to use the footage in the U.S. government's Strategic Bombing Survey. The English-language version of the documentary was completed in April 1946. Akira Iwasaki of Nichi-ei felt that the title given it by the Americans, *The Effect of the Atomic Bomb,* was inhuman. Nichi-ei had intended to show the disastrous damage inflicted by the atomic bomb from the victims' point of view, yet the English title showed that the Americans' primary concern was with the military effectiveness of this new type of weapon.

To guarantee that Nichi-ei's footage would not be used in ways considered dangerous to the occupation, the occupation government ordered the confiscation of all the negatives, prints, and unused footage of the documentary. However, Iwasaki and three of his colleagues were able to hide one rush print from the Americans.

In April 1947, a cameraman who had worked on this atomic bomb film and who later left Nichi-ei after a fight with Iwasaki (and who was probably not an accomplice in hiding the print) informed the military censors that not all of the prints had been submitted to CCD and that film had been sold or shown to the Russians. CCD reported this to the Counterintelligence Section, and an investigation was to be conducted. Yet no further records exist, and apparently CCD could not discover the print that Iwasaki had hidden.

The print that Iwasaki had hidden was returned by the person who had been guarding it to Nichi-ei Shinsha, a newly organized successor to Nichi-ei, in 1952, after the occupation had ended. The new Nichi-ei company has not allowed the print to be shown to the public, except for a few occasions on which they have permitted sections from it to be used in other newsreels and films. Iwasaki guesses that the new Nichi-ei has been afraid of possible pressure from its parent company, Toho.

A 16 mm print of *The Effect of the Atomic Bomb* was returned by the U.S. government to the Japanese government on September 3, 1967. The Ministry of Education, which has been keeping it, has refused to show it in its complete form, despite protests from the filmmakers, from survivors who were in the film, and from the general public. In the early 1980s a Japanese group raised ¥130 million from contributions to purchase 930,000 feet of atomic bomb footage from the U.S. National Archives. This footage was subsequently edited into two films by Susumu Hani, which were released in both countries in 1982.[44]

Shochiku Studio planned to film *Hiroshima*, based on a story written by Ernest Hoberecht of United Press. When the censors examined its synopsis on January 29, 1948, Shochiku explained that the intention of the film was to depict the following:

1. The use of the atomic bombs led to Japan's defeat;
2. The Japanese denounced the war; and
3. The Mo[nu]ment at Hiroshima will be utilized as a symbol of peace.

This transparent attempt to deceive the censors failed. CIE drew attention to the following objectionable points:

1. How would the film depict atomic research in the United States?
2. The use of Japanese war songs;
3. The scene in which a scientist is buried alive, holding a crucifix;
4. Black-marketeers;
5. Atomic bomb is used as an object in the denouncement of war.

The censors believed that "the denouncement of war should be against a system, rather than the implements used in warfare." On May 1, 1948,

Shochiku dropped this project from their production schedule. The studio was forced to state that "this decision was made only after careful consideration, and was not prompted by fear of SCAP censorship."[45]

The treatment of the Hiroshima bombing was critically important to the American government. On May 23, 1949, the U.S. Department of State sent an inquiry to CIE concerning a rumor that the Hiroshima Chamber of Commerce and the Hiroshima Municipal Government were together going to produce a film called *No More Hiroshimas.* Although the stated purpose of the film was to show that "Hiroshima has been reborn as a city dedicated to the struggle for peace," CIE found its inclusion of scenes of "the destruction and human misery which resulted from the atomic bomb" objectionable. Apparently, the film was not allowed to be made.[46]

A similar case is presented in the censorship treatment of Hiroshi Shimizu's *Children of the Beehive.* At the initial scenario conference, the censors strongly emphasized that inclusion of dialogue on the atomic bomb and Hiroshima was unnecessary to the story. The responsibility for the present conditions should be "laid to the war-mongers of Japan, who sought to rule the world." The censors insisted that use of the atomic bomb "came only as a last warning to the people of Japan. Unless this is made clear, reference to the bomb serves no purpose." Nonetheless, the censors felt that, aside from the above-mentioned objectionable dialogue, the picture was an excellent one "on welfare of homeless war orphans and repatriates."[47] Joseph L. Anderson meticulously compared the original script of *Children of the Beehive* written by Shimizu with the completed film and noticed several points where the censors had intervened. The producers of the film had intended to include dialogue concerning a Hiroshima orphan's experience of the bombing. This was deleted from the script by the censors. The censors also compelled the director to replace the background image of the ruins of Hiroshima with a less strikingly devastated scene. Anderson continues:

> Another scene calls for location "in Hiroshima in a bombed out area" [in the script]. While this lengthy sequence is clearly filmed in Hiroshima, what we see [in the complete film] does not go beyond a cemetery. There are damaged tombstones but no damaged buildings.[48]

Kaneto Shindo, who did not experience the bombing but who comes from Hiroshima, made *Children of Hiroshima* [*Genbaku no ko*]. As soon as the occupation was terminated, Shindo's crew headed for Hiroshima in May 1952, and the film was released later that year. Hideo Sekigawa's *Hiroshima,*

Nubuko Otowa (r.) *Children of Hiroshima* [*Genbaku no ko*] (1952), directed by Kaneto Shindo. Courtesy of the Kawakita Memorial Film Institute.

a film about high school students in the city, was made in 1953. Toho Studio head Yoshio Osawa once suggested to director Tomotaka Tasaka, a Hiroshima survivor, that he write a screenplay on Hiroshima.[49] This project, however, was not filmed, probably because of occupation censorship.

On the other hand, CIE permitted the production of *The Bell of Nagasaki* [*Nagasaki no kane*], directed by Hideo Oba and written by Kaneto Shindo, after two revisions of its synopsis. The original synopsis, examined by the civil censors on April 2, 1949, emphasizes the film's intention to portray the "beauty of human love" as personified in a Christian nuclear scientist, Dr. Takashi Nagai of Nagasaki (upon whose book the screenplay was based). The story makes clear that his overzealous laboratory work had already exposed him to fatal doses of X rays before August 9, 1945, when the atomic bomb was dropped on Nagasaki. The censors wrote a note saying that "The decision to use the bomb saved 200,000 Americans here—and turned as many as the Japanese [*sic*, presumably meaning that the use of the atomic bomb in Nagasaki saved as many Japanese as American lives]." The scenes of the destruction of Nagasaki by the atomic bomb were marked as problematic.

In the second draft, Shindo made an apologetic effort in the form of a long written title to justify the dropping of the bombs, and thereby to make the destruction scenes acceptable to the censors. Blaming the tragedy on fanatic Japanese militarism, the writer comes to the following startling conclusion:

> We might say the atomic bomb had been given to Japanese as a revelation of science who prefered savageness, fanaticism and intolerant Japanese spirit to freedom, culture and science. The atomic bomb was an alarm to civilization and an awakening toward peace for Japanese.

After examining this version on April 26, 1949, the censors responded: "story [is allowed] until [the sequence of] atomic bombs. Life of scientist is OK, but one around the bomb is undesirable."

The third and final synopsis, examined by the censors on June 4, 1949, omits the scene of the death of Dr. Nagai's wife after the bombing, and the portrayal of his efforts to rescue the victims. The story resumes in the postwar period, as we see him devotedly continuing his studies, even on his deathbed.

The film was finally completed in 1950, but even then its trailer was found objectionable by the civil censors. Instead of showing "Mitsubishi Ship Building Company, which was making armaments for the Japanese militarists, as being the objective of the bomb," it rather "emphasizes little girls peacefully playing in the park and suddenly being shocked by the dropping of the bomb." The censors felt that, insofar as the story is a biography of Dr. Nagai, it was not necessary to "exploit the phase of the Nagasaki atomic bombing to any great extent," and that the inclusion of scenes such as those described would "not create a better understanding of the reason why the Allies chose to drop the atomic bombs on key military targets in Japan." The trailer was ordered changed, and the complete film was ordered brought in for a screening, upon which occasion "a representative group will be invited for advice and guidance."[50] This case demonstrates the occupation government's adherence to the principle that films should emphasize the military necessity for dropping the atomic bombs, and should not remind the Japanese public that the bombs could not discriminate between military targets and innocent civilians.

The Bell of Nagasaki [*Nagasaki no kane*] (1950), directed by Hideo Oba. Courtesy of the Kawakita Memorial Film Institute.

The original story of *The Bell of Nagasaki* was published in 1949 and immediately became a best-seller. Yoko Ota's *The Town of Dead Bodies* [*Shikabane no machi*], a more realistic description of her experience in Hiroshima, as well as the translation of John Hersey's *Hiroshima*, were permitted to be published in the same year. Media historian Sozo Matsuura presumes that, because the Soviet Union's acquisition of nuclear weapons became known in that year, the Americans realized that it no longer served any purpose to maintain secrecy about nuclear arms. Indeed, they began to permit the claim that America used them to promote peace.[51]

On the other hand, the American censors showed sensitivity toward dialogue that referred to the atomic bombings in a contemptuous, anti-Japanese way in an American film. The censors in 1950 deleted the following dialogue from the Warner Brothers feature film *Cinderella Jones:* "Please, please, please, don't touch it. Don't touch it. Look out for this. One once dropped on Japan—on the Sons of the Rising Sun—would send them on their way to the Happy Hunting Grounds. . . . Just one once, nothing more."[52]

PERIOD FILMS

The realistic practices of commercial cinema gave films a power that the occupation planners had all along tried to harness and control—with grave consequences for the use of traditional Japanese themes in cinema. For instance, feudalistic topics were strictly prohibited in both the traditional Kabuki theater and films. This severely limited the repertoire and made it impossible to show adaptations of certain classic works such as *Forty-Seven Ronin* [*Chushingura*][53] and *Kanjincho,* because of their emphasis on loyalty to lords, or *Terakoya* and *Kumagae-jinya,* for their depictions of cruelty to children.

After the occupation directive of November 1945 effectively banished many classic works of Kabuki from the stage, Faubion Bowers, a serious Kabuki fan who had become General MacArthur's personal aide, decided to try to save Kabuki. Although he had at first hoped to save Kabuki through MacArthur, he soon learned that the general had no interest in this traditional Japanese art form. MacArthur could not be persuaded to appreciate "the wonderful world of Kabuki," according to Bowers. In fact, MacArthur had once seen a Kabuki performance with President Quezon of the Philippines, but "could not make head or tail of it, and walked out."[54] Therefore, Bowers resigned his job in early February 1946 to become an official in charge of theater censorship. Thanks to his personal efforts, once-prohibited programs were gradually cleared once again for stage production. Although in cinema Kurosawa's *The Men Who Tread on the Tiger's Tail,* based on *Kanjincho,* was prohibited from being shown throughout the occupation period, the Kabuki play *Kanjincho* was revived on the stage as early as June 1946. *Kumagae-jinya* and *Terakoya* were again being performed by May 1947. Many prewar film versions of *Forty-Seven Ronin* were banned from the Japanese screen until the end of the occupation, although stage productions of the story had reappeared by November 1947.

Bowers's fundamental idea was that "Kabuki is a traditional cultural property that the contemporary Japanese audience appreciates as a stage art of stylized beauty, therefore they are not influenced by ideas of Kabuki any longer, e.g., revenge, suicide, etc."[55] Film, which depends on the power of lifelike representation rather than "stylized beauty" for much of its impact, could not be similarly claimed to have no influence on the actions of its audience. In this sense, it is understandable why documentaries of Kabuki performances of *Kumagae-jinya* and *Terakoya* were allowed to be made by Masahiro Makino in 1950. Since those films were photographic records of a "stylized" art form, American censors did not worry about their influence.

Feudal loyalty to lords was considered a most dangerous concept, since it represented the opposite of the spirit of individualism, a cherished concept fundamental to American society that was strongly promoted by the occupation. American censors liked to use the Japanese word *oyabun-kobun* (boss-follower) to describe the type of relationship based on blind obedience to authority that was henceforth unacceptable.

Japanese film people deduced that stories like *Forty-Seven Ronin* had been banned because of the revenge theme—that the Americans were afraid of provoking the Japanese people into avenging their defeat in the war. When swordplay scenes were also prohibited, Japanese filmmakers protested that there was no difference between swordplay and gunfighting in American westerns. But the American censors claimed that Japanese swordsmen used their weapons as instruments of personal revenge or to defend the lords to whom they were loyal, and thus were motivated by "feudalistic" values, whereas the gunmen and sheriffs of the Wild West resorted to their weapons only to defend justice and to restore safety to their communities.[56]

Even before the occupation, the American authorities had regarded swords as inherently more cruel than guns. The U.S. Department of War, in the orientation film *Know Your Enemy: Japan* (1944), used many images of swords and swordsmen, compiled from Japanese fictional films and documentaries, to conjure up images of Japanese cruelty in order to bring out the fighting spirit in American soldiers. The film begins with a close-up of a newspaper photo showing a Japanese soldier swinging his sword over an Allied POW. The camera then zooms even closer into the photo, to shock the "civilized" Western mind even more powerfully with the barbarity of this action.

The American fear of the sword is evident in the subsequent scenes, in which a close-up of an ominously shining sword blade in darkness is accompanied by a voiceover, spoken in a rough, Oriental-accented voice, saying that "the sword is our steel bible," a quotation from a Japanese general. The film proceeds to a full shot of a uniformed man slashing straw cylinders. The long shot that follows reveals that he is practicing in front of a Shinto shrine, thus establishing the connection between swordplay and its spiritual origin in Shintoism.

The American suspicion of swordsmanship is a constant theme in this film. The film shows us excerpts from many Japanese period films, while the narration explains that the *samurai* (warriors) are a privileged, idle class that has the exclusive right to carry swords, which they use to "rip off the heads and arms of commoners," sometimes "for practice or amusement," and that short swords were used for committing *harakiri* (ritual suicide by disembowelment) when "captured in disgrace." *Bushido,* the code of samurai rules, is defined as absolute loyalty to one's lord. When we see swordplay scenes on the screen, we are told by the narrator that this code encourages double-crossing and treachery, ambushes, and attacks from behind.

Then, during scenes of samurai attacking Japanese Christians during the sixteenth and seventeenth centuries, we learn that the Japanese are a "bloodthirsty people," unlike Christians, who value "peace" and "equality." Juxtaposed with these images of martyrdom are representations of the concurrent "advances" made in the West by great men such as Voltaire, Washington, Jefferson, Franklin, and Pasteur. We hear self-glorifying phrases such as "the Americans fought for revolution, and the French for equality."

It is easy to see how images of swords are manipulated to suggest that the Japanese were cruel, arrogant, untrustworthy, and backward. If Americans were willing to accept this connection, it is also easy to understand how many could come to believe that swords were inherently evil.

Screenplay writer Keinosuke Uekusa recalls an episode demonstrating how the sight of swords put the Americans into a frenzy during the early period of the occupation. At the end of August 1945, trucks and jeeps of the occupation forces came to the Toho Studio in Tokyo. The Americans collected from the storage rooms all swords, spears, and machine guns used as props. When they noticed that an actor in Kurosawa's *The Men Who Tread on the Tiger's Tail* was using a large sword, they took it away as well, despite the director's protest.[57]

Under such conditions, only four period films were allowed to be made during 1946.[58] The restrictions on their production were gradually relaxed, but until 1949 censorship was tight. The censors complained about a script "loaded with swordplay, intrigues and other objectionable elements,"[59] while they recommended that the Japanese screenplay writers "emphasize the common people," rather than glorify the ruling samurai class with swordplay scenes.[60] The subject of *Swordplay Choreographer* [*Tateshi Danpei*] (1950) was without doubt problematic, but, after the script was rewritten twice, it was allowed to be filmed.[61]

The censorship authorities did not ignore violations in film posters, either. After the civil censors had approved the design for the poster advertising a period film, *The Herd of Gamblers* [*Yukyo no mure*] (1948), the military censors decided to prohibit it. The censors claimed that the portrayal of the men's kimono sleeves, which were tied with string so that they would not get in the way in case of a fight, symbolized revenge among the *yakuza* (traditional gangsters) and thus was not permissible. Shochiku Studio had to redesign and reprint the posters, forcing the postponement of the release of the film, and send the film's star, Kazuo Hasegawa, to the military censorship office for a courtesy call by way of apology.[62] In another case, the censors were concerned with the catch phrases glorifying feudal ideals used in the posters of period films. They also worried about possible inconsistencies between the censored films and the posters advertising them.[63]

Silent films, many of which were period films, were still narrated by benshi or katsuben when exhibited outside the big cities. Because these narrators improvised the dialogue accompanying the images on the screen, the American censors were concerned that they might violate the occupation's guidelines. However, in this case the censors took an uncharacteristically permissive attitude, judging that the popularity of silent films would be temporary, and, in any case, that the old silent prints would not last long, so that a few infringements would not cause any major problems.[64]

Excessive swordplay was forbidden in foreign films as well. In early 1948, the civil censors deleted the scene of sword training but otherwise cleared the American film *The Mark of Zorro* (1940).[65] The military censors then objected to the film, "containing scenes of furious sword fighting," and disapproved of the civil censors' having passed it. Military censor Walter Mihata further complained that the civil censorship section allowed the use of firearms in Japanese films with contemporary backgrounds, and gunplay and swordplay in foreign films, while objecting to swordplay only in Japanese films. Mihata perceived latent feudalism in apparently innocuous scenes, but also objected to the categorical censoring of swordplay scenes, citing a tenet of the samurai code that the best samurai never use their swords against unworthy opponents.[66] On the other hand, the civil censors complained in 1951 that the military censors had early on approved the French film *Taras Boulba* (1936), which had been imported before the war. The civil censors found that this film glorified the martial spirit by showing the leading character using his sword excessively, and advised that it not be released.[67]

The censors wanted the makers of Japanese period films to criticize feudalistic ideas and customs from a contemporary (i.e., American-influenced) viewpoint. For this reason, the synopsis of *Osan and Yohei* [*Osan to Yohei*] was not approved in 1948, as it was seen as lacking criticism of feudalism.[68] Although the censors approved the script of *Heiji Zenigata's Detective Note: Heiji's Golden Coins* [*Zenigata Heiji torimono hikae: Heiji senryo koban*] (1949), they hoped that the film would be more "constructive."[69] The censors twice ordered rewriting of the script of *Great Boddhisattva Pass* [*Daibosatsu toge*] in 1949, not only to eliminate suicide scenes, violent or nihilistic ideas, and the "basic idea of 'Chushingura' [presumably revenge and loyalty]," but also because it was thought insufficiently critical of feudalism.[70] The film was not made until 1953.

ATTITUDES TOWARD WOMEN AND CHILDREN

American censors considered feudalistic the Japanese custom of arranged meetings for prospective marriage partners, *miai*, because the custom seemed to them to downgrade the importance of the individual.[71] Keisuke Kinoshita's very successful comedy, *A Toast to the Young Miss* (*Here's to the Girls*) [*Ojosan ni kampai*] (1949), was problematic for this reason. The film is about the courtship and marriage of a girl from a declining aristocratic family and a man from the nouveau riche. Along with "sequences dealing with war [and] past feudal practice," those portraying the "feudalistic marriage match" were required to be deleted by the censors.[72]

None of Ozu's films on the relationships between parents and their unmarried daughters would have survived if this standard had been applied strictly; thus we are particularly fortunate that these films were actually made. However, in the case of his first postwar film on this subject, *Late Spring*, the censors thought that its story of the daughter's marriage through the miai system was an attempt to preserve feudalistic values. The matchmaker in the film refers to a prospective husband who comes from an old and well-established family from the area. The censors considered this section particularly offensive, and underlined it for deletion in the first script, although it was reinstated in the final version.[73] The script of *The Makioka*

Setsuko Hara (l.) and Shuji Sano in *A Toast to the Young Miss* (*Here's to the Girls*) [*Ojosan ni kampai*] (1949), directed by Keisuke Kinoshita. Courtesy of the Kawakita Memorial Film Institute.

Sisters [*Sasameyuki*] (1950) includes a similar remark on the prospective husband of a daughter of the family, and was marked by the censors.[74]

Just as the American censors expected period films to criticize feudal values from a "modern" moral viewpoint, they wanted these films to show the inequities of the traditional system of marriage. The censors advised the producers of *Love Stories in the Three Generations* [*Ren'ai sandaiki*] (1948), a film that made "an attempt to stress true affection and understanding," to contrast clearly the feudalistic concept of family life in old Japan "as against the present system under the new Constitution."[75] In another instance, the censors suggested that *Crazed Embrace* [*Hoyo*] (1948) emphasize the triumph of love over differences in social status.[76]

Having attempted to legislate the equality of the sexes in the new Japanese constitution, it is only logical that the Americans would not tolerate scenes of physical abuse of women. They demanded that a scene of a man trying to drag a woman up a flight of stairs be cut from a period film, *Five Women from Saikaku* [*Koshoku gonin onna*] (1948).[77]

However, this apparently chivalrous attitude was sometimes carried to extremes. When the popular story *Golden Demon* [*Konjiki yasha*] was filmed by director Makino in 1948, screenplay writer Fuji Yahiro inevitably included the famous scene in which the male protagonist kicks his lover. Having been seduced with a diamond ring from a rich suitor, she wants to break off the affair, and this infuriates him. The American censors first demanded that this scene be cut because of its "contempt of women." After the filmmakers protested, the Americans told them to shoot this scene with "a pair of covers" for his *geta* (wooden sandals). The censors may have justified this slightly bizarre touch by claiming that the covered sandals would not soil her clothes, and might lessen the impact of the blow.[78]

The censors could also be strict concerning more subtle expressions of what they considered the degradation of women. After civil censor Conde had ordered some ten deletions from *Her Voice in the Matter,* a military censor discovered yet another instance of alleged discrimination, and demanded the cutting of a scene in which a wife walks half a dozen paces behind her husband.[79]

In the eyes of the American censors, Japanese women had been consistently and without exception victimized under the traditional social system, and required liberation. The occupation's role was to assist in this process. Thus, when it was shown that Japanese women were sometimes more powerful than men, the Americans could not tolerate it. The civil censorship section disapproved of Shochiku Studio's idea for a comedy, *Liberation of Men* [*Dansei kaiho*], written by Shindo, a satire in which the housewives manipulated and bossed their husbands, and apparently the film was never made.[80]

There was at least one case in which the military censors interfered with a Japanese contemporary stage performance, for depicting the "degradation of women," as well as for describing MacArthur as the "second emperor." An informer suggested that the censors take a look at a show being performed in a Tokyo theater, in which a singer-violinist sang satirical songs, which included such lyrics as the following:

Everybody is talking about democracy, but how can we have democracy
with two emperors?
Women are not equal to men.

Choko Iida (l.) and Tomio Aoki in *The Record of a Tenement Gentleman* [*Nagaya shinshi-roku*] (1947), directed by Yasujiro Ozu. Courtesy of the Kawakita Memorial Film Institute.

If you are a real Japanese, you know who is the real boss at a Japanese
    home.
Seducing Japanese women is easy, with chocolate and chewing gum.

    The singer-violinist seems to have been Ichimatsu Ishida, a comedian whose satirical songs were extremely popular. The censors visited the show on April 29, 1946, and ordered Ishida's performance halted.[81]
    Ishida was featured in Torajiro Saito's *Five Men of Tokyo* [*Tokyo gonin otoko*], produced and released by Toho in December 1945, which included—untouched by the censors—satirical songs with lyrics such as

When the potato ration was announced, many women came,
And let's hope that all of them will come again to vote in the first election
    in which women may participate.
Officials tell us to eat potatoes instead of rice, but what are they
    themselves eating?
They chew their cud lazily, so they are forced to swallow the complaints
    coming from the Allied forces.

Director Yasujiro Ozu. Courtesy of the Kawakita Memorial Film Institute.

In the first postwar election, Ishida won a seat in the Diet.

The censors seem to have been overly sensitive to instances of supposed cruelty to children, as well. Civil censor Clifford Toshio Konno found that the treatment of the boy in Ozu's *The Record of a Tenement Gentleman* [*Nagaya shinshi-roku*] (1947) was too cruel. At issue were scenes such as the one in which a group of neighbors choose by lottery who among them will accompany a boy in his search for his father; in another example, the boy, rather than the woman accompanying him, carries home a heavy bag of potatoes. Nevertheless, these scenes survived in the final version of the film.[82]

ANTISOCIAL BEHAVIOR

Antisocial behavior, such as suicide, gambling, murder, black-marketeering, prostitution, and petty crime, was deemed unacceptable as a film subject. If it could be proved that it was integral to the story of a film, then its portrayal must show that crime does not pay and that justice always wins in the end. Criminals were not to be portrayed as heroes (or antiheroes), and audiences were not to be allowed to sympathize with them. The moral and ethical standards of the censors were modeled after the American Motion Picture Production Code. Harry Slott of CIE's Motion Picture Office once outlined to a group of Japanese film critics the standards of the American Production Code concerning such subjects as illicit sex, vulgarity, obscenity, profanity, costumes, dances, religion, titles, and repellent subjects.[83]

The American belief that suicide is sinful starkly contrasted with the Japanese belief in its acceptability. Not only is suicide taboo according to the Judeo-Christian ethic, but Americans in general have a strong respect for life and physical survival. The American people had been horrified by the war-time kamikaze missions, and, even though some might have recognized and accepted that the Japanese valued honorable death above survival in shame, they rejected the idea that suicide could be a constructive solution to anything. Sharing this attitude, the American censors told the producers that neither showing people attempting suicide, nor expressing the idea that people could solve their problems by committing suicide, was permissible.[84] They further advised that any suicide sequence be replaced by a "more constructive suggestion for the future," be deleted on the grounds that it was unnecessary, or at least be toned down.[85]

In one instance, the American censors complained that the suicide of the husband in Heinosuke Gosho's Once More [Ima hitotabino] (1946) was motivated by the kamikaze spirit, and asked the director to change the scene.[86] In fact, this character is an aristocratic dilettante painter with none of the kamikaze spirit. Because of the censorship, the final version of the film suggests that his death is an accident caused by his mental exhaustion, which makes the scene extremely ambiguous and dramatically incomprehensible.

The censors' special concern regarding this theme is evidenced by the case of Kurosawa's Drunken Angel [Yoidore tenshi] (1948). In the script, the alcoholic doctor's line "To drink is as bad as committing suicide" was underlined as problematic, although suicide was only mentioned in a figurative context.[87]

Murders were objectionable if they were presented without any moral judgments. On seeing Kenji Mizoguchi's Utamaro and Five Women [Utamaro o meguru gonin no onna] (1947), George Gercke of CIE opined that showing a character killing to avenge his failure in love was not desirable because it could influence young people harmfully, even though this partic-

Toshiro Mifune (l.) and Takashi Shimura in *Drunken Angel* [*Yoidore tenshi*] (1948), directed by Akira Kurosawa. Courtesy of the Kawakita Memorial Film Institute.

ular story was not a contemporary one.[88] On other occasions, the censors suggested that a proposed murder scene "must have some cause and should be vital in the plot," and a killing scene was changed in order to emphasize the self-defense motive.[89] Civil censors once suggested that a close-up of a murder with a dagger be changed to a long shot of short duration.[90] They seemed concerned over the shocking impact of such close-ups.

The censors were also concerned that films not give would-be criminals ideas for new offenses and techniques. Hideo Komatsu drew up a set of guidelines that were secretly circulated among the Japanese film studios to help them cope with CIE's policies. In these, he suggested that, for example, pickpocketing scenes should not clearly portray the pickpocket's technique. Furthermore, it should be explained to the censors that all that was being shown was the pickpocket bumping into his victim.[91]

In order for a crime to be portrayed, the filmmaker was required to show that its perpetrators would be brought to justice. The gangster was shown being arrested and tried.[92] The portrayals of the police's efforts to control crime were amplified.[93] The point was made that it is the police force that "maintains law and order legally," and not interfering reporters making private efforts.[94]

The censors complained that the script of Kurosawa's *Drunken Angel*, written by Kurosawa and Uekusa, was full of gangsters' black-marketeering, servile boss-follower relationships, venereal disease, gambling, and prostitution, and suggested: "How about showing the police breaking it up?" Such an obviously moralistic ending was not included. However, the actual ending, an upbeat image of a high school girl who has overcome tuberculosis, replaced the screenplay writers' original idea for an ending. The writers had planned to end the film with a scene of the doctor carrying the dead body of the gangster into a car and driving through streets full of black-marketeers. Furthermore, the way in which the gangster dies was changed several times. In the first synopsis, examined on October 14, 1947, he is killed in a fight provoked by a waitress's jealousy over another woman. In the first script, examined on October 30, 1947, he dies at the hospital of the doctor's friend, after killing his old boss. In the second and final script, examined on November 13, 1947, he is killed in a fight with his old boss.[95]

Gambling was considered an antisocial activity and was required to be portrayed in a "constructive" way, by showing "that it is continually menaced by the law."[96] Similarly, black-marketeering was not to be depicted with "any touch of glamor," but as "an illegal act against the Government and the people," and was not to be shown "unless the sellers are under constant fear of arrest by government authorities." If films dealing with the subject were to be made, they should "offer a solution to the present increasing problem of black-marketeering."[97]

Illegal drug trafficking was not to be shown. Philopon (an amphetamine) had become widely used in postwar Japan, and director Masahiro Makino at one point became an addict after he started using it under the intense pressure of his filmmaking schedule.[98] The censors who had approved the synopsis of Mizoguchi's project *Beauty and the Idiot* [*Bibo to hakuchi*], written by Yoshikata Yoda and Toshio Yasumi, rejected the finished script as too antisocial, for its portrayal of drug trafficking. Although, at the end of the story, the drug users are sent to prison, the censors judged that any reference at all to narcotics or stimulants was too dangerous, and that the film's principal theme of women seduced and turned into prostitutes certainly did not help redeem it.[99] Consequently, the script was never filmed.

The censors similarly advised the producers of a 1947 action film not to glorify opium smuggling or to show it in too much detail.[100] In another film, the censors suggested that the misery caused by drugs was to be emphasized, but the depiction of morphine smuggling was to be toned down, and scenes showing the injection of the drug kept to a minimum.[101]

Repatriated POWs and veterans experienced many difficulties, financial and psychological alike, in adjusting to the postwar life of their homeland. However, these difficulties could not serve as an excuse for repatriates turning to crime, according to the censors. They therefore excised from a film a line of dialogue concerning a returning soldier taking up blackmarketeering because he could not find a job.[102] In the script of another film, a black marketeer character was permitted only after the army uniform he was originally to wear was changed to civilian clothes.[103]

The type of treatment given this issue in Kurosawa's *Stray Dog* [*Norainu*] (1949), written by Kurosawa and Ryuzo Kikushima, must have been exactly what the American censors wanted. In this film, two young returning veterans are robbed of their luggage, each on a crowded train. One of them becomes a criminal, while the other (Toshiro Mifune, who had played the gangster in *Drunken Angel*) becomes a detective, and pursues and finally catches his evil counterpart. The portrayal of the triumph of moral values in this film contrasts markedly with the director's previous *Drunken Angel*, which was criticized by American censors for its glorification of the self-destructive gangster.

When it was unclear in a film how people could live owing to their poverty, the censors sometimes proposed changes calculated to suggest that they would somehow find a way. In *Trial of Love* [Japanese title unknown] (1948), a public prosecutor's line, "Your salary may not be enough to support your mother, but I think you could still live on it," was changed to "Although your salary may not be large, there is enough for you and your mother, without resorting to crime."[104]

Among all possible types of crimes, the Americans must have been most afraid of those that might somehow lead to physical resistance to their own authority. Thus, they forbade portrayals of the theft, illegal possession, or acquisition of arms. Even in the period film *The Sucker* [*Kobanzame*] (1948), the censors suggested that the vocation of one of the characters be changed from arms importer to something else.[105]

A number of films were found objectionable owing to the sensationalism of their depictions of prostitution, venereal disease, and abortion. The

Toshiro Mifune (r.) in *Stray Dog* [*Norainu*] (1949), directed by Akira Kurosawa. Courtesy of the Kawakita Memorial Film Institute.

censors tried their best to discourage this type of exploitative commercialism by ordering deletions and the general toning down of such scenes.[106] They also urged the producers to emphasize the rehabilitation of characters involved in marginal or criminal occupations.[107] In cases in which such depictions were considered too numerous, the censors demanded that lurid titles be changed to less titillating ones, or that the projects be dropped altogether.[108]

It was felt that rape scenes should not incite filmgoers to "morbid curiosity" and should avoid the direct depiction of the act.[109] Civil censors went so far as to attempt to control women's sexual morality when they complained that a nurse who was "violently seduced" by one of the protagonists in the synopsis of a film did not resist his advances firmly enough.[110]

Nude scenes were ordered moderated or eliminated altogether.[111] The scenes of naked women in the hallucinations of the sexually frustrated heroine in Mizoguchi's *The Picture of Madame Yuki* [*Yuki fujin ezu*] (1950),

Michiyo Kogure (l.) and Eijiro Yanagi in *The Picture of Madame Yuki* [*Yuki fujin ezu*] (1950), directed by Kenji Mizoguchi. Courtesy of the Kawakita Memorial Film Institute.

written by Yoda and Kazuo Funabashi, were found objectionable.[112] In an extreme case, even a scene of naked children playing in a ditch in Kurosawa's *Drunken Angel* was marked objectionable by the censors.[113]

It was sometimes hard to draw a line between films considered obscene and those with a scientific or educational purpose. John Allyn of CCD states that his organization took the position that such questions were not in the domain of occupation policy, but rather of Japanese law.[114]

The question of sexual and erotic expression in cinema will be more closely discussed in chapter 4.

XENOPHOBIA

In order for the occupation to succeed, the chauvinistic, nationalistic, and xenophobic ideas that the military government had imposed on or encouraged in the people during the war had to be vanquished. With this in mind, the American censors paid particular attention to any depiction or reference to the Chinese people—who had often been despised and discriminated against in prewar Japan—because China had become one of the Allied countries in charge of the occupation, by virtue of its participation in the Far Eastern Commission and the Allied Council for Japan. References to nationals of the other Allied countries, such as the United States, the Soviet Union, and Britain, were also carefully screened.

The term *dai-sangokujin* (third-nationality people) appeared after the war, referring to Chinese and Koreans living in Japan; their standing changed drastically upon the end of the war, when their previously colonized nations were freed from Japanese rule. In the case of films, it seems that more care was taken to prohibit unfavorable references to the Chinese than was taken regarding the Koreans, perhaps simply because fewer Koreans and Korean territories were portrayed in Japanese films during the occupation period. There was, however, a case of the occupation censors suppressing footage of riots between Koreans and the Japanese police. The censors reasoned that "due to the fact that the coverage contained a good deal of fighting, MPU [Motion Picture Unit] felt that it would only create bitterness between the Japanese and Koreans."[115]

Before the rerelease of the 1941 film *Big City* [*Dai tokai*], a scene of a Chinese restaurant and a Chinese gangster was ordered deleted "on the ground that it concerns Allied personnel."[116] The character of a "Chinese noodle peddler," a good friend of the protagonist, was marked as objectionable in the script of *Chess King*.[117] The fact that the adjective "Chinese" modifies "noodle" and does not necessarily refer to the nationality of the peddler (who at that stage could just as easily have been Japanese) demonstrates the lengths to which the censors went to limit what might be perceived as slights to Allied countries. The Japanese word referring to China as "Shina" was prohibited and required to be changed to "Chugoku,"[118] probably because China regarded the word "Shina" as contemptuous and degrading. In Kinoshita's *Broken Drum* [*Yabure taiko*] (1949), written by Masaki Kobayashi, the tyrannical father's line "I had enough of Japan and I went to Manchuria [to make a fortune]" was found problematic. In the revised script, the line was changed to "I had enough of the mainland and I went to Hokkaido [the northernmost of the four main islands of Japan]."[119]

Clearances from the Chinese Mission and the International Military Tribunal in the Far East were obtained through the civil censorship section before *Mother and Son* [*Haha to ko*] was allowed to be filmed. The film

Tsumasaburo Bando in *Chess King* [*Osho*] (1948), directed by Daisuke Ito. Courtesy of the Kawakita Memorial Film Institute.

portrays a Japanese man who as a soldier commits atrocities in China and is finally persuaded by his mother's love to surrender to the Chinese Mission in Japan after the war.[120]

The project *Burmese Harp* [*Biruma no tategoto*] was presented to the censors by Shin-Toho Studio in early 1950, to be directed by Tomotaka Tasaka and written by Tsutomu Sawamura. The script was marked "British and Indian soldiers" by the censors, probably as a sign that special care should be exercised in its review.[121] Perhaps because of the additional difficulties presented by its setting in Burma and the delicacy required in treating its militaristic subject, this best-seller was not filmed until 1956, in a production of Nikkatsu Studio directed by Kon Ichikawa and written by Natto Wada.

Tsumasaburo Bando (far l.) in *Broken Drum* [*Yabure taiko*] (1949), directed by Keisuke Kinoshita. Courtesy of the Kawakita Memorial Film Institute.

A reference to the break in Russo-Japanese diplomatic relations at the time of the Russo-Japanese War (1904–1905) was marked by the censors in the script of *I Saw Dream Fish* [*Ware maboroshi no uo o mitari*] (1950). A statement that the protagonist's son was killed in the war is also marked in the script.[122] Such references, in this biographical film about a man who succeeds in cultivating trout in a lake, are rather factual and obviously not intended to evoke anti-Soviet feelings. This instance again shows that the American censors were sometimes overly careful.

The occupation government discouraged historical themes with potentially antiforeign elements. When Toyoko Studio proposed making *Townsend Harris and Lord Ii* in March 1951, the censors warned that it must obtain permission through U.S. government channels from the estate of Harris, an American consul who had arrived in Japan immediately after Commodore Perry in the mid-nineteenth century. They also pointed out the anti-Western overtones in the portrayal of the Japanese character Okichi, sent by the Japanese government to serve Townsend Harris, allegedly as a concubine. When the studio returned to the civil censorship office after having attempted for two months to obtain the necessary permission, the legal status of the matter was still unclear. Furthermore, the censors were still concerned over the Okichi character.[123] No film was actually made on this subject until 1954's *Okichi of the Foreigner* [*Tojin Okichi*] produced by an independent company.

Given the censors' extremely sensitive attitudes toward references to things Western, it is easy to understand why they felt that the title of *Passionate Blond under Tender Skin* was deliberately sensationalistic and anti-Western and demanded that it be changed.[124] The following are examples of unintentional violations. In the film *Mother and Son,* a comment by the protagonist's old mother that she does not want to see a foreign film because "the characters lick each other," was ordered eliminated or changed to refer to a Japanese film.[125] The reference to an American cigarette in the script of another film was ordered changed to refer to "other incentive [*sic*] material."[126] In Ozu's *Late Spring,* the daughter's line that her future husband looks like Gary Cooper was marked by the censors, simply because he was an American actor.[127] Perhaps because the censors later realized that he was being referred to in a flattering way, this humorous line survived in the final script.

The following instance of carelessness must have alarmed the censors greatly at the time. In December 1946, a newspaper carried an announcement of the showing of two films at a Tokyo theater, the feature-length British film *The Wicked Lady* (1945) and a newsreel entitled *Princess Elizabeth's Wedding Ceremony* [*Erizabesu ojo goseikon no seigi*]. Owing to improper typesetting, which did not leave any space between the two titles, the ad could be read as *The Wicked Lady Princess Elizabeth's Wedding Ceremony.* The military censors warned the newspaper company that "this ad was most insulting to the British people" and advised that "such a blunder" should never again be allowed to occur.[128]

Despite the taboo against mentioning the social problems created by affairs involving American soldiers and Japanese women (many of which were illicit), in the case of *Sorrowful Beauty* it was established that objecting to an interracial marriage was similarly forbidden "on the ground of racism."[129]

In 1949, Daiei Studio planned to produce a film showing the function of the Civil Affairs Team in Osaka, and CIE asked CCD whether such a subject was permissible. The military censors told the civil censors that they had no objection to occupation personnel appearing in a Japanese film as long as "they were not involved in a disturbance or disorder and this action would not bring discredit on the United States or on the occupation."[130] The next year, when a representative of the Motion Picture Association of Japan requested advice and guidance concerning depictions of foreigners and foreign countries, the censors answered that there was no objection to the use of foreign countries for background or to characterization of any person as a foreigner, as long as they were depicted in a favorable light.[131] However, this policy was not always strictly enforced in the case of depictions of the USSR, as we will see in chapter 7.

RELIGION

Ridicule of religious faith or showing clergymen in an unfavorable light was prohibited.[132] On the other hand, the censors also made it clear that they discouraged the promotion of any particular religion over others. After reviewing the synopsis of *Face of Hell,* the censors recommended that it be changed so as not to promote Christianity, and not to show ministers' clothing or use Christian churches as locales.[133]

The American censors tended to overreact to what they perceived as insults to religion. For example, they objected to the depiction in a film of a Buddhist priest attempting to seduce a girl by confining her in a dungeon, not on general moral grounds, but because they considered the scene a "violation of religious sanctity."[134] In the script of another film, a scene of a priest drinking was marked for deletion.[135] Some other examples seem even less consequential. The protagonist of *Burmese Harp* is a Japanese soldier who becomes a Buddhist priest in Burma after the war. The censors marked the scene of him bidding farewell to his wartime mates as they enter the POW camp, while the latter ask an old Burmese woman to follow him.[136] It is hard to know why this was found objectionable. In *Drunken Angel,* the censors found the doctor's line that he has a "purer heart than [a] Buddhist priest[']s" to be a "questionable statement," although he is speaking figuratively.[137]

OTHER SUBJECTS

In some cases, the American censors pointed out what they considered illogicalities in proposed scripts. Although it is hard to imagine how they could have considered such phenomena dangerous, we shall see in chapter 4 how these deletions were necessitated by the censors' attempt to redirect Japanese cinema according to their own models and concepts.

In a 1947 film, a scene of a woman carrying a man was found illogical. The American censors believed it "possible, yet [it] would have the wrong dramatic effect in this particular scene."[138] In *Broken Drum*, the censors found the portrayal of a young couple climbing up a fire tower unrealistic, because climbing on fire towers was generally prohibited. Screenplay writer Kobayashi and director Kinoshita not only dutifully corrected this sequence as instructed, but ingeniously turned it into the following very humorous scene:

> *While the two lovers are trying to climb the tower, the caretaker appears.*
>
> CARETAKER: What are you trying to do?
>
> *The two are embarrassed.*
>
> SHIGEKI [A BOY]: Because the stars are so beautiful. . . .
> CARETAKER: Then I suppose I can't do anything about it.
> SHIGEKI: Then, will you allow us?
> CARETAKER: Don't jump down.
> SHIGEKI: We may jump up, but never down.
>
> *The two lovers try to climb up, with Akiko [the girl, wearing a skirt] beginning before Shigeki.*
>
> CARETAKER: Wait a minute. It is more polite for the man to go first.
> SHIGEKI: Oh . . . that's right.
>
> *The two change places. The caretaker leaves.*[139]

This scene is a fine example of Japanese filmmakers' ability to view the American censors' suggestions as challenges to be overcome, to the betterment of the final product.

The civil censors were also concerned with the presentation of unscientific notions. In cases about which they had doubts, they contacted the other departments within the occupation government to verify the facts. The Public Health and Welfare Section checked *Blue Flower: Confession of an Abortion Doctor* [*Aoi hana: Aru dataii no kokuhaku*] (1950), and reported to the civil censorship section that the film's presentation of medical issues (i.e., the problems of a family in which the husband is suffering from tuberculosis and the wife is contemplating a legal abortion) were technically correct.[140] In the case of the animated film for children *Octopuses and Snakes* [*Tako to daija*] (1950), the Motion Picture Association of Japan checked its content and found unscientific facts; for example, the film claimed that octopuses emit ink and that a shark expels a shellfish's shell through its fin after eating it. The Association asked the film producer to correct these mistakes, wishing to avoid misinforming children, and reported the matter to the American civil censorship section.[141]

THE CASE OF *DESERTION AT DAWN*

The screenplay of Senkichi Taniguchi's *Desertion at Dawn* (*Escape at Dawn*) [*Akatsuki no dasso*] (1950) was rewritten at least seven times between September 1948, when it was first submitted to CIE, and January 1950, when the film was finally released. For no other film among the cases that I studied from the occupation period were so many rewrites mandated. The various versions of its script, some of whose yellowing pages have started to decay, take up the largest space in the collection of files on Japanese films at the National Records Center in Suitland, Maryland, and are stored in two boxes.[142]

Based on the 1947 popular novel *The Story of a Prostitute* [*Shumpuden*] by Taijiro Tamura, who spent seven years as a soldier in China, the film portrays a love affair between a low-ranking Japanese soldier, Mikami, and Harumi, an army prostitute in China.[143] Mikami is captured by the Chinese army and treated well by them. By allowing himself to be taken prisoner, he has violated a strict rule of the Japanese army, but, nonetheless, he returns to his unit. He is harshly treated by one of his superiors, who is himself making advances toward the beautiful prostitute (later this character was changed to that of a singer). But she loves the protagonist. The two lovers run away together into the Chinese desert, only to be shot by the sadistic officer.

The producer of the film, Tomoyuki Tanaka, visited the civil censorship office for advice and guidance on the synopsis. Tanaka explained that the aim of the film was "to show how the Japanese Army treated Japanese women during the war in China." The American censors suggested that prostitution and sex must not be treated sensationally, and that the causes of the war must be depicted in the film.[144]

It is also noteworthy that the film version made little of the fact that many army prostitutes were Korean. At the Chinese front, Japanese prostitutes were reserved for Japanese officers and wealthy merchants, so the enlisted men had to go to Korean or Chinese prostitutes, many of whom

Ryo Ikebe (l.) and Yoshiko Yamaguchi in *Desertion at Dawn* (*Escape at Dawn*) [*Akatsuki no dasso*] (1950), directed by Senkichi Taniguchi. Courtesy of the Kawakita Memorial Film Institute.

were also forced laborers. In Tamura's original novel, it is suggested that the heroine and many of her colleagues are Koreans. Despite discriminatory remarks from their Japanese soldier customers, these women try their best to be patriotic. Tamura professed himself not only angered by this discriminatory system, but also genuinely appreciative of these Korean and Chinese women, whose affections, he said, sustained the bodies and souls of Japanese soldiers.[145] The changes to make the prostitutes' nationality less obvious may have resulted from the Japanese producers' concern not to provoke the bad feelings of the Koreans.

The first script was written by Taniguchi and Kurosawa, his colleague and close friend. It was examined by the censors on September 11, 1948, and was given a "no good" mark. The censors' record stated that the major objections were to the script's treatment of war and prostitution.[146] The second script, examined on December 9, 1948, was similarly marked "NG. Special requirement forthcoming." The censors' comment, written on a separate form, was, once again, that the subjects of war and prostitution were difficult.

A letter from the Chinese Mission in Japan, written on September 17, 1948, is attached to the form; it concluded that the Mission had no objection to the film, although it suggested some changes in the script. In particular, it asked that "Shina," meaning Chinese, be changed to "Chugoku," the official name for the country; that the Chinese slogan "Destroy Asian Devils" be replaced with "Destroy Japanese Military Clans"; and that the phrase "on the way back from a mission to subjugate guerrillas" be changed to "on the way back from an operation." These changes mitigated expressions that the Chinese felt were insulting or too aggressive.

The third script, examined on December 30, 1948, includes the director's statement of the project's intention: the film was to portray antiwar feeling "through the contrast between the love of a woman from a despised vocation for a soldier of the lowest rank, and his faith in his army, which never rewarded it but cruelly killed him instead." He continues:

> It would be against my will for the heroine to be depicted sensationally as a prostitute. The love in this film is pure, with no calculation or vanity; I would never direct the scenes involving the Japanese army in any way that could arouse the audience's longing for it; Private Mikami is an uncritical character. He is shown as more introspective than the most introspective member of the audience, because I want the viewers to shout at him, "Fool! Why don't you say what you want to, after all this?" I will continue to endeavor until your permission is granted and this film can be shown in public.

Eleven different sections of the script required revisions. The filmmakers decided to emphasize the "exhaustion" of the soldiers (rather than the actual fighting scenes) in a sequence showing "a mission to subjugate guerrillas." The Hinode-kan (Sunrise Inn), an official army house of prostitution, was changed to "a bar." Most significantly, the writers tried to emphasize the questioning of war through the eyes of the prostitutes, using written titles superimposed on the women's faces: "The women never understood what Japan was trying to do in this continent and what good things Japan has done." "They never understood what kind of happiness will come after such a large number of youths kill others and are killed on the orders of a handful of people."

Apparently, this effort by the filmmakers was considered insufficient. Believing that the film was more a sensational depiction of prostitutes than an antiwar statement, the censors demanded another rewrite and decided to discuss the matter with the military censorship section.

Kurosawa's name was omitted as co-writer beginning with the fourth script, examined on January 31, 1949. Yet the redoubled efforts of Taniguchi were evident in written titles proclaiming that this film "is modestly dedicated to the spirits of numerous comrades who were sacrificed in the invasion and war on the continent, without knowing today's glorious Japan of peace and freedom." He also added a shot of the army doctor's death certificate at the end of the film. Describing the soldier's death "on June 7, 1945," as resulting from a wound sustained in battle, this clever device demonstrates the cover-up of the whole event by the senior officer, thereby accentuating more clearly the evils of the army system.

The censors were still not satisfied. They found the story still too sensational, labeling the use of a prostitute in an antiwar picture as "Oriental thinking." They considered the characters "routine," and criticized the negative attitude behind the depiction of the cruelty of war as individual suffering, although they acknowledged that the intention of the film was good.

The prostitute's statement that she came to China as a Red Cross nurse, and the army report noting that she and the soldier were having "sexual intercourse" were among the objectionable points in the script. On February 5, 1949, the civil censors recommended that the filmmakers "revise the story and eliminate the sequences dealing with 'comfort girls' [the Army's official designation for the prostitutes who traveled with soldiers]," which it believed would "only add sensationalism" and would "divert the main emphasis from the antiwar theme." The director argued that portraying them "as women who had been wronged by the imperialist war" would "tremendously enhance the anti-war sentiment." However, in the face of the American censors' disagreement, Taniguchi promised that he would reconsider.

The fifth script is missing from the file. The sixth script was examined by CIE on May 13, 1949. In this version, the heroine's name was for some reason changed from Harumi to Ranko. Several scenes of conversation between prostitutes and officers were still regarded as sensational; the scene of Ranko biting Mikami's finger to seal an agreement in blood was found "savage." The scene of Ranko playfully addressing a portrait of Sun Yat-sen (the first President of postimperial China), as if he were Mikami's mother, was found to lack "political respect." As a whole, the civil censors concluded that the film was over all still too sensational. They particularly found that "the girl meets boy theme is too sentimental"; for example, after being shot, Mikami's last words are "Mother . . . this . . . is . . . my wife . . . Ranko. . . ."

The treatment of the "slaughter of innocents" and the "indictment of [the] destructiveness of war," although it was critical, was thought insufficient to justify making the film. The censors inquired "why do the people of Japan need to be told about the evils of the [Japanese] Army [i.e., outside the context of a more general condemnation of war]?" They wondered why the Japanese surrender was not mentioned at the end of the story. In the attached "Intra Branch Routing Slip" dated May 17, 1949, Harry Slott of CIE remarked to the Motion Picture and Theatrical Branch of the Civil Intelligence Section that "the film seemed intended to be an anti-war story with plenty of sensationalism and accent on sex." Slott's objection that "these stories are allowed on the stage" shows his frustration with the relative liberalism in such matters of other sections of the civil censorship office.

In the seventh version of the script, examined on June 6, 1949, the heroine's name was once again Harumi, and her character was changed to that of a singer. The scene with Sun Yat-sen's picture was deleted, and the date of Mikami's death was pushed forward to July 6, 1945. As one might suspect, the censors were "again disappointed," this time because they considered that the film emphasized a passive "hatred of war" rather than active opposition to it. Merely depicting Mikami as an innocent victim of the Japanese Army was not enough. At the same time, the censors recommended that the film show that the Chinese people were also victims of the war, which they said would do as much to comfort the spirits of the Japanese soldiers as would the portrayal of the ways in which they themselves had been victimized.

As a result, the last version of the script ends with Mikami angrily condemning Japan, after which the camera turns to show the gate from which the officer has shot them. The date of Mikami's death is once again postponed, to August 9, 1945, just before the end of the war, probably to emphasize the sterility of his death.

Many of the major Japanese participants in this film project had had an experience in China of one sort or another. As a soldier in China, novelist Tamura insisted that, through experiencing a life consisting only of "sleeping, eating and fighting," he came to believe that "the flesh" or viscerality was the true basis of human life. After repatriation from China in 1946, Tamura became a forerunner of the *Nikutai-ha* (Flesh School) literary movement because of his free expression of sexual desire, which was first permitted during the occupation. Tamura's sexual expression derived from his philosophy, proclaimed as follows:

> I do not believe in any intellectual system that could not stop this miserable war. I saw Japanese people with plausible intellectual credentials and respectable ideologies transformed into animals. I was one of these animals at the front. How many times did I deplore being a Japanese because of the uselessness of this intellectual system? I was forced to realize that such intellectual thinking has nothing to do with our bodies and will never be able to control them.[147]

Whether or not Tamura's philosophy was conveyed through this film, his advocacy of eroticism naturally helped the film's commercial appeal.

The use of two popular stars, Yoshiko Yamaguchi, with her Chinese flavor, as Harumi, and Ryo Ikebe as Mikami also seemed to help the film's commercial success.

Born to Japanese parents in Manchuria, Yamaguchi was publicized as "Ri Koran [a Japanese pronunciation of her Chinese name Li Hsiang-lan], a Chinese fluent in both Japanese and Chinese" by the Manchuria Film Corporation when she made her debut in 1938. Her popularity immediately increased in Japan. In films such as *Night in China* [*Shina no yoru*] (1940), she was typically cast in the role of a Chinese girl who fell in love with a Japanese man and helped him, symbolizing the Chinese collaboration with the Japanese efforts in China. Upon the end of the war, she once again began to call herself by her Japanese name, escaped execution in China as a collaborator, and returned to Japan in 1946. She returned to the Japanese stage as a singer in the same year, and to the Japanese screen in 1948 with *The Bright Day of My Life*.[148]

Ikebe, popular for his intellectual flair, had started his career as a film actor in 1941, before going to China as an officer the next year. He returned to Japan from the South Pacific in 1946, and began working again as a film actor in 1947.

Director Taniguchi had been a POW in China. He was born in 1912 to an intellectual family in Tokyo. His father had studied at the University of Glasgow and obtained one of the first Doctorates of Engineering conferred in Japan. Taniguchi studied English at Waseda University while active in a leftist theater group. He had to leave Waseda in 1930 upon the suppression of student movements. He came to work for PCL Studio (which later became Toho) in 1933 and worked as an assistant director under Kajiro Yamamoro and Yasujiro Shimazu. He was drafted into the Army in 1943, and, because he knew English, he was often assigned to interrogate Allied POWs

Director Senkichi Taniguchi (front) in 1963. Courtesy of the Kawakita Memorial Film Institute.

during the war. After being repatriated from China in 1947, he reassumed his position as an assistant director at the Toho Studio and was promoted to director in the same year.[149]

Taniguchi believed that the American censors were concerned about *Desertion at Dawn* for two main reasons. First, the project was initiated by the Toho Studio, which was then believed to be "a nest of reds." (When the studio was later struck by a labor union, the project was taken over by Shin-Toho.) Second, the studio had asked the Americans' permission to use old Japanese Army machine guns as props. After the Americans granted permission, the filmmakers went to the fifth floor of Tokyo's Wako department store, where the Japanese Army's abandoned weapons were stored. The Americans sent four officials to supervise the use of the machine guns until the end of the filming. (However, contrary to the Americans' concern, the Japanese crew members were so frightened by the guns that the director had to tell them not to be scared because, without live ammunition, the guns were nothing, "something like scarecrows.")[150]

In this film, Taniguchi wanted to depict how the Japanese Army tried to negate its soldiers' humanity and freedom to love. The director also wanted to portray how a good man came to suffer because of an egotistical officer, based on his own experiences in the Army. Taniguchi channeled his fury over the evils of the Army into his script. But he felt that the American censors' suggestions helped him feel less angry. He was very impressed by the logic of censor Harry Slott when the latter insisted that "any film can attract an audience if it's about war and prostitutes, and isn't it insincere for a writer [to depend on these subjects to make an appealing film]?" Taniguchi appreciated that Slott understood dramaturgy and suggested changes in keeping with the dramatic construction of the script. Thirty-six years later, the director admitted that it might be true that the film's condemnation of the suffering caused by the Japanese Army was limited to the effects on Japanese soldiers, and did not extend to the Chinese people, who had in fact suffered much more. After all, Taniguchi seemed to feel more antipathy toward the wartime Japanese censors than toward the Americans.[151]

Desertion at Dawn was released during the second week of January 1950, and the civil censorship file on the film includes several generally favorable newspaper reviews. *Jiji News* (January 12) found that the Army's hierarchical system was depicted well, although the difference in the characterization of the heroine between the original story (in which she was an army prostitute) and the film (in which she was a singer) "dilut[ed] the passion [of her love]." The Japan Communist Party's *Akahata* (*Red Flag*) (January 11) concluded that the film had been the best yet from Shin-Toho Studio, while *Jiji News* wondered if the film could "console the spirits of the dead."

Desertion at Dawn was ranked third among the ten best films of 1950 by the critics of *Kinema Jumpo* magazine. It was acclaimed for its dramatic intensity, as well as its exposure of the evils of the Japanese Army. The film was selected as an official entry to the Cannes Film Festival of 1951, and became the first postwar Japanese film released in non-Communist Chinese areas and Southeast Asian countries.[152] But on the whole, the film was criticized as much as it was praised.

After mentioning the unprecedented scale of the film's production (it boasted the largest outdoor set and the highest production cost in the history of Japanese cinema), critic Akira Shimizu referred to the observation

of critic Nobuyuki Okuma that, because its antiwar theme was danger-
ously superficial, the film could easily be given a prowar slant if the
political winds were to change. Okuma felt that Mikami's lines reflected
the antiwar theme popular during the postwar period, rather than a more
deeply felt characterization.[153]

Shimizu himself pointed out several problems in the settings and script.
Harumi's characterization as a singer rather than the official Army prostitute
of the original story seemed to result from pressure from Eirin's code of
ethics (see the next section) or from the star herself, he felt. However, it
seemed unnatural for an Army entertainment group to be stranded in a
remote Chinese town. Harumi's attraction to Mikami seemed to Shimizu
very Western, imitating Josef von Sternberg's *Morocco* (1930). Mikami's
character seemed unrealistically naive. In some instances the mise-en-scène
seemed rough, as in the case of the awkward insertion of a serious discussion
into a scene of a wild party. Shimizu concluded that, although the film was
an ambitious, technically excellent treatment of the antiwar theme, its characterizations were not well rounded or insightful.[154]

Despite these criticisms, *Desertion at Dawn* has retained its place in
Japanese film history as a powerful film of passion and antiwar sentiment.

THE RECEPTIVENESS OF JAPANESE FILMMAKERS

Most severely affected by the prohibition of swordplay films during the early
stages of the occupation was Daiei Studio, which traditionally had specialized in this genre, and its stable of actors. In response to this restriction, the
studio began to make films in contemporary settings using the same stars.
Daiei's first attempt, *Brothers of the Meiji Era* [*Meiji no kyodai*] (1946), a film
set in the 1860s and using its four major period stars, was unimpressive
commercially as well as critically. However, the studio's detective film series,
Bannai Tarao [*Tarao Bannai*], which started in 1946, was a great success. The
series used the popular swordplay star Chiezo Kataoka, who had never
before been seen in a Western suit and with a gun in his hand.[155]

Under prewar Japanese government censorship, it had been easy to
include social and political criticism in period films, because the filmmakers
could claim that their films had no relationship to current events.[156] But the
American censors would not accept such claims.

Susumu Fujita (l.) in *Ishimatsu of Mori* [*Mori no Ishimatsu*] (1949), directed by Kozaburo Yoshimura. Courtesy of the Kawakita Memorial Film Institute.

Another strategem the period filmmakers employed was to bring out different themes in traditional stories. For instance, Daisuke Ito was permitted to use the commonly adapted story of Ten-ichibo and Iganosuke as the subject of his film *Humble Masterless Warrior Dares to Pass* [*Suronin makari toru*] (1946) by focusing on the relationships and personal problems of its two protagonists, rather than on action scenes.[157] Director Kozaburo Yoshimura and writer Kaneto Shindo presented a new interpretation of the legendary Edo Period yakuza character in *Ishimatsu of Mori* [*Mori no Ishimatsu*] (1949), which denounced in a satirical comedic style the useless vanity of yakuza loyalty. The protagonist is defined as an antihero, and his swordplay scenes were directed in comic style. Although this film was well received critically (ranking ninth among *Kinema Jumpo* magazine's ten best films of the year), it was a commercial failure. Shochiku Studio head Shiro Kido was not happy with this new trend. He wrote that those directors who introduced new interpretations disregarded mass taste and distorted the traditional values of classic stories, flying in the face of common sense.[158]

When Daiei Studio proposed filming an Edo Period yakuza story, *Chuji Kunisada* [*Kunisada Chuji*] (1946), it feared that the American censors might not pass its project. However, the censors found it acceptable, because screenplay writer Kisho Ogawa emphasized that Kunisada was a hero of the masses and a fighter for justice. This film was the first in which popular swordplay star Tsumasaburo Bando appeared outside the *tachimawari* (swordplay) context.[159] In order to be permitted to make *Utamaro and Five Women*, director Kenji Mizoguchi called on the occupation censors and gave "any number of cogent reasons for making the film. The common man loved Utamaro, he was a great cultural object, really sort of a pre-occupation democrat." Finally, the censors decided that Mizoguchi could make this period film if he agreed to make a modern film about female emancipation in conjunction with it.[160] Mizoguchi's characterization of Utamaro dismayed the writer of the original story, Kanji Kunieda, who had emphasized human freedom through the pursuit of eroticism. Screenplay writer Yoshikata Yoda had done his best to reconcile the different versions, but later confessed that the film was well intentioned but confusing, its ideas not aesthetically integrated.[161]

Sometimes, Japanese filmmakers were able to argue successfully with the American censors. When the idea for the period film *Onatsu and Seijuro* [*Onatsu Seijuro*] was submitted in 1946, censor David Conde did not pass it because it was based on a seventeenth-century story by Monzaemon Chikamatsu and thus considered "feudalistic." Conde suggested that the story be given a contemporary setting. Daiei Studio executives were by now fed up with this kind of argument and ready to give up on the project, but screenplay writer Fuji Yahiro wrote a protest letter to Conde, insisting that Chikamatsu had not been a militarist and that *Onatsu and Seijuro* was purely a love story. He asked, if no one complained that Shakespeare was feudalistic in Conde's country, what was objectionable in this film? After summoning Yahiro and hearing the same argument in person, Conde allowed the story to be filmed, as a period film, in 1946.[162] According to the censors' file, the film is described as the "story of a girl who married a man of her own choice rather than a man of her parents' choice," and its theme is "freedom of marriage." It was thus allowed on the pretext that the film was "democratic."[163]

In June 1949, the Film Ethics Regulation Control Committee was established as an autonomous Japanese censorship apparatus, separate from both American and Japanese political agencies, that assumed the censorship functions of the occupation government's civil and military censors. The committee brought potentially objectional projects to the Americans' attention. Yet even after this changeover, there were examples of civil censorship intervention at the preproduction synopsis and script writing stages. Military censorship activities continued until the end of 1949.

In November 1949, the board of directors of the Motion Picture Association of Japan established a limit on the number of period film productions. Each of the five distribution chains (Shochiku, Toho, Daiei, Shin-Toho, and Toei) was henceforth allowed to exhibit up to twelve such films annually. However, no more than two films could be shown in any given month, and, if two films were shown in one month, none could be shown during the next. The number of period films allowed represented roughly one-quarter of the total number of films produced. During 1950, this standard was adhered to by every company.[164]

The committee's ban on portraying feudalism, militarism, and nationalism was based on its desire to eradicate the ideology that had led to the war, and its regulations governing morality were closely modeled on the U.S. Production Code of Ethics. This code attempted to encourage the depiction of what it considered proper families and decent life-styles—despite the difficulty of maintaining these in the midst of the harsh economic and social situation of postwar Japan.

Such unrealistic idealism notwithstanding, many Japanese filmmakers appreciated the help of the Americans in establishing the committee. Released from the yoke of governmental controls, the Japanese film industry could now begin to police itself, through a committee consisting of representatives from the industry, scholars, and other film professionals. This spirit of autonomy was rather alien to the industry, but Japanese filmmakers realized the importance of being able to develop and pursue their own ideas.[165] Because of the committee's independence, it was to clash with the police and the government, particularly over the obscenity issue, often during the coming decades.

In general, although Japanese filmmakers felt constrained by the prohibitions imposed by occupation film policy, they simply assumed that there was no way to oppose the censors' decisions. They used the words *shinchu-gun machi* (waiting for the occupation forces) to describe waiting until their projects were approved in the same sense that they used the phrase *seiten-machi* (waiting for the sun) to describe waiting for good weather to film.

Japanese filmmakers were subjected to censorship, but, inevitably, they also became participants in determining its policies. The interactions that led to this influence were more frequent and significant than in the case of prewar and wartime Japanese censorship, because the occupiers encouraged and valued the opinions of the Japanese more highly than had their own government. For example, it is highly doubtful that Japanese prewar and wartime censors would have had the patience to allow filmmakers to rewrite their scripts as many as eight times, as the Americans did with Taniguchi's *Desertion at Dawn*.[166]

Almost all of the Japanese filmmakers agreed that the wartime Japanese government censorship had been much worse. In his autobiography, Kurosawa was unsparing in his harsh criticism of the wartime censors, who not only had "no respect for creation" but also "suffer[ed] from sexual manias." He contrasted them with an understanding American censor, of whom he had a very positive impression: "Of course, I am not saying that all the American censors were like him. But they all behaved toward us in a gentlemanly fashion. Not a single one among them treated us as animals, the way the Japanese censors had."[167]

The majority of Japanese film directors and producers share this impression of the "gentility" of the American censors. At the same time, they point out bureaucratic, arbitrary, and sometimes ridiculous applications of the directives, as well as the lack of basic cultural understanding—a situation that seems to have been the worst at the very beginning of the occupation, when both sides were highly suspicious and fearful of each other.

Uekusa recalled that soon after the war he wrote a satire modeled on Nikolai Gogol's *The Inspector General* for Toho Studio. He used a Japanese historical and popular character, Komon Mito, of which the civil censors did not approve. Although the film's producer explained that the script was an attempt to mock traditional feudal authority, he could not persuade the censors. Simply because the project dealt with Komon Mito, who was a symbol of feudalism to the American censors, it was never filmed, according to Uekusa.[168]

Kajiro Yamamoto reported that the American censors forbade him to adapt a particular story written during the war. However much Yamamoto explained that it was an antiwar story and thus had been banned by the wartime Japanese government, the censors would not allow it to be filmed.[169] Clearly, the censors did not always care how the characters or story of a film was actually developed, but often simply forbade films dealing with any subject on their prohibited list.

A case involving Kaneto Shindo illustrates how the censors were incapable of truly understanding uniquely Japanese situations. When Shindo in

1946 wrote *A Woman Kept Waiting* [*Machiboke no onna*] for director Makino, the censor David Conde wanted him to change the characterization of the innkeeper to a negative one. Conde was convinced that all "boss" characters must be portrayed as villainous because they exploited their employees and were thus opposed to democracy. The surprised writer protested that, in Japan, one could not apply such a rule across the board. In small-scale enterprises such as noodle shops, the proprietors had to work among their employees, doing exactly the same kind of work that they did. Thus, not all "bosses" could automatically be portrayed negatively. Although the film was finally made with Shindo's theme almost completely intact, the American censors were reluctant to go along.[170]

Many of the misunderstandings can be attributed to the language problems that resulted from incompetent translations prepared by the Japanese film studios (examples of which include some of the quotations in this book) and the American censors' general unfamiliarity with Japanese culture and customs. Nevertheless, the Japanese filmmakers tried their best to remedy the American censors' ignorance of Japanese culture and customs. The guidelines for Japanese film studios' liaisons with the American censors emphasized the importance of proper translation, recommending the addition of further explanations of difficult to understand Japanese customs for the benefit of the censors.[171]

The occupation scholar Robert E. Ward acknowledges that, while the presurrender planning for the occupation of Japan was conducted by "a small group of the outstanding American experts on Japan," the day-to-day operation of the occupation government in Japan was administered by Americans "who had little, if any, preestablished knowledge of Japan." However, he recognizes that, "had they known more [about Japanese culture], they might have accomplished less," because, owing to their ignorance, they could be more daring and innovative in their policies.[172]

The Japanese complained of the Nisei interpreters' inability to grasp the complicated usage of the contemporary Japanese language.[173] However, this criticism has been disputed by Frank Baba, a Nisei officer who worked for the Broadcast Section of CIE, who said that it was often used as an excuse by the Japanese when they did not want to carry out the occupation government's orders and suggestions.[174]

Nisei censors, who worked as intermediaries between the white Americans who gave orders and the native Japanese who were not happy about those orders but could do little to have them changed, were harshly criticized by the Japanese filmmakers. They complained that the Nisei censors took advantage of their positions to wield power over the native Japanese.[175] John Allyn writes that a few of the Nisei officials were especially anti-Japanese, because of what they and their families in the United States had had to go through amidst the anti-Japanese climate in the days following Pearl Harbor.[176]

One day in March 1947, the military police delivered a summons to Japanese studio executives and liaisons to attend a hearing at the offices of the Criminal Investigation Division. Around fifty or sixty people in all were summoned—not only film company representatives but also the owners and employees of restaurants at which studio executives had wined and dined American film officials, and even some geishas. It was charged that a Nisei official at CIE, Lt. Clifford Toshio Konno, had taken bribes from Japanese studios. After a few days, he was found not guilty, but was nevertheless dishonorably discharged.[177]

CCD first reported on a Japanese bribery case involving a Nisei CIE official in October 1946. A memorandum stated that a "sagacious" Japanese film representative "succeeded in holding in the hollows of his hands, a [CIE] film censor, an American-born Japanese," and thus "has been able to gain definite advantages for himself and those whom he represents." Subsequently, representatives of the Counterintelligence Section, CCD, and CIE held a conference to address the problem.[178] The latter two offices gave the names of all Nisei employees connected with film censorship to the Civil Information Section for investigation.[179] This case is likely to have been Konno's. Another CCD document, written by "W.M." (Walter Mihata) in November 1946, also reported on the case, suggesting bribery between a Japanese film representative and "Lt. Kono" of CIE.[180]

This incident might have been staged as a warning to the Japanese studios, which by then were routinely plying American censors with cash, women, and parties, hoping for favorable treatment in exchange. There are allegations that the studios succeeded in bribing almost every CIE official with women.[181] Other Japanese sources explain that the studios had long been accustomed to bribing the wartime Japanese censors, and that they merely continued the practice with the new authorities.[182] In fact, one critic is of the opinion that Konno was one of the victims of this customary bribery,[183] and racism against Japanese-Americans within the white-dominated occupation government certainly might have speeded his arrest. Surely parties must have helped smooth the sometimes rocky relationship between the American censors and the Japanese film people. It seems likely that the

Japanese side initiated and then gradually increased the scale of the social activities, which included sending actresses to parties, sending stars to the homes of censors, taking censors on a trip to Kyoto, and occasionally organizing baseball games among American visitors, censors, and Japanese film people.[184]

Kajiro Yamamoto had an unpleasant impression of the attitude of some military censors, who used even more disagreeable language than the wartime Japanese censors "to criticize trifling things by bluff, like in an American-style poker game." He recalled that this negative impression was amplified on visiting their office, which had taken over the screening room used during the war by the censors of the Japanese Ministry of Internal Affairs.[185] Yamamoto had had a relatively easy time with the wartime censors, for he had made a number of films promoting the war effort, so it is understandable that he had a hard time with the Americans. However, Marxist producer Akira Iwasaki, who had been harassed by the Japanese government during the war, also complained about the arrogant attitude of the military censors, and the servile attitude of a Japanese receptionist at their office. He concluded that "the 'American gunbatsu [military clique]' is less democratic than the Japanese were."[186]

On the other hand, the civil censors' sincere and enthusiastic efforts to reeducate Japan through film were much appreciated, although the censors' understanding of filmmaking varied, according to the accounts of Japanese film people. Among the CIE staff members, only George Gercke had worked in film in any significant capacity; he had been a branch manager for the *March of Time* in London and was a specialist in music.[187] Gercke once told director Mizoguchi that he had been an assistant director on *Show Boat* (whether the 1929 version, directed by Harry A. Pollard, or the 1936 version, directed by James Whale, is not known) and that he had trained as an assistant director in order to become a producer.[188] Harry Slott was said to have worked as an extra in Hollywood, and Walter Mihata of CCD seems to have worked as a distributor in the United States. These three were probably the only exceptions to the rule.[189]

The censor most discussed by the Japanese film people was David Conde, who was the chief of the Motion Picture section of CIE from its creation until July 1946. He was extremely energetic in his radical attempts to reform Japanese cinema. His extraordinary enthusiasm, hyperactivity, and hot temper led him to bang on the table during meetings and yell at the Japanese, who were disturbed and even threatened by this unusual man. For this reason, Conde was regarded by many as a communist or leftist sympathizer, while some believed he was merely a radical New-Dealer.[190]

At CCD's film censorship section, R. H. Kunzman and Japanese-Americans Arthur K. Mori and Walter Mihata were civilian employees of the War Department.[191] Mihata's father had worked in the early 1910s as a distributor of Japanese films in Hawaii and California, and Mihata himself had visited Japan before the war on business.[192] Hugh Walker, a mixed-blood actor whose Japanese name was Shu Okawa and who was a British national, was employed as of September 1945 in the Press, Pictorial and Broadcasting Division, which sought to take advantage of his familiarity with the Japanese film industry and his bilingual capability.[193] Although Conde and other chiefs of the Motion Picture Division at CIE did not speak Japanese, CCD censors included Japanese experts, such as John Allyn, who had been trained during wartime in the U.S. Army language program. It goes without saying that censors such as Allyn, who knew the language, were more qualified than some of the others.

Japanese film people unanimously liked the idea that they could freely dispute the decisions of the civil censorship officials, as they could not with the military censorship section and had been unable to do with the wartime Japanese censors.[194] Ultimately, however, most of CIE's "suggestions" were actually orders. Interestingly, it was not only Japanese filmmakers who were unhappy about CIE's "orders"; beginning in early 1946, CCD frequently complained about "Civil Information and Education section's interference" on what the former office believed was its bureaucratic turf. For example, CCD stated that CIE's procedure of giving suggestions through pre- and postproduction reviews, "though nominally called one of suggestion, is actually a complete 100% control and as such would be classified as complete censorship control," and that "Civil Information and Education section's action without proper authority" was confusing to the Japanese film industry.[195] We do not know what specific kind of "improper authority," was exercised by CIE, but the remark probably referred to some of the overzealous actions of the civil censorship officials.

Kokichi Takakuwa, a newspaper staff writer working for the liaison section, concluded that journalists felt that working under the occupation censorship was something like experiencing a "severe brown-out," in contrast to the "complete black-out" under wartime Japanese censorship.[196] Japanese film people probably felt similarly about their own situation.

3

THE
DEPICTION
OF THE
EMPEROR

The defeat of Imperial Japan made it possible for the Japanese people to discuss, for the first time in their history, the pros and cons of the emperor and the imperial system. The Showa Emperor Hirohito's reign extended from 1926 to 1989. Although the U.S. government and its occupation government in Japan had already decided not to prosecute Emperor Hirohito as a war criminal, free discussion of his role in the war and the postwar period had been encouraged at the beginning of the occupation. But as the Cold War developed, occupation policy was modified to reflect the new climate, and leftist tendencies in Japan once again began to be suppressed. Since demands to prosecute Emperor Hirohito as a war criminal were most vigorously pressed by the leftists, the Americans began to regard the imperial system as an important bulwark against them and the communist takeover for which they were thought to be working.

The banning of the film *The Japanese Tragedy* in August 1946 was a unique case directly reflecting the American occupation's policy regarding the depiction of the emperor. Directed by leftist Fumio Kamei, *The Japanese Tragedy* is a documentary, compiled from newsreel footage, depicting the Japanese military aggression of the previous fifteen years. After the civilian and military censorship authorities had passed the completed film in June 1946, and it had in fact been shown in several theaters, it was suddenly banned by the military censorship office in August 1946. No reason for this turnabout was given; however, it was believed that it was because the film suggested that the emperor (among other politicians) had been a war criminal.

The International Military Tribunal in the Far East had begun its work in May 1946, and the issue of war criminals was highly controversial. The occupation government's military censorship office ordered that all prints of the film be confiscated, and it was never again shown during the occupation period. *The Japanese Tragedy* thus became the first and only film to be banned after having passed the censors and being shown in public. The banning signaled the new trend toward suppressing leftist sympathizers, not only within Japanese society but also within the occupation government itself.

This chapter will examine the evolution of U.S. policy with respect to the emperor, General MacArthur's media strategy, the backgrounds of the makers of *The Japanese Tragedy*, and the production history of the film, as well as the details of the first and second military censorship reviews of the film.

U.S. POLICY ON THE EMPEROR

The Japanese imperial government would not accept the Potsdam Declaration until it had made certain that the imperial system would be retained after the war. In Washington, the problem of whether or not the imperial system should be retained had been debated by the so-called "Japan Crowd" and its opponents. The former group was centered around former ambassador to Japan and then Under Secretary of State Joseph C. Grew, as well as the diplomats Eugene Dooman and Joseph Ballantine, who had formerly been based in Japan.[1] Based on their experiences of having lived in Japan and their familiarity with Japanese society and culture, they argued that the imperial system was an integral part of Japanese society that held the nation together. They believed that Emperor Hirohito was a peace-loving man, who had been manipulated by militarists against his will. They insisted that, if the emperor were to be executed or the imperial system abolished, Japanese society would fall into great confusion, the resulting antipathy of the Japanese people would hamper the smooth functioning of the occupation, and, as a result, the communists would be able to take over Japan.

The antiemperor group included such prominent figures as Owen Lattimore and Andrew Ross, whose expertise in Chinese matters was greatly valued and influential at the State Department. Sympathetic to China, they demanded severe reprisals against Japan.[2] Others in the group included Assistant Secretary of State Dean Acheson, Office of War Information director Elmer Davis, and columnist Drew Pearson, who expressed the common American sentiment that the imperial system and Emperor Hirohito himself had been the ultimate perpetrators of war crimes.[3]

The military Tojo cabinet, which had been established in October 1941, collapsed in July 1944 as Japan continued to lose battles. Although the succeeding cabinet was also military and did not represent any substantive change in Japanese policy, Washington had for some time been aware of the Japanese government's secret and serious efforts to make peace. The American government, which had also been anxious to avoid more casualties, softened its attitude toward Japan. All of the Japanese wartime cabinets had insisted upon the retention of the imperial system as a precondition for surrender. The U.S. government thus began to consider more seriously the retention of the imperial system, if not the current emperor himself, in order to end the war sooner and to facilitate the postwar occupation.

The argument of the proemperor group was founded on a contradiction: if the emperor had not been responsible for the war policy, how could this practically powerless man now become useful to the occupation? Yet, despite this inconsistency, their position had won over that of the opposing group by the beginning of 1944.[4]

The Potsdam Declaration of July 26, 1945, did not clarify the Allies' plans with respect to the imperial system, but simply stated that "the Japanese Government shall remove all obstacles to the revival and strengthening of democratic tendencies among the Japanese people" and that "the occupying forces of the Allies shall be withdrawn from Japan as soon as these objectives have been accomplished and there has been established in accordance with the freely expressed will of the Japanese people a peacefully inclined and responsible government." This language satisfied both sides in the Allies' internal dispute over the emperor.[5] But in fact the American government, while insisting on the "unconditional surrender" of Japan, informed the Japanese government that it would not insist on the abolition of the imperial house.[6]

This shift in policy was evident in U.S. War Department propaganda films. Early films depicted the emperor as a symbol of Japanese militarism and the nationalist religious cult. In *Prelude to War* (1942), directed by Frank Capra and Anatole Litvak, the first film of the *Why We Fight* series (1942–1945), Emperor Hirohito is portrayed as the Japanese equivalent of Hitler and Mussolini. The images of these three villainous instigators of the war, often in triangular composition, appear over and over again. This trio represents the terror of the Axis. In one scene, the narration vigorously appeals to the audience: "Remember now. If you ever meet them, don't hesitate [to fight back]!"

Similarly, *The Nazis Strike* (1943), the second film in this series, mentions Hirohito, not Tojo, as the force behind the aggressive Japanese policy in China, as the parallel of Mussolini and Hitler.

In the sixth film of the series, *The Battle of China* (1944), an image of the emperor on horseback appears with strident music in the background. In the narration—which provokes the audience with references to "the yellow flood" and "that grinning yellow face," despite the difficulty of differentiating between the "noble" Chinese and the "savage" Japanese—the "God-Emperor" is condemned along with militarists and untrustworthy diplomats, such as Saburo Kurusu (the envoy to the United States just before the Pearl Harbor attack). "The barbarism which produced the Tojos and the slimy Kurusus still intoxicates the little yellow men, still promises them eternity in return for fanatic service to the God-Emperor."

Know Your Enemy: Japan depicts the Japanese system of emperor worship and its historical and psychological background. The film ultimately concludes that the God-Emperor is the source of the Japanese dictatorship and its fanatic militarism. According to Joris Ivens, one of the writers and editors of the film, it was completed in 1944 but was not distributed.[7] Ivens insists that the film was abandoned because of its depiction of the emperor as a war criminal. Even though this view had been shared by the *Why We Fight* series, by 1945, "there had been a policy shift [which resulted in the decision that Emperor Hirohito remain] as an aid to maintenance of order."[8]

Even as the Japanese people wondered what would become of Emperor Hirohito once the occupation began, General MacArthur arrived in Japan. On September 1, 1946, *Asahi Shimbun* published an introduction to the general under the following headline: "Profile of General MacArthur: Working Efficiently, Hobbies are Movies and History Books." The article did not enthusiastically hail the new de facto ruler of Japan, but calmly reported his military achievements in the Philippines and his subsequent popularity in the United States. It portrayed him as "a man of deeds and a very practical person, while some Americans find him showy, enjoying controversy, arbitrary, persistent, aggressive and stern."

After a biographical sketch, the article mentioned that the general liked movies and golf, and that he and his wife had been frequently seen in movie theaters in Manila. It noted that his study was full of history books and that he led a luxurious life of "silver, mahogany tables and thick rugs." (At this point, newspapers were still being censored by the imperial Japanese government rather than the occupation government, which might not have allowed such implied criticisms.)

On September 27, 1945, Hirohito paid his first visit to General MacArthur at the American embassy in Tokyo. The Information Bureau of the Japanese government ordered Japanese newspapers to limit their coverage to announcements and materials from the Imperial Household Agency and the occupation government. The next day, all the Japanese newspapers obeyed this order; however, on September 29, their morning editions astonished the Information Bureau and the Japanese people. There they saw a photograph of Hirohito and MacArthur that had not been released by either the Japanese government or the occupation government, and that was believed to have been obtained from American reporters.

Emperor Hirohito, wearing his morning coat, stands as if at attention. Towering over him is the far larger MacArthur, wearing an open collar, in a relaxed posture, hands resting at his waist. This image finally brought home to the Japanese people the visceral reality that their country had been defeated by powerful foreign countries. Film director Nagisa Oshima has written that the occupation government carefully manipulated this image, to illustrate clearly to the Japanese people that the emperor intended to collaborate with the occupation. The photograph was taken at a moment when the two were looking straight at the camera with serious expressions, rather than when the emperor bowed to MacArthur, or when MacArthur was exchanging pleasantries with the emperor.[9] The Information Bureau immediately

General Douglas MacArthur (l.) and Emperor Hirohito at the American embassy in Tokyo, September 27, 1945. Courtesy of AP/Wide World Photos.

moved to suppress the picture, claiming that it was sacrilegious toward the imperial household. This action, however, in turn provoked the occupation government immediately to nullify the suppression and permit the photograph to be printed.[10]

The clever use of visual elements in this photo was typical of MacArthur's skillful manipulation of his own image. As soon as he landed on Japanese soil, the general impressed Japanese and Americans alike by appearing unarmed—except for his trademark, a corncob pipe—at the Atsugi Military Airport near Tokyo on August 30. His bold posture successfully conveyed his confidence in the overwhelming power of the victors, at a time when all sides were afraid of the turmoil of the period and what it could lead to. The same relaxed manner was to prove effective again on the occasion of his first meeting with the emperor.

After this visit, MacArthur began to feel personally sympathetic toward Hirohito, who, demonstrating his dignity and decency, made clear that he was prepared to meet any kind of fate. The general also realized that the emperor could be very useful to the occupation. MacArthur's telegram to

General of the Army Dwight Eisenhower in Washington on January 25, 1946, emphasized the possibility of serious protests against the occupation forces and a subsequent communist takeover if the emperor were prosecuted.[11]

Emperor Hirohito publicly denied his divinity on January 1, 1946, by order of the occupation government. Again by order of the Americans, the emperor, who had kept strictly out of the public eye before the war, now began to travel all over Japan and for the first time began to be seen by and to some extent mingle with the common people.

Interestingly, MacArthur himself came to be known as "the blue-eyed emperor." While the occupation government tried to destroy the myth of the emperor's divinity and to demonstrate his humanity, it was the general who increasingly withdrew from public life. He carefully restricted the number of Japanese who were allowed to meet him.[12] He met Emperor Hirohito only ten times in the six years before he left Japan, and in that time met only one prime minister, Shigeru Yoshida.[13] MacArthur did not travel and the supreme commander was not closely seen by the Japanese people. This tactic seemed to be effective, in that the Japanese people came to respect and generally love MacArthur.[14] Had he been in any other country but Japan, MacArthur might not have employed such a strategy. But he was well aware of the power he gained by becoming an almost mythic figure in the eyes of the Japanese.

CENSORSHIP PRINCIPLES

The occupation censors prohibited the glorification of the military, religious, and political cult of the emperor. In principle, they allowed criticism of the emperor as a war criminal, and even permitted demands for the abolition of the imperial system, unless these criticisms or demands could in some way lead to criticism of the occupation itself. Thus, both the ultra-rightists and the leftists were restricted in expressing their opinions concerning the emperor.

The *Reporting Guide* of the Press, Pictorial and Broadcasting Division of CCD required reports on any reference in the Japanese news or entertainment media to the following subjects:

1. Divinity of the emperor.

2. Position of the emperor with respect to Shinto.
3. Loyalty to the emperor.
4. Power, authority, responsibility, or function of the emperor under the present Japanese Constitution.
5. Responsibility of Japanese government officials to the emperor.
6. Reports made to the emperor by Japanese government officials.
7. Visits made to the emperor by Japanese, whether government officials or private individuals.
8. Claims of pretenders to the Japanese throne, or claims that the present imperial line is illegitimate.
9. Cost of the present emperor's tours and trips.
10. Cost of maintaining the imperial household.
11. Responsibility of the present emperor for the war.
12. Abolition of the emperor system.
13. Criticism of the emperor, the emperor system, or any member of the imperial family.

The following notes amplified the above-mentioned topics:

A. Reference to subjects 1, 2, 3, 4, and 5 above, and other strongly pro-emperor material may constitute violations of censorship codes (as untrue statements or as rightist propaganda) or of SCAP directives which sharply limit the emperor's position and deprive him of any political, governmental, or religious authority. Such references will be carefully considered by supervisors to determine whether deletion or disapproval is advisable.

B. References critical of the emperor system or any particular emperor or member of the imperial family normally do not constitute violations of any censorship code or regulation, and will be (a) passed in precensored media, (b) approved in postcensored media, UNLESS [sic] they criticize the Allied Powers for failure to depose the present emperor or to try him for war crimes.[15]

At the beginning of the occupation, free discussion of the imperial system was encouraged. Arthur Behrstock of CIE, for example, met with representatives of the major Japanese newspapers, including the *Asahi*, *Mainichi*, and *Yomiuri* papers, to make sure that they understood this.[16]

On "Food May Day" (May 19, 1946), when the Japanese demonstrated to demand food, a man marched carrying a placard upon which was written "Imperial Announcement: The Imperial Entity has been preserved. I, the Emperor, am eating well. You, the people, should starve to death. The Imperial Order." The still-imperial Japanese government decided to prosecute the man for his sacrilege toward the imperial family. The infuriated occupation government thereupon struck the crime of "sacrilege against the Imperial Family" from the criminal code.[17] This action suppressed the imperial law protecting the imperial family from any kind of criticism, and sought to establish basic freedom of speech.

At the same time, the government in Washington and MacArthur in Japan had both decided that Emperor Hirohito would not be prosecuted as a war criminal and that the imperial system should not be abolished. The latter principle was clarified by MacArthur on March 6, 1946, when he announced that the new Constitution of Japan would leave "the throne without governmental authority or state property; subject to the people's will, a symbol of the people's unity."[18] Although the occupation government pretended that this constitution had been prepared by the Japanese government, the draft was in fact hurriedly written by MacArthur's own staff, which had rejected all of the drafts that the conservative Japanese government had proposed.

Mark Gayn reports that at first MacArthur outlined to his staff the three guiding principles for the new constitution, one of which made clear that "while sovereignty was to be vested in the people, the emperor was to be described as a symbol of the state." One of the staff asked if it were to be assumed that Emperor Hirohito would not be tried as a war criminal. Gen. Courtney Whitney and Col. Charles Kades of the Government Section of the General Headquarters, who were engaged in drafting the constitution, confirmed this assumption, saying that Hirohito had rendered service and support to the occupation and therefore should not be tried as a war criminal.[19]

After the Japanese Diet officially passed the draft as the Constitution of Japan, which succeeded the 1889 Japanese Imperial Constitution, it was proclaimed on November 3, 1946, and was put into effect six months later. After unsuccessfully trying to retain as much as possible of the old system and values in the new constitution, the imperial Japanese government at least succeeded in choosing the birthday of the Meiji Emperor (who had reigned from 1868 to 1912) for the proclamation date.[20] Washington and the occupation government clearly understood the emperor's importance in ensuring the success of the occupation, an appreciation demonstrated in the new constitution's description of him as "the symbol of the *unity* of the people [emphasis added]."

MacArthur's early predilection toward retention of the imperial system received strong support from Washington in mid-April of 1946, in the form of a directive from the State-War-Navy Coordinating Committee. As Gayn recalls in his memoirs,

> Although the United States favors ultimately the establishment of a republican form of government in Japan, the Japanese people themselves apparently favor the imperial system. Therefore, General MacArthur is instructed to assist the Japanese people in the development of a constitutional monarchy, and *preservation of the imperial system.*
>
> A direct attack on the imperial system would weaken the democratic elements, and, on the contrary, strengthen the extremists, both communist and militarist. *The Supreme Commander is, therefore, ordered to assist secretly in popularizing and humanizing the emperor. This will not be known to the Japanese people* [emphasis in original].[21]

Truly, the Japanese people did not know. Even those Japanese familiar with the military censorship guidelines outlined previously did not know. In fact, except for the case of *The Japanese Tragedy,* the mere suggestion that Emperor Hirohito had been a war criminal, without even directly criticizing the Allies' failure to prosecute him, was considered sufficient grounds to suppress an entire film.

PRODUCTION HISTORY OF *THE JAPANESE TRAGEDY*

The Japanese Tragedy was made for the weekly news series *The Voice of Freedom* [*Jiyu no koe*] of Nippon Eiga-sha, also known as Nichi-ei. Nichi-ei hired Fumio Kamei as the most suitable director for this forty-minute film. Kamei, born in 1908 and brought up in a liberal and well-to-do family, began his film career when he went to Leningrad in 1928 to study Soviet art. Deeply impressed by the posters he saw there on revolutionary themes, he was soon studying at the Leningrad Film School, where he was further inspired by the Russian techniques of dramatizing human relations under the revolution, and the use of location photography. Sergei Eisenstein's *Battleship Potemkin* (1925) and Vsevolod Pudovkin's *Mother* (1926) were among the most influential films for the young Japanese student, and he studied with Grigori Kozintsev and Friedrich Ermler. Kamei gradually formulated his concept of montage as "not only a technique but a methodology of ideological expression through images."[22]

Director Fumio Kamei. Photo by *Mainichi Shimbun*. Courtesy of Nobito Abe and Yoshio Tanikawa.

After returning home in 1931 because of illness, he began to work at the PCL (Photo Chemical Laboratory) company, which became the Toho Film Company in 1937. He began to make documentary films in 1936, and his *Shanghai* [*Shanhai*] (1937), sponsored by the Japanese imperial navy, was harshly criticized by militarists as too sympathetic to the Chinese. *Soldiers at the Front* [*Tatakau heitai*] (1938) further infuriated the military government. Instead of glorifying the Japanese imperial army's aggression in China, it calmly documents the hardship endured by the Japanese soldiers as well as that of the victimized Chinese. In fact the film was nicknamed *Soldiers in Exhaustion* [*Tsukareta heitai*] since it focuses on the physical and emotional exhaustion of the soldiers rather than their bravery in battle. The film was banned by the Japanese government and was never shown in public.

It appears that *Soldiers at the Front* was the only completed film that was actually prevented from being distributed during the war. The Japanese people were amazed that Kamei, almost alone among Japanese filmmakers,

Soldiers at the Front [*Tatakau heitai*] (1938), directed by Fumio Kamei. Courtesy of the Kawakita Memorial Film Institute.

had succeeded in making such audacious antiwar films in the face of the repressive military government. Kamei then tried to challenge the government's ultrapatriotic policy with respect to "culture films." In such works as *The Ina Song* [*Inabushi*] (1940), about a folk song of the Ina area and *Issa Kobayashi* [*Kobayashi Issa*] (1941), on a Haiku poet of the early nineteenth century, he criticized the socioeconomic exploitation of the people in a rural area "through the depiction of their life, history, custom and culture."[23] Kamei's script for *The Geology of Mt. Fuji* [*Fuji no chishitsu*] (1941) was never allowed to be filmed because its rational, scientific analysis angered the government, which had sought to maintain the mystique of Mt. Fuji as a solemn national symbol.

Kamei was arrested in 1941 and tried on charges of propagating communism through films—charges that appalled him. Although he considered himself an ideological leftist, he had never been a member of the Communist Party or any similar organization. Rather he considered his films humanistic.[24] Kamei was imprisoned and released in 1942; he was one of the very few Japanese filmmakers actually imprisoned during the war. After his release, he quit Toho and joined Nichi-ei, but could not work until the end of the war. Upon Japan's defeat in 1945, it appeared that his time had finally arrived.

On August 15, 1945, Kamei was eating lunch alone while listening to the "important statement from the emperor" declaring the end of the war. (This very attitude was radically different from that of most others, who listened to the broadcast standing stiffly at attention.) When he realized that the war had finally ended, Kamei felt a sudden surge of joy and threw his rice bowl into the air.

Anxious to share his euphoria, he rushed outside, but none of his friends was at home. Finally, he found his old scriptwriter friend Yutaka Yoshimi, packing his things. "What happened?" asked Kamei. Yoshimi murmured, "I don't think I have to be in Tokyo after all this. I'm going back to my home town. . . ." Kamei interrupted by shouting, "Nonsense! Now we can really work!"

From that day on, Kamei began to participate actively in the reorganization of Nichi-ei, believing that the documentary genre would become more and more important in the reborn Japan.[25]

Nippon Eiga-sha, or Nichi-ei, was one of the few newsreel companies that survived under wartime Japanese government controls. Its films conformed to the national policy of glorifying the efforts of the imperial army and navy. After the surrender, the company's executives were expelled, and the Nichi-ei Incorporated Association was disbanded in October 1945. The employees established a new Nichi-ei Corporation that December. They invited Kan'ichi Negishi, who had headed the Nikkatsu Film Company's Tamagawa Studio in Tokyo and then had been a member of the board of the Manchuria Film Corporation, to become one of the new executives. They also asked Akira Iwasaki to join them as a producer.

Iwasaki had participated in the prewar proletarian film movement and had been arrested in 1938 as a Marxist. After his release from prison two years later, it was Negishi who hired Iwasaki as a part-time employee at the Tokyo office of the Manchuria Film Corporation. The job saved Iwasaki and his family from starvation at a time when no one was likely to hire a convicted Marxist. However, this situation gave Iwasaki's enemies a good excuse to attack him after the war. The Manchuria Film Corporation was controlled strictly by the Japanese government's expansionist policy in Manchuria. The corporation consisted of ultrarightists and converted leftists,

Akira Iwasaki, producer of *The Japanese Tragedy*, circa 1950. Courtesy of the Kawakita Memorial Film Institute and the Iwasaki family.

both enthusiasts for reform—a strange mixture of ideological orientations unique to Japanese-occupied Manchuria. The ultrarightists, not content with Japanese wartime government policy, believed that the government was corrupt and the emperor misguided. They had attempted several coup d'etats in the 1930s and, after these failed, some fled to Manchuria, along with their sympathizers, in pursuit of their ideal. So did the leftists and their sympathizers, following the severe suppression of communists and leftists during the decade. The Manchuria Film Corporation embraced both of these trends. Iwasaki was criticized for having been employed by the corporation while he himself was criticizing other Japanese film people after the war for their war crimes.[26]

Thus, Iwasaki felt obliged to Negishi when the latter asked him to join the new Nichi-ei Company. Two other Nichi-ei producers, Masao Shimomura and Tadao Uriu, also helped persuade Iwasaki to join the company. During the war, Iwasaki had developed a deep friendship with these two, who secretly shared his ideological views. Iwasaki soon became the most active producer at the reborn company, which began to make weekly news-reels in January 1946.[27]

THE IMPERIAL MYTH

A month after commencing production, Nichi-ei ran into its first obstacle concerning the depiction of the Japanese imperial system. In early February, Iwasaki planned to make a newsreel proclaiming the negation of the imper-ial national holiday of February 11. According to Japan's imperial myth, February 11 was the date of the foundation of the Japanese Empire "two thousand and six hundred years ago." During the heyday of wartime nation-alistic fascism, this day was most solemnly celebrated. Since the demystifica-tion of the imperial cult was one of the occupation's first steps in its campaign to destroy the wartime militaristic and xenophobic mentality, the occupation government had ordered the Japanese government to forbid the teaching of this nationalistic myth in the schools, and to replace it with a more scientific explanation of the founding of the Japanese nation.

On January 29, 1946, Iwasaki interviewed Minister of Education Yoshi-shige Abe. Iwasaki had expected the minister to clarify the government's new position, as Abe had previously been widely regarded as a liberal, and had in fact been Iwasaki's high school ethics teacher. But Abe disappointed his former student by refusing to disclaim the mythical origins of the holiday. Iwasaki included a portion of this interview in the completed newsreel. After American censors passed the finished film, it was screened at the Ministry of Education on February 7, one day before its scheduled release. After seeing the film, the infuriated Abe demanded the deletion of his interview, claiming that an important statement he had made was arbitrarily shortened by Nichi-ei's editing, and therefore that the meaning of what he had said was changed. When Iwasaki refused to comply, the Ministry of Education brought the matter to the attention of the Americans.

Iwasaki was immediately summoned by Don Brown of CIE and asked to justify his editing of the interview. Iwasaki claimed that time considera-tions forced him to shorten Abe's remarks, but Brown warned that including a quotation without the consent of the interviewed party was grounds for a libel charge. He then asked Iwasaki to delete the whole interview as a special case. Although the partially edited version of the interview was included in the film as it was released on February 8, Iwasaki subsequently agreed to delete the whole interview from the film (probably on February 8) and it was the new version, without Abe's interview, that was shown to the public as of February 9. (The *Asahi Shimbun,* however, reported on the first version on February 9.) In retrospect, Iwasaki saw this episode as symbolizing American protection of the Japanese imperial myth.[28]

Iwasaki reports the following as the complete text of Abe's statement from the interview, the parts in parentheses having been deleted by Iwasaki before the Ministry of Education's interference:

> In the midst of the current confusion and emergency, our country will meet the Imperial National Holiday. (During the war, the nation was so pressured that recently, the value of rationalism has been loudly proclaimed. However, natural phenomena and historical phenomena cannot be treated in the same way. As the eighteenth century's philosophy of enlightenment demonstrated, historical truth is destroyed if you simply apply logic to history.) It was a fashion during the war to conceive of modern-day life in terms of a myth. It is wrong to confuse myth with history; however, we cannot deny the significance of myth in the people's life. It is a current common sense saying that an extra six hundred years are included in the two thousand and six hundred years of the imperial history; however, the proper way to treat this discrepancy has not been academically decided. (The fact that our national history was established around the imperial house will not lose its significance despite this fact's having become half-legendary.) Upon the imperial national holiday, we would like to think of this old national birth along with the spirit of the new national rebirth.[29]

According to the *Asahi Shimbun* of February 9, Abe was interviewed by Nichi-ei on January 29. The film begins with a scene of a classroom, where children are engaged in blacking out the patriotic phrases in their old textbooks. The narration proclaims that the imperial myth that has been forced upon the Japanese people up to that time is unscientific and incorrect. It goes on to say that history has now been taken out of the hands of the fanatic nationalists and is being rewritten. Abe's name is mentioned, and a medium shot of him appears. We hear the edited version of the interview. As soon as it is finished, the camera returns to the classroom, showing children dreamily staring at their teacher, while the narration condemns the ambiguous attitude of the Ministry of Education concerning the imperial myth, a position that confuses teachers and students alike.[30]

It is true that Nichi-ei's editing makes it clearer that Abe was defending the imperial myth, and thus contributing to the confusion over what actually should be taught. However, there is little difference between the complete version and the edited version of the interview. Although it might seem that Abe's real motivation in protesting the inclusion of the interview was his fear of the political repercussions of his candid statement, he was unashamed of his conservative views and unafraid of being purged. It is more likely that he honestly felt he was being misrepresented in the film, and that, thanks to his position, he had the power to rectify the situation.

After a few days, the *Asahi Shimbun* reported a February 11 statement by the General Headquarters concerning the case. The American authorities claimed that, although the film company's freedom to edit must be respected, the company was obliged to report completely and accurately on the subject in question. The American statement further complained that postwar media freedom was often not tempered by a sense of obligation to report correctly and fairly, adding that, because *censorship no longer existed,* reporters themselves were now responsible for the upholding of these principles.[31]

It is strange that the American censors had permitted the inclusion of Abe's statement in the first place, even after Iwasaki shortened it. Did the censors initially allow it to show that the Minister of Education refused to deny the significance of the imperial myth despite the occupation government's earlier order to abolish it? If this was the case, the occupation government's eventual censorship of the statement, at the insistence of the minister who made it, may reflect its (and his) desire to soften the reactionary image that Abe presented, and thus to preserve him in power despite his unacceptable beliefs. The censors had left intact other parts of the film, showing, for example, schoolchildren blacking out nationalistic and militaristic phrases from their old textbooks, and the teacher and students in a history class who were "confused by the ambiguous attitude of the Ministry of Education."[32] Therefore, it seems clear that the censors were not trying to defend the imperial myth as such. At the least, the censors at CIE, and ultimately the entire occupation government, were already moderating their initial crusade against the imperial system. In the end, the Americans left that system untouched.[33]

THE JAPANESE TRAGEDY AND AMERICAN CENSORS

On April 30, the Press, Pictorial and Broadcasting Division of CCD reported the making of a documentary, *The Japanese Tragedy,* by the Nichi-ei Company and pointed out CIE's involvement in the production. Attached to the report was a clipping from the U.S. military's *Stars and Stripes* of April 15. This report drew attention to the statement that the film project had "passed" CIE, reported that "CIE representatives are seeing the 'rushes' and 'suggesting' changes," and noted that the film had originally been entitled *Dark Period* [*Ankoku jidai*][34] but "at the suggestion of Mr. Conde it was changed to *The Japanese Tragedy*."[35]

Iwasaki claims that the title *The Japanese Tragedy* was chosen in a contest within the company, which was won by an employee named Toshiro Takagi, who received a prize.[36] Iwasaki does not mention any suggestions or interference on the part of Conde with regard to the film title or the production of the film itself. However, other Japanese filmmakers have supported the claim that Conde was actively involved in, or even the driving force behind, production of this film.[37] An American journalist, William Coughlin, also stated that the occupation government "instigated and approved" the production of *The Japanese Tragedy*.[38]

Toshio Tokumitsu, the production manager on *The Japanese Tragedy,* described Conde's involvement in planning the film as follows:

> The film officers of CIE section hardly visited Japanese film companies to discuss their business operations. Once, Conde came to Mr. Iwasaki, suggesting that Nichi-ei should take a more enthusiastic attitude toward "culture film" production. At that time, there was little of this. Nichi-ei presented no concrete plan then. Rather, back then, we did not have enough raw film stock even to produce a newsreel and a dramatic film every week. Mr. Iwasaki and I eagerly refuted Mr. Conde's point, explaining this situation. Persuaded by our argument, Mr. Conde soon left our office. Later, Mr. Iwasaki, Mr. Ryuichi Kano [the director of the culture film section of Nichi-ei] and others met and concluded that we should take Conde's enthusiasm into consideration. It was necessary to maintain a good relationship with CIE section. In order to satisfy Conde, we decided to purchase black-market film stock. Somehow, from some sections of General Headquarters, we could purchase "EK [Eastman Kodak] film" stock on the street. Several days later, the plans for *Dark Period* were presented. . . . I was relieved to see Mr. Conde looking extremely satisfied, reading the plan for this film.[39]

Tokumitsu described the process of changing the film's title as follows. *Dark Period* was the working title when the first plan was submitted; it was customary to give films provisional working titles before the official titles were decided upon. Subsequently, several distribution companies told Nichi-ei that the title *Dark Period* was too gloomy and not appropriate for the reborn Japan, and Tokumitsu conveyed this opinion to Iwasaki. Tokumitsu believed that the new title was chosen by Iwasaki, Kamei, and Kano, and he then went to Conde's office to inform them of the change in title. He thus found it hard to believe that Conde was involved in the process.[40]

Shojiro Yabushita, an editor of *Asahi Shimbun,* confirms Iwasaki's claim that it was Toshiro Takagi who came up with the title *The Japanese Tragedy.* In November 1985, Yabushita wrote about *The Japanese Tragedy* in his series on twentieth-century Japanese media history. Mr. Takagi, who was not mentioned in Yabushita's article, subsequently called Yabushita, insisting that it was he who had chosen the title.[41]

Director Kamei remembered that Conde actually suggested that the title *Dark Period* neither represented a positive attitude toward the future nor reflected the previous period objectively. Therefore, Kamei thought it possible that Iwasaki would solicit a new title from the Nichi-ei employees.[42]

A memorandum dated November 6, 1946, from the Press, Pictorial and Broadcasting Division of CCD entitled "Clarification of Statements Made in 'Trends in Motion Pictures,'" included the following statement by censor Walter Mihata:

> At the time *The Japanese Tragedy* was first censored by this department, the Nippon Eiga-sha representative was told that decision would not be rendered until after check by other censors. The Nichi-ei representative [Toshio Tokumitsu] then angrily remarked, "Why should CCD censors make such a fuss over a picture that had been produced under direction and almost daily supervision by Mr. Conde of CIE!"[43]

But Tokumitsu denied this version:

> I never heard at my company that Conde gave suggestions at the editing stage. Any event, however small, that occurred during the process of filmmaking would be discussed among the employees. . . . Moreover, anybody would be suspicious if he saw foreigners accompanied by interpreters coming to see rushes. Therefore, I do not think it was possible that Mr. Conde suggested changes when seeing rushes.[44]

Kamei, who did not remember whether or not Conde came to suggest changes after seeing the rushes, argued that Conde encouraged, but did not demand, the making of a film that would help eliminate militarism and democratize Japan. The American censor and the Japanese filmmakers agreed to make a film to expose the "truth" behind the propaganda that the Japanese military and the wartime government had forced upon the Japanese people. Although the theme and the storyline were Kamei's, Conde provided materials that the Americans had seized from the Japanese. These included news footage of the "Death March of Bataan," a notorious case of Japanese cruelty to Allied prisoners of war; a Japanese officer's memorandum to his men instructing them how to massacre Filipino civilians most efficiently; and an excerpt from the diary of a Japanese soldier on an antiguerrilla mission.[45] Kamei believed that Conde was particularly familiar with the Filipino matters because he had been engaged in anti-Japanese propaganda there during the war.[46]

In addition, Kamei saw all the newsreel and documentary films stocked at Nichi-ei. He selected excerpts for inclusion in the film, while Yutaka Yoshimi wrote the script. It was hard work constructing a persuasive film out of old newsreels and documentaries—the script took more than a month to complete.[47]

THE TECHNIQUE AND CONTENT OF
THE JAPANESE TRAGEDY

The Japanese Tragedy uses newspaper clippings, still photographs, and excerpts from newsreels and documentaries from the prewar and wartime periods provided by Nichi-ei. In addition, Kamei included scenes from at least one fictional film, *The War at Sea from Hawaii to Malaya* [*Hawai Marei-oki kaisen*] (1942), from this period. The director combined excerpts from these films with others from American war documentaries that had been captured by Japanese forces overseas or provided by the occupation authorities. Like the U.S. War Department's *Why We Fight* series, *The Japanese Tragedy* employed the propaganda strategy of attempting "to turn an antagonist's material into an attack on him."[48]

Similarly to the *Why We Fight* series, *The Japanese Tragedy* emphasizes the grave consequences of Baron Giichi Tanaka's memorandum, allegedly submitted to the emperor in 1928 when Tanaka was prime minister, urging

Main title of *The Japanese Tragedy,* set against a background of the International Military Tribunal in the Far East. Courtesy of the Library of Congress
and by permission of Nippon Eiga Shinsha.

the Japanese to invade China as an important step in conquering the
world. The film goes on to explain that, although a variety of government-
controlled political associations supported this expansionist policy, it was
really the economic imperatives of the nationalist capitalistic system that led
to the exploitation of cheap labor at home and the waging of imperialist war
abroad.

The film's many short shots, punctuated in a steady rhythm by written
titles, effectively draw the audience's attention to its rousing condemnation
of the war moguls. We see and hear Emperor Hirohito, the militarists, the
capitalists, the politicians, and the intellectuals glorifying the war. Superimposed titles reveal the huge returns the capitalists realized on their invest-
ments by collaborating in and taking advantage of the war. Juxtaposed with
these scenes are images of exhausted Japanese victims in their villages and
urban slums, of schoolchildren going hungry, and of victims of thought
control, including Professor Yukitoki Takigawa of Kyoto Imperial University,

Banners wave in a gathering to celebrate the Japan-German Anti-Communist Agreement Treaty. Courtesy of the Library of Congress and by permission of Nippon Eiga Shinsha.

who was expelled from his position for his liberal ideas, and proletarian novelist Takiji Kobayashi, who was tortured to death by the Special Higher Police. We are then subjected to images and sounds of mass execution victims in Nanking and the Philippines.

Most intriguing is the presentation of the Japanese government's official reports of its "glorious" war efforts, followed by American documentary footage exposing them as obvious lies. For instance, a jingoistic Japanese newsreel shows a suicide mission of Zero fighter planes en route to attack an American fleet, with the narration reporting that this command attacked and destroyed numerous ships, despite the enemy's counterattack. In the next sequence, we see the fate of this or a similar mission as recorded by the Americans: shot down before reaching the U.S. fleet, and jeered at by happy American sailors. Another "official" wartime narration explains images of fighter planes ditching in the ocean by saying that "these planes did not have enough fuel to return to their carriers." But Kamei's superimposed titles reveal that, in reality, the carriers had been sunk by the Americans and the Japanese planes thus had no base to which to return. Superimposed titles

Professor Takigawa of Kyoto University, from *The Japanese Tragedy.* Courtesy of Yoshio Tanikawa and by permission of Nippon Eiga Shinsha.

also compare the official Japanese and American casualty statistics for one sea battle. They are powerful statements indeed, vividly displaying the lies perpetrated by the wartime Japanese government.

The film spares neither the emperor, the militarists, the politicians, nor the intellectuals, who are seen and heard in wartime newsreel excerpts giving speeches glorifying the war effort. Finally, the film deals with the postwar period, reporting on some of the militarists who were summoned to Sugamo Prison by order of the allied powers. A newspaper headline reading "Kill the Enemy of the People!" appears. The narration declares that many war criminals are still at large, while a newspaper clipping with pictures of prosecuted war criminals is shown. The voice-over argues that many prominent wartime officials and opinion leaders later turned into "pacifists."

Meanwhile, a shot of the emperor in military uniform appears, gradually dissolving into a shot of the emperor after the war, in civilian clothes.

The emperor's new clothes (nos. 1–3) from *The Japanese Tragedy*. Courtesy of the Library of Congress and by permission of Nippon Eiga Shinsha.

The narration continues (the translation hereafter is from Nichi-ei's script): "Already, among the people, the call to pursue war criminals has been raised," as we see a newspaper headline asking about the responsibility of the imperial family.

The scene shifts to a meeting in Tokyo, where a gathering of people demands the prosecution of war criminals. The narration says that "as the testimony against war criminals has progressed, a huge list of as many as one thousand criminals was proclaimed." This is followed by a speech by a representative of a women's organization, accusing the emperor's government of "having driven us into factory labor, telling us that we should sacrifice ourselves in suicidal missions . . . this is the evidence of the crimes of the emperor's government, which so willingly traded our lives for a single bullet and a single warship. . . ." After a round of loud applause, the film ends with several shots of returning soldiers.[49]

Tracing fifteen years of Japanese wartime aggression, *The Japanese Tragedy*, through its powerful visual and auditory images, successfully conveys the filmmakers' antiwar beliefs. A Marxist historical analysis underlies the film's focus on the economic factors behind the Japanese leaders' exploitation of domestic labor and their expansionist policy in Asia. Although it lacks sophisticated technique and its narration may sound crude, the spirit and enthusiasm of its condemnation of warmongering convince viewers not only of the film's argument, but also of the value of such filmmaking.

CCD'S INITIAL CENSORSHIP

Given David Conde's support, it is hardly surprising that *The Japanese Tragedy* easily passed CIE's censorship. When the film and script were submitted to CCD, however, several deletions were demanded. These changes concerned the treatment of war criminals. The parts alleging that Ichiro Hatoyama (who had been purged by the occupation government in May 1946) was a war criminal and the scene with Emperor Hirohito's pictures were underlined, which meant they were subject to deletion.[50] The underlined passages occurred near the end of the film, after the line "However, there are still many war criminals at large, who drove the people to this war of aggression which plunged them into today's miseries." (The translation is from the original script prepared by Nichi-ei.)

(Page 25—First Script)

[Scene] 36. In order to re-mold Japan into a democratic, peace-loving country we have to thoroughly try those dangerous leaders in the past
as well as the system which became the matrix of aggressive war. For
instance, Hatoyama, until the very moment he was purged, had been
telling the nation such nice words to deceive them. (Picture of Hatoyama,
synchronized) "Our Liberal Party recognized the Freedom of Speech, Freedom of Association and Freedom of Economics."

[Scene] 37. There are many people [who] call themselves as the
leaders in the new era, changing their "fronts" like this. (Picture: Newspaper—Kyoto University Affair, Education Minister and President, Picture of
Emperor, shown first in military dress, then in civilian dress). It will be very
serious if we are taken [in] again.[51]

Revisions were made based on these deletions. A second script was
then submitted in which Hatoyama's name was omitted, but the other
critical scene was rearranged into the form in which it appeared in the
final film.

Censors made a notation beside each Japanese name in this script in
blue ink, designating their status as "on trial," "war criminal," or "trial
[awaiting trial?]," and therefore subject to condemnation as war criminals.
Others were designated as "not war criminal," "no record," "released,"
"under arrest," or "cleared." (Unfortunately, we have no way of knowing
who among several censors made these notations.) These categories seem to
have determined whether or not the military censors would allow the officials in question to be criticized as war criminals in the film. Again, the
section with the picture of Emperor Hirohito was underlined, although the
Reporting Guide published by CCD specifically allowed condemnation of the
emperor as a war criminal, as long as such condemnations did not lead to
criticism of the occupation itself.[52]

A part of chief Prosecutor Joseph Keenan's opening address before the
International Military Tribunal in the Far East in Tokyo is marked as follows
(again using the original translation, with deletions underlined):

(Page 25—Second Script)

In stating about the designation of the accused, it is important to call
attention to the fact that there are many who have not yet been designated,
among those comparatively unimportant, as well as those who occupied
the highest of power, in order to arouse the attention of the world.[53]

There is a big cross in red pencil beside Keenan's speech, with the initials R.K. (Richard H. Kunzman). The picture of the emperor is marked "OK" in the same red pencil.

According to the June 13, 1946, report written by the censor K.C., the underlined deletions had been demanded by the censor whose initials were R.H.K. (presumably Kunzman).[54] K.C. noted his opposition to these deletions, insisting that the deleted material did not constitute "criticism of the announced objectives of the occupation or exhortation to undemocratic methods" or a "subject capable of disturbing public tranquility." K.C. actually defended the right to political argument, pointing out that "all political discussion and political change must involve controversy and all controversy must 'disturb public tranquility' to some extent. Obviously it was not the intent of the code to ban all controversial subjects."[55]

The completed film includes none of Keenan's speech, but does include the section about the emperor and condemnations of others not necessarily on trial. Therefore, it seems that, although Kunzman had at one time demanded deletions with his underlining, K.C.'s defense of the right to political argument convinced him to allow the criticism of the emperor and others to stand.

Yet, even after it passed the censors, the filmmakers had trouble arranging for distribution of The Japanese Tragedy. According to Iwasaki, the major film companies, fearful of hostile audiences and thus of losing money, refused to distribute it.[56] David Conde of CIE, in his last weekly report as the chief of the Motion Picture and Theatrical Unit, confirmed Iwasaki's claim, explaining that the film was ready to release that week (the week of July 12, 1946), but that three major production and distribution companies—Toho, Shochiku, and Nikkatsu—"did not wish to book this film. Stated reasons for this reluctance were generally its length (4 reels) and what these companies considered would be its lack of popularity."[57] A later CCD report noted a more serious situation: that these companies had justified their refusal to handle the film on the basis of a fear that "hostile audiences might damage theaters in which it was shown."[58]

The film was nevertheless released independently in a few local theaters in July.[59] Kamei recalled that somebody threw a wooden sandal at the screen during a showing in a downtown Tokyo hall.[60] It is clear that the film's audience certainly included some hostile spectators.

The CCD's file on The Japanese Tragedy includes a clipping of a Tokyo Shimbun film review and its English translation. This review praised the film's theme ("intended to be an objective enlightenment and reflection on our history since the Manchuria Incident") and its audacious technique ("for example, the camera zooms into the emperor after a long shot of an imperial conference"). The review further lamented that the film had been refused distribution by the majors, whose only interest, it declared, was making money.[61]

Another important newspaper, the *Asahi Shimbun*, reported on August 5 that, two months after completion, *The Japanese Tragedy* had been refused distribution by major companies. The excuse given was that the film was too long, but "it is said that the [real] problem is the way that its theme is presented and its ideology. . . ." The article concluded that it was rare for a film to premiere in Warabi City, Saitama Prefecture (north of Tokyo), not in the capital city itself.[62]

Producer Iwasaki claimed that the film was very successful in outlying areas, and that consequently Nichi-ei began preparing for its public premiere in Tokyo.[63] A clipping from a small, seemingly leftist Japanese publication in the censorship file supports this claim, announcing the showing of *The Japanese Tragedy* at the large Kyoritsu Hall in downtown Tokyo for one week, beginning August 15, 1946. Probably in order to build interest, the announcement notes that the film has been "refused release due to various problems."[64] It is unclear whether this line was intended to suggest that the film's release had been held up by the major film companies themselves or by direct interference from American censors.

CCD'S SECOND CENSORSHIP

On August 13, 1946, Iwasaki was summoned to CCD and told that a second military censorship review had found *The Japanese Tragedy* objectionable and that it was therefore to be banned. All the negatives and prints were ordered to be submitted to the censorship office within a week. The appalled Iwasaki asked for an explanation, but received none. Returning to the censorship office every day, he gradually learned that the banning order came from Gen. Charles Willoughby, the head of Military Intelligence Section. His request to meet Willoughby was denied. A Colonel Bishop, an assistant to General Willoughby, listened to Iwasaki's protest and request for an explanation, made through Nichi-ei's interpreter, Shigeji Narahara. Bishop answered that he had not heard of the case and that he would speak with Willoughby and give Iwasaki an answer later. Yet Iwasaki received no response.[65]

Tokumitsu offers another version of how Nichi-ei protested to the military censorship section. As soon as he heard about the banning of *The Japanese Tragedy*, he went to CIE to demand an explanation. Conde, in a discouraged tone, referred him to CCD.[66] Tokumitsu immediately went there, but was told by Mihata that no explanation could be given there. "Where can I get an answer?" asked Tokumitsu. The distressed Mihata replied, "I cannot answer anything, but can only say that it came from General Headquarters." Tokumitsu urged that Iwasaki, as the producer of *The Japanese Tragedy*, go to General Headquarters.

When Iwasaki and Tokumitsu visited General Headquarters, they were met by Willoughby, accompanied by two subordinates. Iwasaki, reading from a prepared statement "slowly, in clear English," again asked for an explanation. Willoughby did not even open his mouth, but merely stared at them, while one of his subordinates took notes. The Japanese filmmakers asked the Americans to send an answer later if they could not answer on the spot, and left. They never received a response.[67]

Iwasaki had heard that Premier Shigeru Yoshida was complaining about the film; however, since it had passed both civil and military censorship two months before, he had never imagined that it would be banned. Iwasaki heard the following account from Mark Gayn and other foreign journalists: Premier Yoshida saw *The Japanese Tragedy* at a regular private screening at his residence on August 2 and was enraged by what he considered a devastatingly critical film. He asked General Willoughby, who happened to be one of the guests that day, to convey his request to ban the film to General MacArthur. Willoughby supported Yoshida's request, and consequently the film was banned.[68]

On September 10, 1946, Mark Gayn accompanied David Conde on a visit to Iwasaki, who had been assaulted during the controversy and was recovering at home.[69] Akira Ando, a notorious right-wing gangster boss, is said to have wanted to buy the financially distressed Nichi-ei subsequent to the banning of *The Japanese Tragedy*. Iwasaki declined this offer, and he believed that it was Ando who then sent two assassins, carrying Japanese swords, to attack him. However, Iwasaki is generally believed to have been attacked by or at the behest of right-wingers who were infuriated by the treatment of the emperor in his film. Gayn suggests that there was a close relationship between Ando and Michael Bergher, Chief Film Officer at the Central Motion Picture Exchange in General Headquarters. He describes a scheme on the part of the American film industry, with the help of Ando, to monopolize the Japanese film market.[70]

Iwasaki recounted the case as follows: "The American censors stopped it [The Japanese Tragedy]. I asked why. They said it was orders from General Willoughby. Then my friends told me the picture was shown secretly at Premier Yoshida's residence, and there were some American guests from the Military Intelligence Section, and Yoshida asked them to ban the picture."[71]

Interestingly, Iwasaki attributed to Gayn his information that Yoshida saw the film, and Gayn gave Iwasaki as his source. The undeniable fact we may deduce from these statements is the close relationship among Iwasaki, Gayn, and Conde.

Iwasaki's information was in fact generally correct, with a few emendations. The military censorship documents show that Yoshida had known what kind of film The Japanese Tragedy was before the August 2 screening, and was careful to invite American officers. Willoughby himself was not present at the screening, but two of his subordinates, Lt. Col. D. S. Tait and Lt. Col. Thomas P. Davis, reported back to him on the film and Willoughby then initiated the second censorship review.

Tait and Davis saw The Japanese Tragedy at the Premier's residence on August 2 at 12:30 P.M. Both of them wrote reports on the same day, Tait to Willoughby and Davis to Col. W. S. Wood of the Military Intelligence Section.[72] They were told that Brig. Gen. Frayne Baker of the Public Relations Office, a very influential and conservative assistant to MacArthur,[73] and Lt. Col. D. R. Nugent, the top officer of CIE, had also been invited but did not attend. Davis felt that "it is patently obvious that we had been invited to the showing in the hope that SCAP might be influenced to take some action in banning this and other films of its kind." Jiro Shirasu, Chief of the Liaison Office of the Japanese imperial government, who was also there, explained to the Americans that the film had been made "with the collaboration of Mr. Conde of CIE, whom he believed had been relieved of his post because of the film."[74]

The two American officers found the technical quality of the film poor ("cheaply made by pasting together old stills and bits of newsreels" [Davis] and "a political propaganda film thinly disguised as a 'documentary,' . . . . poorly put together and badly printed" [Tait]). Both outlined the film's content, and finally gave fairly close descriptions of the emperor scene. Davis wrote as follows:

> News clipping headlining [the] Philippine demands for the trial of the emperor as a war criminal, a communist gathering at which a young woman makes a fanatical appeal for the trial of the emperor, a photograph of the emperor in all his glory and medals which fades into a recent picture of the man in slouched hat and stooped shoulders, after which the show ends with the photos of soldier's ashes [sic] being unloaded from a ship.

Tait wrote more concisely: "It shows the surrender ceremony on the 'Missouri,' then, Japanese war criminals arriving at Sugamo Prison, and at last a picture of the emperor, saying 'This is the man who should be punished.'"

The two American officers concluded in their reports that the film should be banned "in the interests of public order," because "its radical treatment of the emperor" might "well provoke riots and disturbances."[75] Their logic is congruent with General MacArthur's decision that, because the emperor had supported the occupation and because abolishing the imperial system would threaten the nation's stability, the imperial institution should be protected.

The Military Intelligence Section then verified that the print shown at Yoshida's was the version that had passed its censorship. CCD was greatly annoyed by the delay in the delivery of the print from Shirasu's office and concluded that he deliberately delayed for three days his report on how the government had obtained its print—a report that would make clear that the print was the version once approved by CCD. This delay resulted in CCD's own initiative to bring in a print and to have Davis determine whether the print he had seen on August 2 was "identical with the print as passed" by CCD.[76] This episode reveals the ambiguous attitude of the Japanese government, which obviously wanted to manipulate the Americans to achieve its purpose, yet did not know exactly how quickly and aggressively it should act to respond to the Americans' own demands.

CCD then decided to revise its previous evaluations of the key people mentioned in the film. Their judgments once again varied, and included the classifications "probably unquestionable" (concerning Hideki Tojo and his successor as premier, Kuniaki Koiso), "justifiable" (two major *zaibatsu* [family-owned conglomerate] entrepreneurs), "bad taste" (another two entrepreneurs), "even more dubious taste" (Ichiro Hatoyama, a politician "who has been purged but who has never been arrested"), "tantamount to political libel" (two politicians), and "the inference is obvious" (the emperor).[77]

Subsequently, on August 7, the censor whose initials were W.S.W. (possibly W. S. Wood) recommended to Col. Rufus S. Bratton, Chief of the Civil Intelligence Section of G-2 (military intelligence) that, "In view of the reports made on this film by two experienced officers, I recommend: That the film be suppressed as one which is detrimental to the aim of the occupation."[78]

On August 9, W.B.P. (William Benjamin Putnam) of CCD expressed an opposing opinion. He argued that the film includes no "violent criticism, vituperation [or] ridicule which go[es] beyond legitimate discussion of the emperor." Noting that "the discussion of the Imperial System and of the present emperor is allowed, including both defense and criticism," Putnam concluded that the film did not indulge in criticism "which necessitates [its] suppression." He insisted that, if this type of discussion of the emperor were found in other places, it might require a change in policy in all public media, but that the present policy did not require change, in that

　a. It insures the freedom of speech and press which is encouraged by SCAP.
　b. It protects the emperor from ridicule, vituperation or virulent criticism which would:
　　1. Disturb the public tranquility.
　　2. Undermine the position of a ruler, for whom the majority of the Japanese people have deep affection, and whose cooperation has eminently assisted the smooth and successful progress of the Occupation.[79]

The final paragraph speaks directly to the usefulness of the emperor and his new image, as shaped by the American authorities. Putnam, hewing to the General Headquarters policy on the emperor, concluded that suppression of the film was not necessary, compared to the importance of protecting the basic right of freedom of expression and the potential danger of causing a disturbance of public tranquility.

The next day, W.S.W. sent a brief to Colonel Bratton arguing that, although CCD's statement that the film "does not violate censorship policy is correct," the film should nonethelesss be suppressed. He based his argument on the judgment of the two officers who had seen the film at Yoshida's on August 2 that it might result in rioting or other disorders. He continued that the suppression of this particular film "does not necessarily mean that we must revise the censorship code."[80]

This opinion must have been evaluated and then supported by General Willoughby. On August 12, the Civil Intelligence Section sent a "check sheet" to CCD recommending the suppression of the film and noting that "That recommendation has been concurred in by General Willoughby." It attached Wood's notes as "authority for suppressing the film" and called it a "necessary action."[81]

Thus, censors at every level had differing opinions as to whether or not *The Japanese Tragedy* should be suppressed, even during the second round of censorship. The following facts are clear: (1) CCD and the Civil Intelligence Section conveyed their opinions independently; however, the latter's position prevailed. (2) Their final conclusions were subject to approval by General Willoughby. (3) In this case, the decision was a choice between freedom of expression, which the occupation government ardently advocated as a necessary element of a democratic society, and potential damage to the smooth functioning of the occupation. In the end, the necessity for the latter was used to justify banning the film, undercutting the occupation's idealistic philosophy.

THE SEIZURE OF THE PRINTS

Iwasaki hurriedly arranged screenings of *The Japanese Tragedy* during the last week before the film was to be confiscated by the censors. He found a 250-seat auditorium at the Traffic Culture Museum in downtown Tokyo, and screened the film three times a day for seven days.[82] Another screening was arranged by a student group on or about August 15 at a large classroom at the Law School of the University of Tokyo. The print was borrowed for the occasion from the Traffic Culture Museum.[83]

Once the deadline for the confiscation, August 20, had passed, CCD promptly began to track down every existing print of the suppressed film. (According to a military censorship document, inconsistent with Iwasaki's account, Nichi-ei was "ordered to bring in to Motion Picture Department of CCD all the negative and positive prints" by August 16, not August 20.) The censorship office also supposedly notified the Nichi-ei Company by letter on August 15 of their decision finding *The Japanese Tragedy* "unsuitable for showing to the public," without further explanation. This letter threatened subsequent action in case of "any instances of non-compliance," based on the occupation government's directive of January 28, 1946, regarding the film censorship.[84]

On August 16, the military censorship office discovered that, among Nichi-ei's ten 35 mm positive prints, one had been made "on raw film stock furnished by the Soviet Mission, which intends to send the print to the U.S.S.R.," and had been delivered to the Russian embassy. The censors pointed out the illegality of reproducing Japanese films and importing raw film stock "without SCAP's clearance and without obtaining an import permit." The censorship office recommended that the Foreign Liaison Sub-Section impound the print, thus enlarging its own involvement into the diplomatic sphere.[85] Whether or not the print was ever delivered from the Russian embassy to CCD is not known. Kamei believes that this print eventually arrived in Moscow, and that another print was also requested by the New Zealand Mission, although whether or not the latter actually received it is not known.[86] In addition to the Soviet Union, New Zealand was among the countries (also including Australia, the Philippines, and China) whose press was expressing the view that the emperor should be brought to trial.[87] Another 35 mm duplicate print had been sold to the leftist Korean Association of Japan and its Minshu Eiga Company, which turned it in to CCD on August 30.[88]

In addition, the military censors learned that Iwasaki had ordered three 16 mm prints on June 26, 1946, all of which were handed over to CIE on July 15. In response to CCD's inquiry, CIE answered that it had returned the three prints to Nichi-ei. Nichi-ei brought them to CCD on October 10. The reason given by Nichi-ei for the delay was that Iwasaki had been hospitalized and absent from his office from August 28 to September 25 as a result of the attack, and did not know that the prints were in his desk.[89] Iwasaki does not mention anything in his book about these 16 mm prints. It is unlikely that this delay was an attempt by Nichi-ei to sabotage CCD's efforts, because Nichi-ei and Iwasaki must have been well aware of the censorship office's powerful intelligence network. However, it must be remembered that this same Nichi-ei managed to hide one rush print of the Hiroshima documentary footage throughout the occupation period, despite the order of the occupation government. Thus, although Tokumitsu believes it impossible that any print escaped from CCD's search, Kamei thinks that somebody at Nichi-ei, perhaps whoever had hidden the Hiroshima print, may also have hidden a print of *The Japanese Tragedy*, perhaps even with Iwasaki's knowledge.[90]

The case was not reported in the Japanese media because of occupation censorship. On August 20, the Press, Pictorial and Broadcasting Division of CCD announced the following procedures "per instruction from Colonel Putnam":

a. There will be no discussion of the film, "Tragedy of Japan" with other SCAP agencies or personnel.
b. The views of CCD or of anyone else as to the action taken on this film will not be discussed and there will be no conflict between our actions and another proposed action.
c. Although *there will be no change in present proceedings of film censorship*, no film will be encouraged released *finally* until it has been approved by G-2 and this section will constitute final decision [emphasis is in original].[91]

These measures confirmed CCD's position as concurrent with the recent decisions of top military intelligence officials.

Tokumitsu has stated that Japanese journalists became interested in this case but realized it was unwise to intrude into the affairs of the American authorities. However, many of these journalists secretly agreed that the Japanese government had indeed pressured the American authorities into banning the film. An informer called Nichi-ei saying that, although he did not know exactly how it had been done, the Imperial House Agency had complained to the Japanese government that a film caricaturing His Highness was being shown, and that the Japanese government had then asked the Military Intelligence Section of General Headquarters to ban it.[92]

At least one Tokyo film periodical managed to print the story somehow untouched by censorship. In its question and answer section, a correspondent initialed Y.S. asked the editor of *Shukan Giga Times* the reason that further showings of *The Japanese Tragedy* were prohibited after its screenings at the Traffic Culture Museum from August 11 to August 15. This reader had heard that the major film companies had refused to distribute the film, and that on August 16 it was suppressed "by order of the authorities." The editor answered that the authorities had judged that such a gloomy documentary would not be appropriate for contemporary Japanese, who were supposed to be "bright and cheerful."[93] Although the response did not mention the censorship literally, it certainly indicated that the "authorities" had interfered with freedom of expression. It would seem that the censors overlooked this revelation unintentionally.

According to Tokumitsu, Nichi-ei considered demanding indemnification from the Japanese government and the Imperial House Agency. However, the idea was abandoned because Nichi-ei's parent newspaper companies, realizing that such demands would be futile, offered no support.[94]

CCD reported on September 2 that Nichi-ei had asked it for compensation for the suppression of *The Japanese Tragedy,* which cost the company an estimated ¥557,000. The censors came up with their own estimate of ¥300,000 based on news stories, but decided that no indemnity should be paid.[95] This decision must have been a serious financial blow to Nichi-ei, a relatively small company that already had difficulty coping with inflation.

The same report stated that, after three months, the question of lifting the order suppressing the film would again be opened, "because of the possibility that the attitude of the Japanese people at that time may be less hostile to the type of critical discussion of the emperor which this film contains." However, there is no further mention in the military censorship files as to whether the question was ever in fact reopened.

Of course, "again" could be taken to mean that the question had been raised once more *prior to September 2.* In fact, in the censorship file, there is a letter from General Willoughby to Nichi-ei (attention: Mr. Akira Iwasaki) dated August 22, 1946. Strangely enough, this letter declares the lifting of the ban:

> Upon thorough investigation, the danger that the "Tragedy of Japan" will disturb public tranquility does not seem sufficiently grave to require suppression of this film.
>
> It is the desire of the Supreme Commander for the Allied Powers that the fullest freedom of speech and thought be allowed in Japan, so long as the security of the occupation or its objectives are not endangered.
>
> Accordingly, the temporary suppression of the film "Tragedy of Japan" has been lifted.[96]

Of course, quite to the contrary, the ban was not lifted then or later. *The Japanese Tragedy* was never again shown during the occupation period. Although there might have been further discussion in late August 1946 as to whether or not the ban should be lifted, it clearly was not, and a review of *The Japanese Tragedy* by Naosa Togawa for *Kinema Jumpo* magazine was deleted in full from its September 1946 issue.[97]

CONCLUSION

The case of *The Japanese Tragedy* is unique: no other film, Japanese or foreign, passed the censorship of CIE and CCD, only to be recensored, found unsuitable for public consumption, and suppressed. The critical issue was the film's treatment of the emperor, which had been a great concern of the occupation forces and most particularly of General MacArthur.

The Japanese Tragedy suggests that Emperor Hirohito was responsible for starting the war with the United States in 1941, and he is occasionally described as having uttered "honorable words" encouraging the war effort. For director Kamei, the view of the emperor with its dissolve had a special meaning. Before and during the war, portraits of the emperor and the empress were required to be posted in public places, and to some extent this practice extended to private homes as well. Kamei later stated that he used the dissolve between portraits of the emperor in two different outfits as a way to represent his suspicion that the postwar trend toward "democracy" was also a fashion, like changing costumes.[98] Kamei also points out that, until the end of the war, cameramen had been allowed to shoot the emperor only from the front, so that his slightly stooped posture would not be revealed. But in his film, Kamei used a postwar portrait of Hirohito, whose angle showed his true posture.[99] The message was quite clear to both the Japanese audience and the American censors.

The director Masahiro Shinoda (born in 1931), who made *MacArthur's Children* [*Setouchi shonen yakyudan*] (1984), a film on the occupation period, perceived the imperial system as having been all-powerful during that period:

> It is certain that the emperor was prepared to follow the destiny of the Romanov Family. Even if he had been executed, however, the core of the Japanese state would not have accepted a grafted-on American democracy. The republican government would have quickly collapsed, and we might have experienced a civil war more miserable than the war with the Americans.[100]

Was *The Japanese Tragedy* really likely to provoke civil disturbances? Over forty years after the fact, it is difficult to know for certain, but it seems highly unlikely, even considering that Emperor Hirohito was generally popular at that time among the Japanese people. Two newspaper opinion polls on the imperial system were conducted a few months after the end of the war. A *Yomiuri-Hochi Shimbun* poll on December 9, 1945, resulted in a 95% proemperor response, and an *Asahi Shimbun* poll of January 23, 1946, showed a 92% proemperor reaction. Between 90% and 95% of the Japanese people, then, are believed to have favored the newly liberalized postwar imperial system, as opposed to the wartime regime.[101] Although the effect of *The Japanese Tragedy* must have been, and still is, powerful, the belief that it would move the Japanese public to riot may have been rooted in paranoia of a kind all too prevalent among the American occupiers.

On the other hand, the threat of riots may have only been a cover for the anticommunist feeling that was the underlying rationale for the banning. The direct involvement of the communist producer Iwasaki and the leftist director Kamei, as well as the interest of the Russian embassy and the Korean Association of Japan (both of which Iwasaki completely ignored in his otherwise detailed account of this case), must have provided the American censors with a good reason to suspect the influence of the Soviet Union.

Moreover, Conde's resignation from the occupation government, voluntary or forced, coincided with the banning of *The Japanese Tragedy.* Whether Conde's departure was related to the banning of the film remains unclear. Although Tokumitsu did not believe that there was a connection, he recounts one episode that gives good grounds for suspicion of Conde as a communist or a communist sympathizer. Conde complained to Tokumitsu that Nichi-ei's newsreels did not include enough close-ups and long takes of the Japan Communist Party leaders released from prison by General MacArthur after the war.[102] Indeed not only some Japanese filmmakers, but also some American occupation officials suspected that Conde was a Communist Party member.[103] After leaving the occupation government, he started working for the International News Service and Reuters. After an article of his criticizing MacArthur's policy appeared in *The St. Louis Dispatch*, his visa was not renewed, and he was deported from Japan in 1947.[104]

If Conde's resignation was tied to his political views, it would indicate the presence of anti-Soviet and/or anticommunist feeling among the American occupation forces at an early stage of the occupation. Such red-baiting reached its height around 1950, at the start of the Korean War. However, the suppression of *The Japanese Tragedy,* along with Conde's departure from the occupation government, signaled the start of the trend in the sphere of cinema barely one year after the beginning of the occupation.

Another important point is that the intelligence-gathering abilities of both the occupation forces and the Japanese film community were highly developed. The Americans monitored practically every action of those Japanese film people of whom they were suspicious. For instance, Iwasaki is on the list of one hundred individuals under CCD surveillance. Other film people on the list include directors Heinosuke Gosho and Teinosuke Kinugasa, and screenplay writer Yusaku Yamagata, all of whom were active in the Toho union's strikes. Critics Kiichi Sasaki and Kiyoteru Hanada and theater and film actor Yoshi Hijikata are also on the list.[105] Japanese filmmakers also managed to collect highly reliable information concerning the relationships between, and the actions of, the Japanese government and top-level officers of the American occupation forces, with the help of foreign journalists.

The most ironic element of this story is that the same Iwasaki and Kamei who had suffered greatly at the hands of the wartime Japanese government suffered again under the American occupation forces, which had been considered the liberating army of democracy. In marked contrast, most Japanese filmmakers who had made films throughout the war were able to continue making films under the occupation without any serious problems.

The suppression of The Japanese Tragedy resulted from an intrinsic contradiction within occupied Japan: the Americans decided to rule the country by means of the existing Japanese governmental and bureaucratic system, rather than destroying it, as they did in occupied Germany. The most vocal Japanese critics of the emperor were communists, and the Americans thus equated all antiemperor feelings among the Japanese people with communism, in many cases without justification.

The banning of and information blackout concerning the film were extremely upsetting to the Japanese filmmakers involved. Being unable to count on Japanese media support, they could not even speak out in their own defense. Furthermore, the ban was financially costly and had a chilling effect on the Japanese film industry and on the kinds of subjects filmmakers might tackle in the future. When Kamei, along with several other Japanese film people, attended a screening of The Japanese Tragedy arranged by the author in 1984, some of the viewers argued that it was around the time that the film was banned that the Japanese people stopped actively discussing the responsibility of Emperor Hirohito as a war criminal. They recalled that, until then, the discussion of that topic had been heated.[106] The shock treatment that suddenly silenced the discussion concerning the emperor as a war criminal was ultimately very effective.

The conflict in this case was between freedom of expression, which the American occupiers ardently advocated as a necessary element of a democratic society, and the potential danger of hampering the smooth operation of the occupation. It is encouraging to know that some among the American censors believed that the necessity of protecting freedom of speech outweighed the possibility that the film would provoke public disturbances. The fact that such idealistic beliefs could not survive against the American anticommunist mentality may in itself be considered a Japanese tragedy.

The author reported her research on the censorship process for *The Japanese Tragedy* in early 1986 to director Kamei. He first recalled that the period when the film was made was an uncertain time and that everyone in both the occupation government and the Japanese government was extremely nervous. He himself never thought at the time that he was doing anything unusual, but believed that an ordinary matter was the object of overreaction by both sets of authorities.

Concerning the possibility of his film's causing riots among the Japanese people, Kamei admitted that the proemperor feeling had been so strong that the American occupation forces were very concerned, because they sincerely hoped to carry out the occupation smoothly. Kamei also believed that certain mass protests must have worried the Americans. These included the first postwar May Day, part of which turned into a serious demonstration in front of the Imperial Palace, as crowds demanded rice.

Kamei, Iwasaki, and other Japanese filmmakers recognized that there were two opposing sides within the occupation government: those who were trying idealistically and radically to democratize Japan—the so-called "New Dealers," who included Conde—and the more conservative forces, who triumphed in this case. Kamei recognized this opposition as an example of the American democratic tradition in action. He also praised the American government's release of its once-classified documents on the case (as usual, earlier than the Japanese government would have) as another example of that tradition.

On the other hand, the director was more critical of his own people, believing that "Japanese people are, at heart, still trying to conquer the world, and nowadays their ambition has taken the form of economic warfare." He insisted that "Japanese business practice is basically very violent, although on the surface Japanese businessmen may seem polite." His observation has appeared more and more accurate, particularly as the economic tensions between Japan and the United States have grown more serious in the course of the past decade.

Kamei then began to see things from a wider viewpoint than the strictly national. "Instead of thinking about our problems in terms of territorial units, such as Japan, America, the Soviet Union, and China, or the emperor and such," he said, "I believe that the essential problem that surrounds us is global. I have been extending the scale of my way of thinking." In the winter of 1986, he was making an ecology film titled *All Living Beings Are Friends* [*Seibutsu mina tomodachi*], believing that the time had come to make people realize that "rather than making war to defend our own countries, we must stop war to defend our own planet." He continued: "The greatest task imposed on science now is to make people realize that we cannot depend on science."[107]

Prior to 1986, Kamei had continued making both dramatic and documentary films until 1963. His most recent film, following a hiatus of over twenty years, was an intriguing step forward for the principled and ever-energetic director.

Kamei passed away after an illness on February 27, 1987, on the day of the Tokyo premiere of *All Living Beings Are Friends*. In the United States, two of his films, *Solders at the Front* and *Between War and Peace,* were at that point being premiered in fourteen cities. The overdue introduction of this little-known Japanese director to those outside of his native country had just begun.[108]

4

RECOMMENDED
SUBJECTS

As soon as the war ended, Japanese filmmakers began to make so-called "democratization films" or "democratization enlightenment films," in line with the recommendations made by CIE. This agency proposed subjects to treat and directions to pursue—including condemnation of the crimes of the militarists and "war-mogul" zaibatsu, the equality of women, and civil and human rights—with the purpose of encouraging the democratization and demilitarization of Japan. Because almost no producers, directors, or actors had been purged as war collaborators, the same filmmakers who had promoted the war effort up until August 1945 immediately began to make films promoting democracy.

As the Cold War proceeded, subjects such as the condemnation of capitalist-militarist alliances, promotion of the labor union movement, and criticism of the imperial system (which was officially abolished by the new

Constitution of Japan) were more and more frowned upon by the Americans, who were increasingly concerned with communist influences in Japan.

This chapter will discuss the themes that were recommended by CIE as appropriate subjects for Japanese films. In the following chapter, we will closely analyze an archetypal democratization film made according to these guidelines: Akira Kurosawa's *No Regrets for Our Youth* (1946).

DEMOCRATIZATION

The speed with which the Japanese studio heads changed their policy from promoting war to promoting democracy frequently astounded their employees. Yumeji Tsukioka was the female star of *Separation Is Also Pleasure* [*Wakare mo tanoshi*], which was being produced by Daiei Studio during August 1945. The film was about the separation of the heroine from her lover, who was drafted. On August 15, after the Japanese defeat, the young actress was convinced that she would have to change her profession. She could not imagine that Daiei Studio, which had actively promoted the war, could survive under the new political system.

After a tearful visit to the outer garden of the Imperial Palace, she went to see Masaichi Nagata, the president of Daiei, at the studio's business office to say good-bye. Nagata had been dutifully giving speeches at his studio every month, preaching the importance of the film industry's contribution to the war effort. He thus surprised her with his reaction: "What are you talking about? The time for Japanese cinema has just arrived." He had decided to change the character of the draftee in her film to a sailor and to start reshooting immediately. The sections of which the new authorities approved remained, and Daiei hurriedly released the film, now transformed into a harmless musical, on September 13, 1945.[1]

Director Kiyohiko Ushihara submitted his new project, *Repairs for Everything: The Magic Shop* [*Yorozu shuri-ya: Maho Shokai*] to Daiei on August 23, barely a week after the Japanese defeat. Studio production chief Masashi Soga was pleased with it, and assigned Hideo Oguni to write the screenplay. The title was then changed to *The Deceived Man* [*Damasareta otoko*].

In October, David Conde, chief of the Motion Picture and Theatrical Branch of CIE, visited Daiei Studio and its president's home to discuss the new policy with studio executives, directors, and producers. Following up on the September 22 directive, Conde explained his agency's policy more con-

Masaichi Nagata, producer
and head of Daiei Studio.
Courtesy of the Kawakita Memorial Film Institute.

cretely, emphasizing the educational value of filmmaking. His suggestions
elaborated the following points:

1. Depict the Japan-China war from a critical viewpoint, and make clear the
   struggle between militarists and antiwar activists and its results.
2. Do not confine women to roles consisting only of childbearing and
   housework, considering their newly upgraded social status.
3. Treat the subject of war orphans carefully, keeping in mind the good
   examples of *Road to Life* [1931, directed by Nikolai Ekk] and *Boys
   Town* [1938, directed by Norman Taurog].
4. Do not feature Japanese-American characters.

Trying to conform with these suggestions, Ushihara asked the advice of a
Japanese journalist on current problems of political corruption, the release of
political prisoners, and exposés of militarists and zaibatsu. Thereupon Oguni
came up with a script condemning a wartime zaibatsu chief, profiteering from

supplying war materiel, who attempts to control the postwar political scene by manipulating the hero's mentor. The hero fights against the corrupt scheme, and the daughter of the zaibatsu chief falls in love with him.

The American censors wanted to associate with this film project the promotion of the first postwar general election, which was scheduled for the following April. When the script was submitted on December 21, 1945, Conde immediately approved the project, suggesting changes in its title and some of its narrative structure and situations. He wanted the script to clarify the responsibility for war crimes and the hero's political aim to reconstruct Japan as follows:

1. The hero is awakened by the truth, so the title should be changed to a more positive one;
2. Make it clear that the factory workers were drafted to work producing war supplies;
3. It is fine that the hero works for others, but his pursuit of private happiness and individual profit must also be emphasized;
4. Clarify the purposes of the hero's establishing a new political party by presenting his solutions for the imminent problems of people, including those of housing and food;
5. Insert shots of newspaper articles condemning the crimes of the *zaibatsu;* and
6. In the last scene, emphasize the hero, and not his lover.

Conde proposed communicating these ideas in a number of ways, ranging from techniques as crude as showing close-ups of newspaper articles to more general suggestions, such as not making the protagonist appear too idealistic or heroic to be believable. Ushihara was impressed by these suggestions, and the film's title was changed to *Popular Man in Town* [*Machi no ninkimono*].[2] The film was released on March 27, 1946, but won little critical attention.

Tadashi Imai is another director who remembers the strong influence of Conde's suggestions. Imai's first postwar film, *People's Enemy* [*Minshu no teki*] (1946) is a condemnation of zaibatsu. Written by leftists Toshio Yasumi and Yusaku Yamagata, the film depicts corrupt capitalists who, in collusion with the military, exploit their workers and make great profits by converting their factory from fertilizer production to the manufacture of bombs. Clear moral contrasts are made between a good girl and a bad girl, and between the sincere, antiwar workers and the war moguls. Upon the end of the war, the workers finally defeat the capitalists.

Akitake Kono (l.) and Susumu Fujita (c.) in *People's Enemy* [*Minshu no teki*] (1946), directed by Tadashi Imai. Courtesy of the Kawakita Memorial Film Institute.

Thirty-six years later, Imai recalled Conde's influence on the making of *People's Enemy.* According to his account, Toho Studio decided to make this film under Conde's "order." Conde was not content with the original synopsis, and pressured Imai to change some twenty sections, suggesting, for example, the inclusion of a poster saying "Down with Zaibatsu and Capitalists." Imai ignored every one of his suggestions, believing that a film should not be an ideological diatribe. When the film was completed, Conde was reluctant to see it, and it took Imai and producer Naozane Fujimoto several hours to persuade him to go. At the beginning, Conde seemed dissatisfied, but gradually he began to show interest in the film, and ended up singing the "Internationale" along with the hero. Conde was extremely happy with the finished work, and that night he treated Imai, Fujimoto, and Yamagata to some expensive whisky.[3]

The film was released on April 25, 1946, to great critical acclaim. It received the Director's Prize in the newly established Mainichi Film Competition and was ranked eighth on the *Kinema Jumpo* critics' list of the ten best films of the year. Yet Imai himself was not happy with the film, maintaining that Akira Kurosawa's *No Regrets for Our Youth* was much better and that his film did not deserve an award.[4]

At the top of the *Kinema Jumpo* critics' list was Keisuke Kinoshita's first postwar film, *The Morning of the Osone Family* [*Osone-ke no asa*]. This film was also a harsh critique of wartime militarism, and, as its title suggests, projected a new start for postwar Japan. Written by Eijiro Hisaita, who had been active in the proletarian literature movement in the 1930s, the film is about a family whose militaristic uncle exploits everyone in the family. The eldest son is arrested and imprisoned for his liberal beliefs, and the second son, influenced by his uncle, becomes a commando and is killed. As the war ends, the uncle still tries to turn a profit by making a corrupt deal, but the widow of the family finally stands up to him with a long speech condemning the evils of the militarists. The film ends with a scene of the family celebrating the release of the eldest son, followed by a shot of a glaring sun rising over the ocean, as if to hail the triumph of justice. The American censors had strongly recommended the inclusion of this ending, which also mentions that Americans liberated political prisoners. Although Kinoshita was not happy about the idea, he had to include the scene.[5] In addition, Kinoshita tried his best, against the suggestions of the Americans, not to portray the "enemy," the militarist uncle, as thoroughly evil. The director and the screenplay writer were convinced that "there could not be such an evil human being."[6] Nonetheless, the film emerged as a powerful drama with a strong message. This film, too, particularly pleased Conde, who held a party at his own expense for the people involved in its making.[7]

Despite directors' reservations about making political films, *People's Enemy, The Morning of the Osone Family,* and *No Regrets for Our Youth,* along with Kiyoshi Kusuda's *As Long as I Live* [*Inochi aru kagiri*], a biography of an antiwar activist executed as a spy, are considered more mature and successful than most of the other films to be described subsequently. These latter films, simplistically condemning wartime militarists and their collaborators and promoting freedom fighters, were criticized by critics as crudely made and propagandistic. For example, a mere four months after Daiei Studio made

From left to right, Eitaro Ozawa, Haruko Sugimura, and Mitsuko Miura in *The Morning of the Osone Family* [*Osone-ke no asa*] (1946), directed by Keisuke Kinoshita. Courtesy of the Kawakita Memorial Film Institute.

Songs of Allied Destruction [*Eibei gekimetsu no uta*], it released, on December 20, 1945, a film called *The Last Chauvinist Party* [*Saigo no Joi-to*]. The latter film portrays the kindness of the British and American troops who helped modernize Japan in the mid-nineteenth century.

Other examples of crudely propagandistic works include the following films made between 1945 and 1946. *A Descendant of Taro Urashima* [*Urashima Taro no matsuei*] is an exposure of wartime profiteers. *Unexpected Dividend* [*Hyotan kara deta koma*] and *The Comedy Was Finished* [*Kigeki wa owarinu*] are satirical comedies about those who sided with the war effort and militarists. *Who is a Criminal?* [*Hanzaisha wa dareka*] is a biography of an antiwar activist.

Green Home Country [*Midori no kokyo*] and *Thunderstorm* [*Raiu*] deal with the problems of rehabilitating POWs and repatriates. *Brothers of the Meiji Era,* on civil rights activists in the 1880s, is a historical allegory. *The Pioneer of Love* [*Ai no senkusha*] is a biography of a scientist, and *The Man*

Who Strips Off His Gloves [*Tebukuro o nugasu otoko*] is about the liberation of medical science in the late nineteenth century.

Almost any film could achieve commercial success during the immediate postwar period, even films of this type, which flooded the market from late 1945 through 1946. However, considering the complete ideological turnaround that had immediately preceded production of *The Last Chauvinist Party*, it is unlikely that most democratization films were made out of deep conviction or understanding of their subjects. Indeed, this lack of conviction and understanding was probably the reason that most of the democratization films were critical failures.

KISSING AND SEXUAL EXPRESSION

As we have seen in chapter 2, the slightest amorous expression had been condemned as a symbol of Western decadence in the austere atmosphere of wartime Japan. Kissing scenes in foreign films had been cut, and Japanese filmmakers had not dared to include them in their films. An exception was reported by Shochiku star Ichiro Yuki. Yuki maintained that he performed a kissing scene with actress Hiroko Kawasaki in *Women Are in Every World* [*Onna wa itsuno yo mo*] (1931) at the request of director Keisuke Sasaki (unrelated to Yasushi Sasaki). At the critical moment during its censorship session, Yuki intentionally distracted the censor, whom he knew personally, and the scene slipped by unnoticed. But four days after the film's premiere in June 1931, a policeman on duty in a downtown Tokyo theater caught the kissing scene and reported it, which resulted in an immediate halt to the screening and the confiscation of the film. Yet Yuki believes that thousands of viewers all over Japan saw his infamous scene during those first four days.[8]

It is of course unthinkable that Japanese people had never kissed before the end of the war; if nothing else, literature and woodcuts prove the opposite. However, love tended not to be physically demonstrated in public, either in daily life or on the screen. Family members never kissed either, and kissing was for all practical purposes invisible in Japanese culture.[9]

Early in 1946, David Conde read the script of Shochiku Studio's new film *Twenty-Year-Old Youth* [*Hatachi no seishun*]. The film portrays the romance between a girl (Michiko Ikuno) whose father wants her to marry the son of his boss and the young man (Shiro Osaka) whom she really loves.

Shiro Osaka (l.) and Michiko Ikuno in *Twenty-Year-Old Youth* [*Hatachi no seishun*] (1946), directed by Yasushi Sasaki. Courtesy of the Kawakita Memorial Film Institute.

It was thus considered "antifeudalistic" because of its depiction of youths choosing their spouses according to their own free will.[10]

According to Shochiku's liaison, Hideo Komatsu, Conde wanted the producers to include kissing scenes, and instructed Komatsu to convey his suggestion to the producer and director of the film, which he did.[11] The film's director, Yasushi Sasaki, had made the first postwar film to be released in Japan, *Breeze* [*Soyokaze*], which was released on October 11, 1945.[12] This film included "The Song of Apples," which became an overnight hit. However, his next film, *New Wind* [*Shimpu*] (1945), enraged Conde, who claimed that the completed film differed from the script that he had approved. The director thus felt obliged when Conde ordered him to include kissing scenes in *Twenty-Year-Old Youth*. Sasaki states that Conde rationalized his suggestion by saying "Japanese tend to do things sneakily. They should do things openly."[13]

Other sources support this view. Film critic Toru Ogawa writes that the occupation government had quietly suggested that the Japanese studios make "kissing films," pointing out that "Even Japanese must kiss in private." Thereupon Shochiku and Daei, as if they had been waiting for this suggestion, responded by each making a kissing film.[14] Film historian Jun'ichiro Tanaka claims that an American censor and a Nisei officer one day recommended to a Shochiku employee that kissing scenes be included in the studio's films, remarking "We believe that even Japanese do something like kissing when they love each other. Why don't you include that in your films?" In order to try to satisfy the new authorities, Shochiku cautiously began to include kissing scenes. They were rather awkward at first, but the censors were nonetheless pleased to see them.[15]

Walter Sheldon reports that Michiko Ikuno had to receive special instruction in kissing techniques for *Twenty-Year-Old Youth*—"from a prominent American wire-service correspondent (whom she had been dating) as the nearest available probable expert."[16] Whether this was true or not, these landmark scenes were shot in an atmosphere of tension. The star was said to have used a small piece of wax paper[17] or a piece of gauze[18] on her lips, or a piece of cotton inside her mouth,[19] to avoid direct contact, probably for sanitary as well as moral reasons.

Finally, on May 23, 1946, came the historic release of *Twenty-Year-Old Youth*. The critical scenes appear at two points in the film. Foreshadowed by the male lead's touching the lips of the heroine with his finger, the first "official" kiss seen on the Japanese screen occurs in an interior scene, in which he kisses her from behind while she is seated. The scene is associated with the image of flowers in a vase and cherry blossoms outside the house. (The film's theme song, in an animated rhythm, also mentions the "cute flowers of the sweet pea," accompanying romantic images of lovers and flowers.) In the second kissing scene, the lovers are in a boat on a lake. A close-up of him looking down at her while she looks up at him is followed by a kiss in the same position. This idyllic and romantic image, backed up with the theme song, closes the film. These were sensational moments in Japanese cinema history. In 1984, Masahiro Shinoda used the first kissing scene in his *MacArthur's Children,* with the cheering children eagerly awaiting the moment in a local theater.

The more provocatively titled *A Certain Night's Kiss* [*Aruyo no seppun*], directed by Yasuki Chiba, was released on the same day by Daei Studio.[20] The film is about the romances, frequently accompanied by songs and music, of three young couples: a poet and a singer, an architect and a secretary, and an inventor and a hairdresser.[21] At the end of the film, the poet and the singer stand face to face, staring at each other in the rain. The kiss suggested by the title, however, is in fact obscured by her dropped umbrella, as the studio lost its nerve at the last moment.[22] Yet, despite this lingering reticence, the simultaneous appearance of two movies with kissing scenes broke the dike. Henceforth, film after film proudly displayed kissing and embracing.

This new phenomenon elicited both negative and positive responses from filmmakers, critics, and the public. Director Kajiro Yamamoto indignantly wrote that "Mr. C" of CIE now insisted inflexibly that there could be no lovers who did not kiss, despite his own protest that Japanese actually did not kiss in public and that kissing scenes would not be enjoyed.[23] *Stars and Stripes* reported that the leftist Free Film Workers Group severely criticized "irresponsible" producers whose films included "unnecessarily passionate love scenes with kissing, hugging, squeezing, clinging, etc.," for purely commercial reasons. The group felt that these films took advantage of the abolition of prewar censorship to engage in sensationalism, rather than to produce films with a "truly democratic spirit."[24]

Some critics hailed the freedom of amorous expression finally and unexpectedly granted by the occupation. Kyoichiro Nambu, for instance, wrote, "This occupation order startled moviemakers. It was like a blessing from heaven. For how many decades have we aspired to this!" He added that audiences at *Twenty-Year-Old Youth* were enormously excited.[25] Another source described audiences as "gulping, sighing, and yelling."[26]

Sheldon, on the other hand, claims that the first kissing scene of *Twenty-Year-Old Youth* elicited only "nervous laughter" from its audiences.[27] *Stars and Stripes* reported a mixed response from viewers, some of whom were holding their breath or covering their faces with their hands, while young students were giggling and "yelling 'banzai,' which led to a roar of laughter in the theater."[28]

On the other hand, Jun Izawa, *Asahi Shimbun*'s film critic, gave an extremely harsh review to the first two Japanese kissing films:

> *Twenty-Year-Old Youth* and *A Certain Night Kiss* are so-called "kissing films," making a big deal out of kissing scenes. . . . In general, the acting is so bad that the kissing seems forced, and it looks as though these scenes were included merely for the sake of showing kissing. The true level of the actors' skill became evident at this point. Japanese cinema is degraded by the making of films relying on showing a few seconds of kissing for commercial appeal.[29]

Other critics also opposed the sensationalism of the kissing films. Tadashi Iijima wrote that the "kissing film" phenomenon was insane, and that he absolutely agreed with the resolution of the Free Film Workers Group. He believed that those who made kissing films certainly knew that they were merely products of commercialism.[30] Ichiro Ueno labeled kissing films a shameful result of the exploitation of the liberties granted under democracy.[31] Some critics argued that, because kissing in Japan was not customary among family members or friends as an expression of greeting, it was regarded exclusively as amorous or a form of foreplay by the Japanese; this made kissing on the screen seem lurid and unnatural.[32] Another writer accused producers of imitating the self-indulgence of popular American films, with their emphasis on titillation, rather than courageously taking advantage of their new freedom of expression.[33]

Three months after the release of the first kissing films, the *Yomiuri Shimbun* solicited its readers' opinions concerning them. Out of 411 responses, 73% were pro and 27% were con. The defenders of the kissing films advocated kissing as a candid expression of love. In response to those opposing kissing as nontraditional for Japanese, they insisted that it was time for Japanese to liberate themselves from feudalistic ideas, let love out of the closet, and emotionalize the Japanese cinema. Some of the criticisms of these films included the following:

1. Kissing is not a Japanese habit;
2. If public kissing is not recommended, films should not encourage it;
3. The acting is unskillful and foolish;
4. Superficial commercialism is evident;
5. Kissing films are saccharine, and of no help to those trying to combat postwar decadence and nihilism;
6. Japanese do not know how to kiss, and merely showing kissing to appeal to the viewer's libido is foolish;
7. Kissing is an authentic expression of love only between mothers and children.[34]

Another opponent of public kissing, writer Bunroku Shishi, justified his beliefs with an analysis of Japanese physiognomy. He believed that the high noses of Westerners made their kissing attractive, but felt that the Japanese must have realized centuries ago that their own kissing would not be aesthetically appealing to others, and claimed that this must be the reason why public kissing had become unpopular.[35]

Responding to the criticism that kissing was not Japanese, Ren Yoshi-mura and Eiichi Koishi's 1946 film *Brilliant Revenge* [*Kenrantaru fukushu*], based on Tolstoy's *Resurrection*, included a kissing scene, but one set on a stage, where Japanese actors were performing the roles of westerners.[36]

American cinema, in contrast, has a long history of kissing scenes. As soon as the cinematic medium was introduced to the United States, Ameri-can producers immediately thought of filming a kiss as a novelty. Edison Kinetograph thus brought the famous kiss of May Irwin and John C. Rice from Broadway to the screen in 1896. In close-up, the kiss of this fat, middle-aged couple may look comical to the modern eye, but *The May Irwin–John C. Rice Kiss* became a roaring hit. Its commercial success may have backfired, though, for the film also occasioned one of the first attempts at screen censorship.[37] This kissing film became a sensation in 1897 Osaka, where the benshi explained that kissing was the accepted mode of Western salutation.[38]

Although by the mid-1940s Hollywood had firmly established kissing scenes as the crowning moments of love between its handsome heroes and beautiful heroines, not all of the American authorities in Japan were in favor of public kissing scenes. On March 22, 1946, two months before the first Japanese kissing scenes appeared on the Japanese screen, the occupation government ordered Allied soldiers not to hold women while walking in the street, or otherwise demonstrate physical affection in public.[39] In a 1946 film magazine, mention of "the showing of exaggerated kissing scenes in the American style" was at one point marked for deletion as "crit[icism] of U.S.," but subsequently given an "O.K." by the censor.[40] On the other hand, as we saw in chapter 2, the promiscuous public kissing scenes in *Between War and Peace* were deleted by order of the military censors, who claimed that they constituted criticism of the occupation, suggesting that decadence re-sulted from American influences.

As kissing scenes became common, directors and actors alike were increasingly able to bring them off realistically and maturely. Keisuke Kino-shita's *Phoenix* [*Fujicho*] (1947) was praised as the first Japanese film to show a kissing scene as a natural and necessary element of the plot. Jun Izawa attributed this success to the skill of actress Kinuyo Tanaka and director Kinoshita.[41] Akira Shimizu further perceived in this "beautiful kissing scene" a strong antiwar feeling, in contrast to earlier scenes, which were merely "nervous, guilty, embarrassing, or obscene, coquettish, and base, trying to achieve commercial appeal."[42]

Kinuyo Tanaka (front) and Keiji Sada in *Phoenix* [*Fujicho*] (1947), directed by Keisuke Kinoshita. Courtesy of the Kawakita Memorial Film Institute.

It was Kinoshita's intent to portray kissing as natural and pleasant; however, Ken Uehara, the star who had originally been cast opposite Tanaka, declined to appear in the film. He believed that kissing scenes were not yet necessary in Japanese films, reflecting the current custom of not kissing in public. As a result, newcomer Keiji Sada was cast in his place.[43] Cautious star Setsuko Hara had also declined to appear in kissing films on the grounds that the Japanese did not kiss in their everyday life; she would wait until the time when kissing became more natural among Japanese.[44]

Although Japanese actors and actresses may have become more relaxed in and accustomed to kissing scenes over the years, some still have felt that they could not perform them well enough. Popular actress Yoshiko Yamaguchi was already regarded as an expert for her passionate kissing scenes in *The Bright Day of My Life* and *Desertion at Dawn*. However, when asked her purpose in visiting the United States in 1950, Yamaguchi answered that she wanted to study the technique of kissing, which was underdeveloped in

Yoshiko Yamaguchi (front) and Masayuki Mori in *The Bright Day of My Life* [*Waga shogai no kagayakeru hi*] (1948), directed by Kozaburo Yoshimura. Courtesy of the Kawakita Memorial Film Institute.

Japan.[45] She had become convinced that Japanese were not good at kissing, whereas kissing in American films and plays was "natural, enjoyable, necessary, beautiful and skillful."[46]

Although some Japanese did feel it odd that kissing was now shown on the screen while it was hardly seen in real life in public, particularly between Japanese, the Americans encouraged such scenes purposely to force the Japanese to express publicly actions and feelings that heretofore had been considered strictly private. The American censors felt that the Japanese in general had a tendency to keep thoughts and actions hidden, and that this was wrong. Ever since the surprise attack on Pearl Harbor, Americans had condemned the Japanese more for their "sneakiness" than for any other quality. "Inscrutable" was an adjective widely used in condemnations of the Japanese. They felt uneasy when they perceived that the Japanese were not expressing themselves openly. Thus, if Japanese kissed in private, they should do it in public, too.

Such ideas may reflect the predictable arrogance or cultural imperialism of the conqueror. The Americans, coming from a culture that valued frankness and explicitness, probably could not imagine that Japanese often felt more eroticism in the hidden or the implicit, a preference that is one of the essences of Japanese traditional literature and art.

However, on the whole, most Japanese seem to have welcomed the liberation of sexual expression. The case of kissing scenes was unique in that they were not merely permitted, but in fact strongly suggested by the occupation authorities. Nonetheless, if the Japanese people had not actually enjoyed them, such scenes would not have continued to appear for long on the Japanese screen. Despite all the criticism of the kissing film producers' commercialistic motivations, and the argument that such films degraded morality and decency, the new freedom was in general appreciated by the filmmakers and their audience alike.

The advent of kissing scenes definitely contributed to the emancipation of sexual expression in other media. In October 1946 the first sexually oriented magazine, *Ryoki* (meaning "In Search of the Bizarre"), appeared. Unlike the kissing films, this magazine had no pretensions of educating or enlightening its readers concerning values. By the end of the first half of 1947, some thirty such magazines were being published, and the boom continued until the end of 1948, during which period more than 150 of these publications had been put out. These pulp magazines were known as *kasutori zasshi,* or "dregs magazines," named after a cheap (and illegal) alcoholic beverage made from sake dregs. The popular belief was that it was safe to drink as much as two *go* (one go is around 0.18 liters). Similarly, although none of these cheap magazines lasted past the second go (*go* also means issue), they were widely read all over the country.[47]

The kasutori magazines concentrated on pornography, crimes, grotesquerie, and exposés. Kissing soon became their main theme. Like the kissing films, they were immediately criticized by those who insisted that kissing was not a Japanese tradition. The magazines, in response, began to defend kissing as modern and antifeudalistic.

One of the magazines, *Riibe* (after the German word for love, *Liebe*) published a cover story on how to kiss in its first issue, in November 1947. The article attempted to instruct readers in how to achieve the maximum enjoyment in kissing, and affirmed the significance of kissing to the liberation of humanity,[48] thus supplementing the opportunities for visual instruction afforded by the kissing films.

Yukiko Todoroki (l.) and Chiaki Tsukioka in *The Gate of Flesh* [*Nikutai no mon*] (1948), directed by Masahiro Makino. Courtesy of the Kawakita Memorial Film Institute.

The kasutori magazines began to disappear around 1949, with the advent of more family-oriented publications that promoted an idealized conception of sex within the limits of the family unit. Around the same time, as we have seen, control over Japanese cinema was transferred from the American preproduction censors to the Eirin, whose regulations (closely modeled on the American Motion Picture Production Code) sought to protect conventional family values.

The first public striptease show was staged in November 1947 in a small theater in Tokyo, and was received enthusiastically. It was produced by the Toho Theatrical Company in a "frameshow" format, in which young women posed on the stage behind a large frame, imitating famous Western and Japanese seminude paintings and thus imparting an artistic, pseudosophisticated flair to the show. The same theater followed this spectacle with a sensational theatrical piece called *The Gate of Flesh*, based on a popular story by Taijiro Tamura. Portraying the harsh conditions of the lives of streetwalkers, this piece achieved enormous popularity, playing more than a thousand times, and was made into a film by Masahiro Makino in 1948.[49]

Flush with the newly granted freedom to portray sex (as long as the genital areas were not actually exposed), Japanese filmmakers flooded the market with so-called "*ero-guro*" (erotic-grotesque) films full of titillating sexual appeals. Subgenres such as striptease films and "*pan-pan*" (street-walker) films also arose. The attitude of the American and Japanese author-ities toward these films is discussed in chapter 2, in the section on the depiction of antisocial behavior.

The line between obscenity and sensationalism on the one hand and the sincere pursuit of sexual expression on the other has of course always been ambiguous. For example, some critics condemned Kenji Mizoguchi's *Women of the Night* [*Yoru no onna-tachi*] (1948) as sensational and claimed that his *The Picture of Madame Yuki* was titillating. The former film portrays the lives of women in Osaka City who have to resort to prostitution in order to survive; the latter is about the wife of a declining aristocrat who does not love her husband but cannot resist his sexual appeal. Censor Harry Slott was particularly happy with *Women of the Night,* believing it would arouse the public consciousness, and several health and welfare agencies promised their cooperation in its filming.[50] *Women of the Night* was called a "streetwalker film" by some, but was praised by others for its realistic and powerful portrayal of a woman's struggle for survival in the difficult postwar period.[51] The film placed third on the *Kinema Jumpo* critics' list of the ten best films of 1948.

The Picture of Madame Yuki, containing more bed scenes than any previous Japanese film,[52] was condemned by some as a typical erotic-grotesque film, but, at the same time, the significance of its portrayal of eroticism and sexual emancipation, particularly of women, was well appre-ciated.[53] Based on Seiichi Funabashi's popular contemporary novel, the film conveyed the idea that women, too, have sexual desires, which have nothing to do with spiritual values—a concept that could finally be discussed openly in the postwar atmosphere of freedom.

Toshimi Aoyama, a liaison at the Towa Film Company, writes of an episode that shows the enthusiasm of American censors for free sexual expression. Prewar Japanese censors had deleted many sexual scenes from Gustav Machaty's *Ecstasy* (1932, released in Japan in 1935). The American censors wanted to retrieve the deleted scenes, including one in which Hedy Kiesler (later known as Hedy Lamarr) runs in the nude, and another show-ing a close-up of her ecstatic face during a sexual encounter. They promised Aoyama that they would pass these scenes. Unfortunately, Aoyama could not

Kinuyo Tanaka (l.) and Sanae Takasugi in *Women of the Night* [*Yoru no onna-tachi*] (1948), directed by Kenji Mizoguchi. Courtesy of the Kawakita Memorial Film Institute.

find them, as the original negatives of the scenes had been sold to a Hong Kong dealer when the cuts were first made in 1935.[54]

WOMEN'S LIBERATION

Kenji Mizoguchi made a trilogy of "women's liberation films": *The Victory of Women* [*Josei no shori*] (1946), *The Love of Actress Sumako* [*Joyu Sumako no koi*] (1947), and *My Love Has Been Burning* [*Waga koi wa moenu*] (1949). All three straightforwardly advocate women's liberation, and feature Kinuyo Tanaka portraying spiritually and politically conscious heroines. The heroine of the first film is a lawyer who has an affair with a liberal. As a result of his wartime imprisonment, he becomes seriously ill and eventually dies. Meanwhile, she confronts her brother-in-law, a reactionary public prosecu-

Kinuyo Tanaka in *The Victory of Women* [*Josei no shori*] (1946), directed by Kenji Mizoguchi. Courtesy of the Kawakita Memorial Film Institute.

Mitsuko Mito (l.) and Kinuyo Tanaka (second from left) in *My Love Has Been Burning* [*Waga koi wa moenu*] (1949), directed by Kenji Mizoguchi. Courtesy of the Kawakita Memorial Film Institute.

Director Kenji Mizoguchi. Courtesy of the Kawakita Memorial Film Institute.

tor, in court when she defends an unfortunate woman whose distressed circumstances forced her to commit a crime. In several monologues, she attacks the feudalistic Japanese family system that has oppressed women.

The second film is a biography of a pioneering actress in the New Theater movement of the early twentieth century. Her ardent passion for art and uncompromising romantic pursuit of her married mentor have impressed the Japanese. *My Love Has Been Burning* is a biography of a female activist of the "freedom and people's rights movement" in the late nineteenth century. Kaneto Shindo, who cowrote the screenplays of the first and third films, has said that *The Victory of Women* was consciously planned by Shochiku Studio as a "democratization" film, but that *My Love Has Been Burning* was a project that the occupation government forced the studio to make.

Shindo regarded Mizoguchi as incapable of capturing the true meaning of women's liberation, as evidenced by the cardboard personality of the

So Yamamura (l.) and Kinuyo Tanaka (c.) in *The Love of Actress Sumako* [*Joyu Sumako no koi*] (1947), directed by Kenji Mizoguchi. Courtesy of the Kawakita Memorial Film Institute.

lawyer in the first of these films. In the last film, Mizoguchi was again superficial in portraying the activist heroine. Shindo believes that Tanaka's best performance was in the role of the actress Sumako because she could draw on more of her own life in portraying the enthusiastic lover of her art and her man; in contrast, the other two roles required more abstract and intellectual characterizations.[55]

Yoshikata Yoda, a lifelong collaborator of Mizoguchi's and a writer on the second and third films of the trilogy, admits that he could not success-fully dramatize these heroines in his screenplays.[56] Yoda also believes that Mizoguchi did not really understand postwar democracy, probably because he was too concerned with trying to transform himself to catch up with the changing times: "At the historical moment at the end of the war, Mizoguchi was at a loss. He was in the middle of a slump in his career, too. . . . He could not understand postwar democracy, and because the world was drastically changing, he was probably obsessed about changing himself, too. . . . Finally, he realized that he could not grasp anything."[57]

Yoshi Hijikata (l.) and Isuzu Yamada in *Actress* [*Joyu*] (1947), directed by Teinosuke Kinugasa. Courtesy of the Kawakita Memorial Film Institute.

These films, laden with textbook moralizing, were critical failures, although another similar film, Akira Kurosawa's *No Regrets for Our Youth,* achieved great critical and commercial success owing to its impressive portrayal of a strong-willed heroine—one more complete and more dramatically well-rounded than those of Mizoguchi.

An interesting off-screen episode illustrates how postwar ideas affected a female film worker during this period. Actress Isuzu Yamada was the star of Toho Studio's *Actress* [*Joyu*], directed by Teinosuke Kinugasa, which was being made simultaneously in 1947 to compete with Mizoguchi's *The Love of Actress Sumako.* While playing the role of a passionate lover, Yamada actually did fall in love with the director, a married man, who became her mentor. But this was not the only parallel between the on- and off-screen stories. Like the heroine of Mizoguchi's *My Love Has Been Burning*—who becomes aware of the private egotism and chauvinistic attitudes of a lover who preaches on behalf of civil rights in public—Yamada gradually began to feel disillusioned by the "contradiction between what [her mentor] says and what he does." She eventually parted from Kinugasa and married the leftist actor Yoshi Kato, whom she found she could genuinely respect and under whose influence she herself became a leftist activist.[58]

PROMOTION OF THE NEW CONSTITUTION

During the summer before the Constitution of Japan was proclaimed on November 3, 1946, the Japanese Ministry of Education contacted Japanese film companies to discuss a plan to propound the principles of the new constitution. Film producers did not generally show much enthusiasm, believing that such projects would hardly be entertaining and that the government should underwrite them.[59]

After some negotiation, the producers became more cooperative. When the Committee for Promoting the New Constitution proposed making films to commemorate its proclamation, each of the three major studios decided to submit a film. Taking the traditional characteristics of the studios' work into consideration, the Committee proposed that each focus on a different aspect of the new constitution. Civil rights would be treated by Daiei Studio, which specialized in period films, while the theme of equality was assigned to Shochiku Studio, which was known for its melodramas and films about women. Toho Studio, which specialized in contemporary subjects, would make a film on the renunciation of war. The committee would contribute only limited funding, and each studio would take financial responsibility for the completion and distribution of its film. All other details were left in the studios' hands.

The committee was headed by Hitoshi Ashida, then Minister of Foreign Affairs, who served as Premier from February to October of 1948. During the initial discussions, Ashida stated that he was not worried about the films seeming crude or commercialistic, because they were indeed to be commercial productions and, after all, the studios knew best how to attract the public. In contrast, one of the other participants in the discussion, Masaichi Nagata of Daiei, emphasized how important it would be for the producers to really understand the significance of the event they were depicting.

The new constitution was to be effective as of May 3, 1947. In order to reduce the conflicts that might result from releasing all three films simultaneously, the studios decided that the first film would be released during the

Tsumasaburo Bando in *The Political Theater* [*Soshi gekijo*] (1947), directed by Hiroshi Inagaki. Courtesy of the Kawakita Memorial Film Institute.

week of April 29, the second the following week, and the third two weeks later.[60]

Shochiku released *Flames of Passion* [*Joen*] on April 29, as agreed. Written by Eijiro Hisaita and directed by Minoru Shibuya, the film features Shochiku's two popular stars, Shuji Sano and Mitsuko Mito. It tells the story of a couple who had married for the sake of their families. They are thinking of getting a divorce but are gradually awakened by genuine human affection. On May 6, Daiei released *The Political Theater* [*Soshi gekijo*]. Featuring the studio's swordplay stars, Tsumasaburo Bando and Ryunosuke Tsukigata, as well as female star Takako Irie, the film was directed by period film specialist Hiroshi Inagaki and written by swordplay master Fuji Yahiro. It is a biography of Sadanori Sudo, who produced political theatrical pieces extolling the Freedom and People's Rights movement in the 1880s, which resulted in the promulgation of the Constitution of Imperial Japan in 1889 and the first nationwide election of the Lower House in 1890. This movement was led by

Ryo Ikebe (l.) and Hatae Kishi in *Between War and Peace* [*Senso to heiwa*] (1947), directed by Satsuo Yamamoto and Fumio Kamei. Courtesy of the Kawakita Memorial Film Institute.

visionaries who struggled with the severe oppression and restrictions imposed by the Meiji imperial government, and it became one of the favorite themes for films promoted by the occupation government.

Although these first two films were released successfully as scheduled, the third and final film was not released until July 10. At Toho Studio, the company labor union had taken over the production administration (see chapter 6). The studio's project for the Committee for Promoting the New Constitution, *Between War and Peace*, was assigned to two directors, the communist Satsuo Yamamoto and the leftist Fumio Kamei. The producer, Takeo Ito, explained the unusual arrangement as a reflection of the cooperative spirit of Toho's labor union movement of that time.[61] It also seems to reflect an experimental streak in Toho's of filmmaking methodology, combining the talents of the documentarist Kamei and the powerful dramatist Yamamoto.

Kamei had made *The Japanese Tragedy,* which, as we have seen in chapter 3, was banned by the occupation military censors in the summer of

1946. The others involved in the production of the film were also communists or leftists. Ito, a Japan Communist Party member, was the chairman of the Nichi-ei-en or Japan Movie and Theater Workers Union, which was leading the Toho labor union strikes. Cinematographer Yoshio Miyajima, also a Communist Party member, was one of the core unionists at Toho, and writer Toshio Yasumi was also known for his leftist-oriented work. The American suspicions as to the ideological backgrounds of these filmmakers were obvious: the military censors' memorandum on the production of the film in May 1947 stated bluntly that producer Ito and director Kamei were "confirmed 'Reds.'"[62]

As the title suggests, *Between War and Peace* portrays scenes from both wartime and peacetime; its story was inspired by D. W. Griffith's *Enoch Arden* (1911).[63] A ship carrying the draftee hero (Hajime Izu) to the Chinese front is bombed and he is reported killed. His wife (Hatae Kishi), left alone with a baby at home, undergoes many hardships. A good friend of her husband (Ryo Ikebe) helps her, and eventually they marry. But after the war, to their surprise, the husband returns. He had in fact been a POW in China, where he was well treated and came to realize the evils of Japanese militarism. Despondent at first, he soon decides to help the new couple.

One day, a psychological aftershock from a wartime air raid drives the new husband into delirious behavior. Unappreciative of the efforts of his wife and his friend to help him, the jealous and desperate man is tempted by criminals and is almost hired by an oppressive capitalist to help break a strike. At the last minute, however, his conscience is awakened by friendship and love. Upon seeing the problem resolved, the first husband leaves the two to become a teacher, to help inculcate in children the spirit of peace.

The completion of the film was delayed for twenty days, owing to the large scale of the production, which required the construction of numerous sets.[64] After passing CIE's censorship, it was submitted to CCD on May 14, 1947. Because there was no sign for several weeks that the military censors had passed the film, both the filmmakers and the managers of Toho became concerned, and began to visit the censors to make inquiries. They also visited CIE, and attempted to pressure the civil censors into helping them by saying that, if the new film were held up much longer, the studio would have to rerelease films made before the war.

At the same time, the management and antiunion workers at Toho emphasized to the censors that they had had nothing to do with the film, and had no control over the communist-dominated labor union that had produced it. Indeed, they would welcome the censors' action to suppress the film, which might in turn help them to get rid of the communists and unionists. Toho's public relations executive told censor Walter Mihata that the studio was prepared to "wipe off the 7,000,000 Yen" production expense if the suppression of the picture would make the Toho labor union realize that the "production policy on pictures must be the responsibility of management." Antiunion director Kunio Watanabe and others who left Toho for Shin-Toho Studio told the censor that "the whole basis of the picture is to belittle the Americans and the loyalty to the emperor idea."[65]

In late May, CCD decided that the complete suppression of *Between War and Peace* would be inadvisable because it had already been widely publicized as a so-called Constitution Commemoration Film. The censors hoped that the film would eventually be shown, with revisions and deletions minor enough not to be noticed by the public. The deletions included scenes that the censors considered to be critical of the occupation, as discussed in chapter 2.[66] In mid-June, the military censors learned that rumors were circulating that the American censors were holding up release of the film. These reports came not only from Toho, the Committee for Promoting the New Constitution, and CIE, but, most importantly, from the Telepress Section of the military intelligence section that was monitoring Japanese correspondence.[67] A local film weekly attempted to report that *Between War and Peace* had been suspended by the censors and that it had even been said that the film would not be released. Consequently, this description was deleted.[68]

By now the censors were receiving visitors daily from both the production and business offices of the studio seeking information on the censorship action. The delay must have been difficult for all parties. A minor Japanese official in the Committee for Promoting the New Constitution, obviously embarrassed by the situation and hoping not to offend the censors, had tried to disassociate the committee from the film by telling an occupation official that the committee was rather disappointed with the film in its completed form.[69]

The film was finally passed on June 13, 1947, after the deletion of seventeen sections, amounting to around thirty minutes.[70] Producer Ito claims that the film was passed after twenty-four deletions, totaling more than thirty minutes, which made the film harder to understand;[71] the studio may have been ordered to make the additional revisions so that the initially deleted parts would not be noticed by the public. The film was released on July 10. Although it won both praise and condemnation from the critics,

Between War and Peace was definitely the most successful of the three films made to promote the new constitution. It placed second on the *Kinema Jumpo* critics' list of the ten best films of 1947, and was particularly praised for its excellent combination of dramatic sections (directed by Yamamoto) with documentary and semidocumentary sections (directed by Kamei), as well as its earnest antiwar appeals. Toho had had to use unknown actors and actresses after its big stars left for Shin-Toho because of the strikes, and the three young leads were praised for their fresh talent. On the other hand, critical dissatisfacton with the film stemmed from a perceived crudeness in its expression of the theme without fully developing its characters and its presentation of a passive hatred of war rather than an active and more constructive antiwar ideology.[72] Ironically, Shochiku's *Flames of Passion* and Daiei's *The Political Theater,* which had not had any trouble with the censors, were almost completely ignored by the critics and the public alike. Research established that audiences preferred *Between War and Peace* in part because the film's theme was a familiar one, its antiwar message was well developed, and it took an optimistic view of the situation of war widows.[73]

BASEBALL

Among the more unusual subjects that American censors tried to promote was the game of baseball. During the war the sport had been persecuted in Japan as a symbol of the enemy's culture, but it immediately regained its substantial prewar popularity as soon as the war ended. Masahiro Makino's timely response was his 1946 light comedy *Carefree Father* [*Nonkina tosan*], in which he featured twenty-five professional baseball players in scenes of the game.[74] Old and young, rich and poor alike, practically every Japanese enjoyed the sport, as a spectator and/or a participant. Even when amateur players could not find proper gloves and balls, owing to the depressed postwar economic conditions, they still played enthusiastically. In an attempt to capitalize on the situation, RKO Studios in 1949 conducted a promotional campaign that gave away "a half dozen baseball gloves and bats as presents from Gary Cooper" on its Japanese release of Sam Wood's *The Pride of the Yankees* (1942), in which the actor portrays Lou Gehrig.[75] And we can feel the fans' excitement captured in the baseball stadium scene in Kurosawa's *Stray Dog.*

In January 1948, Harry Slott of CIE recommended that a baseball sequence be included in *Bridal Champion* [*Hanayome senshu*], a "frothy love comedy" involving professional baseball players. He felt that such a scene would "add a good deal to the spirit of democracy."[76] Several weeks later, upon reading the script prepared by Toyoko Studio, his office recommended that the baseball sequence be lengthened, "insomuch as it is representative of a good old sport."[77] As far as we know, the American censors never explained what made baseball a "democratic" sport, other than its being American. A similarly chauvinistic assumption seems to underlie the censors' suggestion that, because baseball was the American national sport, "something should be done to bring out the fact that the Japanese have borrowed this sport from the United States," when Toyoko submitted the synopsis of Torajiro Saito's *The Age of Baseball Fever* [*Yakyukyo jidai*] in July 1948.[78] The film, featuring many popular comedians, includes appearances by two popular baseball players. At the same time as this film was being planned, Shin-Toho Studio decided to produce *Enoken's Home Run King* [*Enoken no homuran-o*] (1948), featuring famous comedian Kenichi Enomoto and including scenes of professional baseball games.[79]

The baseball craze of this period later became the subject of such Japanese films as Kihachi Okamoto's *Dynamite Bang Bang* [*Dainamaito don-don*] (1978) and Shinoda's *MacArthur's Children*. The former is a comedy about a baseball game between Japanese gangsters and Americans in a small town, and the latter is the story of an enthusiastic group of boys living on an island who form their own team and end up playing against a team of American soldiers. Nagisa Oshima considered baseball a spiritual symbol of the postwar period, and includes several scenes of the protagonist playing catch in *The Ceremony* [*Gishiki*] (1971), a chronology of a family through the postwar period.

Director Kirio Urayama remembers that the occupation's policy of democratization was based on the three Ss: screen, sports, and sex. He believes that this policy could be interpreted either as an enlightened attempt to liberate Japan from its feudal value system or as an attempt to degrade mass morality to the lowest common denominator. Yet he too admits to being crazy about all three Ss when he was a small-town teenager during the occupation.[80] Indeed, many other filmmakers are also well-known baseball lovers. Perhaps this is because the all-important team—according to which mentality the manager leads the team with authority but must also possess the special talent of being able to encourage the selfless cooperation of each player—is similar to that necessary in their own work.

JAPANESE RECEPTIVENESS

The "democratization films" were also called "idea pictures." CIE officials pressured the film industry to emphasize this type of film, at the expense of "escapist films," which it considered purely entertainment-oriented and therefore devoid of "reorientation value." As always, the censors maintained that their judgments were conveyed as "suggestions," not orders. However, many Japanese film people have pointed out that, because the censors had the authority to cut off the supply of raw film stock to studios that did not make enough "idea pictures," they wielded enormous power.

With recommended subjects as with prohibited subjects, Japanese filmmakers were both appreciative of and annoyed by censor David Conde's enthusiasm for detailed suggestions on each new project. Director Ushihara appreciated Conde's attempts to understand the Japanese filmmakers' disputes. At the same time, the director admitted that it was a great nuisance to go through the complex process of conveying Conde's suggestions to the studio head, after which screenplay writers would try to come up with new versions that would satisfy all concerned.[81] Setsuo Noto, then a Toho Studio liaison, also stated that it was easy to talk with Conde, because he was willing to discuss everything thoroughly until the filmmakers understood, but that it was hard to write scripts with which he would be satisfied.[82]

Conde's unique viewpoint, which, as we have seen, could be interpreted as communistic, also dismayed many Japanese. Kajiro Yamamoto recalled that "Mr. C. of CIE" became infuriated on seeing a scene in which a farmer's face looked dirty. He claimed that a farmer must be a "good man" and thus should have a clean face to match, and required the studio to reshoot the scene, with the farmer played by another actor. The censor approved of the reshot scene, but the Japanese audience burst into laughter upon seeing it.[83] Hideo Komatsu wrote that a civil censor was especially pleased to see Ichiro Sugai in a Mizoguchi film because this actor resembled Kyuichi Tokuda, the secretary of the Japan Communist Party.[84]

America's earnest desire to replace as quickly as possible the militarist mindset with the democratic mindset was reflected in its early film policy, which required Japanese filmmakers to produce rather crude films propagating democracy. As in the case of forbidden subjects, the degree to which desired subjects, themes, and images were recommended gradually decreased as the occupation proceeded. Wielding the double-edged sword of prescription and proscription, American censors were able to advance their goal of democratizing postwar Japan through film.

In general, the Japanese public enthusiastically accepted the liberation of the Japanese film industry, the production of films treating novel ideas and subjects, and the new freedom to see previously prohibited foreign films. Despite the grinding poverty and rampant inflation of the period, people willingly paid high admissions to see films. It is true that during the immediate postwar era there were few public entertainment forms to compete with cinema, but, if the Japanese public had not really supported it, the industry would of course not have flourished as it did.

Japanese nationalists have claimed that America's democratization programs and policies destroyed the unique abilities and character of the Japanese people. Yet even if this is true, the Japanese people's enthusiasm for the occupation's reforms makes them at least partially responsible for their loss.

5

NO REGRETS FOR OUR YOUTH

A Case Study of a "Democratization Film"

After the Japanese film industry had been "liberated" from wartime military institutions and placed under occupation censorship, the newly "democratic" film industry, in emulating its American counterpart, soon became the exact opposite of that which had produced the militaristic films of preceding years. It seems surprising how quickly and easily this transformation occurred; however, it was typical of the Japanese spirit of cooperation with, or perhaps obedience to, the occupiers.

This chapter will examine how a "democratization film" was made, taking as a case study Akira Kurosawa's *No Regrets for Our Youth*,[1] which was produced during the early stage of the occupation period and released by Toho Studio in October 1946.

THE BACKGROUND OF THE FILM

No Regrets for Our Youth had a great impact on the audience of this period, which had a highly developed (although idealized) notion of democracy.[2] The importance of this 1946 film stems not only from the powerful impression it made on the general public, but particularly from its influence on the youths who would become the next generation of Japanese film directors. For instance, Nagisa Oshima, who was then fourteen years old, later wrote at length on this film, as we will see later in this chapter. It was the first postwar film seen by thirteen-year-old Yoshishige Yoshida. When it was screened for his small-town junior high school class, its portrayal of the heroine laboring in a field particularly impressed him.[3] Kei Kumai and Kazuo Kuroki were both sixteen years old at the time. In fact, it was Kumai's realization that a film artist could express himself so powerfully despite the harsh realities of postwar life that motivated him to become a filmmaker.[4] Kuroki found it very refreshing that this fictional film employed a "documentary touch."[5]

It was a period in which, at least on a superficial level, the values of the past were totally rejected. The Japanese people, who had been thoroughly mobilized for the war effort, were now told that they must reject all of the political doctrines and objectives for which they had fought and died, and accept their conqueror's ideas instead.

Although Emperor Hirohito followed the occupation government's mandate and repudiated his divinity in a statement to the nation on New Year's Day, 1946, political prisoners had already been released the previous fall, including some ten survivors of the Ozaki-Sorge Spy Ring case. The nation saw Japan Communist Party leaders hailing their "liberators" in front of the occupation government's building in central Tokyo. In February 1946, the purge of antidemocratic elements began. The first postwar general election since the institution of universal suffrage (mandated the previous October) sent thirty-nine women to the national Diet.

Two days after the first May Day celebration in many years in 1946, the International Military Tribunal in the Far East opened. It continued for two and a half years, and condemned seven A-class war criminals to death. October 1946, the month of the release of *No Regrets for Our Youth*, also saw the handing down of the verdicts at the Nuremberg Tribunal, newsreels of which were commercially distributed in Japan during the Japanese trials.[6]

No Regrets for Our Youth is considered one of the most representative of the postwar democratization films, a perfect response to requests from the occupation government to make films that would help democratize the Japanese mind. The film deals with the famous case of Professor Yukitoki Takigawa of Kyoto Imperial University (in the film, Yagihara, played by Denjiro Okochi), who was persecuted in 1933 by the military government for his liberalism. Takigawa later testified at the International Military Tribunal in the Far East, condemning his persecution. By the time the film was made, he was considered a hero for his struggle against wartime militarism.

The film also depicts a character modeled on Hotsumi Ozaki of the Ozaki-Sorge Spy Ring, who was later executed as a Soviet spy (in the film, he is Yagihara's student, Ryukichi Noge, played by Susumu Fujita). Ozaki, an ex-journalist, expert on China, writer, and consultant on Chinese problems to the government, was arrested by the Japanese police as a top member of the ring in October 1941. After the trial, only German journalist Richard Sorge and Ozaki were executed, in November 1944; others, including a Yugoslav journalist, a German couple, and twelve Japanese, were sentenced to prison. Ozaki had delivered to Sorge confidential Japanese diplomatic and military information, believing that Sorge was working for the Comintern; in reality, Sorge was working for Department Four (Intelligence) of the Red Army.[7] The real Ozaki was not a student of Takigawa's, but, along with Takigawa, he came to be regarded as a martyr of the fascistic military regime as soon as the war ended. During the war, the details of the case were not publicized, probably because there were no real grounds for executing Ozaki and Sorge as "enemy" spies, since Japan was not yet at war with the USSR. Their execution was shocking for several reasons. First, this was probably the only case of treason against Japan during the war. Second, Ozaki was a high-class intellectual closely associated with top government officials. Third, Ozaki was a pacifist who believed that only he would be able to save Japan and the Japanese people from the misery of war through his actions.

The characters of Yagihara and Noge represent the type of "figures in Japanese history who have stood for freedom and representative government" that CIE was advocating as the desirable kind of hero for Japanese films. Like the real-life Takigawa, Yagihara is discharged from his university under pressure from the government. Furthermore, just as Takigawa resumed his position at the university after the war, upon his return to his old position Yagihara gives a lecture to an auditorium full of students. The professor praises the sacrifices and efforts of his student Noge in the face of this quintessential example of the suppression of liberalism by the militarist government.

One of the most successful occupation programs was agrarian reform. Embodied in two laws passed in 1946, it redistributed the land previously owned by absentee land owners into the hands of tenants. The poverty of prewar Japanese farmers is clearly contrasted in the film with the bright and hopeful images of the postwar village to which the heroine decides to dedicate herself at the end. Kurosawa added a scene in which a line of trucks passes; one of them picks up the heroine and drives on. The image of these trucks passing in the dust of the village road gives a stark impression of the villages that had been "newly born" thanks to the modernization brought about by the occupation policy. The film thus testifies to the reforms then occurring in villages all over Japan.

The theme of idealistic youths abandoning urban life to rediscover the simple values of the farming life may also illustrate the social consciousness of the period. Interestingly, the dramatization of the background of Noge's character drastically differs from that of the model on this point. In the film Noge's parents are poor, hardworking peasants, whereas Ozaki's father was a successful journalist, although his family led a rather modest life.

Kurosawa created an unusually strong character in the professor's daughter, Yukie (played by Setsuko Hara), who becomes Noge's lover. After Noge is arrested for his antiwar activities and dies in prison, she goes to live and work with his parents in their poor farming village. The film is positive in its portrayal of Yukie, an individualistic woman who pursues her idealism to the end.

As we have seen, the emancipation of women was one of the occupation's top priorities, and, in fact, equality of women was mandated by the 1947 Constitution of Japan (even though equal rights for women are still not formally guaranteed by the U.S. Constitution, on which the Japanese document was modeled).[8] General MacArthur himself suggested the emancipation of women as the highest of the five priority reforms to then–Prime Minister Shidehara as early as October 11, 1945.[9] Women's issues were always a focus of CIE policy throughout the occupation and in September 1947 the Women's and Minors' Bureau was created in the Japanese Ministry of Labor thanks to the efforts of the occupation government. The occupation government also brought about the extension of suffrage to women, the elimination of the sexist prewar adultery law, and the opening of national universities to women.

As Kurosawa himself admits that it is rather unusual for him to concentrate on heroines, *No Regrets for Our Youth* stands out among his films. He claims that, out of his entire body of work, the only films that have women as central figures are this one and *Rashomon* (1950).[10] The casting of Toho star Setsuko Hara in the role of this "unusual" heroine was very effective, although Hara has been quoted as saying that she had not wanted to appear in such a film.[11] Hara became very popular for her rather Western physical features. She has exceptionally large eyes and sculptured nose and mouth lines and is very tall, all of which are atypical of Japanese. It is believed that one of her grandparents was German. Hara's film career began at the age of fifteen, in 1935. After playing several cute, innocent girls in contemporary and historical settings, her real recognition came when the German director Arnold Fanck chose her to play the heroine in the first Japanese-German co-production, *The New Earth* [*Atarashiki tsuchi*]/*Die Tochter der Samurai* in 1937. This film was a great commercial success. Because of her exotic physique, she played many roles in Japanese film adaptations of Western literary classics, such as *Les Misérables, The Pastoral Symphony,* and *Stella Dallas,* in the late 1930s.[12]

This trend was interrupted by the war, which forced her to play the roles of patriotic wives and courageous women at the front. Some directors, like Satsuo Yamamoto in *Hot Wind* [*Neppu*] (1943), exploited Hara's Western characteristics in casting her as an individualistic heroine who speaks her mind and acts according to her desires and beliefs. (The latter film was criticized by Tadashi Iijima, who felt that Hara's character was too "American" and that her relationship with the hero was also "American.")[13]

No Regrets for Our Youth was the first major film in a series of postwar depictions by Hara of well-bred, intellectual, strong-willed bourgeois girls and wives. However, the role of Yukie carries these attributes to an extreme unmatched by other female roles in postwar Japanese cinema. For example, in Kurosawa's other films, we often see women characters who try to improve themselves and struggle positively with the problems of life, such as the schoolgirl in *Drunken Angel* and the nurse in *The Quiet Duel* [*Shizukanaru ketto*] (1949). The dancer in *Stray Dog,* the wife in *Rashomon,* the young girl in *The Idiot* [*Hakuchi*] (1951), and the princess in *The Hidden Fortress* [*Kakushi toride no san-akunin*] (1958) all have flaming tempers and stubborn wills. Yet the character of Yukie is a synthesis of all of the overwhelmingly strong examples of these tendencies.

The film was the first in which Hara worked with Kurosawa.[14] Her unique beauty contrasts with the plump, short, and more ordinary looks of the actresses, such as Chieko Nakakita, Noriko Sengoku, Teruko Kishi, and

Miki Sanjo, that Kurosawa frequently used in his subsequent films. Hara's striking features are well suited to the strong-willed heroine she plays, partly because the Western resemblance hints at a Western-style liberal feminism almost unknown in Japan. Moreover, Kurosawa successfully draws previously unseen expressions out of her, showing her as a prisoner with untidy hair and an exhausted face, or as a laboring woman struggling in the field with joy radiating through the dirt on her face. This radical change in the actress's image was in keeping with the revolutionary spirit of the period.

As may be guessed from the foregoing description of the film's themes, the idea for *No Regrets for Our Youth* may have originated within CIE itself, or, if not, within a company very conscious of and responsive to this occupation agency's suggestions. According to the screenplay writer, Eijiro Hisaita, "the idea and research were totally from [Keiji] Matsuzaki, and Mr. Kurosawa cordially collaborated in the writing, above and beyond his role as the director of the film."[15] Another account came from a critic who insisted on the strong influence of the producer, saying: "This film is full of defects. Hisaita did not know what to do. It was obvious that the producer Keiji Matsuzaki took the initiative and Hisaita could not find a clear idea."[16] Matsuzaki, who was a student of Takigawa's at Kyoto Imperial University, states that he wanted to make a film modeled after the Takigawa incident and asked Hisaita to write a script. Then the producer met Kurosawa, with whom he had worked before, and the three of them worked together on the storyline. Matsuzaki went to Kyoto in December 1945 to do research and interview the people involved in the case—except Takigawa himself, perhaps to avoid unduly influencing the character he was creating by meeting the real-life model, but also because the producer wanted instead to concentrate on the younger generation (Takigawa's students) who had fought for academic freedom.[17]

In an interview in 1985, Kurosawa did not remember the details of the production history of *No Regrets for Our Youth*. However, he did not recall that CIE had had a significant influence on the project, insisting that it was he himself who, as always, had decided on the film's subject.[18]

Both Matsuzaki and Hisaita were active in the proletarian literature and film movements of the late 1920s and early 1930s. Hisaita's strong antagonism toward the wartime government, which suppressed the leftist movement, is obvious in the screenplay he wrote for this film, as it is in another very successful film whose screenplay he wrote in the same year, *The Morning of the Osone Family* by Keisuke Kinoshita. According to Matsuzaki, he

Eijiro Hisaita, screenplay writer of *No Regrets for Our Youth* and *The Morning of the Osone Family,* in 1963. Courtesy of the Kawakita Memorial Film Institute and the Hisaita family.

chose Hisaita for his film because he was the "most suitable" for the job, being "a colleague with a perspective on the development of Japanese intellectual history similar to mine." The producer was excited since both Hisaita and Kurosawa were very eager to work on this project.[19]

Kurosawa had also participated in the proletarian art movement in the late 1920s, as a painter. Gradually he began to feel alienated by the crude political messages conveyed in these works, but he continued to be involved in the more overtly political side of the movement until 1932. Kurosawa confesses:

I had tried reading [Karl Marx's] *Das Kapital* and theories of dialectic materialism, but there had been much that I couldn't understand. For me to try to analyze and explain Japanese society from that point of view was therefore impossible. I simply felt the vague dissatisfactions and dislikes that Japanese society encouraged, and in order to contend with these feelings, I

Director Akira Kurosawa in 1952. Courtesy of the Kawakita Memorial Film Institute.

had joined the most radical movement I could find. Looking back on it now, my behavior seems terribly frivolous and reckless.[20]

He lost contact with the members of the group after a long and serious illness, and did not seek them out thereafter. He concludes that "It was not a case of the leftist movement's fever dying down; it was a case of my own leftist fever not having been a very serious one."[21] Even though Kurosawa frankly admits that his leftist commitment was not very deep, his antipathy for the wartime special police, and the danger he felt in challenging the authorities, are portrayed in this film. For example, the thrilling scene of Noge's arrest in a coffee shop in the film reminds us of Kurosawa's own narrow escape from arrest in a coffee shop.[22] Kurosawa's statement notwithstanding, this kind of turnabout was not unusual during a period when many Japanese filmmakers proclaimed themselves Marxists or leftists while it was popular to do so, only to reject such beliefs when the government began to suppress them.[23]

THE OPENING TITLES

No Regrets for Our Youth begins with opening titles bravely proclaiming the film's objective of depicting those who lived and struggled under Japanese militarist-fascist rule. The original titles read as follows:

> Taking the Manchuria Incident as a start, militarists, zaibatsu, and bureaucrats condemned as "red" anyone opposing the invasion, thus trying to create a national consensus. The "Kyoto University Incident" was an example: in 1933, Minister of Education Hatoyama, with such an intention, tried to expel the liberal professor Takigawa from Kyoto University, and met the resistance of the whole university. This became a grave problem unprecedented in the field of education. This film is based on this incident; however, all the characters in the film are creations of the filmmakers, whose intention is to depict the history of the development of the soul of the people who lived according to their principles during the age of persecution and disgrace that followed this incident.[24]

It is significant to see how these titles were related to the current political scene, as director Nagisa Oshima points out.[25] Ichiro Hatoyama was at that time the president of the Liberal Party, which received the largest number of votes in the first postwar general election, and he would establish his own cabinet as prime minister in 1955. But he was suddenly expelled from public office by the occupation government on May 3, 1946,[26] as a result of his actions as Minister of Education between December 1931 and March 1934, when he was said to have been behind the persecutions and arrests of many liberal and leftist professors. The verdict of the occupation government order read in part: "The dismissal in May 1933 of Prof. Takigawa from the faculty of Kyoto University on Hatoyama's personal order is a flagrant illustration of his contempt for the liberal tradition of academic freedom and gave momentum to the spiritual mobilization of Japan which, under the aegis of military and economic cliques, led the nation eventually into war." Hatoyama was replaced by ex-diplomat Shigeru Yoshida, who held the position from May 1946 to April 1947 and again from October 1948 to December 1954.

Oshima claims that there must have been many intrigues within the occupation government and the Japanese government that led to the expulsion of Hatoyama, and that the decision to make a film about the "Kyoto University incident" at that point was partly due to these as well as to the policy of encouraging the making of democratic films.[27] The titles give the impression that Hatoyama was almost solely responsible for the incident and the subsequent suppression of liberalism.

Arthur Behrstock, who was at that time working for the Plans and Operations Section of CIE, claims that he played the main role in the Hatoyama purging. Behrstock's Nisei assistant, Taro Tsukahara, found a book that Hatoyama had written before the war, in which he praised Hitler and Mussolini. This fact was dramatically disclosed at the press conference at which Hatoyama was expected to announce his appointment as premier, and General MacArthur decided to prohibit Hatoyama from taking the office only 48 hours before he was expected to assume it.[28] Journalist Burton Crane confirms that Hatoyama was purged for having written this book, but claims that it did not praise Hitler or Mussolini and that it was brought to the attention of the occupation government by the Japanese communists, who were trying to establish a leftist government.[29]

Joseph Gordon, who was head of the interpreting group of the Government Section of the occupation government, believes that Hatoyama was purged because his book, written in 1940, "express[ed] rather enthusiastic admiration for Hitler." Gordon does not remember who brought the book to his section, but he believes it was a political enemy of Hatoyama's. Gordon was given a copy, and he had to translate it in a rush because Hatoyama was about to take office. He translated the table of contents, the introduction, and some random sections, including a passage expressing the author's admiration for the German labor front for its organizational efficiency and weeding out of dissident elements.[30]

Hatoyama himself later wrote, in a self-righteous defense of his book, that his editor had had to suppress his liberalism in order not to provoke the wartime government, and that he had never been impressed by the fascist system. As for Germany, he wrote:

> Of course, I was greatly interested in Germany, which produced Goethe and Kant. Without expressing admiration of this nation's intelligence, we cannot talk about modern history. The Nazi system, which had ruled over this intelligent nation for less than one fifth of a century, must have some good points. However, I felt strongly the craze of the period.[31]

Akira Iwasaki, a communist filmmaker, claims that the book at issue was discovered by foreign correspondents, including Mark Gayn and Wilfred Burchett.[32] It is true that Hatoyama was one of the main targets of the leftists in those days. Faubion Bowers mentions that "the Russians concentrated on Hatoyama and the various people who were to be purged."[33]

An interview with Professor Takigawa is included in the 1946 film *The Japanese Tragedy* (directed by Fumio Kamei and produced by Akira Iwasaki):

> In 1933, the so-called Kyoto University Incident originating with my dismissal occurred and the then Minister of Education, Mr. Ichiro Hatoyama, bravely [*sic*] suppressed the liberal movement in accordance with the militarists and the rightwingers, which resulted in the aggressive wars which followed.[34]

This paraphrasing of Takigawa is very similar to Hisaita's original text for the opening titles of Kurosawa's film.

The situation becomes even more interesting when we note that the present version of the film in circulation in Japan and the United States does not include the following two parts of the original titles: "in 1933, Minister of Education Hatoyama, with such intention, tried to expel the liberal professor Takigawa from Kyoto University, and met the resistance of the whole university" and "whose intention is to depict the history of the development of the soul of the people who lived according to their principles during the age of persecution and disgrace that followed this incident." Without these two lines, the present titles lose the combative spirit of the original version.

Kurosawa has confirmed what many suspected: that Toho would not allow such politically charged statements as this personal attack on Hatoyama to remain in the completed film. Kurosawa explains that "I wanted to demand that these people, such as Hatoyama, take responsibility [for the Takigawa and Ozaki incidents]. However, the Toho company told me to delete [Hatoyama's name] because it would have been upsetting."[35] Even if these sentences had actually been allowed to remain in the titles and to be read by the immediate postwar Japanese audience, they would surely have become unacceptable by 1954, when Hatoyama returned to power as premier. In any case, the episode of the opening titles suggests how *No Regrets for Our Youth* was influenced by the crosswinds of contemporary politics.

THE CONTENT AND TECHNIQUE OF THE FILM

The images of "shining" youth are most effectively and powerfully presented in the opening picnic scene, in which a babbling brook reflects the sunlight, flowers are blooming, and students and the heroine run up a wooded hill in the sunlight. Oshima explains how much he was impressed by this imagery when he first saw the film in 1946. He believes that, by defining youth as "shining"—a concept with no direct relation to the propaganda of the occupation government—Kurosawa subverts the notion of the "idea picture" that had been imposed by the government. He also attributes this visualization of "shining youth" to Kurosawa, not Hisaita.[36] Kurosawa indeed talked of his excitement at being able to shoot these "shining" images of youth, under the new freedom from wartime censorship.[37]

In fact, Hisaita's script describes the "swift sunlight coming from among the young leaves reflected on the faces and bodies of the young people," but does not elaborate further. Kurosawa's exceptional talent is already obvious in the dazzling sensation he creates by deftly combining the static, peaceful images of water and flowers with the dynamic effect of the swiftly ascending movements of the youths. The rhythmical repetition of this movement in the same direction (from screen left to screen right and upward) alternately shows Yukie running up among the trees and the students following her.

In the previous sequence at the brook, Kurosawa intriguingly establishes the triangular relationship of Yukie with two students, Noge and Itokawa. When Yukie (whom we see from behind) shows reluctance to cross the water, the camera shows both men extending their hands toward her, i.e., toward the camera, thus enhancing the spectator's identification with Yukie. Then follows a close-up of Yukie's face. In the next shot, Noge takes the initiative and carries her across the water. The camera then shows the cheering group of students, followed by a close-up of the sullen face of Itokawa. Yukie teases Itokawa as she playfully turns his hat backwards on his head. A close-up of her face smiling and a long shot of her running away follow. In this subtle sequence, without the help of any dialogue, Kurosawa establishes Noge's straightforwardness and quickness to act, and Itokawa's contrasting indecisiveness. Yukie's ambivalent affection for both students is shown at the same time.

The next sequence makes even more clear the meaning of this opening scene, when the camera shows Noge and Itokawa alternately running after Yukie. At the same time, the soundtrack repeats the melody of the slow, minor-key Kyoto University student song that accompanied the opening titles. This well-known tune is heard repeatedly during the film, both with and without its lyrics, heightening the emotional surge by associating the notion of "freedom of learning" with that of "shining youth."

The peaceful moments of the students on the hill are suddenly interrupted by the noise of a gun from the soldiers' training field nearby. The pace of the film then accelerates to portray the heightened tensions of the "age of persecution and disgrace," beginning with the discharge of Yagihara. Out of the film's 110 minutes, some 10 minutes in the first scene and another 10 in the last are set in peacetime, leaving the 90 minutes in between to portray the war era.

Kurosawa's style is grounded in contrasts. Yukie's two student suitors are clearly opposite types. Noge seriously pursues his idealism by courageously involving himself in the student protest movement, and later in the antiwar movement, dying a martyr. The weak and unprincipled Itokawa crumbles in the face of any authority. He submits in humiliation to Yukie's caprice, hesitates to participate in the students' actions, and makes excuses in front of her. He finally becomes a public prosecutor, helping to repress Noge's liberalism. Itokawa's middle-class background is contrasted with Noge's proletarian origin through the images of the comfortable and neat room of the former's mother[38] and the hut in a poor farming village where Yukie goes at the end of the film.

Of course, the heroine chooses Noge, and she herself changes dramatically, from a protected bourgeois girl into a passionate lover and finally into a laboring peasant unwelcomed by Noge's persecuted parents. Her comfortable urban middle-class life is strikingly contrasted with her hardships in the dirt of the field in the scene in which, dressed in peasant attire, she sinks her hands into a brook—a shot superimposed on a close-up of her hands playing the piano.

This iconography of hands is further developed in the next scene. Yukie shows her silent obstinacy before Itokawa, who visits her in the country to persuade her to come home. Instead of responding to his selfish remarks, Yukie begins to squeeze the rainwater out of the cloth around her waist. This scene is followed by her determined refusal to accept Itokawa's suggestion.

This remarkable scene, created with intense imagery of her hands, is associated with the image of the pouring rain behind her. Kurosawa used the technique frequently in his subsequent films, such as *The Quiet Duel, Stray Dog, Rashomon,* and *The Seven Samurai* [*Shichinin no samurai*] (1954), in which he sets the scene of emotional climax against the image of pouring rain.

If this hard rain symbolizes the storms and winds of wartime, flowers are frequently used as the symbol of peacetime. The opening picnic scene

Setsuko Hara in *No Regrets for Our Youth* [*Waga seishun ni kui nashi*] (1946), directed by Akira Kurosawa. Courtesy of the Kawakita Memorial Film Institute.

and the postwar scene in which Yukie revisits the picnic spots, are filled with blossoming flowers. After Yukie and Noge begin to live together (it is unclear whether or not they were ever officially married), we see four successive shots of different flowers in vases, set in various places in their house, accompanied by peaceful and joyous music. These illustrate the passing of time. The scene of Yukie and Noge sitting together in a field full of white flowers shows the momentary happiness they are allowed before their inevitable tragedy.

After Noge is arrested, Yukie is arranging flowers at home when the detectives come to arrest her, their passing feet ominously blocking our view of her work. It is also symbolic that the flower-loving Yukie, in an earlier scene, plucks the blossoms from the chrysanthemum's stems and throws them into a flat bowl at her flower-arranging class. Her disturbed state of mind is neatly conveyed by the image of the plucked flowers floating on the water.

Setsuko Hara (l.) and Susumu Fujita in *No Regrets for Our Youth*. Courtesy of the Kawakita Memorial Film Institute.

As part of his plan, Kurosawa effectively (if simplistically) alternates images of Yukie in the traditional Japanese kimono and in Western dress, according to her emotional state. When prosecutor Itokawa comes to dinner to try to discourage her father from promulgating his liberal ideas, she wears a kimono and remains uncharacteristically taciturn throughout the scene. This is the first time we see her in traditional costume. Previously, she has appeared in Western dress, playing the piano and arguing with her father's students in their Western-style house. We see her in a kimono again after she begins to live with Noge, assuming the role of a housewife. On the other hand, she wears Western dress during all the scenes focusing on important decisions and actions, such as her love scene with Noge at his office, her visit to Noge's parents in the village, and her decision to go back to the village after the war.[39]

The scenes of field labor and of the villagers' persecution of the family are skillfully developed. Oshima insists that Kurosawa employs a documentary-style montage in the field labor scenes. He also claims that, by employing a documentary style at the climax of the heroine's pursuit, Kurosawa deliberately destroyed the theatrical and social dramatic style at which Hisaita was so good, ultimately subverting the form of the "idea picture" and trying to supersede it.[40] The rhythmic movements of the plowing by Yukie and Noge's mother (played by Haruko Sugimura) are shown alternately in mid-shots, close-ups, and full shots. (One long shot of the field with a low horizontal line and clouds extending to the horizon reminds us of the work of John Ford, a director much admired by Kurosawa.) In the scenes of planting rice in the paddy, the combination of long shots, mid-shots, and close-ups of the two working, taken from various angles and often using superimpositions, dramatizes the monotony of the labor. Accompanied only by rhythmic music, these scenes, consisting of relatively short shots, seem to employ a silent film style of montage.

As for the villagers who persecute Noge's parents and Yukie for their relationship with a spy, another long sequence most vividly evokes the stifling atmosphere of their closed-minded society. As Yukie walks down the village road, her subjective shot shows a few children running parallel to her movement (and to the camera). Then several shots of children running in all directions are intercut with shots of Yukie walking, with the sound of the jeering children's voices heard throughout.

This is followed by a series of swift tracking shots showing standing men, crouching children, women, and aged men, all of whom silently stare at her (and the camera) and some of whom turn their faces and shut their doors. Into this series are occasionally inserted mid-shots of Yukie walking, taken from various angles. The gloomy music gradually gets louder. Finally, Yukie collapses under the heavy burden she is carrying, and, as the camera shows her trying to stand up, two shots of trees and one shot of roadside grasses moving in the wind are inserted as her subjective views, with loud laughter on the soundtrack. This strange sequence is an expression of the helpless psychological state of the heroine, to whom even the nature around her seems hostile and derisory. It is at this point that, for the first time, Noge's mother silently comes to the aid of Yukie; after this incident, the feeling of solidarity between the two women gradually grows.

CRITICAL RESPONSE

Yukie's transformation from amateur pianist to committed laborer led to criticism of her extreme and unnatural characterization. Among those voicing such objections was Fuyuhiko Kitagawa:

> This film is full of defects. Hisaita did not know what to do. It was obvious that the producer Keiji Matsuzaki took the initiative and Hisaita could not find a clear idea—it is obvious in the creation of the heroine's character, so superficial and forced, and also in their arbitrary interpretation of the Takigawa Incident. Director Kurosawa indulged himself, saying that he will create a new woman character.[41]

Tadao Urii is quoted as saying: "The reason why Yukie became unhappy must be her own eccentric imagination and thus her unhappiness is not anybody else's responsibility."[42] Tadashi Iijima considered that "the heroine of this film is terribly abnormal and lacks humanity."[43]

Another reviewer wrote:

> The devious heroine looks like a mad person. It is ironic that she simply looks like a hysterical girl. The film is proud of itself as progressive; however, it is fatal that the film in reality praises the conventional morality. The theme that a woman has to stay with her husband's family even after he dies is very obsolete. When Yukie Yagihara rushes to plant rice despite her fever, it is as if she were saying "No regrets for a mad person."[44]

Naoki Togawa attributed the failure of the film to the gap between Hisaita's intention to depict "youth with no regret" as sentimentalism and Kurosawa's interpretation of it as heroism.[45]

Several years later, Kurosawa responded to his critics: "I believed then that it was necessary to respect the 'self' for Japan to be reborn. I still believe it. I depicted a woman who maintained such a sense of 'self.' Those who criticized and hated her would have approved if the protagonist of the film had been a man."[46]

On the other hand, the American censors were very happy with the film that resulted. In 1985 Kurosawa remembered as follows:

> The American censors all came to the screening. They were talking to each other until the middle of the film. Then, after the sequence of the heroine going to the countryside, everybody stopped talking. After the film ended, the applause began. Everybody offered to shake my hand.[47]

David Conde of CIE praised the film as the best among all those to which he gave guidance.[48] The film was completed after Conde's departure from CIE, and the agency's officials, including his successor, George Gercke, gave a special party to celebrate the success of the film.[49]

However, Kurosawa maintains that the finished film differs markedly from his original plan—which was directly influenced by the Toho labor union's production administration committee—to his dissatisfaction. Kurosawa claims that he was attacked by the Scenario Review Board "because my script resembled one to be shot by Kiyoshi Kusuda [*As Long as I Live*], based also on the Sorge-Ozaki case,"[50] and because it was felt that Kurosawa was trying to interfere with the new director's start. Kurosawa continued, "Rather, I hope to make a better film than Kusuda's," a remark that seemed to upset the board enough for it to force Kurosawa to change the latter half of the scenario, despite Hisaita's reluctance. So Kurosawa maintains that the original scenario by Hisaita on Hotsumi Ozaki was better than the one for the completed film.[51]

The depth of Kurosawa's indignation is clear even forty years later, when interviewed by the author. He still criticized the union leaders who forced him to change the plot:

> The unionists and the communists, all of them forced me to change the story. So, I had to change the latter half, from the point when the heroine goes to the countryside. Since I had to change it, I wanted to do it drastically and surprise them. After my film was completed, it turned out that the other film was totally uninteresting. Therefore, they began to say that they should have let me make my film as I had wanted to. I yelled at them, "What are you talking about now?" The unionists and communists were really lording it over us then. A communist screenplay writer was repatriated, and he insisted on incorporating the device of syllogism into screenplay writing. However, I replied that an uninteresting screenplay is uninteresting despite all such devices. I argued often because I was young.[52]

Kurosawa is not as critical of American occupation censorship as he is of wartime Japanese censorship. For instance, his first film, in 1943, *Sanshiro Sugata,* was criticized by the military board, which demanded many cuts. Donald Richie writes that one officer even asked (a question incomprehensible to us today) "if the young Kurosawa was not interested in aiding and abetting the enemy."[53] However, he is quite critical of the Toho studio labor union's production administration committee, which was established at the occupation's behest. To promote the idea of unionization, the committee initiated the production of *Those Who Create Tomorrow* [*Asu o tsukuru hitobito*] in 1946 with three directors: Kajiro Yamamoto, Hideo Sekigawa, and Kurosawa. Kurosawa has refused to include this film in his filmography, and thus *No Regrets for Our Youth* is officially his first postwar film.

As it turned out, *No Regrets for Our Youth* was further influenced by the labor union movement. The film was released on October 29, 1946, in the middle of the second strike by the Toho labor union, which had begun on October 25, and therefore had to be shown in the Nikkatsu company's theaters instead—an unusual measure that Toho management decided to take against the protests of the filmmakers.[54] This second strike provoked a group of those who opposed the strike and the communist union leadership, led by Toho's ten top stars, to form their own union, known as the "Society of the Flag of Ten."

Ironically, it was the stars who had played the roles of hard-core antiwar liberals in *No Regrets for Our Youth,* including Setsuko Hara, Susumu Fujita, and Denjiro Okochi, who were among the ones who founded this new, antileftist organization. Conversely, Akitake Kono—who had played the opportunistic student Itokawa, who later becomes a wartime government public prosecutor—remained one of the most active of leftist unionists.

IDEOLOGICAL VACUOUSNESS

As we can see, in *No Regrets for Our Youth,* the heroine's self-sacrifice in the face of the tribulations of wartime is splendidly depicted. On the other hand, it is never clearly shown for what ideals she sacrifices herself. Those who criticized Yukie's character had a point in that the film does not give enough explanation of her motivation—why she comes to act so forcefully. It is clear that Yukie, seeking the meaning of life, falls in love with Noge, and follows him. Even after his death, she tries to pursue his idealism and, for reasons that are not quite clear, decides to live with his parents, asking them to let her stay with them because she claims to be Noge's wife. Her decision may have originated in the scene in which Noge remorsefully shows Yukie a picture of his old parents, saying that they are his "weak point."

During the scene of Yukie's laboring in the field, her monologue "No regret whatever . . ." is heard on the soundtrack followed by her father's voice repeating his previous advice to her: "You must fight for freedom. Behind its struggle there will be sacrifice and responsibility." Noge's voice is then heard: "What I am doing will only be appreciated by the people ten years later." These statements as remembered by Yukie are very obviously to be seen as motivating her actions, but (as will be explained shortly) we are hardly given any idea of what Noge actually believed. No further explanation is given. Perhaps Yukie's actions would be more understandable if Kurosawa had not been forced to change the latter part of the film. Similarly, the ideals for which Professor Yagihara gives up his job, and Noge his life, are not described. Kurosawa's achievement lies not in an analysis of their political views, but rather his very skillful demonstration of the consequences of their having expressed those views.

We see newspaper headlines reporting that academic freedom is in danger, that Yagihara has been forced to leave his position, that professors are protesting the Minister of Education's decision, and that students will hold a protest meeting. Quasi-documentary footage of banners hanging from buildings, and students' meetings and their disruption by mounted police, increase the suspense. The suspenseful pace is accelerated by close-ups of the running feet of students and hooves of the police horses, and long shots of students gathering and being arrested by the police, along with slogan-filled banners and handbills.

Newspaper headlines go on to report the decision of some professors to compromise with the Minister of Education, and the suppression of the students' protest movement, to the detriment of academic freedom. The film technique used to portray these sensational events is superb, but there is no explanation of why Yagihara's ideas are dangerous or subversive.

The film is similarly unsatisfactory concerning its depiction of Noge's philosophy. We are shown the title and byline of his magazine article, "A Thought on the Sino-Japanese Relationship," as Prosecutor Itokawa shows it to Yukie. It is the film's only clue to Noge's political leanings, except for a brief conversation in the beginning of the film in which Noge proclaims the importance of the "China problem."

Again we see newspaper headlines, reporting the arrest of the members of an international pacifist espionage organization, and, in the next scene, Yagihara protests to Itokawa that what the newspaper reports is contradictory to what Noge is actually doing. But Noge himself simply explains to Yukie that what he is doing now will only be appreciated by the people ten years later.

When Yukie confronts him and asks him to reveal his secret ideas, Noge's figure leaves the frame, leaving only his shadow on the office wall. He then says: "If there is such a man, and he is going to do something . . . ," as if he is afraid of confronting the fact that he himself is going to undertake some important action. This use of the third person, alluding to himself, corresponds to the ambiguous visual image of his shadow on the wall, and to Kurosawa's refusal to present a specific political viewpoint.

The crucial love scene between Yukie and Noge follows. This scene is also suggestive in that it does not show the two embracing each other. In the original script by Hisaita, these scenes are set in a field near a shipyard rather than in Noge's office. Kurosawa's decision to move this important scene indoors, at dusk, creates a claustrophobic feeling, with a dominant dark imagery that heightens the tension.

Some critics of the period, such as Iijima, also complained that the film does not explain what Noge and Yukie believed in,[55] as did filmmaker Oshima.[56] The critics argued that the Japanese audience was expected to flesh out the characters of Yagihara and Noge with what they already know of Takigawa and Ozaki. Oshima believed that *No Regrets for Our Youth* should have depicted these characters not as heroes but as resisters who would eventually be forced to compromise. His condemnation is harsh:

> However, they [Kurosawa and Hisaita] did not do so, and they absolved all Japanese, including themselves, of responsibility by using the phrase "live according to their principles." By pretending that there was "total resistance," which certainly did not exist, they rewrote history, trying to show that there existed a certain antiwar power among the Japanese people.
>
> Thus, on the one hand, they excused themselves, and on the other hand, they were incapable of depicting their enemy's images. Content to merely indicate the enemy by such words as "militarists, zaibatsu, and bureaucrats," in the opening titles, they were incapable of creating images of such people, or they could never think of creating visual images of such an enemy's thoughts.
>
> This is the natural result of Kurosawa and Hisaita making a film according to their own images of their own easy survival during the war and their own postwar viewpoints. They did not subjectively accept the problems presented in the form of the "idea pictures." The film, which does not reveal their own subjective responsibilities, and does not clearly present the enemy, must have been welcomed by the film capitalists, who were then scared of the occupation's purges.[57]

(In fact, thirty-one film industry leaders were expelled from their positions by the occupation government's purge directives, issued in October 1947. They were company presidents and executives who had held their positions between July 7, 1937, and December 8, 1941, and were thus held responsible for assisting with war preparations between the Sino-Japan Incident and Pearl Harbor. All of them were rehabilitated and returned to their positions in October 1950.)

Years after the events in question, it is easy to condemn the older generation for having been opportunistic. As many have observed, these filmmakers had to survive during the war as well as after the war. Kurosawa himself rather simply and honestly admits as much in his 1978 autobiography:

> After the war my work went smoothly again, but before I begin to write about that, I would like to look back once more at myself during the war. I have to admit that I did not have the courage to resist in any positive way, and I only got by, ingratiating myself when necessary and otherwise evading censure. I am ashamed of this, but I must be honest about it.
>
> Because of my own conduct, I can't very well put on self-righteous airs and criticize what happened during the war. The freedom and democracy of the post-war era were not things I had fought for and won: they were granted to me by powers beyond my own. As a result, I felt it was all the more essential for me to approach them with an earnest and humble desire to learn, and to make them my own. But most Japanese in those post-war years simply swallowed the concepts of freedom and democracy whole, waving slogans around without really knowing what they meant.[58]

As for the ideological content of *No Regrets for Our Youth,* Kurosawa complains about the pressure from the labor union's production committee to change the first script, and mentions his particular desire to shoot the scenery of "the grassy hills, the flower-lined side streets, the brooks reflecting the sun's rays," which "had special meaning for us" when the film, "the first to be made in the post-war atmosphere of freedom,"[59] was being made. But there is no argument on the specific ideological significance of this film.

Donald Richie defends Kurosawa as follows:

> What appealed to Kurosawa in the story was not the suppression of a certain kind of political thought, but the fact that thought of any kind was suppressed; not that a possible leftist was executed but that any man was executed. . . . His sense of injustice and outrage provided the initial decision to make the picture. . . . As is usual with Kurosawa, he is so interested, is so engrossed in *how* something such as lack of freedom affects a person, how a living character reacts in all of its richness and humanity, that he forgets the social issue or, better, finds it irrelevant. He is not at all interested in

what forces have made people what they are; he is completely interested in what people make out of what the forces have made of them.[60]

The producer Matsuzaki seems to affirm a similar intention: "This film does not intend to portray the Takigawa incident accurately, but I hoped to depict what was essential in the fight for learning and freedom in that case and the theme of the development of young people through this struggle."[61]

These arguments might just as well have been used to justify the Japanese war-collaboration films, which were not so much concerned with depicting the ideology behind what Japan was fighting for as with portraying the "suffering" of the people through their "self-sacrifice." Similarly, in *No Regrets for Our Youth*, we see the heroine and uncompromising protagonists suffer persecution without our being told why and for what. The theme of *No Regrets for Our Youth* is again "self-sacrifice," depicted with great technical skill. Kurosawa in fact stated his ambition to "accomplish expression that is really filmic in this film."[62]

The move from the production of war-collaboration films to that of postwar democracy films is still a highly sensitive area. The general public was disillusioned to see so many Japanese appear to change so quickly from ardent defenders of the imperial system, and the war that was being fought to defend it, into enthusiastic pacifists espousing democracy. There was even an initiative by leftist filmmakers to list the war criminals at whose hands they had suffered during the war. In response, some filmmakers began to attack those in the leftist group on the grounds that they themselves had also compromised with the wartime government and made war films.

Film critic Tadao Sato argues that most Japanese filmmakers were not particularly enthusiastic about collaborating with the wartime government, but still chose not to oppose it actively. They were not happy about its militaristic and fascistic policies, but nonetheless did their best to work within the limitations prescribed by those policies. A rare exception was Fumio Kamei.[63] Kamei continued as an exception to the rule under the occupation, which banned his film *The Japanese Tragedy*. Victimized by both regimes, Kamei was a prominent example of a filmmaker who maintained his principles regardless of the political climate.

Fighting to the death for one's principles is highly esteemed in Western culture. Similarly, Westerners have traditionally expected artists to struggle against hide-bound traditions, conventional values, and authority in general in order to express new visions. Therefore, those Japanese filmmakers who collaborated with both the Japanese and the American authorities must appear unprincipled to Western eyes. Japanese, however, while admiring the rare courage of filmmakers such as Kamei, might hesitate to condemn the others as mere "collaborators."

Perhaps more sensible is the position of director Mansaku Itami, who neither collaborated with the wartime government nor condemned afterwards those who did. Itami simply refused the invitation to join the group, saying that he had made no films during the war, not because of his political convictions, but rather owing to a physical illness. He went on to warn the Japanese public against claiming that "we were deceived [by militarists]." Itami felt that those who proclaimed loudly that they had been "deceived" bore as much responsibility for the war as did the "deceivers."[64]

In this regard, Kurosawa's position in *No Regrets for Our Youth*, which refused to advocate any concrete political position, might be regarded as prudent rather than opportunistic. He may well have understood the puerility of condemning the wartime regime in order to advance fashionable ideas about democracy self-righteously. In addition, although the Ozaki case was receiving great attention from the media at the time the film was being made,[65] many aspects of this espionage case were still ambiguous, and it might have been difficult to depict the political motivation of Ozaki's character clearly in the film. As for the Takigawa case, however, everyone clearly understood the whole story.

Kurosawa hesitated to condemn even the villagers who, during the war, persecute Yukie and Noge's parents. In the film's last sequence, which is not in Hisaita's script, Yukie climbs into the back of a pickup truck and sees several villagers there. A close-up follows, showing the embarrassed smiles of the villagers. Then, the camera takes in Yukie's benevolently smiling face, followed by shots of the villagers bowing slightly. Yukie obviously (although tacitly) forgives the villagers for their mistreatment of her during the war, not condemning them for their faults. This generous behavior may heighten our perception of Yukie's nobility, yet it seems out of character for one who has showed such iron-willed dedication in the face of wartime persecution. Because the ideological background for her dedication is not sufficiently explained in the film, it remains easy for the audience to believe that her dedication was merely obstinacy or impulsiveness.

Moreover, it was not just any thoughts that were suppressed during the war, as Richie claims, nor was merely "anybody" subject to persecution. Only those thoughts and individuals who opposed the war effort or made themselves unwanted in other ways were persecuted. It must have been very odd to see the same stars who had once portrayed patriotic fighters and selfless workers suddenly and on the same movie screens appear to be struggling *against* the wartime government after August 1945. For example, the stars of this film—Denjiro Okochi, Setsuko Hara, Susumu Fujita, and Akitake Kono—had performed impressively in the roles of generals, patriotic women, and war heroes.

Film critics of the time had little praise for their acting, except for Hara's. They complained that Okochi's character did not look like a real professor, and attacked Fujita's acting as almost ridiculously superficial, saying similarly that he did not look like an intellectual. Yet many of these criticisms must be related to the fact that actors in those years indiscriminately played any roles given to them without regard to ideological principles.

Fujita's case was the most extreme. He was well known for his portrayal of *gunshin* (military gods): heroes whose noble dedication to the war effort led them to sacrifice their lives and thus made them respected as godlike figures.[66] Fujita himself states that he wanted to quit his profession upon the end of the war because he felt guilty for having played so many heroes during the war; but, because he could not think of another suitable occupation, he just continued acting.[67] Leftist film producer Takeo Ito argues that Fujita was most active performing gunshin roles because his face was perfectly suited to those parts.[68] Fujita naturally felt the contradictions inherent in the abrupt change in roles from wartime patriotic heroes to postwar antiwar heroes. Somewhat apologetically, he argues that, as a result of this conflict, he was reluctant to give a speech at an early labor union meeting, although it had been demanded that he do so, as the actors' representative in the union.[69] The tide was strong and swift, and Fujita was one of many actors and filmmakers who did not swim against it. Besides, there has been no really serious argument against this trend among Japanese actors.

In a very similar way, many Japanese directors were able to make any kind of film, regardless of ideology, including war films and postwar democratic films. It is widely argued that most Japanese directors were (and are) not really artists, but rather artisans catering to the demands of their superiors without seriously questioning the political and ideological implications of their work. Japanese filmmakers were obsessed with making technically brilliant portrayals of the theme of self-sacrifice, no matter what the political climate. Once assigned a task, the filmmakers simply worked hard until the film was completed, with relatively little concern for the reason for it. This kind of obsession with work is very strong in the Japanese national character, and the wartime regime had exploited and encouraged it for its own ends.

There is a Japanese proverb, "Nagai mono niwa makarero," which may be roughly translated as "If you can't beat 'em, join 'em," reflecting the traditional prizing of harmony over conflict rooted in the nation's geographical and sociological imperatives. This aspect of the Japanese psyche doubtless influenced the behavior of film directors.

We might imagine that the ideological vacuousness of many films made during and after the war results from the directors' conscious strategy to preserve their integrity by avoiding meaningful collaboration with either of the two governments. In any case, the crucial point is that these films were nonetheless effective in mobilizing their audiences to support the war effort and (to a lesser extent) postwar democratization.

6

THE
STRIKES AT
TOHO
STUDIO

Organized labor had been severely suppressed by the prewar Japanese government, but was strongly encouraged during the early stage of the occupation. Proud and idealistic unionists, taking advantage of the newly bestowed rights of assembly and collective bargaining, immediately set to work organizing their constituencies. Unions quickly sprang up in every sector of the Japanese economy, and the film industry was no exception.

Among those at the major studios, the union at Toho Studio became the most powerful. Demanding salary increases, improved working conditions, and more power in decision-making, this union struck the company three times in two and a half years. Considering its close ties with the wartime government and its collaboration in producing the most successful war films, it is ironic that Toho also produced the most radical and active unionists and many of the most successful "democratization" films immediately after the war. This chapter will begin by reviewing the history of Toho, through its transition from a war film factory into a democratization film factory. This account considers the problem posed by the modernization of the film industry, its correlation with the changing Japanese economy, and the increasingly intimate relationship with the various government regimes. At the same time, this modernization required, and is a noteworthy example of, the typically Japanese flexibility (some would call it lack of principles) that allows the most politically radical and conservative elements to coexist within a company.

We will then closely examine the development of the postwar labor union at Toho. An interesting result of this movement was *Those Who Create Tomorrow,* produced in mid-1946 by the union's labor administration committee, inspired by the heady atmosphere of the period. Set in a film studio and a theater, it vividly reflects the course of the unionization of the film industry.

The unionization movement reached its climax during the third strike at Toho in the summer of 1948, the suppression of which, with the aid of the U.S. military, dealt the movement a near-fatal blow. This event itself became an exciting spectacle in the eyes of the Japanese public. The internal struggles among the management, the labor union, and dissident forces within the union were less visible, but nonetheless full of intrigues, betrayals, and human drama.

The importance of the unionists' role in laying the foundations of postwar Japanese cinema has heretofore been ignored and unappreciated in the Western literature. In order to understand thoroughly the cinema of this period, the unions' role must be explained.

TOHO FILM COMPANY

Toho Film Company was established in 1937 as the result of the merger of four companies: Shashin Kagaku Kenkyu-jo (Photo Chemical Laboratory), PCL (Photo Chemical Laboratory) Studio, JO Studio, and Toho Film Distribution Company. The first of these companies had been founded in 1932 by Tokyo businessman Yasuji Uemura to experiment with the new technology of sound in film. Although PCL Studio had been established in 1933 to specialize in producing sound films, the first company continued to provide sound system and laboratory services to other studios, to rent studio space, and to produce industrial and documentary films. The studio made many films sponsored by the companies that had provided its initial capital, including Meiji Candy and Dai-Nippon Beer. Its initial production was the first Japanese musical, *Intoxicated Life* [*Horoyoi jinsei*], directed by Sotoji Kimura in 1933. It was an American-style musical intended to promote beer drinking.[1]

JO Studio had been founded in 1934 in Kyoto by Yoshio Osawa, who was the Japanese representative of the American Bell and Howell camera company and of the German Agfa film company. The *J* in JO refers to Jenkins, an American sound system that Osawa represented, and the *O* is from his own family name. JO Studio also specialized in sound films.

The Toho Film Distribution Company had been established in 1936 by Ichizo Kobayashi, with the participation of the three above-mentioned companies. Railway mogul Kobayashi had made his debut in the entertainment business by founding the Takarazuka Theater, featuring an all-girl revue, in a town that he had developed on his railway line in the Kobe-Osaka district in 1911. Kobayashi himself would write the scripts for the revue's numbers. He later expanded into the Tokyo area, constructing the Tokyo Takarazuka Theater and the Hibiya Movie Theater in 1934. ("Toho" is the abbreviation for "Tokyo Takarazuka," because the Chinese character for "takara" may also be pronounced as "ho.") He built and purchased more major theaters in 1935. Thus, by 1937, Kobayashi—who already controlled the Tokyo Electric Company and the Hanshin Railway Company, and had a financial interest in Shashin Kagaku Kenkyu-jo and PCL Studio as well—had come to monopolize the theater district in the central area of Tokyo.

Toho Film Distribution Company released not only the films produced at PCL and JO Studios, but also American films from Paramount, 20th Century-Fox and Warner Brothers, as well as European films imported by Nagamasa Kawakita's Towa Film Company. But in September 1937 the foreign cinema was suddenly crippled by the government's decision to stop importing foreign feature films. The China-Japan war had begun in July of that year, and the annual importation of some three hundred foreign titles fell victim to the nationalistic policies of the wartime period. On September 11, 1937, Toho Film Company was established, with Uemura as president, Osawa as an executive, Kobayashi as a consultant, and Iwao Mori as the studio chief.[2]

PCL had been successful in hiring directors away from other studios. When Nikkatsu Studio's employees illegally struck in 1932, sympathetic directors such as Minoru Murata, Daisuke Ito, Tomu Uchida, and Tomotaka Tasaka and actors Isamu Kosugi and Koji Shima (both of whom later became directors) left Nikkatsu and joined PCL. Director Sotoji Kimura was invited to join PCL after producing his own film, *Youth across the River* [*Kawamuko no seishun*] (1933), at PCL; the film is regarded as the last prewar "proletarian film." Kajiro Yamamoto also quit Nikkatsu to join the studio, and Mikio Naruse, Yasujiro Shimazu, Teinosuke Kinugasa, and Kunio Watanabe came over from Shochiku Studio. The new studio's innovative spirit, and particularly its use of the new technology of sound, were great attractions to directors who were dissatisfied with their old studios and sought more challenging jobs; its successor, Toho, was similarly attractive.

On the other hand, other major studios represented the conventional world. Nikkatsu Studio, the abbreviation for Nippon Katsudo Shashin (Japan Moving Picture) Company, was established in 1912, with close ties to Kyoto's yakuza organization, the Senbon-gumi. Masaichi Nagata, who later became president of Daiei Film Company, had belonged to this organization when he was young. Shochiku Studio was organized in 1920 by twin brothers Matsutaro Shirai and Takejiro Otani, who also owned traditional kabuki theater troupes. (Shochiku's "sho" comes from the Chinese character for "matsu" and "chiku," from the character for "take.")

In an industry that was still highly influenced by feudal practices and traditions,[3] Toho's self-proclaimed "modernity" distinguished it. Its high initial capitalization enabled the new studio to afford high-quality facilities and equipment, along with a nationwide chain of large theaters. By the end of 1938, the Toho chain included twenty-seven theaters nationwide, half of which were large halls with capacities of between 1,500 and 2,000 with the newest facilities and innovative concessions and restaurants attached to the theaters. By the end of 1939, this number had increased to sixty-three, and by 1942 it stood at ninety-one. The number of noncompany theaters showing Toho's films also increased annually—from 501 in 1938 to 668 in 1941—despite the efforts of the more established film companies to stop Toho's growth.[4] It became the first studio to employ only university graduates as assistant directors.[5] Many leftist filmmakers, such as Kimura, came to work at Toho.

The studio also employed the "producer system," as opposed to the traditional "star" and "director" systems typical of Shochiku and Nikkatsu. Mori had decided to organize the studio on the Hollywood model, assigning the artistic responsibilities to the directors and the financial and administrative responsibilities to the producers. According to film critic Naoki Togawa, Mori had traveled to Hollywood to study, and discovered a role model in producer Irving Thalberg. Traditionally, Shochiku, Nikkatsu, and other studios had concentrated power in a few hands—those of the studio heads, the executive producers, and a few important directors. The powerful directors selected crew members and actors to work with them in *kumi* or groups. The work of each kumi had a consistent personality, but this modus operandi encouraged authoritarian master-apprentice relationships. This system was effective in producing in quantity the type of films that the theaters demanded, but made it difficult to change directions when business faltered.

In another significant departure from common industry practice, tasks that had traditionally been given to assistant directors at the other studios were assigned at Toho to production managers.[6]

On the negative side, Toho was sometimes forced by fierce competition within the industry to resort to bribery and dirty tricks to steal directors and stars from other studios. Every other studio had done the same to establish itself, but Toho's great wealth gave it unprecedented power. Its "modernistic" philosophy allowed it to cloak its actions in the claim that it was helping combat the old feudalistic practice by which directors and stars were bound for life to a single studio.

A typical example was the decision of Shochiku period film star Chojiro Hayashi to move to Toho. Before completing the shooting of a period film at Shochiku, Hayashi made a joint announcement with Toho that he would join the new studio in October 1937. The following month, when Hayashi had just finished his first day of shooting at Toho's Kyoto Studio, a ruffian attacked him and slashed his face with a razor. Shooting was canceled and Hayashi was hospitalized. After he recovered, scars were still visible on his left cheek, and Hayashi decided to "give his stage name back to Shochiku" and to begin his career anew under his real name, Kazuo Hasegawa, with a new film for Toho. Both studios tried hard to manipulate the publicity surrounding these events for their own interests. After the attack, the public response was transformed from indignation over the star "who forgot his sense of obligation to his old studio," into sympathy for his plight. Hasegawa asked the police not to investigate the matter, apparently feeling guilty about his own actions. The public was shocked at what it had seen of the dark side of the film business.[7] Director Masahiro Makino knew the young yakuza who had attacked Hasegawa, and was himself rather critical of Toho for stealing not only Hasegawa but also directors Kinugasa and Watanabe from Shochiku with offers of more money.[8]

Another dark side of Toho's modernity was its ready adherence to the government's war policy. Kobayashi became Minister of Commerce and Industry in July 1940, significantly increasing Toho's ties to the government. Shochiku and Toho began to compete to take over Nikkatsu, which finally was absorbed into Masaichi Nagata's Dai-Nippon Eiga Seisaku Gaisha (Daiei Studio) in 1941, as the result of the government's new policy of consolidating small film companies into oligarchical structures for easier centralized control. Daiei engaged period film directors and stars and began to specialize in such films, while Shochiku continued its traditional specialization in family-oriented films and melodramas for the female audience. Toho, a new company without a traditional specialization, was thus in a position to act promptly in response to the expectations of the government, and it began to concentrate on war films. The studio's wealth also enabled it to deploy the special effects required by this genre. Furthermore, Toho's producer system was well suited to the newly bureaucratized central governmental control over the industry.[9]

Army in Shanghai [*Shanhai rikusentai*] (1939), directed by Hisatora Kumagai and written by Tsutomu Sawamura, included location sequences shot immediately after the real battles. *Flaming Big Sky* [*Moyuru ozora*] (1941), directed by Yutaka Abe, written by Yasutaro Yagi, photographed by Yoshio Miyajima, and featuring nine hundred fighter planes, became a great hit. Even more spectacular, owing to its unprecedented scale, was Kajiro Yamamoto's *The War at the Sea from Hawaii to Malaya*. Planned jointly with the imperial navy, its shooting took six months. Large-scale sets and cranes were used; all the top Toho cameramen, including Akira Mimura, Mitsuo Miura, Hiroshi Suzuki, and Yoshimi Hirano were recruited for the task; and Eiji Tsuburaya (who would in 1954 participate in the production of *Godzilla* [*Gojira*]) orchestrated the special effects. As if this were not enough, documentary footage was inserted into the battle scenes. Toho spent ¥770,000 for production and ¥150,000 for publicity. The film was released on December 3, 1942, to commemorate the first anniversary of the successful attack on Pearl Harbor, and attained record-breaking commercial success, earning ¥1,115,000 during the first eight days.[10]

Other popular battle films included *Flowers of the South Sea* [*Nankai no hanataba*] (1942), directed by Yutaka Abe, set in the South Pacific; *Victory Songs of Wings* [*Tsubasa no gaika*] (1942), directed by Satsuo Yamamoto and

The War at Sea from Hawaii to Malaya [*Hawai Marei-oki kaisen*] (1942), directed by Kajiro Yamamoto. Courtesy of the Kawakita Memorial Film Institute.

written by Akira Kurosawa, on the war in the air; and *Suicide Troop of the Watchtower* [*Boro no kesshitai*] (1943), directed by Tadashi Imai and written by Yusaku Yamagata and Ryuichiro Yagi, set on the border of Korea and Manchuria. As soon as the war ended, before the Allied occupation forces landed in Japan, Toho destroyed the negatives and prints of two more of the war films they had made so proudly: *Fire on That Flag* (1944), directed by Yutaka Abe, written by Hideo Oguni and Yagi, photographed by Yoshio Miyajima and produced by Takeo Ito and Kazuo Takimura, and *I Believe I Am Being Followed* (1945), directed by Kunio Watanabe and written by Toshio Yasumi. The former had been shot in the Philippines, with a cast including Allied POWs and Filipino actors, and told the story of Japan's liberating that country from cruel American colonialism. The latter film was a biography of a soldier killed in battle in the Philippines.

Toho was also skillful at producing melodramas, into which the requisite wartime ideology was injected. *The Song of the White Orchid* [*Byakuran no uta*] (1939), directed by Watanabe; *Night in China* (1940), directed by

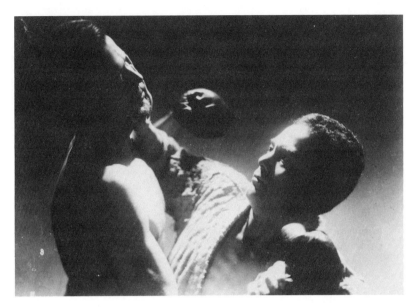

Susumu Fujita (r.) in *Sanshiro Sugata Part II* [*Zoku Sugata Sanshiro*] (1945), directed by Akira Kurosawa. Courtesy of the Kawakita Memorial Film Institute.

Osamu Fushimizu and written by Oguni; and *The Pledge of Burning Sands* [*Nessa no chikai*] (1940), directed by Watanabe, were among the extremely popular melodramas starring Li Hsiang-lan (Yoshiko Yamaguchi's Chinese name) and Kazuo Hasegawa, who portray lovers from the two nations. These films were made as ideological propaganda for the Japanese and the peoples under Japanese military rule. *Night in China*, for example, had three endings, each intended for a different national audience: the Japanese, the Chinese, and those in the South Asian colonies. In the Chinese version, the story ends with the wedding of the Chinese heroine and the Japanese naval pilot. The Japanese audience saw a more complex ending: before the wedding, the hero is called up to active duty, is wounded in battle, and eventually dies. On learning the news, his fiancée commits suicide by drowning. In the version seen in Malaya and the Philippines, the story is further complicated: the news of the soldier's death proves false, and, although he is wounded in a battle with communist guerrillas, he returns to save the heroine just as she is about to throw herself into the river.[11] Besides the obvious lesson of cooperation between Japan and China (and other Japanese colonies) in all three versions, the ending for the Japanese audience reflects its strong preference for tragic romances.

Historical allegories included Kurosawa's *Sanshiro Sugata* and *Sanshiro Sugata Part II,* about a judo master fighting Japanese and Western enemies in the Meiji Era (1868–1912), and Makino's *The Opium War* [*Ahen senso*] (1943), a remake of D. W. Griffith's *Orphans of the Storm* (1921) set against the background of the nineteenth-century Opium War. Seeing Toho's success, Shochiku and Daiei Studios soon began to release their own films in these genres.

Surprisingly, many of those making war films at Toho, including producers, directors, screenplay writers, cinematographers, and actors, had been active in the prewar Proletarian film movement, and would again become active in the union movement after the war, as we saw in chapter 5.

THE POSTWAR LABOR UNION MOVEMENT

Thanks to the early occupation policy of encouraging labor unions, initiated by David Conde of CIE, Japanese filmmakers responded to their formation with immediate enthusiasm. Legalization of workers' rights had been codified in the Labor Union Law, which took effect on March 1, 1946, and the Labor Relation Arbitration Law of October 13, 1946. Shochiku's Ofuna Studio was the first to organize an employees' union, on November 9, 1945; it was chaired by Kogo Noda, the studio's most respected scenario writer, known for his collaboration with Yasujiro Ozu. The union asked for and won a salary increase, and successfully contested the company's decision to accept executives from the government. These victories stimulated filmmakers at the other studios, and by the end of 1945, all six film companies (three studios producing dramatic films and three producing newsreels and documentaries) were unionized. All of the unions asked for salary increases to keep pace with the rampant inflation, and demanded labor's participation in management. Unions at two of the newsreel companies, Nichi-ei and Asahi, won on the issue of labor participation in management.

On January 13, 1946, the All-Japan Film Employee Union Association (Zen Nippon Eiga Jugyoin Kumiai Domei, known as Zen-ei) was organized as a parent organization for the unions formed at each of the studios, with 2,700 unionists from the entire industry participating. This umbrella unionization was necessitated by the fact that, immediately after the war, following the American model, only industrywide craft unions, as opposed to company unions, were acceptable.[12] Chaired by Toho screenplay writer Yasutaro Yagi, it announced demands such as adequate salaries and benefits for all, labor participation in the industry's administration, democratization of film exhibition and distribution, and unification of the labor movement.[13]

The union at Toho first organized the workers at the studio, and soon brought in workers at the main and branch offices, until its membership numbered 5,600. It first struck on March 20, 1946, when its demand for improved working conditions was refused by the company. After a fifteen-day strike, the union won a minimum monthly salary of ¥600 (plus overtime) and the establishment of a production administration committee consisting of union members, which allowed the union to participate in decision-making.[14]

On April 16, 1946, the central committee of Zen-ei decided to compile a list of war criminals in the film industry, in response to a request by CIE. Later that same month, Zen-ei expanded and changed its name to Nichi-ei-en, an abbreviation for Zen Nippon Eiga Engeki Jugyoin Kumiai Domei or the All-Japan Film and Theater Employee Union Association. It now had 18,000 members, and joined the communist-dominated All-Japan National Congress of Industrial Unions (Zen Nippon Sangyobetsu Rodo Kumiai or San-betsu).

On April 28, after the new organization was established, it made public the list of war criminals, as a first step toward the democratization of the film industry, following the release of a similar list ten days earlier by the leftist Free Film Workers Group. The war criminals on the Nichi-ei-en list were divided into three categories. Class A included twenty-three former officials of the Ministry of Internal Affairs and the Bureau of Information, along with film company presidents and executives (including Otani and Kido from Shochiku, Osawa and Uemura from Toho, Nagata and Kikuchi from Daiei, and Kyusaku Hori from Nikkatsu, among others). They were recommended for permanent exclusion from the film industry. Temporary suspension was sought for ten film executives and director Hisatora Kumagai,[15] grouped in Class B. Thorough self-criticism was recommended for those in Class C, who included the makers of such films as *The War at the Sea from Hawaii to Malaya* and *Fire on That Flag*.

Film workers also had to fight the postwar inflation, exemplified by the dramatic escalation of film admission prices. During wartime, cinema admission had been fixed at ¥0.95 for first-run films. After the war, this rate increased rapidly. Immediately after the surrender, it was around ¥1, but by March 1946 it had already increased to ¥3. Two months later, admission to a first-run Japanese film cost ¥4.50, ¥5 for first-run foreign films. By March 1947, first-run admission had risen to ¥10, and it doubled again over the next six months. By August of the following year, it had doubled yet again. The tax on film admissions was also extremely high at the beginning of the postwar period: 100 percent for admissions below ¥1 and 200 percent for those above. In March 1946, the tax rate was reduced to 50 percent for admissions below ¥3.50, 100 percent for those above, and no tax on admissions costing less than ¥0.50.[16]

Despite the serious postwar inflation and the rising price of tickets, the film industry enjoyed huge profits because the Japanese audience was hungry for entertainment. Capitalists who were looking for new investment opportunities after the dismantling of the arms industry began to invest in the construction of new theaters.[17]

Ninety-three of Toho's 120 theaters had suffered from wartime air raids (sixty-three had been completely burned out), but all the major ones had survived. The company reopened these surviving theaters immediately after the war, and seventy more were renovated by the spring of 1946. However, the occupation government took over Toho's Tokyo Takarazuka theater in December 1945 for its own use, renaming it the Ernie Pyle Theater after the Allied war reporter who had been killed in battle. Soon after this, Toho's other major theaters in Kyoto and Osaka met with the same fate, which led to a serious decrease in the company's income.[18]

THOSE WHO CREATE TOMORROW

On May 2, 1946, the day after the first May Day celebration permitted in many years, Toho released *Those Who Create Tomorrow*, directed by Hideo Sekigawa, Kurosawa, and Kajiro Yamamoto and written by Yamagata and Yamamoto. At Conde's suggestion,[19] this film was planned by the union to promote the idea of unionization, beginning with the organization of a film studio, and spreading through the entertainment field and then to other industries. Its main theme is the conflict between the feudalistic sense of obligation the worker was supposed to feel toward his benevolent employer, and the awakening sense of workers' unity in the fight to improve their working and living conditions.

The story revolves around a family with two working sisters, the elder (Chieko Nakakita) a script girl and the younger (Mitsue Tachibana) a revue dancer. Their father (Kenji Susukida), a white-collar worker in an iron-manufacturing company, is an antiunion traditionalist. They rent the second floor of their house to a railway engineer (Masayuki Mori) and his family. The film thus not only reflected the labor situation at Toho's film studio, but also the theatrical section of the company and the railway company that was one of Toho's parent companies.

Over the film's opening credits, we hear on the soundtrack the union's song, hailing the unity of the workers. The difficult economic situation of modest households is emphasized through the family's conversation about prices and food rationing. The driver upstairs is troubled when his concern over his son's illness conflicts with his feeling of obligation to participate in the strike at his factory. But his wife recommends that he join his colleagues, and the camera follows him to his factory, which has been occupied by a group of strikers, singing and demonstrating with banners.

The union's songs and music accompany the visual images of striking workers at various times throughout the film. Close-up shots show signs with militant slogans: "Democratization of Cinema Is for the People," "Let's Win Our Daily Bread through Struggle at the Studio . . . ," and so on.

At the studio, while a scene is being shot featuring "Actor Fujita" (one of Toho's biggest stars, Susumu Fujita, playing himself), the camera pans up to where the lighting technicians are standing near the ceiling. They converse about the problems confronting them: "Only the company is making money." "They never think about our audiences." "We don't like commercialism." "We are happy to work on this excellent project, but we need economic security." Then, an actress (Toho star Hideko Takamine) joins Fujita on the set below, saying "We can never make 'rich' films under such conditions."

The director's shouting "Cut!" leads directly into the next scene, backstage at the theater where the younger sister works. One of the dancers is sick from overwork and her colleagues complain about the hard working conditions.

In the next scene, back at the studio, the spectators hear the workers saying that the railway company (at which the driver works) was struck, and the management has been taken over by labor. A lighting technician, slowly and in plain language, begins to express the "common people's opinion": "This is a problem for working people . . . the problem of our conscience . . .

the responsibility to our customers . . . something new has to be done . . . . We are in a different field, and we want to make good movies, but the fighting spirit should be shared."

At this point, someone suggests that they all should join in supporting the strikers at the railway company. After the discussion, the elder sister suggests that they should go that night. We then see studio unionists singing in front of the railway company offices.

At home, the father expresses his opposition to the labor movement, naively believing that "our company president would never do something so inhuman [as to fire company employees]," and claims that his daughters have come under the bad influence of the engineer upstairs. But unionization finally spreads to the father's company, and when the company fires the unionists, the father is fired, too. He sees the sign on his office wall urging "Struggle!" and is strongly impressed when the engineer continues the struggle with his comrades after the death of his child.

At the younger sister's theater, the dancers decide to organize when one of them is fired by an inhumane manager (Takashi Shimura) because of illness. Outside the theater, a group of workers is marching and singing with banners, and the younger sister finds her father in the group. The camera captures the old man's shining face in a close-up from a low angle, and gradually he joins in singing revolutionary songs. The film ends as the strikes at the studio and the railway company continue.

The press screening of *Those Who Create Tomorrow*, accompanied by the singing of the "Internationale," impressed Conde very favorably.[20] Shigemi Hijikata of the Toho publicity department drew the poster for the film. It portrayed workers carrying red flags and signs and, unlike the publicity for most films, did not feature portraits of the film's stars. Conde so liked this poster that he asked Toho if he could have the original, and Toho presented it to him after May Day.[21]

However, the critical and commercial response was not very sympathetic to this crude propaganda film. Even Kyuichi Tokuda, the secretary of the Japan Communist Party, found the film "too intellectualized and uninteresting."[22] Rather than effectively dramatizing the unionists' struggle, the film resorts to clichéd dialogue and relies for its effect on close-up shots of strikers singing militant songs. It is too simplistic in dividing the world into exploitative capitalists and noble, hard-working employees.

Akira Kurosawa, one of the co-directors of the film, later dismissed his participation as follows:

This film cannot be described as mine more than anybody else's. In sum, it is a film made by the Struggle Committee and it is a good example of how uninteresting such films could be. It was made in a week, and even now, when I hear their [the demonstrators'] songs on May Day, it reminds me of this film and it makes me sleepy. It might be a good film considering it was made in a week.[23]

TOHO'S SECOND STRIKE

On September 1, 1946, the Toho labor union demanded a salary increase, from the minimum of ¥600 to ¥1,000, to keep up with inflation, and the company management granted it. Then in October, Nichi-ei-en planned a general strike, asking the following:

1. Each company should recognize Nichi-ei-en as its employees' collective bargaining agent.
2. Each company should sign a contract with Nichi-ei-en.
3. Each company should participate in industrywide organizations to negotiate and work with Nichi-ei-en to solve the problems inherent in the development of film and theater:
   a. To maintain full employment.
   b. To improve the methods of distributing newsreels and culture films and rationalize distribution fees.
   c. To respect the opinions of film crews in deciding which films were to be rereleased.

The companies were most disturbed by the first demand, believing that granting it would infringe on their right to bargain with their employees, and would lead to Nichi-ei-en eventually taking over the management. In the executives' eyes, these demands constituted "communist subversive activities." The managements of Toho, Shochiku, and Daiei announced collectively that they would not negotiate with Nichi-ei-en because its activities had become extremely political.[24]

A general strike in the film industry was planned for October 15. On October 6, the Toho labor union split into two groups, one of which insisted on striking and a second that wanted to avoid a strike in order that the distribution of their own films not be interrupted. The latter group, numbering fifty people, left Nichi-ei-en to establish an alternative union.

On October 15, the rest of Toho's employees, Shochiku's Ofuna studio, and Nichi-ei-en went out on strike. Daiei's union joined the strike on October 18, and Shochiku's Kyoto studio was struck on October 26. On October 20, film and theater people met at a stadium in Tokyo to hold the "Art Revival Festival," a demonstration on behalf of their cause.

The companies' managements met with Nichi-ei-en, demanding that it withdraw from the communist-oriented San-betsu and negotiate with them peacefully. On October 25, Nichi-ei-en abandoned collective negotiation on behalf of its member unions, each of which began to negotiate individually with the companies. Daiei settled on October 30, and Shochiku on November 6. Toho's negotiation was prolonged because its president, Yoshio Osawa, went out of his way to understand and accommodate the union, despite pressure from the company's owners. Educated at Princeton University, Osawa was familiar with American labor laws, and highly praised by Toho's unionists for his liberal views.[25] But in the meantime, Toho's studio and theaters were completely shut down, and those anxious to work again and opposed to the original, communist-oriented union gradually left it to join the new organization.

On November 13, Toho's top ten stars, under the name the "Society of the Flag of Ten," led by Denjiro Okochi (who had played the role of the liberal university professor Takigawa in Kurosawa's *No Regrets for Our Youth*), left the first union and established yet another union. Dissatisfied with the "politicization" of the union and the "dictatorial attitude" of the union leaders, and frustrated by not being able to work, Okochi had composed an antiunion pronouncement and circulated it among the studio employees.[26] Nine stars (Kazuo Hasegawa, Susumu Fujita, Setsuko Hara, Hideko Takamine, Isuzu Yamada, Takako Irie, Toshiko Yamane, Ranko Hanai, and Yataro Kurokawa) followed Okochi, along with directors Kunio Watanabe and Yutaka Abe, and 445 other employees.[27] This mass exodus from the original union brought the combined total membership of the two splinter unions to nearly two-thirds of the active membership of the original union. Nonetheless, the core union continued its strike.

On November 18, Toho management and Nichi-ei-en reopened their negotiations. The management offered a new contract based on that used by the American auto industry, as well as a sample contract provided by the occupation government. The union, headed by producer Takeo Ito, presented its own version, also based on occupation government materials, demanding labor's participation in management and a closed-shop system, requiring that all employees join a single union and forbidding the company to employ anyone who would not join. Ito claimed that the occupation government had given both sides the same sample, sent from the USA, of a collective bargaining agreement. Thus the content of the contracts from both sides was much the same, in particular in setting up the grievance machinery to avoid future strikes.[28]

On November 30, the two sides came to terms, and signed a contract on December 3, bringing an end to the 51-day strike. Management gave in to almost all of labor's demands: it agreed to significant labor participation in administration and personnel affairs by the routing of major decisions through a council on which both sides were to be represented. Additionally, the agreement limited the work day to eight hours, and instituted the shop steward system, which was touted by the occupation government as a democratic system of management. If the workers could not agree with their shop steward, they were free to negotiate directly with the company president, then with the local labor committee, then with the central labor committee. Ito praised this contract, as did Osawa, saying that Toho's labor and management hoped to rely on collective bargaining to avoid future strikes.[29] On the other hand, the union was unsuccessful in its attempt to eliminate a clause providing for arbitration of disputes.

The management signed similar contracts with the second and third unions, which also provided for arbitration of disputes. All three contracts were for a single year.[30] Because of the closed-shop provision in its contract with the first union, Toho established Shin-Toho ("New Toho") on March 8, 1947, using Toho's facilities and buildings, for the members of the other unions. The new company had 478 employees.[31]

After losing its big stars to Shin-Toho, Toho had to depend on former bit-part players and up-and-coming actors and actresses. In June of the previous year, Toho had sponsored a search for "New Faces." Four thousand young people applied, out of whom the studio chose sixteen men and thirty-two women.

Among them was a sullen young man named Toshiro Mifune. His defiant attitude at the interview repelled most of his interlocutors. However, one of them, along with actress Hideko Takamine, liked this wild man and called in Akira Kurosawa to take a look at him. Kurosawa was deeply impressed by his unique character and insisted that he should be selected.[32] Three months of training helped prepare Mifune and the other young recruits, including actresses Hatae Kishi, Setsuko Wakayama, and Yoshiko

Ichiro Ryuzaki (l.) and Mieko Takamine in *Once More* [*Ima hitotabino*] (1947), directed by Heinosuke Gosho. Courtesy of the Kawakita Memorial Film Institute.

Kuga and actors Hajime Izu and Isamu Numazaki, for the Toho productions of 1947.

Among these new actors and actresses, as well as the directors, writers, and producers who had remained at Toho, there developed a spirit of competition with Shin-Toho, and they set out to better the new company's films, despite its stable of former Toho stars. Other factors also contributed to the new high standards of quality at Toho. For example, the contract with the union specified that the company only make films that had been approved by a committee including union members. This gave some filmmakers undreamed-of control over the content, style, casting, and budget of their films. Many directors, communist and noncommunist alike, appreciated this new freedom.[33] The yoke of commercial pressure from the company having been loosened, filmmakers could choose their themes and experiment with styles. Budgets and shooting schedules were generous.

Isao Numasaki (l.) and Chieko Nakakita in *One Wonderful Sunday* [*Subarashiki nichiyobi*] (1947), directed by Akira Kurosawa. Courtesy of the Kawakita Memorial Film Institute.

Partly as a consequence, Toho produced only thirteen films in 1947. In 1946, it had produced eighteen films, and before that, under wartime control, each of the three companies was making two films a month. Yet the critical response to the 1947 releases was almost uniformly enthusiastic. Six films were ranked among the ten best films of the year by *Kinema Jumpo* magazine's critics: *Between War and Peace*, directed by Satsuo Yamamoto and Fumio Kamei won second place. In third place was *Once More*, directed by Heinosuke Gosho and written by Keinosuke Uekusa, the story of a wartime romance between a bourgeois girl and a doctor who works in the slums. *Actress*, directed by Kinugasa and written by Hisaita, placed fifth, and *One Wonderful Sunday* [*Subarashiki nichiyobi*], directed by Kurosawa and written by Uekusa, a neorealist film portraying a young couple's struggle amidst postwar poverty, gained sixth place. *To the End of the Silver-Capped Mountains* [*Ginrei no hate*], directed by Taniguchi and written by Kurosawa and Kajiro Yamamoto, an action film with a human touch, was seventh, and the film that came in eighth was *Four Stories of Love* [*Yottsu no koi no monogatari*], consisting of four episodes, respectively directed by Shiro Toyoda, Naruse, Kajiro Yamamoto, and Kinugasa and written by Kurosawa, Oguni, Kenta Yamazaki, and Yasumi.

Despite this critical success, the new system of filmmaking, although ideal for many of the filmmakers, was seen as a disaster by the owners. The company had hoped to make twenty-four films, the same pace as it had maintained during the war, but the union would not compromise. At a time when the average budget for a film was about ¥5 million, *Once More* cost ¥8.9 million, *Between War and Peace* ¥9 million, *To the End of the Silver-Capped Mountains* ¥10.1 million, and *Actress* ¥15.3 million. None of these expensive films earned back its cost, and Toho ended up losing ¥75 million in 1947.[34] Miyajima states that, according to a Toho announcement of the time, the company lost ¥78.2 million during the first quarter of 1947, of which ¥30.5 million was attributed to the production and distribution departments.[35] Pressure from major investors forced Osawa and other executives out in March 1947. Katamaru Tanabe, a younger brother of Ichizo Kobayashi, became the new president. After a series of negotiations with the union—as many as eighty-three all-night meetings during his eight-month tenure—he became ill and was replaced by Tetsuzo Watanabe in December 1947.[36]

TOHO'S THIRD STRIKE

Tetsuzo Watanabe, was a former professor of law at Tokyo Imperial University, a delegate to the International Labor Conference, and a well-known anticommunist. He was considered favorably by the U.S. planners of the occupation. When the Office of Strategic Services listed those in Japan (both natives and foreigners) who could be expected to be cooperative and helpful in future occupation activities, the list of liberal scholars and Christian missionaries included Watanabe. In the report, Watanabe is described as an authority on labor law, a cultivated scholar in the European tradition (living in a Western-style house and playing the violin), and a man with significant potential to help in the unification of Japanese labor and the aristocracy.[37] The characterization of Watanabe as liberal contains elements of truth: he was investigated by the police for independently publishing a pamphlet critical of a Ministry of Education pamphlet in 1941. In February 1944, he criticized as inaccurate the government's statements on the success of the war effort, and said that Germany would be defeated: for this, he was informed upon and then arrested and imprisoned for a year.[38]

Watanabe was not ashamed of his ignorance of filmmaking. Asked at the press conference after his appointment what kind of films he liked among the recent ones he had seen, Watanabe answered that he had not seen any films since the early French detective film *Zigomar* (released in Japan in 1911!).[39] On the other hand, he took pride in his firm sense of mission to "defeat the two kinds of reds at Toho: communists and red budgets." In an interview, Watanabe boasted that anticommunism had long been his principle, and stated that, if Toho allowed a handful of communists to agitate, the resulting unrest would harm the company. Of course, the company could not fire employees just because they were communists. Watanabe did not mind anyone putting his political principles into practice per se, as long as he did so only in his private life and not at the company. Asked if the antiunion movement within the studio would not be similarly harmful, Watanabe disagreed, pointing out that Toho was only working to stop the union's "destructive communist activities" and that it had the right to do so.[40] Nonetheless, Watanabe sometimes demonstrated surprising ignorance of his communist opponents. When he first visited Toho's studio, he was welcomed by red flags and unionists singing the "Internationale." He said to his aide: "I don't like red flags, but I like that nice song. Is it Toho's company song?"[41]

Watanabe's position was strengthened by the appointment of his aide, Takeo Mabuchi, to the newly established position of managing director specializing in labor negotiations. Kurosawa described the new president as "a notorious 'red-hater,'" and the new director as "a strike-breaking specialist," who was "willing to engage in the lowest imaginable tactics to win the strike battle," and "a genius of foul play."[42] The new regime immediately announced that Toho would resume making twenty-four films annually, and that production costs for each film would be limited to ¥6.5 million. Furthermore, it informed the union that the company wanted to change their contract to restore to the company total power over management and personnel issues, and to limit the union's rights of negotiation and strike. The union refused. At this time, Kurosawa's *Drunken Angel* and Gosho's *Visage* [*Omokage*] were in production; Imai's *Blue Mountains* [*Aoi sanmyaku*], Taniguchi's *Jakoman and Tetsu* [*Jakoman to Tetsu*], and Kamei's *The Life of a Woman* [*Onna no issho*] were at the planning stage.

Watanabe abolished the shop steward system and restored the section chief system. He also vetoed three projects submitted by the union, all of which were to be produced by Takeo Ito, the union chairman. One of these was *The Man of Flame* [*Honoo no otoko*], which communist Kiyoshi Kusuda was scheduled to direct, a cooperative project with the Japan Railway Corporation's union. The others were to be directed by communist Satsuo Tamamoto. Watanabe pressured the union by saying that Toho would not mind closing its studio and concentrating on distribution and screening if the union would not cooperate.

As the union continued to refuse management's new contract, Toho in April 1948 announced the dismissal of 1,200 employees (278 from the studio), including "known communists, and individuals active in the Nichi-ei-en."[43] The studio's union asked management to reconsider, claiming that the studio could return to profitability by making eighteen films annually, but the company disagreed.

The negotiations soon fell apart, and, on April 15, the union occupied the studio facilities to protest the dismissal. Sympathetic groups from outside, including activists from the Japan Communist Party and members of the Communist Youth League, the Industry Labor Association, and the North Korean Association, joined the unionists at the studio. They sang revolutionary songs, made speeches through loudspeakers condemning the company, erected barricades, and closed the front and rear gates of the studio.[44]

President Watanabe explained the situation as follows:

> After the war, Toho had to reabsorb former employees returning from the front and from conscripted labor. Toho's studio, with its 1,200 employees, is producing only 13 films annually, while Shochiku's Ofuna and Kyoto studios, with 1,020 employees, are [together] producing 42 films. This means that Toho has surplus employees and is wasting money on personnel. In addition, despite the decrease in revenues, production costs have been increasing. With the company two billion yen in the red, it will have to be disbanded in less than half a year. This is why we decided to dismiss employees to rebuild our company.[45]

But Ito refuted these claims:

> It is the company's responsibility to retain the surplus employees, because it was created by a merger between several companies. The company should realize who it was who actually built the Toho company of today. President Watanabe continually talks about the inefficiency of production, but he ignores Toho's important mission in the advancement of mass culture by

producing good films that are also awakening the notion of basic civil rights.[46]

The company then announced a one-month halt in studio operations, effective May 1. Funds for the five films then in production were frozen. Management demanded the closing of all buildings, the return of the facilities to company control, and prohibition of entry by unauthorized people. The union refused every one of these demands. Two to three hundred outside supporters entered the studio every day, and films were screened for their entertainment. Dance parties were held, the "Internationale" was sung, and group discussions and demonstrations were conducted inside the studio itself, to the delight of the young unionists.[47]

On June 1 the company announced the indefinite closing of the studio and stopped paying salaries. The unionists and their families were forced to take temporary jobs, such as selling candies and dolls, doing carpentry, repairing radios, painting signs, and arranging costumes at weddings. The actors and directors organized theater troupes to tour the country to raise funds. Kurosawa directed Chekhov's *Proposal,* and adapted his just-completed film *Drunken Angel* into a play and traveled with its two stars, Takashi Shimura and Toshiro Mifune.[48] Naruse and Taniguchi also directed theater pieces. Actors and actresses, including Ryo Ikebe, Yuriko Hamada, Takashi Shimura, and Ichiro Ryuzaki, supported the union by contributing their fees for appearing in the films of other studios. Kazuo Hasegawa, one of the ten stars who had left Toho during the second strike to join Shin-Toho, quit his new studio. When he appeared in a period film, *The Sucker,* at another studio, he insisted that it be assigned to unionist director Kinugasa, and that an all-Toho crew be used.[49]

On July 5, twenty-two employees established the Toho Democratization Club, to oppose the communist domination of the union.[50] It would eventually absorb other dissatisfied employees from the main office and the Nagoya branch office, and develop into the Toho Employees Union. The club demanded the reopening of the studio, and received the company's immediate support. This in turn encouraged others to join the club, whose members began to wear blue ribbons to distinguish themselves from the original union members, who wore red ribbons. The groups soon came to be known as the Blue Ribbon and Red Ribbon clubs. Both Toho's official company history[51] and Ito[52] state that the new organization numbered about one hundred members, although Uekusa counted only sixty, led by the same people who had organized the group that had left for Shin-Toho.[53] The core union members believed that management supported the formation of the club in order to divide the union members.[54]

The members of the two organizations quarreled fiercely at the studio. The Tokyo Municipal Labor Arbitration Committee tried to intervene, but its efforts were rejected by both sides. On August 10, the Red Ribbon members constructed barriers around the studio, protected the gates with fire hoses and large fans, and tried to prevent the Blue Ribbon members from entering.

The Nichi-ei-en had on May 8 filed a protest before the Tokyo District Court, opposing the company's decision to close the studio. The company filed a counterprotest before the same court on May 11. On August 11 the court sent a judge to take a firsthand look at the situation and invited representatives of management and the leaders of the two unions to speak before the court.

On August 13, the Artist Group—consisting of fourteen directors (Kinugasa, Gosho, Naruse, Toyoda, Kamei, Kurosawa, Kusuda, Sekigawa, Imai, Taniguchi, Kajiro Yamamoto, Satuso Yamamoto, Eisuke Takizawa, and Motoyoshi Oda), four screenplay writers (Yasumi, Yamazaki, Yamagata, and Uekusa) and six producers (Ito, Iwasaki, Sojiro Motoki, Tomoyuki Tanaka, Dan Yoneyama, and Toshio Ide)—issued a statement asking the company to reconsider, and resolving not to work for Toho unless Watanabe and Mabuchi resigned. It was decided that members would be sent to other studios and to the Tokyo District Court to explain the situation at the studio and to publicize the statement.

On the night of August 13, the court issued its decision, in the company's favor. The following morning, company lawyers and seven representatives of the court arrived at the studio to execute the order, but were prevented from entering by Nichi-ei-en members. On August 16, the Tokyo Municipal Labor Arbitration Committee presented an arbitration plan, which was rejected by all parties. Early on the morning of August 18, an actor who belonged to the Blue Ribbon union climbed up the chimney of the laboratory building to demonstrate against the strike, and stayed there for the next thirty-four hours. Nicknamed "the chimney man" thereafter, he had supposedly been persuaded to perform this stunt by the Blue Ribbon union, which had promised to make him a producer when it took power.[55] Around seven o'clock the next morning, a fire started inside the laboratory building, but it was soon put out; Nichi-ei-en members believed that it had been caused intentionally by the company or members of the Blue Ribbon Club.[56] Some officials of the occupation government believed that the fire was "put out by union members" and reported that the union strikers would not let firemen clear the barricade to extinguish the fire, because they feared that "the police may follow firemen onto the studio grounds."[57] The Tokyo District Court finally decided to execute the order to remove the unionists from the studio itself.

At 9:20 on the morning of August 19, the district police chief arrived at the front gate of Toho Studio and read the decision of the court. The company's lawyers and the court officials arrived at 9:30. They had been preceded by a platoon from the First Cavalry Division augmented by three aircraft (possibly reconnaissance planes) and several tanks sent by the U.S. Eighth Army.[58] The Americans claimed that the Japanese police had requested the Army's presence, to protect the Americans who lived around the studio and to defend Japanese democracy.[59] On the other hand, Akira Iwasaki claimed that the American families living near the studio had been ordered to move out by the morning of August 19.[60] Fifty or sixty trucks full of Japanese policemen, totaling two thousand men, followed and surrounded the studio.[61]

The tense atmosphere was broken by the appearance on a platform above the front gate of actor Tokue Hanazawa, the "defense captain" of the union, wearing a cowboy hat and accompanied by two or three young assistant art directors. Hanazawa gave a signal, and suddenly a blue mist poured down from the platform, accompanied by an ear-shattering noise. After a moment, he ordered a halt and, with a laugh, addressed the astonished authorities below through a loudspeaker: "Sorry, it was just a test!" It was a demonstration of how the union could deploy the studio's own props and facilities to defend their position.

The night before, the union leaders had discussed how to defend the studio from an attack by the police. They wanted above all to shock the police, and someone suggested using the studio's huge fans (used to simulate windstorms) to blow red pepper powder into the attackers' faces, temporarily blinding them. Another replied that this tactic would only further exasperate the already excited policemen, who might then become more violent. An art director suggested spraying red paint at the policemen, whereupon Kurosawa asked them to use blue paint, which he thought would antagonize the police less.[62]

Kurosawa explains that these tactics, childish though they were, were intended as deadly serious gestures in the struggle to protect the studio that the employees loved so dearly.[63] Kamei, on the other hand, insists that the paint-spraying idea was conceived as a psychological warfare tactic: the union had discussed the idea with journalists who had visited the studio, stating that those who attacked the studio would thus be marked as "oppressors." Thus the policemen carried extra uniforms on August 19 to be prepared in the event of a spray-paint attack.[64]

The American occupation forces took these "defense" measures as seriously as they were intended. A document on the "Toho Dispute" dated August 19 reads as follows: "The communists had erected a barricade [at] the front and rear entrances of the Number One studio, and a large blower was [at the] rear of the barricade to blow broken glass and sand into the path of anyone attempting to enter the studio. The fire hoses of the studio were laid out to the front entrance."[65]

The court officials granted the union representative fifteen minutes to go inside and discuss with his colleagues what the union wished to do. The front gate was then closed, and all present wondered what would happen next. Suddenly, the gate opened, and Kamei and unionist Yukie Kikuchi came out, carrying a large sign, freshly lettered: "Culture Cannot Be Destroyed by Violence." The two walked slowly in front of the silent policemen and onlookers, and back through the gate. Shigeo Kume, a lighting technician, then handed out fliers addressed to the "democratic policemen," which the policemen surrounding the front gate accepted silently.[66]

At 10:40, a police loudspeaker urged the four hundred unionists inside the studio to come out without resisting.[67] Opinions are divided over how long it took for the union to reach its decision. According to some, the members decided within ten minutes to leave the studio, on the condition that they could retain their jobs and keep their union.[68] Other sources claim that it took longer.[69] But eventually the unionists, after occupying the studio for 134 days, gathered in a procession and left the studio through the rear gate, carrying a red flag and singing the "Internationale." Actresses Nakakita, Kuga, Kishi, Setsuko Wakayama, and Sayuri Tanima were seen in tears. The court officials entered the studio, and the Blue Ribbon members removed the barricades. Thus ended the events of August 19, 1948, which would be summed up in the history books with the phrase, "Everything Came But the Battleships."[70]

THE RESOLUTION

The Nichi-ei-en unionists continued to use their office at the studio, and demanded that the company renounce its planned dismissal of 270 unionists, but the company continued to refuse to negotiate with the communist-dominated union. The leaders of Nichi-ei-en, Ito and cinematographer Yoshio Miyajima, met unofficially with company executives Watanabe, Tanabe, and Mabuchi on the night of October 18. The union leaders declared that they had ordered a nationwide strike against Toho theaters starting the following day, and suggested that some twenty unionists would quit the company voluntarily if the company gave up its dismissal plans. Originally, Ito had prepared a list of eighteen names: himself, Miyajima, directors Satsuo Yamamoto and Kiyoshi Kusuda, writers Yusaku Yamagata and Zenpei Saga, editor Akikazu Kono, art director Shigeru Miyamori, studio technician Seiji Tsuchiya, and Mikio Majima of the theater section, along with eight others. When the company pressed for additional names, those of director Fumio Kamei and Akira Iwasaki, who were not actually employed by Toho but were active in the union movement, were added.[71]

Early the next morning, the company representatives finally agreed to the union leaders' plan. The union returned to the company complete management control, but the company acknowledged the union's rights to organize and represent its workers. Management gained the right to limit political parties' activities within the studio, and promised not to discriminate against the Nichi-ei-en unionists. The union leaders then called off the strike, and the company released ¥15 million to finish the union's production of *The Life of a Woman*.[72]

Both sides had been exhausted by the long strike, and were ready to reach an agreement. The union won the cancellation of the dismissal plan, and management successfully excised the core of the communist influence at the studio, so both sides could claim success. However, the strike left unhealable wounds and bitterness in the hearts of the filmmakers who had once worked together at Toho. Some remained at Toho, and some chose to leave. Kurosawa explains the destruction of morale caused by this long struggle, blaming the company executives, but admitting that the union also sometimes went too far:

> For me the most painful moments of this strike were when I was caught between the employees of the Toho studio and the employees of Shin Toho.

Director Fumio Kamei (r.) during the shooting of *The Life of a Woman* [*Onna no issho*] (1949), with Hatae Kishi (l.) and Isao Numasaki. Courtesy of the Kawakita Memorial Film Institute.

... At this sight I felt an irrepressible rage welling up inside me. Far from learning from experience with their blunders in the second strike, the management were heaping more errors on top of what they had done. They were tearing to shreds the cooperating work force of precious talent we had nurtured for so long.[73]

Toho filmmakers felt that president Watanabe and labor executive Mabuchi, the two top managers brought in from outside, showed no feeling for the studio or for filmmaking. Iwasaki wrote that the barbaric plan to fire 270 employees could only have been conceived by managers hired from outside, and could never happen at Shochiku or Daiei, whose top management people really cared about filmmaking.[74] Kurosawa was determined never to work under the two executives.[75] Described by Kurosawa as a "genius of foul play," the latter employed tactics that outraged his foes. Mabuchi intentionally misquoted the directors for the convenience of management and later, when confronted by the directors, readily apologized, knowing that the correction in the news media would have little impact.[76] Mabuchi also insulted female unionists by saying at a Diet hearing that they might have engaged in sexual misconduct, another statement for which he was later forced to apologize.[77] Similarly, Watanabe upset filmmakers, critics, and even the American censors with his witch-hunting for communists. He once labeled as "communist propaganda" six Toho films, including Imai's *People's Enemy, Those Who Create Tomorrow,* Kusuda's *As Long as I Live,* Oda's *Eleven High School Girls* [*Juichi-nin no jogakusei*] (1946), Kamei and Yamamoto's *Between War and Peace,* and Kurosawa's *One Wonderful Sunday.* Watanabe's statement that the films were undesirable for export annoyed the American censors, who interpreted the remark as a subtle criticism of the civil and military censorship bodies, which had passed all of the films.[78] Indeed Watanabe and Mabuchi succeeded in pleasing only the company's investors.

The union leaders' rigid and combative attitude also alienated some employees. One of the top Toho stars who had helped to found the "Society of the Flag of Ten," Hideko Takamine, was troubled by the way in which normally capable, friendly, and quiet employees were transformed into aggressive, polemical demagogues who stirred their listeners with militant rhetoric and histrionics. She felt repelled by the authoritarian attitude of the leaders, and decided to quit the union, along with other stars and employees who felt the same way.[79]

Another star, Isuzu Yamada, recounted that she left Toho because she did not really understand the need for the strikes, and did not agree with the union's demand for salary increases. In addition, she felt obliged to follow film director Kunio Watanabe, who had introduced her to the film industry, when Watanabe left Toho for Shin-Toho. She recalled an example of the "ill effects of unionism" on filmmaking at Toho: during the making of Kinugasa's *Actress,* the crew sometimes spent only two or three hours a day shooting, because of staff conferences; furthermore, the crew stopped shooting at exactly 5:00 P.M. even if only one shot was left. Soon after moving to Shin-Toho, she left that studio, too, along with Yoshiko Yamaguchi, and became a free agent. Gradually, Yamada came to realize the importance of unionism, and committed herself to leftist film and theater projects, returning to Nichi-ei-en in May 1950.[80]

Yamada stated that the stars felt somewhat ostracized within the union, and that this feeling led them to quit, although it was also true that they did not understand the significance of the union movement to begin with.[81] For their part, the other unionists felt that the stars, in fact, were indifferent to workers whose status, salary scale, and life-style were enormously different from theirs. For instance, one unionist recalled how shocked she was when Denjiro Okochi, at a meeting, yelled at his fellow members: "How dare you decide to strike without asking my permission?" She felt as if she were watching him in one of his period film appearances.[82] To try to include in a single union the highly visible and individualistic stars and the replaceable technicians and workers was in some ways valuable, but in other ways reckless.

The union's ideological immaturity and inexperience was another problem, especially during the early stage of the occupation. Kenji Mizoguchi, selected as the union chairman at Shochiku's Kyoto Studio, appalled his fellow union members by making a speech saying "I am now your union chairman, and therefore I will give you orders. Please be prepared to follow my orders."[83] The division between labor and management was not well delineated; director Masahiro Makino admitted that at different times he operated on both sides of the fence.[84] Screenplay writer Yoshikata Yoda stated that, until the Toho strikes, the unions and the companies had often merely pretended to oppose each other.[85] Makino also pointed out that the most vociferous union speechmakers often did not know the meaning of the terminology that they used.[86]

What appeared to be a lack of principles among the union leaders sometimes confused and dismayed the union members. Documentary film director Shinkichi Noda expressed this feeling upon visiting the home of cinematographer Yoshio Miyajima, one of the most active union leaders. Noda saw displayed on the wall awards that Miyajima had received for his war films, such as *Flaming Big Sky* and *Fire on That Flag*. Takeo Ito was the producer of such anti-Allied films as *Fire on That Flag* and *Straight to the Americans* during wartime, and screenplay writer Yusaku Yamagata had also worked on similar projects. Female unionists perceived the sexist attitudes that the union leaders' political radicalism could not disguise. One woman was shocked to hear a communist union leader talking about "awakening his wife by kicking the pillow out from under her when he found her sleeping upon his returning home." She believed that most of the male activists must have shared his attitude.[87]

Ironically, even after Toho successfully rid the company of the most influential of the communist workers, it was to be troubled by Shin-Toho, the company that it had itself established for its anticommunist former employees. The problems began when Toho president Osawa was forced out of office and Shin-Toho became a publicly held company. Toho lost its firm control over Shin-Toho's management, which began to demand independence. When Toho established Shin-Toho during its second strike, it reserved for itself the exclusive right to distribute Shin-Toho's films, and claimed 25 percent of the profits in exchange for advancing all production costs, interest-free.[88]

Shin-Toho's first production was *One Thousand and One Nights of Toho* [*Toho sen-ichi ya*], directed by newcomer Kon Ichikawa and released in February 1947. It introduced Shin-Toho's big stars, who had all come over from Toho. The decision to set it in a film studio seemed to be the anticommunists' response to the Toho unionists' *Those Who Create Tomorrow*, also set in a studio. Neither this film, nor any of Shin-Toho's films made during that year, won critical favor.

After the company and the union reached agreement, Toho started shooting new films again in November 1948, but on a different basis than before. Management decided to retain as employees only office workers and supplementary technical department staff: all actors, studio technicians, directors, and screenplay writers were organized into independent subcontracting groups.[89] Even the four main producers (Sojiro Motoki, Kazuo Takimura, Naozane Fujimoto, and Nobuyoshi Morita) were made independent. In spite of the goal of twenty-four films per year that it proclaimed during the third strike, Toho released only four films, including Kurosawa's *Drunken Angel,* in 1948. This reduced output perhaps reflected top management's indifferent attitude toward producing any new films at all, which had been implicit in Watanabe's threat to turn Toho into a film distribution and exhibiting company.

In 1949, Toho released only five films, three of which were significant. These included *The Life of a Woman* (directed by Kamei, shot by Miyajima, and produced by Ito and Fujimoto) about a woman's problems with her work and with the feudalistic conventions of the family system. A fisherman in the north country was the subject of *Jakoman and Tetsu*, which was produced by Morita, written by Kurosawa, and directed by Taniguchi, and starred Mifune. *Blue Mountains (Parts I and II)* were light comedies criticizing the repressive attitudes toward sex prevailing at a small-town high school. They were directed by Tadashi Imai, shot by Asaichi Nakai, and produced by Fujimoto, and starred Setsuko Hara, Ryo Ikebe, and other new

From left to right, Hajime Izu, Setsuko Wakayama, Yoko Sugi, Ryo Ikebe, Setsuko Hara, and Ichiro Ryuzaki in *Blue Mountains* [*Aoi sanmyaku*] (1949), directed by Tadashi Imai. Courtesy of the Kawakita Memorial Film Institute.

actors and actresses developed at Toho. The Blue Mountains films were record-breaking commercial hits, and were also tremendously successful with the critics.

It was the success of Blue Mountains that brought the conflict between Toho and Shin-Toho to a head. In July 1949, after the first film's release, Shin-Toho demanded that Toho, weakened financially by its strikes, stop producing films. However, in September the board decided to start producing its own films again. At the same time, Watanabe resigned the company presidency to become chairman of the board, and was replaced by Ukichi Yonemoto, a shrewd stockbroker who held a significant investment in the company.

Shin-Toho, upset by Toho's renunciation of its earlier pledge, announced that it would not allow Toho to distribute its films any more. In November, Toho filed suit against Shin-Toho, claiming ownership of the sixteen films that Shin-Toho then had in production. After a fierce court battle, the parties came to terms in March 1950. According to their agreement, Shin-Toho would give eight of the sixteen films to Toho, as well as one year's distribution rights to the forty-three films released by Shin-Toho between August 1948 and December 1949. In exchange, Shin-Toho won complete independence from its parent company.[90]

One of the main reasons for Toho's problems was the conflict between the companies that had merged to form Toho in the first place. There was a fundamental power struggle between the Toho Film group, based on the merged film companies, and the Takarazuka group, based on Kobayashi's theater enterprises. Among the presidents of Toho, Osawa was from the former camp, and Watanabe was from the latter. After the occupation government "rehabilitated" the executives from the Toho Film group whom it had accused of being war criminals, they tried to return to their old positions, but found that the Takarazuka group had already monopolized them. These executives then hoped to make films at Shin-Toho, and Watanabe had the idea of assigning all production work to Shin-Toho, while retaining exclusive control over distribution and theaters at Toho. However, the Takarazuka group, which believed that the Toho Film group was responsible for the strikes, was unhappy with the plan and with Shin-Toho, which was taking production money from Toho. Thus, the Takarazuka group ousted one of its own, Watanabe, from the presidency, and chose Yonemoto to succeed him.[91]

In addition, those in the theater group were paid less than those in the film studio, a fact that caused the former group to resent the latter, who dominated the union movement and whose "superior" attitude was also upsetting.[92]

Within the Toho Film group itself, there was another struggle, between the production people (mostly from the old PCL) and the distribution people. The latter were mostly experts in foreign film distribution, and had been working for Toho when the importation of foreign films was stopped owing to the war. Most of the active unionists belonged to the production group at the studio, and those in the distribution department were among the first to become antiunion. Distribution people were said to be unlikely to share the workers' sensibilities, as they were businessmen rather than craftsmen or laborers.[93] In addition, outside the big cities, the distribution people had long-standing ties with theater owners; such relationships might have been impeded by unionization.[94]

AMERICAN CONCERNS

Owing to the occupation's censorship policy, it was not reported in the Japanese media that troops and materiel belonging to the American occupation forces had been mobilized to help the Japanese police remove the unionists from the studio and to help bring to an end the third Toho strike. The *Asahi Shimbun* newspaper reported that 2,000 policemen, the largest number yet mobilized in postwar history, had gone to the studio to execute the court order. The police chief announced that they had been sent to assist in the peaceful implementation of the order by preventing "violent" actions by the unionists, and not as a tactic of political oppression. The photo accompanying the article shows a crowd of men in uniforms and helmets, presumably from the police.[95] A film magazine similarly limited itself to mentioning "2,000 policemen," with not a word about the Americans.[96] The occupation censors were careful not to allow any scenes showing American troops or equipment to be included in the Japanese newsreels reporting the Toho dispute.[97]

On the other hand, English-language newspapers, which presumably few Japanese would read, reported that the eviction was helped by American military forces. *Stars and Stripes* reported that "troops of the First Cavalry Division were instructed to back up the Japanese police in carrying out the court order to evacuate strikers" from the studio.[98] The *New York Times* reported the news via United Press as follows:

> TOKYO, Thursday, Aug. 19—Communist-led sit-down strikers agreed today to leave the grounds of Toho movie studios after United States tanks and troops were called out in the first serious labor demonstration since Gen. Douglas MacArthur banned strikes. About 1,000 Japanese workers, many of them carrying red banners, immediately began leaving the property after their leaders capitulated. The surrender came after morning-long attempts by Japanese police to force an entry into the barricaded studio grounds and carry out a court order to evict the sit-downers. Workers inside the gates and along the barbed wire fence defied the court directive and the 100 police who originally planned to carry out the eviction order found themselves powerless. The call for a show of force brought out three United States tanks and fifty infantrymen armed with carbines.[99]

Despite the American attempt to keep images of American military force out of Japanese eyes, the American military's interference made them seem like oppressors in the eyes of those Japanese who knew what had really happened. One unionist claimed that he and his colleagues campaigned around Japan, displaying pictures showing American soldiers surrounding the studio, to raise the people's consciousness.[100]

American concern over this big strike at the largest film studio in Japan is evident in the close intelligence surveillance accorded the events at Toho.[101] Spot intelligence reports were sent from the strike scene by the Military Intelligence Section almost hourly on August 19, relating the situation and dispatching the news to other concerned agencies within the occupation government.[102] The Americans understood the powerful psychological effect of their military presence, reporting that "occupation personnel made a show of force and observed the operation, but took no part in it." When it became obvious that no violence would occur, the commanding general of the Eighth Army ordered the commanding general of the First Cavalry Division to withdraw all troops, indicating that "this incident was one of concern only to the Japanese and no Occupation forces should interfere in its current status."[103] Although no one was arrested, either by Japanese police or by American military personnel, a union leader making a speech in front of a railway station condemning the repression of the strike was arrested later by an MP for engaging in "criticism of occupation policy." He was found guilty by a U.S. military court, and was imprisoned.[104]

The unionists alleged that the Americans had begun to pressure them psychologically even before August 19. One of the more active union leaders, Seiji Tsuchiya, claimed that he had been summoned to meetings with both the Seventh Corps in Yokohama and the Fifth Corps in Tokyo, at which he was pressured to settle with the company soon.[105] Unionist Masako Ishikawa spoke about her experience of having been interrogated by a Nisei intelligence officer after she made a speech on the nationalist independence movements of Southeast Asia at one of the big meetings.[106] To prepare for the inevitable confrontation with the Japanese police and the American military forces, the union members collected as much information as possible on their opponents' actions. Through their network of sympathizers and spies, the unionists knew as of the early morning hours of August 19 about the scale of the Japanese police action and also that American military forces were heading for the studio.[107] They also spied on company executives and the antiunion members of the Blue-Ribbon Club.[108]

General MacArthur's antilabor attitude was demonstrated as early as May 20, 1946, when, in referring to the May Day demonstrations, he cautioned against "the growing tendency toward mass violence and physical processes of intimidation" by "disorderly minorities."[109] This attitude informed overall occupation policy, as he prohibited the general strike scheduled for February 1, 1947. The following year, MacArthur suggested in an open letter to Prime Minister Yoshida that he take away collective bargaining rights from government employees (national and local), and his suggestion became law through an act passed by the Japanese Diet on July 31, 1948.[110]

The anticommunist Truman Doctrine, granting economic assistance to Turkey and Greece, was announced in March 1947, and the Marshall Plan was proclaimed three months later. In early 1948, the American government announced that its policy goals for the Far East included setting up Japan as a shield against communism, an end that it would bring about by deemphasizing the demilitarization of Japan, and by working to help stabilize the Japanese economy. In January 1948, U.S. Secretary of the Army Kenneth C. Royall made the "Japan as anticommunist Shield" speech; in March, the second "Strike Report" was announced, which reduced the amount of reparations covering purely military losses; and in October, National Security Report 13-2 announced a new policy toward Japan, which called for limited democratic policies, the rehabilitation of accused war criminals, and economic stabilization.[111] The nine-point Dodge Plan for stabilization was announced in December.

Large-scale strikes led by communists and their sympathizers had also been broken by management at the *Yomiuri Shimbun*, backed by Maj. Daniel Imboden, the chief of the occupation government's Newspaper and Media Division, and Brigadier General Frayne Baker, the public relations officer. (The tactic of the *seisan kanri*, or union takeover of management administration, was first used in 1945 in this dispute. This policy spread throughout the labor movement until the fall of 1946 and thereafter declined, gradually disappearing after 1950.)[112]

The Toho unionists were prepared to become the target of the antiunion movement. However, nobody could have predicted that the American military would also appear in a show of force. Indeed, after the third Toho strike, they were never again used. But the Americans' decision to use military force in this instance demonstrates their particular concern over the ideological power of Japanese films, as well as the effect on the national consciousness of the studio strike itself, which held the attention of the Japanese public owing to its profound interest in films and the stars who made them.

Hollywood had also experienced strikes, in 1945 and 1946. The first, an eight-month strike by the Conference of Studio Unions, was broken when police dispersed picketers with tear gas and fire hoses in October 1945. The second, shorter but more violent, occurred in the fall of 1946. These strikes awakened in American studio heads strongly antilabor attitudes.[113]

By 1947 Hollywood came under fierce attack from another quarter: the House Un-American Activities Committee. News of the testimony of American stars and directors at its hearings was reported in Japanese film magazines.[114] Japanese unionists saw the parallels between their experiences and those of their American counterparts, but Takeo Ito, for one, confessed that he did not attach much importance to them at the time.[115] By that time, leftist and prolabor film people on both sides of the Pacific had been routed by the anticommunists, suffering a defeat from which they would not soon recover.

7

AMERICAN
COLD
WAR
POLICY

ANTILABOR POLICY

With the growing dominance of the Cold War mentality in American foreign policy, the American censors in Japan became increasingly cautious
about the portrayal of labor disputes and the "communist slant" that they
perceived in both Japanese and imported films. No sooner had the Chinese
communists defeated the Nationalists and founded the People's Republic of
China in October 1949 than the Korean War broke out in June 1950. Japan
was just across the sea from both countries, hence the Americans' concern
over the spread of communism.

CIE claimed that labor disputes were under the jurisdiction of the
Labor Division of the Economic and Science Section.[1] However, CIE, along
with CCD, closely monitored any portrayals of such disputes in films, and

ordered that they be handled carefully, so that organized labor and mass demonstrations would not be glorified and capitalists would not be portrayed as villainous. Sometimes they ordered such scenes completely eliminated.[2] CIE's purview extended to scenes of labor disputes in newsreels as well, and such scenes were deleted or revised. For example, a scene of a hospital from which twelve communist staff members had been discharged was deleted from one newsreel by the censors,[3] and the treatment of the dismissal of several unionist school teachers in another was found "leftist inclined" and "one-sided" and revisions were demanded.[4]

The concerns with labor disputes had of course existed in the immediate postwar years as well. CCD had deleted such scenes from Nichi-ei's *This Year: 1945–1946* [*Kono ichinen*] as early as August 1946, the same month during which the censorship agency banned Nichi-ei's *The Japanese Tragedy*. Dismissing *This Year: 1945–1946* as "supposedly a documentary presentation of the twelve months following V-J Day," the censors eliminated fifteen objectionable sections that they found "distorted" and "slanted."[5] In 1948, CIE judged "unnecessary" several sections of Nichi-ei's *The World in Cartoons* [*Manga no yononaka*] that dealt with the third Toho strike and thus deleted them.[6]

In making such judgments about which scenes had "communist" content, the most obvious symbol for the censors was the red flag. "A close-up, full view, of a waving 'red flag'" was therefore ordered eliminated from a 1949 film on the governmental railway workers' union entitled *The Whistle Keeps Blowing* [*Goteki nariyamazu*].[7] Similarly, a scene with a "display" of a red flag and "communist marchers" was eliminated by the censors from Yoshimura's 1948 *The Bright Day of My Life*.[8] Another communist symbol, a poster saying "Workers of the World Unite!", was found not only unnecessary to the storyline but also "tinged with communistic ideology," and was therefore deleted upon the censor's recommendation from *Platform of the Night* [*Yoru no purattohomu*] (1948).[9] In an extreme case, a Russian-style building was regarded as "communist" by the censors in Heinosuke Gosho's *Once More* (1947). Thus, the lovers' meeting place was changed from in front of the "Nikolai Hall," a popular downtown building, to a building with a nondescript Western architectural style.[10]

The American censors considered a variety of events "communist," "subversive," or "destructive." For instance, the censors deleted a reference to the banning of "meetings and cultural festivals" from a newsreel that also had shots of policemen standing in front of the palace grounds.[11] Also eliminated from two newsreels were scenes of riots and of injured persons in the wake of the implementation of a new rotation system at governmental agencies.[12] The censors even deleted a newsreel's coverage of a free lunch program for schoolchildren, because the institution of this program had been one of the demands of the communist-dominated teachers' union.[13]

As for foreign films, scenes of famous revolutions and uprisings from history were carefully scrutinized. The dialogue of the 1940 American film *The Mark of Zorro*, in which a character encouraged the peons (Mexican tenant farmers) to revolt, was ordered to be more "clearly defined."[14]

ANTICOMMUNIST POLICY

The occupation government's program of showing American newsreels before the feature films in Japanese theaters ran into trouble in October 1948, when a controversy concerning the inclusion of anticommunist scenes arose among the American governmental and civilian agencies responsible for selecting the newsreels. The agencies included the Civil Affairs Department of the U.S. Army; the occupation government's own CIE and CCD; and the Central Motion Picture Exchange, by then a civilian agency.

The Civil Affairs Department's New York field office was responsible for selecting and sending out films suitable for reeducation programs in occupied areas. The Central Motion Picture Exchange had been established in November 1946 to handle American films shown in Japan, through the Motion Picture Export Association in the United States. The Central Motion Picture Exchange was headed by Michael Bergher, who had been CIE's chief film officer in charge of imported motion pictures until November 3, 1945. He had been in Japan before the war as a branch manager for Columbia Pictures and MGM, and he returned to Japan after the war as an employee of the U.S. State Department's Office of International, Informational, and Cultural Affairs (OIC), where he worked until he left Japan in June 1946. Because the office ceased operations the same month, Bergher's successor, Charles Mayer, was not a State Department employee, but instead worked as the representative of an association of nine major American film companies (Paramount, MGM, Warner Brothers, Universal, RKO, Columbia, Twentieth Century-Fox, United Artists, and Republic).[15] He had been scheduled to be transferred from his position as branch manager of Twentieth Century-Fox in Java to serve as branch manager in Tokyo when the Pacific war broke out.[16]

CCD noticed that anticommunist stories had been prominently featured in American newsreels during recent weeks, including coverage of the Pope's anticommunist campaign, horror stories of refugees from communist countries, the blockade and airlift in Berlin, and the Federal Bureau of Investigation's arrests of communists as suspected spies. These newsreels were compiled in Japan by the Central Motion Picture Exchange using sequences from American newsreels, and Mayer instructed the newsreel production staff to include all of the "anticommunist" sequences. During a censorship session, CIE asked the exchange to delete a scene of a communist country's sports festival. CCD felt that CIE should have made its opinions known at the initial editing stage, so as not to waste money on valuable film stock.[17]

Several months later, Mayer suggested that some of the scenes of and commentaries on communist activities in American newsreels that might be readily understood by American audiences would not be effective in Japan. His remarks upset the Civil Affairs Department, which was responsible for sending over the original American newsreels. An example of the kind of scene to which Mayer was referring was one showing the arrival of a socialist delegation in New York, accompanied by narration saying that the "Reds will present communism's views on world peace—are guarded by New York police—they may be unwelcome—but they get American protection while they spill their communist propaganda on democratic soil." Although Mayer believed that the Japanese "would never understand our way of doing things," the Civil Affairs Department argued that an important purpose of the reorientation program was to make those in the occupied areas understand "our American way of practicing democracy." The department insisted that showing such scenes was consistent with the policy of Maj. Daniel Imboden (chief of the Newspaper and Media Division of CIE) to show the American attitude toward communism, the American way of treating communism, and the American style of democracy and freedom.[18]

Such arguments became more prevalent. Later in 1949 Mayer asked CIE for advice about how to treat the newsreel scenes of communist riots in Paris and Trieste. CIE's chief, Lt. Col. D. R. Nugent, answered:

> Unless the commentary makes it clear that communists everywhere employ violence, even when it involves innocent individuals in clashes with the police, to further their dark ends, it is suggested that such riot scenes

continue to be deleted. No useful purpose is seen in risking stimulation of Japanese communists to imitate the trouble-making of communists in other countries.[19]

Several years later, in 1952, the New York field office of the Civil Affairs Department sponsored the production of an anticommunist propaganda newsreel series, *The Big Lie*. Each segment attempted to convey images of the terror in communist countries, although CIE's Office for Occupied Areas recognized that this series was weak "due to lack of suitable footage." For propaganda effect, the producers hoped to include scenes showing "unfavorable conditions behind the 'Iron Curtain' such as slave labor camps, Japanese POW's, collectivism, etc." Scenes showing the Soviet leaders together with the leaders of the satellite countries were considered effective in conveying the image of the Kremlin's dominance over its "allies," and scenes of military pageantry and parades were used to show audiences that "so-called peace moves are merely smoke screens to hide actual conditions."[20]

To the extent that the makers of postwar American foreign policy regarded the communist countries as their enemies, they had to suppress references in films to the fact that Americans had fought side by side with communists and leftists during World War II. Such a reference, to collaboration with the Chinese communists, was deleted from Kamei's 1949 *The Life of a Woman*.[21] The American censors also eliminated references to an Italian partisan prisoner being a communist and having "fought with the Reds in Spain" from the Japanese version of an Italian film, possibly *Open City* [*Roma, Città aperta*] (1945, released in Japan in November 1950).[22]

The first Italian neorealistic film introduced to Japan by Italifilm, the Italian film representative, was Rossellini's *Paisan* (1946). Released in September 1949, it evoked a sensational response from audiences and critics alike. Subsequently, Luigi Zampa's *To Live in Peace* [*Vivere in Pace*] (1946) was released in October 1949, Vittorio De Sica's *Shoeshine* [*Sciuscia*] (1946) in March 1950, Giuseppe De Santis's *Tragic Hunt* [*Caccia tragica*] (1947) in June 1950, and De Sica's *The Bicycle Thief* [*Ladri di Biciclette*] (1948) in September 1950. The American censors had no objections to any of these films.

However, in June 1950, the censors questioned the suitability for release of two other Italian films, Rossellini's *Germany Year Zero* [*Germania Anno Zero*] (1947) and De Santis's *Bitter Rice* [*Riso amaro*] (1949). In its March 1950 response to an inquiry from the Diplomatic Section of the occupation government conveying the Italian diplomatic mission's concern over the delay in clearing them for import, CIE stated that the films "present a peculiar problem." The censors believed that, despite their high artistic quality, the films' content "lends itself to exploitation by Japanese communists." They continued:

> If it is unfair to give credence to the accusation that many Italian producers and directors "have one foot in Moscow," at least they tend to present life in terms which make it easy for the communists to use them as evidence of the truth of the party's assertions about injustice and other imperfections in democratic societies, just as they use *The Grapes of Wrath* and *Mr. Smith Goes To Washington*.[23]

The two Italian films were not released in Japan until 1952. As for the American films mentioned by CIE, *Mr. Smith Goes to Washington* (1939), directed by Frank Capra and released in Japan in October 1941, shortly before the attack on Pearl Harbor, had been a source of concern to the military censors as early as August 1946. They were afraid that the film might give a "misleading and unfavorable" impression of the American democratic system that the Japanese were supposed to be emulating through its depiction of "American democracy as a system of corrupt political machinery, financial graft, dictatorial control of all the newspapers of a state to distort news, and the manipulation of governmental offices extending through governor to a U.S. Senator who is supposedly the probable next president."[24]

Another socially conscious American film, John Ford's *The Grapes of Wrath* (1940), about the predicament of a poor migrant family during the Depression, was not released in Japan until 1960. However, we cannot be certain whether this delay can actually be blamed on lingering traces of American anticommunist attitudes, or was due to a simple problem in copyright clearance.

Portrayals of the extremes of poverty and luxurious decadence in America were similarly forbidden by the censors. A montage showing "young Americans joy-riding, drinking home-made liquor, operation of Speak-Easies, rum runners, etc." was eliminated from *The Great Gatsby* (1949) by order of the censors.[25] *Miss Tatlock's Millions* (1948), a "wacky comedy" about a millionaire family, was judged by CIE to be without reorientation value and likely to give a distorted picture of an "American family of wealth" to Japanese audiences. Also disturbing to the censors were this film's lines of dialogue ridiculing a character who condemns another (a self-styled "fighting liberal") as a communist. The civil censors suggested that the Information Division not release this film in Japan, advice that was apparently followed.[26]

Other American films the military censors considered "questionable" were those that might suggest to the Japanese audience an "incorrect meaning of democracy," those portraying "certain objectionable practices or elements of American life," and those glorifying war heroes. Among the thirty-six films imported between August 1945 and December 1946, eight were judged as of this type, and one was suppressed for its glorification of the war. The eight films classified as "questionable" were The Men in Her Life (1941), Casablanca (1942), Now, Voyager (1942), The Spoilers (1942), Watch on the Rhine (1943), Enter Arsene Lupin (1944), Tall in the Saddle (1944), and Captain Eddie (1945). Although it was not specified, the reason for the suppression of Counter-Attack may have been its subject, Russian guerrilla fighters. Both the civil and the military censorship sections were more concerned about the "reorientation value" of films than about their role as mere entertainment.[27]

Indeed, the military censor who wrote the above report was concerned that, while Japanese filmmakers were being forced to pursue reorientation subjects, American films with more box-office appeal were coming to dominate the market for entertainment films. He believed that Japanese filmmakers should be given more chances to make such entertainment films, and regretted that a Central Motion Picture Exchange official could be such a blatant advocate of American business interests. A truly "democratic" policy would allow the Japanese public to see a representative cross-section of both "suitable" and "questionable" films, he argued.[28]

However, as the Cold War reached its height, the censors' attitude toward any element that could be construed as anti-American became even more strict. One of the characters in the French film Manon was an American officer, who was regarded by the censors as representing his country; thus they decided in 1950 that, in the Japanese version of the film, he could not be portrayed as having any negative characteristics. Scenes of him being seduced by the heroine and overlooking illegal trafficking in the surplus goods of which he is in charge were deleted, and references to such events were eliminated from the soundtrack and from the Japanese subtitles.[29]

In another more extreme instance, the name of a certain kind of caterpillar, the Amerikan shirohitori (American white bird), caught the ears of the censors reviewing the narration of a 1950 Japanese newsreel describing these insects as having damaged crops. Noting that East Germany had released a propaganda statement referring to an American insect as having destroyed its potato crop, the censors asked the Forestry Division of the Natural Resources Section of the occupation government whether the usage of "American" in the insect's name was technically correct. Several days later, the department reported that the caterpillar had originated somewhere on the North American continent, but that there was no proof that it came from the United States. Therefore, the censors ordered that it be referred to as "a North American insect."[30]

After the outbreak of the Korean War, excessive depictions of bombed-out areas were also eliminated from American newsreels by order of the censors.[31] Into a Japanese newsreel's statement about refugees "who have lost all, victims of the aggression, and are swarming on the highways day after day," a censor inserted the phrase "of North Korea" after "aggression," to make it clear to Japanese audiences which side was the aggressor.[32]

In the case of Japanese domestic affairs, the censors decided that news-reels should make no reference to Japanese police actions in security cases. Certain phrases regarding police attacks on the Japan Communist Party were deleted from Japanese newsreels. For instance, the censors eliminated a reference to the Japanese police having "made sudden raids" on the Communist Party's newspaper offices on June 26, 1950 (the day after the Korean War broke out), when the police were in fact delivering an occupation government order banning the paper from publishing for thirty days.[33] The censors were aware that such coverage would bolster the case of those who argued that Americans were suppressing freedom of speech.

In another instance, the censors were concerned with protecting the image of the new "Police Reserves," which the occupation government had ordered the Japanese government to establish as a kind of defense force in response to the Korean War. The censors were careful not to allow "communist propagandists the opportunity to utilize this to our disadvantage" in newsreels, by emphasizing that the new organization was not actually an arm of the police force (which might stigmatize it), that the reservists were well paid, and that they were not being mobilized to fight in Korea.[34]

ANTI-RUSSIAN POLICY

At a time when the slightest hint of anti-Americanism was carefully screened out, obviously anti-Russian films were more than welcome. When the Central Motion Picture Exchange announced in August 1949 the release of *The Iron Curtain,* directed by William Wellman and released in the United States in May 1948, based on the case of an alleged Soviet spy in Canada, the USSR member of the Allied Council in Japan went before the occupation government to protest its release. But the Soviet protest was ignored and the film was released.[35] A film made in 1949 by the antiunion Shin-Toho Studio, *Can-Can Girls of the Ginza* [*Ginza kan-kan musume*] used a huge, visually arresting sign advertising this American film as the background to a street fight sequence, as if it was a message of support from the filmmakers. On the other hand, an angry letter from a Japanese to General MacArthur, arguing that such a reactionary film would hamper the cause of international peace, drew the attention of both the military and civil censorship sections.[36] Furthermore, critic Ichiro Ueno wrote a harsh review of the film in which he described it as an artistic failure.[37] However, CIE did not find any difficulty in selecting the sensationally titled American film *I Was a Communist for the FBI* as a film of merit in September 1951.[38]

Japanese filmmakers did not miss the opportunity to compete with American-made anti-Russian films. *Homecoming* [*Damoi*], portraying the predicament of Japanese POWs in the Soviet territories and their families waiting in Japan, was produced by Shin-Toho in 1949, directed by Takeshi Sato, and supervised by famous antileftist director Kunio Watanabe, and featured such antiunion stars as Yoshiko Yamaguchi and Susumu Fujita. While the film was being produced, the Soviet member of the Allied Council, as well as the Soviet Repatriate Livelihood Welfare Union, protested, requesting the occupation government to order a halt to the production. Yet CIE chief Nugent found that "the film would appear to be no more anti-Soviet or 'defamatory' than the repatriation facts themselves," and decided that no reply would be sent to the protesting organizations. After the film was completed, he found it not only of topical interest but also a "good entertainment" and suggested that it be subtitled in English for circulation among American soldiers throughout the Far East Command, although his suggestion was ultimately rejected by the Special Service Section.[39] The film was released to the Japanese public in November 1949. Toho produced *I Was a Siberian POW* [*Watashi wa Shiberia no horyo datta*] on a similar subject in early 1950. A duo famous for their popular and flashy collaboration films made during the Pacific war, screenplay writer Tsutomu Sawamura and director Yutaka Abe, also participated in this project.

The Americans' anti-Russian policy was also demonstrated by their attempt to minimize the impact of Russian films on the foreign film market in Japan. An American film that had been imported before the war, *Call of the Yukon* (1938), was released in Tokyo on December 7, 1945, thus becoming the first foreign film released in Japan after the war. The first two foreign films imported into Japan after the war were also both American-made, and were released on February 28, 1946, by the Central Motion Picture Exchange: *Madame Curie* (1943), directed by Mervyn LeRoy, and *His Butler's Sister* (1943), directed by Frank Borzage and starring Deanna Durbin.[40] Although the cost of admission to each of these two films (¥10) was more than three times that for domestic films (¥3), the Japanese were avid for foreign films, and swamped the theaters. Deanna Durbin immediately became their favorite foreign star. Soon, more American films arrived in the theaters, such as *Watch on the Rhine,* Charlie Chaplin's *The Gold Rush* (1925, first released in Japan in 1926, but rereleased in 1946, this time accompanied by music), and John Cromwell's *Abe Lincoln in Illinois* (1940).

Other foreign films began to appear in the Japanese market as well. A British film that had been imported before the war, *The Ware Case,* was released on December 26, 1945. The only other non-American foreign films released in 1946 were two French films that had been imported before the war, then banned by the government censors: *Yoshiwara* (1937) and *Mayerling* (1936).[41] The first postwar British production released in Japan, on December 2, 1947, was Compton Bennett's *The Seventh Veil* (1945), and the first postwar French production released in Japan, on January 27, 1948, was Jean Cocteau's *Beauty and the Beast* [*La Belle et le Bête*] (1946).[42]

The first postwar Russian film, *Sports Parade in Moscow,* a documentary about an August 1945 sports pageant, was released on November 5, 1946, becoming the first color film released in Japan. But nearly one whole year passed before the next Russian film, *They Met in Moscow* (also called *Moscow Music Girl,* 1941) was released, on September 30, 1947. *The Stone Flower* (1946) was released on November 4, 1947. Nine Russian films were released in 1948, but 1949 and 1950 saw the release of only two per year.[43]

According to the yearly quota system approved by the occupation government on May 9, 1948, the number of films from any single country could not exceed the maximum number of films imported from that country in any prewar year.[44] The Russians claimed that sixteen Soviet films had been imported in 1934 and that the Russian quota of six films per year should thus be increased.[45] Owing to the loss of prewar Japanese records, CIE could neither substantiate nor refute the Russian claim. It thus concluded that the yearly quota of six films should be increased, but hoped to "hold this [number] down to the lowest possible figure, possibly seven."[46] In 1949, the Russian quota was officially increased from six to seven.[47]

The censors frequently delayed and quibbled over clearances for Russian films.[48] When a Kyokuto Film Company (Kyokuto eiga-sha) representative in 1950 brought in a prewar Russian film, *Safe Guidance into Life* (presumably 1931's *Road to Life*) for clearance, the censors stated that at least half of the film was objectionable "due to the lack of respect for law and order." Furthermore, the censors found the condition of the print to be poor, which made this film undesirable for release. The Japanese agent replied that the film would make a powerful anti-Russian statement by showing the miserable conditions of life in the USSR, whereupon the American censors answered with a straight face that it was not the occupation government's desire "to exploit any one country," and that, according to the Japanese Motion Picture Code of Ethics, respect for all nations was to be maintained.[49]

The Soviet representative to the Allied Council complained that CIE "in every way is delaying the screening of Soviet films by keeping a period of a year or more and not giving any answer [*sic*]." The Russians pointed out that films from other countries were passed "within one or two weeks." Nevertheless, four Russian films were found unsuitable in 1949, and nine in 1950.[50] The American censors paid particular attention to Russian films because they believed that Russian films received "special and intensive promotion" by "Japanese communists and fellow-travelers." They were convinced that almost all the Soviet films were propaganda, full of misleading images of a wonderful life in the USSR as compared with the horrors to be found in America. They were also concerned with the powerful full-color images of such Soviet films as *Far Away from Moscow, Bountiful Summer,* and *Mussorgsky*[51]—and with the grasp of film technology on the part of the Russians that they implied.

CIE and Military Intelligence frequently discovered Russians engaged in covert anti-American activities in Japan. In March 1949 CIE reported to Military Intelligence that teams from the League for Protection of the Livelihood of Repatriates from the USSR would tour the country to hold meetings at which *They Met in Moscow* would be shown, without clearance from CIE.[52] An informer belonging to the Japan Communist Party reported that footage showing American soldiers' violence toward Japanese (for example, MPs beating Japanese) had been sold by Japanese newsreel cameramen to the Russians, who had then combined it with footage obtained from other sources and made anti-American documentary films, which they screened privately at the Soviet embassy.[53] While they emphasized the effectiveness of the Soviet films in promoting communism, and attacked these films and Soviet activities as propaganda, the American censors conveniently ignored the blatantly propagandistic intentions of many of the American films they were approving at the same time.

THE RED PURGE AND THE BIRTH OF THE
INDEPENDENT PRODUCTION

While the war raged in nearby Korea, a Red Purge of the film industry was begun in Japan in September 1950 that would eventually lead to the firing of 137 employees. Beginning in May 1950, General MacArthur had issued several directives forcing the expulsion of Japan Communist Party members from their jobs. On May 3, MacArthur condemned the party as potentially dangerous to the public peace. On June 6, twenty-four of the party's top leaders were purged and went underground; on July 18, publication of the party's newspaper, *Red Flag*, was suspended indefinitely.[54] On this basis, the newspaper and broadcasting industries also began a harsh anticommunist campaign, which discharged 704 employees from fifty companies. Seventy-seven employees were relieved of their posts in central and local governments and public corporations, and 1,700 more were dismissed from school positions. The lists of those to be purged had been compiled from the list of party members registered at the Japanese government's Special Investigation Bureau, as well as from information provided by spies and informers in each company.[55]

The occupation authorities considered the film industry particularly important owing to its high visibility. Therefore, sixty-six employees from Shochiku Studio, thirty from Daiei, thirteen from Toho, twenty-five from Nichi-ei, and three from Riken were purged as communists on September 25. The antiunion Shin-Toho was unaffected by the purge. Mitsuo Makino, the president of Toyoko Eiga (which became Toei in 1951), decided not to submit any of his employees' names as communists, insisting that his company did not have any.[56] Makino (brother of director Masahiro) had produced films using communist and leftist directors such as Tadashi Imai and Hideo Sekigawa for Toei when they could not work anywhere else. Kaneto Shindo claims that some noncommunists were also included in the list at

Daiei, citing a statement by a Daiei executive, and mentioning the names of some who had been purged despite the fact that they were not party members. These included director Tai Kato, a friend of an active unionist, and an actor who had upset the company with his complaints.[57]

Some of the purged filmmakers eventually returned to their companies after long court struggles. Four out of eleven former Daiei employees who brought a suit against the company in 1951 won their case in 1958 in the Osaka High Court; the other seven eventually lost. But the four soon resigned from Daiei, citing psychological pressure brought to bear by the company. Eleven purge victims from Shochiku Studio brought suit in 1956, but lost their case in 1973 in the Tokyo High Court.[58]

However, many of those purged chose to work with independent companies outside the main studios. They, along with other leftists, were blacklisted and would not work in the major media companies for at least the next decade. For example, it has been argued that the reason for Kon Ichikawa's being chosen to direct the documentary of the 1964 Tokyo Olympic Games was his antiunion position during the Toho strikes. (Ichikawa was made a director as soon as he moved from Toho to Shin-Toho after Toho's second strike in 1947.) Originally, the assignment had been given to Tadashi Imai, a famous leftist director, but he was opposed by the Committee for the Tokyo Olympic Games. This episode shows how long the aftereffects of the Red Purge were felt in the Japanese film industry.

Many victims of the Red Purge joined the independent film production companies formed by leftist filmmakers who had quit Toho Studio after its third strike. Thus, the number of films independently produced doubled from seventeen in 1947 to thirty-eight the following year, and again to sixty-seven in 1949.[59] The new companies pursued innovative themes and styles that would never have been approved by the major studios.

One of the most acclaimed independent companies was the Eiga Geijutsuka Kyokai or the Society of Film Artists, established in March 1948 by producer Sojiro Motoki and directors Kajiro Yamamoto, Akira Kurosawa, and Senkichi Taniguchi. Backed by this organization, Kurosawa made a series of successful films: *The Quiet Duel,* concerning the dilemma of a moralistic doctor infected with venereal disease while operating on a patient; *Stray Dog,* a fast-paced, documentary-style drama about a young policeman searching for his stolen pistol; and *Scandal* [*Sukyandaru*] (1950), a harsh condemnation of yellow journalism. Meanwhile, Taniguchi made *Desertion at Dawn* in 1950.

Director Heinosuke Gosho. Courtesy of the Kawakita Memorial Film Institute.

Hiroshi Shimizu independently produced and directed *Children of the Beehive,* a semidocumentary film about war orphans, a serious social problem that was beginning to draw wide attention. Heinosuke Gosho, who had been sympathetic to the Toho strikers and participated in the demonstration on August 19, 1948, when strikers were ejected from the studio's premises, was regarded as a dangerous leftist by the occupation government and the major film companies long after that time. He established Studio Eight Productions in October 1950, along with several fellow Toho refugees and others, including director Shiro Toyoda, cameraman Mitsuo Miura, and writers Jun Takami, Junji Kinoshita, and Sumie Tanaka. Its first production was Gosho's *Dispersing Clouds* [*Wakare-gumo*] (1951), a poetic story of human relationships set at a local inn.

Kindai Eiga Kyokai or the Society of Modern Cinema was established in April 1950 by director Kozaburo Yoshimura and screenplay writer Kaneto Shindo when their project, *Deceiving Costume* [*Itsuwareru seiso*], a critique

Left to right, Hiroko Kawasaki, Ken Mitsuda, Keiko Sawamura, and Yoichi Numata in *Dispersing Clouds* [*Wakare-gumo*] (1951), directed by Heinosuke Gosho. Courtesy of the Kawakita Memorial Film Institute.

Machiko Kyo (l.) in *Deceiving Costume* [*Itsuwareru seiso*] (1951), directed by Kozaburo Yoshimura. Courtesy of the Kawakita Memorial Film Institute.

Ganemon Nakamura (l.) and
Chojuro Kawarazaki in *Oh!
We're Still Living* [*Dokkoi
ikiteiru*] (1951), directed by
Tadashi Imai. Courtesy of the
Kawakita Memorial Film In-
stitute.

of the world of geisha, was turned down by Shochiku. They were soon joined
by actor Taiji Tonoyama, Shochiku's communist producer, Hisao Itoya, and
a communist Toho director, Tengo Yamada. Their first film, directed by
Yoshimura and written by Shindo, was a romance, *Beyond the Battlefield*
[*Senka no hateni*] (1950), co-produced with Daiei. *Deceiving Costume*, also
co-produced with Daiei, was completed in late 1950 and released in early
1951. The duo co-produced with Daiei a number of other critically acclaimed films, including a contemporary satire called *School of Freedom* [*Jiyu
gakko*] (1951) and *The Story of a Loving Wife* [*Aisai monogatari*] (1951),
Shindo's first effort as a director, which told the story of his own youth.

The leftist company Shinsei Eiga-sha was founded in February 1950 by
ex-Toho unionists, who used their severance pay as seed capital. Helped by
audience contributions, it produced Satsuo Yamamoto's *City of Violence*
[*Boryoku no machi*] (1950), based on the true story of a journalist's struggle
with a local gangster boss, and Imai's *Oh! We're Still Living* [*Dokkoi ikiteiru*]
(1951), about the life of laborers.

The modest budgets of such independent films forced their makers to rely on many location shots, lending the film a heightened sense of realism similar to that seen in the products of such other national cinema movements as postwar Italian neorealism and the Brazilian cinema nôvo of the early 1960s. The leaders of all of these movements had in common a success in conveying their sense of mission through their films, despite their tight financial restrictions. The high morale sustained by their idealism enabled them to produce a number of ambitious, high-quality films, many of which won awards for excellence. The uplifting effect of the independent movement on Japanese cinema as a whole was to last far beyond the occupation period.

8

THE
LEGACY
OF THE
OCCUPATION

The story of Japanese cinema under the American occupation is as complex as that of the most famous film made during the period, Kurosawa's *Rashomon.* Just as in the film, an objective account of events during the era we have examined is almost impossible to establish. Looking at a single incident through the eyes of the filmmakers, the American policymakers, the film censors, and the film critics in turn reveals the great differences (not to mention conflicts) in their perspectives, and hints intriguingly at how their widely divergent motivations may have determined what and how much they remember today. Although I have tried to reconcile the differences, to the extent that my account is based on these stories, it is merely yet another such story. Like any storyteller, I have tried to show both the comic and the tragic sides of the tale; I am happy to have found more of the former than the latter.

Machiko Kyo (front) and Toshiro Mifune in *Rashomon* (1950), directed by Akira Kurosawa. Courtesy of the Kawakita Memorial Film Institute.

Censorship under the American occupation, a process planned and carried out by human beings, was inevitably fraught with inconsistencies and contradictions, which made life difficult for those involved at the time but are interesting to study over four decades later. The process of agreeing upon policy and then attempting to put it into practice immediately revealed the fundamental differences among the American censors themselves, as well as those between the censors and the Japanese filmmakers. Despite their legal authority and underlying military and economic power, the Americans were inevitably forced to compromise, not only because of the lack of unity in their own ranks, but also because of the problems inherent in trying to change the millennia-old thought and behavior patterns of a proud people in its native land.

Although the occupation and its censorship programs were officially terminated on April 28, 1952, their influence was to continue long afterward. This influence was strengthened and perpetuated by the bilateral U.S.-Japan defense treaty signed before the occupiers left, which effectively excluded the Soviet Union and China, former allies who were now rival powers. The departing occupation authorities helped Japanese filmmakers to form the Film Ethics Regulation Control Committee, an autonomous industry organization intended to regulate film policies. Perhaps just as important, they encouraged American-style independent thinking by the filmmakers much more than the wartime Japanese authorities had.

American film policy clearly reflected the victors' overall goals for their vanquished enemy: disarming and democratizing Japan in order to rehabilitate it as a member of the world community and help ensure world peace. Not so explicitly stated as a reason for this democratization, but nonetheless an important American goal, was the enlistment of Japan as an ally in defending American interests amidst the uncertainties of the postwar international scene. Some of the occupiers wanted to inculcate the Japanese people with respect for individualism, freedom of expression and thought, and basic human and civil rights simply so that they would resist future indoctrination by fascist militarists or by America's communist foes.

Nonetheless, there was also an idealistic spirit among those members of the occupation authorities who genuinely wanted to help the Japanese, and they in turn were glad to take advantage of this assistance. In order to inspire the Japanese to democratize, and not to be lured by the siren song of communism, the Americans quickly relaxed their severe economic policies and quickly rehabilitated many of Japan's major capitalist powers. A long-term result of this decision was, of course, the "miraculous" Japanese economic growth that has led in recent years to economic warfare between the two countries. As the previously banned zaibatsu who had collaborated with the Japanese militarists were allowed to return to the scene, leftists began to be purged by the occupation government. Japan's decision (with American encouragement) not to extirpate the wartime zaibatsu sacrificed a significant opportunity for economic democratization on the altar of economic growth. As Japan's economic power grew, U.S. pressure to spend more and more on her military increased, to the point that, by 1991, Japan had the second highest military budget in the world.[1] This is indeed a curious position for a country whose constitution prohibits it from possessing any offensive military capability, and it is ironic that its former enemy bears much of the responsibility for it.

On the other hand, in the sphere of education, the ideal of egalitarianism brought about by the occupation inspired Japan's antielitist education policy. Although a persistent sense of hierarchy still distinguishes some elite schools, the vast majority of schools use the same curriculum and apply identical standards of performance. Within each class, every pupil is expected to learn the same material in the same way, with little regard for individuals' natural talents or abilities, the aim being for every student to reach the same level. Whether this educational philosophy is truly democratic or merely conformist is a complex issue. The concepts of individualism and free thinking, essential to democracy although not always consistent with egalitarianism, have been inculcated in modern Japanese youth, with debatable success. To the extent that these new ideas have taken hold, they have been criticized by an older generation brought up on unquestioning obedience to authority. For example, former Minister of Education Setoyama criticized the policies of the American occupation thus:

> The occupation policies were explicitly intended to destroy Japanese morals, traditions, customs, and habits. In the constitution, many splendid things are written; however, none of them is reflected in the educational process. Human rights or freedom really means, e.g., feeling pain when you pinch yourself, or not doing things to others that you don't want done to yourself. Such things are not taught. No books teach one to take care of one's parents. It was the occupation policy to regard such morals as wrong. If such things had been taught, there would not have been so much juvenile violence recently.[2]

Ironically, the mass demonstrations against the 1960 renewal of the Japan-U.S. Security Treaty may be considered an important legacy of the freedoms encouraged by the occupation.

It was around that time that a group of young filmmakers burst onto the scene with a totally new style. Oshima, Yoshida, and Shinoda took advantage of the popularity of "youth films" and, by portraying the life-style and sentiment of rebellious youth, manifested their ideological concerns in innovative ways. Oshima's *Night and Fog of Japan* [*Nihon no yoru to kiri*] (1960) is of particular interest. This film questions the failure and disillusionment of the left when the 1960 treaty was signed despite their protests, using a unique narrative strategy full of flashbacks, long tracking shots, and spotlit scenes. Shinoda's *Dry Lake* [*Kawaita mizuumi*] (1961) also depicts the involvement of the student movement during this national political upheaval. Yoshida began in 1960 to make films about the alienation, frustration, and detachment of outlaws, proletarian youth, and cutthroat businessmen. By the mid-1960s, all three had left Shochiku Studio to further pursue their ideological and stylistic concerns at their own independent production

THE LEGACY OF THE OCCUPATION   263

companies. Their work soon began to be described as the Japanese Nouvelle Vague, corresponding to the contemporaneous French movement. Discontent with the ideological stance of the older generations of filmmakers, who refused to portray their "enemies," this group of directors intended to define "why they fought" in their films. Their active assertion of their own political ideas, conveyed by their audacious sense of film form, may be considered one of the positive results of the new philosophy of education mandated by the occupation.

This generation of Japanese, born in the early 1930s, were youths during the wrenching social and political upheavals of the transitions from wartime militarism to occupation democratization to Cold War militarism. It is thus no surprise that the filmmakers who grew up during this critical period should tirelessly explore in their films the meaning of nationalism, with particular concern for the imperial system, disillusioned revolutionary idealism, and the new emphasis on individualism. The intense involvement with and public debate of such themes is part of the intellectual legacy of the postwar occupation and the Cold War period.

In marked contrast, the work of filmmakers born during the early to mid-1950s, such as Yoshimitsu Morita and Sogo Ishii, is not so overtly political, despite its attention to social problems. Morita made the internationally successful *The Family Game* [*Kazoku geimu*] (1983), a stylistic satire on the family and education, and *Sorekara* (1985), an innovative interpretation of a classic novel. Ishii's *Crazy Family* [*Gyakufunsha kazoku*] (1983) is an explosive black comedy about the shortage of housing space. This new generation grew up during the "economic miracle" and takes for granted the freedoms and material comforts for which previous generations had struggled. Yet, in another sense, this generation has brought to fruition the American occupation of Japan, by integrating American popular music, fashion, eating habits, and the like into their culture in a new and thorough way. They no longer question the origins of these cultural products but embrace them naturally. Their wholesale adoption of foreign customs and values, radical though it may seem, is yet another example of the same phenomenon that helped the film industry survive the transition to the occupation period, albeit in changed form: the peculiarly Japanese adaptability to things new when confronted by a foreign culture. This adaptability gives us confidence in the prospects for the survival of Japan and its cinema into the future.

NOTES

INTRODUCTION

1. In 1946, an estimated 465,000 American soldiers were stationed in Japan. By 1948, there were only 125,000. With the outbreak of the Korean War, the number increased to between 210,000 and 260,000 throughout the early 1950s. Shiela K. Johnson, *American Attitudes Toward Japan 1941–1975* (Washington, D.C.: American Enterprise Institute for Public Research, 1975), 62.

2. Carl Hovland, Arthur Lumsdaine, and Fred Sheffield, *Experiments on Mass Communication* (Princeton: Princeton University Press, 1949), cited in Joseph T. Klapper, *The Effects of Mass Communication* (Glencoe, Ill.: Free Press, 1960), 85–87. Also see Charles Burgess Ewing, *An Analysis of Frank Capra's War Rhetoric in the "Why We Fight" Films,* Ph.D. dissertation, Department of Speech, Washington State University, 1983. For the relationship between Hollywood studios and the U.S. government, see Clayton R. Koppes and Gregory D. Black, *Hollywood Goes To War: How*

Politics, Profits, and Propaganda Shaped World War II Movies (Berkeley and Los Angeles: University of California Press, 1990).

3. "Japanese Films: A Psychological Warfare," OSS Research and Analysis Branch Report No. 1307 (March 30, 1944), National Archives, Washington, D.C.

4. For an excellent comprehensive review of this subject, see Carol Gluck, "Entangling Illusions: Japanese and American Views of the Occupation," in Warren I. Cohen, ed., *New Frontiers in America–East Asian Relations* (New York: Columbia University Press, 1983), 169–236.

5. For example, see Jun Eto, *Mo hitotsu no sengo-shi* [*Another History of the Postwar Period*] (Tokyo: Kodansha, 1978); "The American Occupation and Postwar Japanese Literature: The Impact of Censorship upon a Japanese Mind," *Hikaku Bungaku Kenkyu* 38 (September 1980), 1–18; "Genron tosei: Senryo-ka Nippon ni okeru ken'etsu [Media Control: Censorship in Occupied Japan]" in Ray Moore, ed., *Tenno ga baiburu o yonda hi* [*The Day the Emperor Read the Bible*] (Tokyo: Kodansha, 1982); and *Tozasareta gengo kukan: Senryo-gun no ken'etsu to sengo Nippon* [*The Closed Space: The Occupation Forces Censorship and Postwar Japan*] (Tokyo: Bungei shunju-sha, 1989).

6. Peter Frost, "Reverse Course," paper presented at the International Conference on the Occupation of Japan, Amherst College, Amherst, Mass., August 1980. Sections of some of the other conference papers are included in Moore, *Tenno ga baiburu o yonda hi.*

7. My attempt to see Conde's file at the FBI under the Freedom of Information Act has been unsuccessful to date.

8. Mark Gayn, *Japan Diary* (Tokyo: Charles E. Tuttle, 1981), 234–240; Eiji Takemae, *GHQ* (Tokyo: Iwanami shinsho, 1983), 116.

9. See, for example, Noel Burch, *To the Distant Observer: Form and Meaning in the Japanese Cinema* (Berkeley and Los Angeles: University of California Press, 1979); and Joseph L. Anderson and Donald Richie, *Japanese Film: Art and Industry* (expanded edition) (Princeton, N.J.: Princeton University Press, 1982).

10. It would be interesting to compare the Japanese experience with that of other national cinemas under foreign military and political control. See, for example, H. Mark Woodward, *The Formulation and Implementation of U.S. Feature Film Policy in Occupied Germany, 1945–1948,* Ph.D. dissertation, University of Texas at Dallas, 1987; and Evelyn Ehrlich, *Cinema of Paradox* (New York: Columbia University Press, 1985), on the French cinema under the German occupation. In Japan, Tadao Sato has written on the national cinemas of other Asian countries—such as Korea, Taiwan, Manchuria, the Philippines, and Indonesia—while under Japanese occupation. See, for example, his *Kinema to hosei: Nicchu eiga zenshi* [*Cinema and Gunfire: The Prehistory of Japanese and Chinese Cinema*] (Tokyo: Libro Porto, 1985).

11. Chikara Ouchi, most notably cited in Rinjiro Sodei, *Senryo shita mono sareta mono* [*The Occupiers and the Occupied*] (Tokyo: Simul Press, 1986), 55–56.

12. Interview with Yoshikata Yoda by the author on June 3, 1984, in Kyoto; interview with Kaneto Shindo by the author on June 25, 1984, in Tokyo.

13. John Dower, "Japanese Cinema Goes to War," *Japan Society Newsletter* (July 1987), 9.

14. The series ran from February to April 1987 at the Japan Society, New York. I had the privilege of working as the assistant curator, program coordinator, and subtitling supervisor.

CHAPTER 1

1. Chieo Yoshida, *Mo hitotsu no eiga-shi: Katsuben no jidai* [*Another Film History: The Age of Katsuben*] (Tokyo: Jiji tsushinsha, 1978), 51–52; Nagisa Oshima, *Taikenteki sengo eizo-ron* [*The Theory of the Image of Postwar Cinema Based on Personal Experience*] (Tokyo: Asahi shimbun-sha, 1975), 23, citing Taro Tajima, *Ken'etsu-shitsu no yami ni sasayaku* [*Whispering in the Darkness of the Censorship Room*] (n.p., n.d.).

For the prehistory of the nationwide institutionalization of film censorship, see Mamoru Makino, "Wagakuni ni okeru eiga ken'etsu no seido-kaizen no jokyo [The Situation Until the Legalization of Film Censorship in Japan]," *ICONICS* 2-13(33) (January 1986), 43–55.

2. Kikuo Yamamoto, *Nihon eiga ni okeru gaikoku eiga no eikyo* [*The Influence of Foreign Films on Japanese Cinema*] (Tokyo: Waseda Daigaku shuppan, 1983), 32–34. Other sources list different years for the banning of the film, as in Teruo Hata citing early 1912 in his "Eiga-ho ga seiritsu: Eiga no kokka-tosei hajimaru [The Film Law Established: National Film Control Started]," in *Sekai eiga jiken jinbutsu jiten* [*Encyclopedia of World Film Events and People*] (Tokyo: Kinema Jumpo-sha, 1970), 151; and Gordon Daniels citing 1911 in his "Japanese Domestic Radio and Cinema Propaganda, 1939–1945: An Overview," *Historical Journal of Film, Radio and Television* 2(2) (1982), 121.

3. Hata, *Eiga-ho ga seiritsu*, 151.

4. Interview with Masaru Shibata by Kenji Iwamoto and Tomonori Saeki for the Oral History of the Japanese Cinema series, no. 4, *Image Forum* (March 1984), 133; Richard Mitchell, *Censorship in Imperial Japan* (Princeton, N.J.: Princeton University Press, 1983), 348.

5. "Senzen no eiga-ho [Prewar Film Law]," in *Eiga no jiten* [*Encyclopedia of Film*] (Tokyo: Godo shuppan, 1978), 462–464.

6. In July 1937, war broke out near Peking between the Japanese army and Chinese nationalist government forces, which were under pressure from the Chinese communist regime to resist furthur Japanese encroachment. The Japanese cabinet announced its reluctance to widen the scope of the war, but it could not stop the military's expansionist strategy. In Japan, the event was first called "the North Chinese Incident," then "the China Incident," and finally "the Sino-Japan Incident."

Although it was called an "incident," it was actually a full-scale war. Edwin O. Reischauer, *The Japanese* (Cambridge, Mass.: Harvard University Press, 1982), 338; Keigo Hogetsu and Kunihiko Fujiki, *Nihon-shi* [*Japanese History*] (Tokyo: Yamakawa shuppan, 1970), 299–300.

7. Joseph L. Anderson and Donald Richie, *The Japanese Film: Art and Industry* (expanded edition) (Princeton, N.J.: Princeton University Press, 1982), 129; Daniels, "Japanese Domestic Radio and Cinema Propaganda," 125; Oshima, *Taikenteki*, 22; Kazuo Yamada, *Nihon eiga no gendai-shi* [*The Modern History of Japanese Cinema*] (Tokyo: Shin Nihon shuppan-sha), 61.

8. Oshima, *Taikenteki*, 22.

9. "Senzen no eiga-ho," 465–477.

10. Anderson and Richie, *Japanese Film*, 129; Tadao Sato, *Currents in Japanese Cinema*, translated by Gregory Barrett (Tokyo: Kodansha International, 1982), 101.

11. Shibata interview, 133.

12. Toshimi Aoyama, who worked for the Towa Film Company, a foreign film import company, in an interview with the author on July 23, 1984, in Tokyo. Mr. Aoyama was described as a master of the difficult surgery demanded by prewar censorship. Ichiro Ueno, "Meijin Aoyama Toshimi san [Master Toshimi Aoyama]," in *Towa Eiga no ayumi* [*The History of Towa Film*] (Tokyo: Towa Film Company, 1955), 244–245.

13. "Eiga ken'etsu yowa" [Extra Story of Film Censorship] in *Film Center* [Tokyo: National Film Center] 18 (1973), 42; Toshimi Aoyama, "Eiga ken'etsu no omoide [The Memoirs of Film Censorship], no. 1," in *Eiga-shi kenkyu* 21 (1986), 1–12.

14. Daisuke Ito, *Hige to chonmage* [*The Beard and Topknot*] (n.p., n.d.), cited in Shibata interview, 133.

15. Akira Kurosawa, *Something Like an Autobiography*, translated by Audie Bock (New York: Alfred A. Knopf, 1982), 118; interview with Kazuo Miyakawa by the author on June 3, 1984, in Kyoto; Aoyama, "Eiga ken'etsu," 7.

16. Ibid., 10.

17. Shibata interview, 133.

18. Shibata interview, 133. Kenji Mizoguchi's *The City Symphony* [*Tokai kokyokyoku*] (1929) was released only after 2,000 feet were deleted from the completed film, while Shigeyoshi Suzuki's *What Made Her Do So?* [*Nani ga kanojo o so sasetaka*] (1930) was released without cuts. *Nihon eiga kantoku zenshu* [*Encyclopedia of Japanese Directors*] (Tokyo: Kinema jumpo-sha, 1976), 389.

19. Anderson and Richie, *Japanese Film*, 64.

20. Yoshikata Yoda, *Mizoguchi Kenji no hito to geijutsu* [*The Personality and Art of Kenji Mizoguchi*] (Tokyo: Tabata shoten, 1970), 55–56.

21. Reported by Akira Kurosawa, who was the second unit director who shot the scene and who fought with the Army Information Officer over it. Kurosawa, *Something Like,* 111.

22. Interview with Masahiro Shinoda by the author on June 23, 1984, in Tokyo.

23. Tadao Sato, *Kinoshita Keisuke no eiga* [*Films of Keisuke Kinoshita*] (Tokyo: Haga shoten, 1984), 124.

24. Interview with Masahiro Makino by Kenji Iwamoto, Tomoki Saeki, and Atsuko Saito for the Oral History of the Japanese Cinema series, no. 7, *Image Forum* (July 1984), 56–57.

25. Tadao Saito, *Toho koshinkyoku: Watakushi no sendenbu 50-nen* [*The Toho March: My 50 Years of Publicity Work at Toho*] (Tokyo: Heibon-sha, 1987), 89–92.

26. Rentaro Kyogoku, "Toruko maachi: Todoroki Yukiko koshinkyoku [Yukiko Todoroki's March]" *Eiga Goraku* (March 1, 1948), 2.

27. Isuzu Yamada, *Eiga to tomoni* [*Together with Cinema*] (Tokyo: San'ichi shobo, 1953), 97–98.

28. Kurosawa, *Something Like,* 111, 131.

29. Makino interview, 55–58. However, Makino in his autobiography, *Eiga tosei* [*Film Life*] (Tokyo: Heibon-sha, 1977), 2:107–110, states that, after an eleven-hour discussion with the censor, the film was released with "no cuts." The current videocassette version does not include the allegedly deleted scenes.

30. Kurosawa, *Something Like,* 134.

31. Kajiro Yamamoto reports that one censor was jealous of the filmmakers because he himself had wanted to become a filmmaker and had failed. "Katsudo-ya bifun-roku [The Record of the Slight Anger of a Movie-Maker]," *Bungei Shunju* (June 1952), 189.

32. For example, see Kajiro Yamamoto's *Torpedo Squadrons Move Out* [*Raigekitai shutsudo*] (1944) and Yutaka Abe's *Flaming Big Sky* [*Moyuru ozora*] (1941).

33. Hiroshi Kikuchi and Yusuke Tsurumi, "Eiga hodan [Free Discussion on Cinema]," *Eiga Hyoron* (October-November 1944), 11.

34. Sadamu Kumanomido, "Genka no Nihon eiga-kai ni atou [Giving to the Present Japanese Film Industry]," *Eiga Hyoron* (January-February 1944), 3.

35. Tsutomu Sawamura, "Shinario zuiso: Eiga no hyogen ni kansuru hansei [On Screenplay Writing: Reflections on Cinematic Expression]," in *Eiga Hyoron* (December 1944), 8–11; and "Daitowa eiga o meguru sonen [On the Great Asian Cinema]," *Eiga Hyoron* (January-February 1945), 3–5.

36. See Otis Cary, ed., *From a Ruined Empire: Letters—Japan, China, Korea, 1945–1946* (New York: Kodansha International, 1975), a compilation of letters written among those who had been trained in the U.S. Navy Japanese Language School and were stationed in the intelligence sections in the Pacific and Far East during and

immediately after World War II. Also, Herbert Passin, in *Encounter with Japan* (Tokyo: Kodansha International, 1982), writes about his experiences at the U.S. Army Japanese Language School and his assignment in Japan during the occupation.

37. *SCAP Non-Military Activities in Japan and Korea,* Summation no. 1, September/October 1945, 174, U.S. Government Section, Law School Library, Columbia University.

38. Masayo Duus, *Tokyo Rose,* translated by Peter Duus (Tokyo: Kodansha International, 1979), 170–172.

39. One of the results is Ruth Benedict's *The Chrysanthemum and the Sword: Patterns of Japanese Culture* (New York: Meridian, 1946), a classic study of Japanese culture.

40. OSS Research and Analysis Branch Report no. 1307, March 30, 1944, National Archives, Washington, D.C.

41. This notion is also found in Tadao Sato, *Currents in Japanese Cinema,* translated by Gregory Barrett (Tokyo: Kodansha International, 1982), 100–106; Nagisa Oshima, "Eiga ni totte senso towa nanika [What Is War for Cinema?]," in *Nihon eiga o yomu* [*Reading Japanese Cinema*] (Tokyo: Daguerreo Press, 1984), 28–38; and Anderson and Richie, *Japanese Film,* 132–135.

42. The best example is Frank Capra's *Why We Fight* series (1942–1945), made for the OSS. See Charles Burgess Ewing's *An Analysis of Frank Capra's War Rhetoric in the "Why We Fight" Films,* Ph.D. dissertation, Department of Speech, Washington State University, 1983. Also see John W. Dower, *War Without Mercy: Race & Power in the Pacific War* (New York: Pantheon, 1986), which discusses the racist basis of much of the propaganda created by both sides during the Pacific war.

43. Alexander Korda was based in Hollywood between 1940 and 1943. Samuel Spewack (Spevak) made a documentary, *The World at War* (1942), for the Office of War Information.

44. Capra was among the most-imitated of American filmmakers during the postwar democratic film period. The first postwar film by Mikio Naruse, *A Descendant of Taro Urashima* [*Urashima Taro no matsuei*], released in March 1946, was a Capra-esque social satire along the lines of *Mr. Smith Goes to Washington* (made in 1939 and released in Japan in 1941 and again after the war) and *Meet John Doe* (made in 1941 and released in Japan in 1951). The story even includes a Jean Arthur-ish woman journalist character. (In the filmography of Mikio Naruse from unpublished manuscript by Audie Bock on Naruse.)

45. "Japanese Films: A Psychological Warfare," 15.

46. Naozane Fujimoto, "Ichi purojusa no jijoden [A Producer's Autobiography]," in Hotsuki Ozaki, ed., *Purojusa jinsei: Fujimoto Naozane eiga ni kakeru* [*A Producer's Life: Naozane Fujimoto Challenges Film*] (Tokyo: Toho Printing, 1981), 165–166.

47. Daniels, "Japanese Domestic Radio and Cinema Propaganda," 129. Also see Oshima on the effect of Tomotaka Tasaka's *Five Scouts* [*Gonin no sekkohei*] (1939) on the Japanese audience in "Eiga ni totte," 34–38; and Sato's account of the effect of Kajiro Yamamoto's *The War at Sea from Hawaii to Malaya* [*Hawai Marei-oki kaisen*] (1942) on himself in *Currents in Japanese Cinema,* 109.

48. Marlene J. Mayo, "Psychological Disarmament: American Wartime Planning for the Education and Re-education of Defeated Japan, 1943–1945," in *The Occupation of Japan: Education and Social Reform,* proceedings of a symposium sponsored by the MacArthur Memorial, Old Dominion University, and the MacArthur Memorial Foundation, October 16–18, 1980, Norfolk, Va., 24.

49. It is the opinion of many occupation scholars, such as Mayo, that the war did not end in 1945; the ideological "war" between the United States and Japan continued through the occupation period.

50. Jun'ichiro Tanaka, "Nihon eiga sengo-shi [The Postwar History of Japanese Cinema]," in *Kinema Jumpo* (October-III, 1964), 48.

51. Kyushiro Kusakabe, "Jitsuroku sengo Nihon eiga-shi: Hito to jiken to [Documents of Postwar Japanese Film History: People and Events]," no. 1: "Sengo zero-nen [The Postwar Year Zero]," *Hoseki* (1982), 191; Kyoichiro Nambu, "Genba sengo-shi: Gosippu de tsuzuru katsudo-ya no ayumi [Postwar History on the Spot: The Movement of Moviemakers Written with Gossip]," no. 1, *Tokyo Times* (March 12, 1972), 15.

52. Yamamoto, "Katsudo-ya," 188; Kusakabe, "Jitsuroku sengo Nihon eiga-shi," 191.

53. Hideko Takamine, *Watashi no tosei nikki* [*My Professional Diary*] (Tokyo: Asahi shimbun-sha, 1980), 1:273–282.

54. Makino, *Eiga tosei,* 2:168–169.

55. Kurosawa, *Something Like,* 141–142.

56. Kusakabe, "Sengo zero-nen," 191.

57. Kiyohiko Ushihara, *Kiyohiko eiga-fu 50-nen* [*The Fifty-Year Film Story of Kiyohiko*] (Tokyo: Kagamiura shobo, 1968), 236.

58. Yamamoto, "Katsudo-ya," 191.

59. On September 18, 1931, a group of Japanese army officers in Manchuria, with the tacit approval of their army superiors in Manchuria and Tokyo, staged an attack on the railroad near the Manchurian capital, which was then blamed on the Chinese. It gave the Japanese army an excuse to invade the whole of Manchuria and to set up a puppet state called Manchukuo the following February. The civilian government was unable to control the situation and finally led Japan out of the League of Nations, which had condemned the situation. Reischauer, *Japanese,* 98.

60. Kurosawa's *Something Like an Autobiography* is replete with examples: see pp. 111–112, 117–120, 130–131, and 142–143. Other examples include Makino, *Eiga tosei,* 2:101–102, 107–110; Yamamoto, "Katsudo-ya," 189; Keinosuke Uekusa, *Waga*

seishun no Kurosawa Akira [*Akira Kurosawa of My Youth*] (Tokyo: Bungei shunju-sha, 1985), 58–66; and the Aoyama interview.

61. William E. Daugherty, in collaboration with Morris Janowitz, *The Psychological Warfare Casebook* (Baltimore, Md.: Johns Hopkins University Press, 1958), 505.

62. Akira Iwasaki, *Senryo sareta sukuriin* [*The Occupied Screen*] (Tokyo: Shin-Nihon shuppan-sha, 1975), 22.

63. Kurosawa, *Something Like,* 143–144.

64. *Kurosawa: A Retrospective* (New York: Japan Society, 1981), 34.

65. Memorandum for GHQ/SCAP from Toho and Daiei Motion Picture Co., Ltd., April 19, 1951, in CIE file, National Diet Library, Tokyo (hereafter NDL).

66. GHQ/SCAP, CIE, memorandum to Director of Social Education Bureau, Ministry of Education, February 29, 1952, in CIE file, NDL.

67. Mayo, "Psychological Disarmament," 83–84.

68. Ibid., 85; Takemae, *GHQ,* 116.

69. Mayo, "Psychological Disarmament," 123; *Declassified Reports of the Official Intelligence Research as of July 1, 1950,* July 7, 1950, Department of State, bibliography no. 53, National Archives, Washington D.C., 9.

70. Mayo, "Psychological Disarmament," 56–57.

71. Kokichi Takakuwa, *Makkaasaa no shimbun ken'etsu: Keisai kinshi sakujo ni natta shimbun kiji* [*MacArthur's Newspaper Censorship: Suppressed or Deleted Newspaper Articles*] (Tokyo: Yomiuri shimbun-sha, 1984), 38.

72. Takemae, *GHQ,* 41.

73. Takakuwa, *Makkaasaa no,* 38.

74. Mayo, "Psychological Disarmament," 88–89.

75. Ibid., 90; *GHQ bunsho ni yoru senryo-ki hoso-shi nenpyo* [*The Chronicle of Broadcast History during the Occupation According to the GHQ Documents*] (Tokyo: NHK Hoso Bunka Chosa Kenkyu-jo, 1987), 16.

76. Takemae, *GHQ,* 88–89.

77. Mayo, "Psychological Disarmament," 89; Takakuwa, *Makkaasaa no,* 39–40.

78. Ibid., 89; Takakuwa, *Makkaasaa no,* 39–40; Sozo Matsuura, "Ken'etsu seido to sogo zasshi no fukkatsu [The Censorship System and Revival of General Magazines]," in Saburo Ienaga, ed., *Showa no sengo-shi* [*The Postwar History of the Showa Era*] (Tokyo: Shobun-sha, 1976), 269–270.

79. Akira Shimizu, "20.9.22 kara 23.8.19 made: Senryo-ka no eiga-kai no kiroku [From September 22, 1945, to August 19, 1948: The Record of the Film Industry under the Occupation]," in *Film Center* [catalogue of a retrospective of Japanese films made under the occupation] (Tokyo: National Film Center, 1973), 9.

80. *Eiga Engeki Jiten* [*Encyclopedia of Film and Theater*] (Tokyo: Jiji tsuhshin-sha, 1947), 45.

81. Shimizu, "20.9.22 kara," 9; Ushihara, *Kiyohiko eiga-fu 50-nen*, 238; *Toho Eiga 30 nen-shi* [*Toho Film's 30 Year History*] (Tokyo: Toho Printing, 1963), 171; Shiro Kido, *Nippon eiga-den: Eiga seisakusha no kiroku* [*The Story of Japanese Cinema: The Record of a Film Producer*] (Tokyo: Bungei shunju-sha, 1956), 209–211; Iwao Mori, "9.22 no shuki [Note of September 22]," *Eiga Hyoron* (September 1945), 4–6.

82. *SCAP Non-Military Activities in Japan and Korea*, Summation no. 1, 160.

83. Shimizu, "20.9.22 kara," 9–10; *Toho Eiga 30 nen-shi*, 170–174.

84. Takakuwa, *Makkaasaa no*, 53.

85. Yoshinobu Ikeda, "Senryo-seisaku no nisan [A Few Things about the Occupation Policy]," *Eiga Jiho* (November 1953), 22.

86. Anonymous discussion, "Senryo-ka no eiga gyosei no uchimaku [The Inside Story of Film Administration under the Occupation]," *Eiga Jiho* (November 1953), 17.

87. Takemae, *GHQ*, 104–105. However, Jay Rubin writes that CCD totally stopped its censorship operation in October 1949, citing Eizaburo Okuizumi, ed., *Senryo-gun ken'etsu zasshi mokuroku: kaidai* [*The List of the Occupation's Censorship of Magazines: Retitled*] (Tokyo: Yushodo Shoten, 1982), 10–14. "From Wholesomeness to Decadence: The Censorship of Literature under the Allied Occupation," *Journal of Japanese Studies* 11(1) (Winter 1985), 85.

88. GHQ/SCAP, CIE, "Memorandum Concerning Motion Picture Censorship," January 28, 1946, in CIE file, NDL.

89. Yamamoto, "Katsudo-ya," 190.

90. "Memorandum Concerning the Elimination of Undemocratic Motion Pictures," November 16, 1945, in CIE file, NDL.

91. Kazu Adachi, "Purojusa gunyu-den [The Group Portrait of Producers]," no. 7, *Kinema Jumpo* (August-I, 1988); anonymous discussion, "Senryo-ka no," 16.

92. "Eiga-kai kyutenkai no GHQ seisaku [The Drastic Change in GHQ Policy toward the Film Industry]," *Yomiuri Shimbun* (September 20, 1982).

93. Mayo, "Psychological Disarmament," 82–83.

94. Anonymous discussion, "Senryo-ka no," 16. For Conde, see Matsuura, "Ken'etsu seido," 276; Kusakabe, "Sengo zero-nen," 194; and Takemae, *GHQ*, 124–125. In a telephone interview with the author on January 9, 1985, in New York, Behrstock described himself as "liberal" while describing Conde as "radical."

95. For example, Kido, *Nihon eiga-den*, 210–211, 213; Matsuo Kishi, *Jimbutsu Nihon eiga-shi* [*The History of Japanese Film Personalities*] (Tokyo: Dabiddo-sha, 1970), 290; interview with Kaneto Shindo by the author on June 25, 1984, in Tokyo; and Yoshio Miyajima, "Kaiso-roku [Memoirs]," no. 27, *Kinema Jumpo* (April-II, 1986), 109–110.

96. Ikeda, "Senryo-seisaku," 22.

97. For example, ibid.; Shimizu, "20.9.22 kara," 10; and "Eiga-kai kyutenkai." The latter listed fifteen newsreels and animated films, while Shimizu stated that "countless newsreels and culture films were added to the list" (p. 10).

98. David Conde, "Nihon eiga no senryo-shi [The History of Japanese Cinema under the Occupation]," *Sekai* (August 1965), 252.

99. "Elimination of Undemocratic Motion Pictures," memorandum from the Central Liaison Office of the Japanese Government to GHQ/SCAP, November 26 and December 15, 1945, in CIE file, NDL.

100. "Elimination of Undemocratic Motion Pictures," memorandum from the Central Liaison Office of the Japanese Government to GHQ/SCAP, December 27, 1945, in CIE file, NDL.

101. Later, several prints of the last two films were discovered. "Report on Suppressed Films Which Were Burned," Ministry of Internal Affairs, May 8, 1946, in CIE file, NDL.

102. Saito, *Toho koshinkyoku,* 118–120.

103. "Memorandum Concerning Destruction of Seized Japanese Feature Films" from Motion Picture and Theatrical Division, CIE, to General Dyke, January 19, 1946; "Memorandum Concerning the Disposition of Banned Japanese Motion Pictures" from CIE to Commanding General, Eighth Army, February 14, 1946; "Memorandum Concerning Action Regarding Banned Japanese Motion Pictures" from CIE to the Imperial Japanese Government, January 28 and February 17, 1946; "Memorandum Concerning the Disposition of Banned Pictures" from the Chief of Press, Pictorial and Broadcasting Division, through CCD to CIE, May 7, 1946, all in CIE file, NDL.

104. "Memorandum Concerning the Disposition of Banned Japanese Motion Pictures."

105. Press Release from GHQ/USAFPAC, CIE, November 19, 1945, in CIE file, NDL.

106. Anderson and Richie, *Japanese Film,* 161.

107. "Information Sheet of CIE, MPU [Motion Picture Unit] Concerning Banned Undemocratic Films," December 1, 1950, in CIE file, NDL.

108. "Memorandum Concerning Application for Release of Japanese Feature Films" from Toho Motion Picture Co., Ltd., and Daiei Motion Picture Co., Ltd., to GHQ/SCAP, April 19, 1951, in CIE file, NDL.

109. Letter from the Motion Picture Association of Japan to CIE Section, GHQ/SCAP, November 13, 1951, in CIE file, NDL.

110. Memorandum from CIE to the Director of the Social Education Bureau, Ministry of Education, February 29, 1952, in CIE file, NDL.

111. "Eiga-kai kyutenkai."

112. Press release from GHQ/USAFPAC, CIE, November 19, 1945.

113. Rubin, "From Wholesomeness to Decadence," 97.

114. Editor's Note, *Zaisei* (May 1946), 64, Prange Collection, McKeldin Library, University of Maryland.

CHAPTER 2

1. Press, Pictorial and Broadcast Division memorandum on "Plan for Censorship of Motion Pictures Reported Pursuant to Directive of 28 January 1946," March 26, 1946, CCD file on Movie Films (Censorship) of 1946, Box 331-8579, National Records Center, Suitland, Md. (hereafter NRC); CCD memorandum on "Documentary Intelligence Value of Suppressed Japanese Motion Picture Films," April 7, 1948, in CCD file on Suppressed Military Films, Box 331-8579, NRC.

2. Summary of conference between CIE and CCD concerning "Possible Duplication of Manpower in CIE and CCD Motion Picture and Theatrical Branch," September 3, 1948, in CIE file, National Diet Library, Tokyo (hereafter NDL).

3. CIE file on the film, its first script, examined on May 5, 1949, and the second and final script, examined on September 12, 1949, Box 331-5291, NRC.

4. Hideo Komatsu, who worked as a liaison between Shochiku Studio and the occupation government, kept a work diary. He has retained one volume, covering the period between September 1946 and April 1947, in his private collection, and was kind enough to show it to the author. This example appears in the entry for November 13, 1946. See also CIE file on the film, its first script, examined on May 5, 1949, and the second and final script, examined on September 12, 1949, Box 331-5291, NRC.

5. CIE comment on the synopsis of the film, February 13, 1948, in CIE file, NDL. Other examples include CIE comment on the synopsis of *Badger Walks Down Ginza* [*Tanuki Ginza o aruku*], January 12, 1948, and CIE comment on *Male Virgin* [*Dotei*], its first script examined on December 27, 1948, and the second script (which was marked "N.G."), examined on March 14, 1949, Box 331-5267, NRC.

6. Kajiro Yamamoto, "Katsudo-ya bifun-roku [The Record of the Slight Anger of a Movie-Maker]," *Bungei Shunju* (June 1952), 192–193.

7. CIE comment on Nichi-ei newsreel, March 31, 1950, in CIE file, NDL.

8. CIE file on the film, and intrasection memorandum to Office of International, Informational, and Cultural Affairs, Motion Picture and Theatrical Branch, from Political Affairs Information Officer, May 26, 1950, Box 331-5297, NRC.

9. Examples include a character in *Women's House* [*Onna no ie*] (CIE comment on the script of the film, examined on January 7, 1948); a purged character in *Together with Passion* [*Honoo to tomoni*] (CIE comment on its first script, examined on April 3, 1948, and its second script, examined on May 14, 1948); and a war criminal character in *Mother and Son* [*Haha to ko*] (CIE comment on its synopsis, examined on January 10, 1948), in CIE file, Box 331-5267, NRC. Similarly, the

description of the Imperial Navy officers with "shining medals" at a wartime party was deleted from film star Kanjuro Arashi's memoir in a film magazine. Kanjuro Arashi, "Seishun aishi: Utakata no koi [The Sad Story of Youth: An Ephemeral Love]," *Eiga Club* (February 20, 1947), 32–33.

10. CIE comment on the synopsis of *A Struggle in the Alps* [*Arupusu no shito*], February 19, 1948, in CIE file, NDL.

11. CIE comment on the script of *Fiery Rose* [*Hi no bara*], July 23, 1948, in CIE file, NDL.

12. Press, Pictorial and Broadcasting Division memorandum, July 15, 1946, in CCD file on Relations with CIE, Box 331-8579, NRC.

13. CCD checksheet on International Military Tribunal in the Far East Newsreel, December 20, 1948, in CCD file on *Satsujinki* [Murdering Demon: perhaps an early title of the documentary about the Tribunal], Box 331-8579, NRC.

14. Ibid. The translation is from the script prepared by the producer.

15. File on *Tokyo War Criminal* [perhaps another early title of the documentary about the Tribunal], Box 331-5788, NRC.

16. Memorandum from Press, Pictorial and Broadcasting Division District II to Press, Pictorial and Broadcasting Division on "Exhibition of Pro-military Feeling at a Movie Showing on November 24, 1948"; CCD checksheet on International Military Tribunal in the Far East Newsreel, December 20, 1948; and memorandum from Press, Pictorial and Broadcasting Division to Press, Pictorial and Broadcasting Division District II on the same matter, December 28, 1948, CCD file on *Satsujinki*, Box 331-8579, NRC.

17. Motion Picture and Theatrical Branch intrasection memorandum to Policy and Program Branch concerning the film, August 17, 1950, in CIE file, NDL.

18. CIE comment on the film, February 12, 1948, in CIE file, NDL.

19. Masahiro Makino, *Eiga tosei* [*Film Life*] (Tokyo: Heibon-sha, 1977), 2:182–183. Another example of the prohibition of Mt. Fuji is seen in CIE comment on the synopsis of *Map of New Tokyo* [*Ginza shin-chizu*], May 29, 1948, in CIE file, NDL.

20. According to Setsuo Noto, who was a liaison between Toho Studio and the occupation government, in an interview with the author on June 5, 1984, in Tokyo.

21. CIE comment on the second script of *Together with Passion*, examined May 14, 1948, Box 331-5267, NRC.

22. CIE comment on the film, July 15, 1948, in CIE file, NDL.

23. CIE comment on the first script of the film, examined on May 5, 1949, and on the second script, examined on September 12, 1949, Box 331-5291, NRC.

24. CIE comment on the synopsis of *That Dream and This Song* [*Ano yuke kono uta*] (1948), examined on February 2, 1948, and on *Super Express for a Bride* [*Ren'ai tokkyu*], examined on May 24, 1948, in CIE file, NDL.

Similarly, in the field of literature, the American censors prohibited descriptions that might evoke antipathy to Japan's past enemy. Novelist Shohei Ooka (the author of *Fires on the Plain* [*Nobi*], which was filmed by Kon Ichikawa in 1959), stated that when his *Record of a POW* [*Furyoki*] was first published in a magazine in February 1948, the word *teki* (enemy) had been replaced by *aite* (opponent). This measure had been initiated by his publisher, after the suppression in January 1947 of Mitsuru Yoshida's memoir, *The Last of the Battleship Yamato* [*Senkan Yamato no saigo*], which CCD thought was militarist propaganda. Jun Eto, "The American Occupation and Postwar Japanese Literature: The Impact of Censorship upon a Japanese Mind," *Hikaku Bungaku Kenkyu* 38 (September 1980), 1–18.

Ooka recalled that when *Furyoki* was first published in book form, in December 1952, the word *teki* was used. Letter to the author, October 2, 1985.

25. Press, Pictorial and Broadcasting Division memorandum on "Recommended Deletion for 'Senso to heiwa,'" June 5, 1947, in CCD file on the film, Box 331-8579, NRC. Also, Jun Eto, "Genron tosei: Senryo-ka Nippon ni okeru ken'etsu [Media Control: Censorship in Occupied Japan]," in Ray Moore, ed., *Tenno ga baiburu o yonda hi* [*The Day the Emperor Read the Bible*] (Tokyo: Kodansha, 1982), 139.

26. Telephone conversation with the author on July 12, 1984, in Tokyo.

27. Eto, "Genron tosei," 138–144. Eto added that the Press, Pictorial and Broadcasting Division suggested that the film use photos of Toho Studio's actresses instead of Hollywood stars, and substitute pictures of clothed Japanese women for those of the white women. He concluded that this measure illustrates that occupation censors were not only puritanical but also racist. Ibid., 144.

The author could not find this particular section in the CCD's file on this film, but found the order to change a scene with a child selling pictures of nude foreign women so that the pictures were of clothed Japanese women. Press, Pictorial and Broadcasting Division Review Sheet, June 13, 1947.

28. Press, Pictorial and Broadcasting Division memorandum on "Toho's New Production 'Senso to Heiwa' for Censorship on 22 May," May 26, 1947, signed by R.K. (Richard Kunzman), in CCD file on the film, Box 331-8579, NRC.

29. Checksheet from Press, Pictorial and Broadcasting Division to CCD on "Senso to Heiwa," June 6, 1947, signed by J.J.C. (John J. Costello), in CCD file on the film, Box 331-8579, NRC.

30. Press, Pictorial and Broadcasting Division memorandum for record on "Senso to Heiwa," May 22, 1947, written by W.Y.M. (Walter Y. Mihata), and Press, Pictorial and Broadcasting Division memorandum on "Recommended deletions for 'Senso to heiwa,'" June 5, 1947, CCD file on the film, Box 331-8579, NRC. Also Eto, "Genron tosei," 142.

31. Memorandum from Chief, Government Section, CCD to CIE, July 18, 1947, in CIE file, NDL.

32. Interview with the author on June 3, 1984, in Kyoto.

33. Komatsu work diary entry for December 16, 1946. One of the largest PX facilities was at a department store on the busiest corner in Tokyo's Ginza district, which was also a famous photo site. The phrase "in front of the PX building" was deleted from a magazine caption of a photograph of two female stars standing in front of the Ginza PX building. *Sinemagurafiku* (August 10, 1947), 14, Prange Collection, McKeldin Library, University of Maryland.

34. Yamamoto, "Katsudo-ya," 190.

35. Joseph L. Anderson's letter to the author, December 1986. However, in the same film, the following English sign is shown: "This Area Off Limits to Occupation Personnel By Order of the Provost General." Similarly, in Akira Kurosawa's 1950 film *Scandal [Sukyandaru]*, a sign saying "Loading Space for Special Service. Chusha Kinshi, Beigun Kenpei Shireibu [No Parking, US Military Police Headquarters]," is shown.

36. CCD checksheet on CI&E, February 4, 1946, in CCD file on Relations with CIE, Box 331-8579, NRC.

37. CCD memorandum on "Deletion made in Daiei production 'Nusumare-kaketa Ongakusai' at the request of CI&E," December 20, 1946, in CCD file on Relations with CIE, Box 331-8579, NRC.

38. Yamamoto, "Katsudo-ya," 190; Noto interview. Yamamoto claimed that a conversation scene with the sound of airplanes flying overhead had to be reshot.

39. Komatsu work diary entry for January 23, 1947.

40. CIE file, NDL.

41. According to Kazu Adachi, Imai could not make the film not only because of occupation government policy, but also because of the reluctance of Japanese studios, bowing to commercial pressure. See his "Purojusa gunyu-den [The Group Portrait of Producers], no. 36," *Kinema Jumpo* (November-I, 1989), 124–127, and no. 38 (December-I, 1989), 130–133. Imai remade this film in 1983. This time, he could make a color film shot on location in Okinawa, an approach that had not been allowed by the American military authorities on the island in 1953.

42. Uriu suspects David Conde's involvement in the confiscation of the Hiroshima documentaries. See his *Sengo Nihon eiga shoshi [A Short History of the Postwar Japanese Cinema]* (Tokyo: Hosei Daigaku Shuppan, 1981), 2–20.

43. CCD file on Atomic Bomb Films, Box 331–8578, NRC.

44. Akira Iwasaki, *Senryo sareta sukuriin [The Occupied Screen]* (Tokyo: Shin-Nihon shuppan-sha, 1975), 113–118; Kyushiro Kusakabe [a film journalist and a Nagasaki atomic bomb survivor], "Jitsuroku sengo Nihon eiga-shi: Hito to jiken to [Documents of Postwar Japanese Film History: People and Events], no. 8," *Hoseki* (1982), 190–194.

Eric Barnouw of Columbia University's Center for Mass Communication compiled Iwasaki's footage, obtained from the National Archives, into a 16 mm film entitled *Hiroshima-Nagasaki: August 1945* in 1970. This film has been widely circulated in the United States by Columbia University and the Museum of Modern Art. Eric Barnouw, *Documentary: A History of the Non-Fiction Film* (New York: Oxford University Press, 1974); Iwasaki, *Senryo sareta*, 180–209; interview with Kazuko Oshima (who collaborated with Barnouw in the making of his film) by the author, on August 29, 1986, in New York.

Akira (Harry) Mimura, a cameraman who had worked in both Hollywood and Japan, was assigned to shoot Hiroshima by order of the occupation government, according to Kazu Adachi. See his "Purojusa gunyu-den, no. 33," *Kinema Jumpo* (September-II, 1989), 168.

45. CIE comment on *Hiroshima*, in CIE file, NDL.

46. Letter to CIE from B. B. MacMahon, Colonel, Infantry, Acting Chief, Reorientation Branch, Civil Affairs Division, May 23, 1949; CIE report to Chief, Civil Affairs Division, Special Staff, United States Army, Washington 36, D.C. (attention: Reorientation Branch), June 11, 1949, in CIE file, NDL.

47. CIE comment on the film, July 13, 1948, in CIE file, NDL. CCD's memo on this film, July 15, 1948, reported the CIE (George Ishikawa's) request to CCD to delete dialogue on Hiroshima and the atomic bomb. This measure seems to have been CIE's double check on this important matter. CCD file on Movie Films (Censorship) of 1948, Box 331-8579, NRC.

48. Anderson letter.

49. Yoshio Osawa, Yasutaro Yagi, and Takeo Ito, "Nippon eiga no unmei [The Fate of Japanese Cinema]," *Kinema Jumpo* (Fall special issue, 1949), 14.

50. CIE file on the film, Box 331-5267, NRC; CIE comment on the trailer of the film, September 8–12, 1950, in CIE file, NDL.

51. Sozo Matsuura, "Senryo-ka no genron dan'atsu [Media Oppression under the Occupation]," in Ryusuke Sagara, ed., *Dokyumento: Showashi [Document: Showa Era History]* (Tokyo: Heibon-sha, 1975), 6:266. Keisuke Kinoshita filmed *Children of Nagasaki [Kono ko o nokoshite]*, an adaptation of Dr. Nagai's book, in 1983.

52. CIE comment on *Cinderella Jones*, May 1, 1950, in CIE file, NDL.

53. John Allyn believes that the wartime *Life* magazine article on *Chushingura* or *Forty-Seven Ronin* did much to tarnish the image of this story in American eyes, because of its criticism of the "glorification of loyalty, self-sacrifice and bloody revenge." "Motion Picture and Theatrical Censorship in Japan," *Waseda Journal of Asian Studies* 7 (1985), 24.

The story of *Forty-Seven Ronin* has been one of the most popular and profitable film subjects in the history of Japanese cinema. Between 1926 and 1962, twenty-four versions were made, including Teinosuke Kinugasa's 1932 version and Kenji Mizoguchi's *Forty-Seven Ronin [Genroku Chushingura]* (1941–1942). It is said that whenever a film studio fell into financial distress, it would produce a film based on this story, for a guaranteed hit. *Sekai eiga sakuhin daijiten* [*Dictionary of World Motion Pictures*] [Tokyo: Kinema Jumpo-sha, 1970], 134–135.

54. Interview with Faubion Bowers by Beate Gordon on the occupation, for the Oral History Research Center at Columbia University, on October 23, 1960, in New York.

55. Toshio Kawatake, "A Crisis of Kabuki and Its Revival Right after World War II," *Waseda Journal of Asian Studies* 5 (1983), 41. See also Allyn, "Motion Picture and Theatrical Censorship in Japan."

56. David Conde, Akira Iwasaki, and Naozane Fujimoto, "Shidoshita Nippon eiga to no saikai: GHQ shodai eiga engeki hancho Debiddo Konde shi to kataru [Reunion with Japanese Cinema: Discussion with Mr. Conde, the First Chief of the Motion Picture and Theatrical Branch of GHQ]," *Kinema Jumpo* (November-III, 1964), 28–29; Kusakabe, "Jitsuroku, no. 1," *Hoseki* (1982), 194.

57. Keinosuke Uekusa, *Waga seishun no Kurosawa Akira* [*Akira Kurosawa of My Youth*] (Tokyo: Bungei shunju-sha, 1985), 93–94. Kurosawa himself downplayed this incident, stating that the American visitors enjoyed taking pictures and 8 mm films and that "some even wanted to be photographed while being slashed at with a Japanese sword. Things got so out of hand I had to call a halt to the day's shooting." Akira Kurosawa, *Something Like an Autobiography,* translated by Audie Bock (New York: Alfred A. Knopf, 1982), 142.

58. Kusakabe, "Jitsuroku, no. 1," 195.

59. CIE comment on the script of *The Sucker* [*Kobanzame*], July 12, 1948, in CIE file, NDL.

60. CIE comment on the synopsis of *Princess Sen's Palace* [*Sen-hime goten*], July 13, 1948, in CIE file, NDL.

61. CIE file on the film (the first script, examined on May 26, 1949, and the second one, on June 3, 1949), Box 331-5297, NRC.

62. Interview with Hideo Komatsu by the author on May 28, 1984, in Tokyo; Komatsu, "Sengo eiga shiriizu [Series on the Postwar Cinema], no. 1," *Tokyo-eki* (n.d.), 21.

63. CCD memorandum on "Exhibition of objectionable movie advertising posters," June 27, 1947, and memo from J.J.C. (John J. Costello) to CCD, July 19, 1947, CCD file on Movie Films (Censorship) of 1947, Box 331-8579, NRC.

64. CCD memorandum on "Silent Picture Shows gaining popularity," on April 5, 1948, CCD file on Foreign Films, Box 331-8579, NRC.

65. CIE comment on the film, February 12, 1948, in CIE file, NDL.

66. CCD memorandum for record on "Motion Picture Section of CI&E policy on sword fighting scenes in pictures" by W.Y.M. (Walter Y. Mihata), March 2, 1948; memo from J.J.C. (John J. Costello) of Press, Pictorial and Broadcasting Division to CCD, March 9, 1948, and return memo from B.J.W., March 11, 1948, CCD file on Relations with CIE and on Movie Films (Censorship) of 1948, Box 331-8579, NRC. The film apparently was not released.

CCD suppressed the release of Universal's 1942 film *The Spoilers* because of "too much gunplay and unnecessary killing" and for its glorification of the outlaw character. Checksheet from Motion Picture Department to Pictorial Section and from Pictorial Section to Press, Pictorial and Broadcasting Division District I, October 10, 1946. CCD file on Foreign Films, Box 331-8578, NRC.

67. CIE comment on the film, May 11, 1951, in CIE file, NDL.

68. CIE comment on the synopsis of the film, July 6, 1948, in CIE file, NDL.

69. CIE comment on the film, on September 17, 1949, in CIE file, NDL.

70. CIE file on the film, the first script, examined on July 18, 1949, the second, on August 20, 1949, and the third, on September 12, 1949, Box 331-5297, NRC.

71. The incidence of marriages through miai has been decreasing in Japan, although miai is not necessarily anti-individualistic, since participants now have the freedom to refuse the arranged partner. However, in prewar Japan, it was more difficult for a young lady to refuse an interested suitor once she had agreed to attend a miai.

72. CIE comment on the film, December 28, 1948, in CIE file, NDL.

73. CIE file on the film (the first script, examined on May 5, 1949, and the second, on September 12, 1949), Box 331-5291, NRC. See also "Senryo-ka no eiga gyosei no uchimaku [Inside Story of Film Administration under the Occupation]," by three anonymous film company liaisons, *Eiga Jiho* (November 1953), 16.

74. CIE file on the film (its script, examined on March 7, 1949), Box 331-5297, NRC.

75. CIE comment on the synopsis of the film, February 20, 1948, in CIE file, NDL.

76. CIE comment on the film, February 25, 1948, in CIE file, NDL.

77. CIE file on the film, Box 331-5297, NRC. Other examples are seen in the CIE comment on *Chess King* [*Osho*] (the first script, examined on February 24, 1948, and the second, on April 8, 1948), Box 331-5290, NRC; and the CCD comment on *Four Stories of Love* [*Yottsu no koi no monogatari*], March 10, 1947, in CCD file on Relations with CIE, Box 331-8579, NRC.

78. Fuji Yahiro, "Jidaieiga no ki jusan-nen [The Record of Period Films for Thirteen Years]," *Kinema Jumpo* (March-I, 1964), 40.

79. CCD checksheet on CI&E from R.H.K. (Richard H. Kunzman) to W.P. (Walter Putnam), February 4, 1946, in CCD file on Relations with CIE, Box 331-8579, NRC.

80. CIE file on the film, (its script, examined on April 14, 1949), Box 331-5267, NRC.

81. Interview with Seymour Palestin by the author on January 10, 1985, in New York. Palestin worked in the theater section of CCD from January to November 1946.

82. Komatsu work diary, entries for December 2–7, 1946. Konno's objection was filed on December 2. The final "OK" was given by Konno's colleague, George

Ishikawa, in Kyoto when Komatsu took a trip there on December 6. It is not clear what the precise nature of the trip was, but Komatsu evidently had to go to Kyoto to get the necessary approval. As will be described later in this chapter, this could be one case in which the studio bribed the censors so that they would pass the script.

83. CIE record on "Motion Picture Critics' Role in the Democratization of Japanese Motion Picture," July 9, 1948, in CIE file, NDL.

84. Note on *One Night,* Komatsu work diary entry for December 16, 1946.

85. CIE file on *Sorrowful Beauty* [*Kanashiki bibo*] (its script, examined on March 2, 1949), in CIE file, NDL; CIE comment on the synopsis of *Crazed Embrace,* February 25, 1948, in CIE file, NDL; CIE comment on *Chess King* (the third script, examined on July 26, 1948), in CIE file, NDL; CIE comment on the script of *The Romantic Stone Lantern* [*Roman doro*], December 31, 1948, in CIE file, NDL.

86. Tadao Sato, *Obake entotsu no sekai: Eiga kantoku Gosho Heinosuke no hito to shigoto* [*The World of the Strange Chimneys: The Personality and Work of Film Director Heinosuke Gosho*] (Tokyo: Noberu shobo, 1977), 204.

87 CIE file on the film (its script, examined on October 30, 1947), Box 331-5290, NRC.

88. Komatsu work diary entry for December 10, 1946. Gercke allowed the inclusion of the scene at issue "only this time" because he realized its importance to the narrative.

89. CIE comment on *The Fourth Lady,* July 15, 1948, in CIE file, NDL; CIE comment on the script of *Three Hundred and Sixty-Five Nights* [*Sanbyaku rokuju go-ya*], July 22, 1948, in CIE file, NDL.

90. CIE comment on *Twenty-One Fingerprints* [*Nijuichi no shimon*], July 6, 1948, in CIE file, NDL. Its script (examined on October 30, 1947), is in Box 331-5290, NRC.

91. Komatsu private collection, n.d.

92. CIE comment on *Fiery Rose* on July 23, 1948, NDL.

93. CIE file on *Brand* [*Rakuin*] (its script, examined on May 18, 1949), Box 331-5267, NRC.

94. CIE comment on the revised script of *The Bright Day of My Life* [*Waga shogai no kagayakeru hi*], May 20, 1948, in CIE file, NDL.

95. CIE file on the film, Box 331-5290, NRC. Some Japanese critics wrote negative comments on *Drunken Angel,* claiming Kurosawa's criticism of the gangster world was not harsh enough. (See Miyoo Imamura's review in *Eiga Hyoron* (June 1948), 23; Shimbi Iida's review in *Kinema Jumpo* (June-II), 20; and Chiyota Shimizu's review in *Kinema Jumpo* (July-III), 11.

96. CIE comment on the script of *Nightless Castle of Flowers* [*Hana no fuyajo*], July 8, 1948, in CIE file, NDL; CIE comment on the script of *Gonbei, the Nameless* [*Nanashi no Gonbei*], February 14, 1948, in CIE file, NDL; CIE comment on the script of *The Fourth Lady,* July 15, 1948, in CIE file, NDL.

97. CIE comment on the synopsis of *The Conflict between Love and Hatred* [*Ai to nikushimi to no tawamure*], February 20, 1948, and on its script, February 28, 1948, in CIE file, NDL; CIE comment on *Ah! The Bell Rings* [*Aa, kane ga naru*], February 19, 1948, in CIE file, NDL; CIE comment on *The Romantic Stone Lantern*, December 31, 1948.

98. Makino, *Eiga tosei*, 1:226, 230, 244–245, 251–265. He states that the drug that he was using was the kind that had been given to kamikaze fliers during the war.

99. CIE file on the film (its script, examined on August 15, 1949), Box 331-5296, NRC.

100. Note on *Face of Hell* [*Jigoku no kao*] in Komatsu work diary entry for October 10, 1946.

101. CIE comment on the revised script of *The Bright Day of My Life*, May 20, 1948, in CIE file, NDL.

102. CIE comment on *The Conflict between Love and Hatred*, February 28, 1948, in CIE file, NDL.

103. CIE comment on the script of *Super Express for a Bride*, May 24, 1948, in CIE file, NDL.

104. CIE comment on the film, May 22, 1948, in CIE file, NDL.

105. CIE comment on the synopsis of the film, June 15, 1948, NDL.

106. CIE comments demanding the deletion of the dialogue referring to selling one's body for money in the synopsis of *Nightless Castle of Flowers* (July 8, 1948, in CIE file, NDL); demanding deletion of the locale of Yoshiwara, an official red light district from the script of *The Fourth Lady* (July 15, 1948, in CIE file, NDL); demanding the deletion of the sequence in which a man-on-the-street radio interviewer discusses social problems with a streetwalker from the script of *Miss Top-Shell* [*Sazaesan*] (July 22, 1948, in CIE file, NDL); and demanding the deletion of the scene of the prostitutes' lynching from the synopsis of *The Gate of Flesh* [*Nikutai no mon*] (January 3, 1948, in CIE file, NDL). CIE comments ordering the producer to tone down the cynicism of streetwalkers and useless emphasis on money in the revised script of *The Gate of Flesh* (April 28, 1948, in CIE file, NDL); to tone down sensationalistic references to prostitution, venereal disease, and the "yen-motive" in the revised script of *Pitiful Resistance* [Japanese title unknown] (July 6, 1948, in CIE file, NDL); to tone down the past of the streetwalker in the synopsis of *Sand on the Eyes* [Japanese title unknown] (February 25, 1948, in CIE file, NDL); to treat the dancer's scene with caution in the script of *Absolutely Welcome Each Other* [*Zettai aishite*] (July 16, 1948, in CIE file, NDL); to treat the subject of abortion with care in the synopsis of *The Life of a Woman* [*Onna no issho*] (February 17, 1948, in CIE file, NDL); and to film the sensational subject with care, reacting to the synopsis of *Mermaid of the Night* [*Yoru no ningyo*] (February 14, 1948, in CIE file, NDL).

107. CIE directives that the script of *Fiery Rose* be changed to replace the streetwalker with a rehabilitated one (July 23, 1948, in CIE file, NDL); to emphasize a

minister's speech proclaiming "citizens' responsibility [for the problem of prostitution]" in the revised script of *The Gate of Flesh* (April 28, 1948, in CIE file, NDL); to emphasize the need for a proper institution for prostitutes, under government guidance and inspection, in the synopsis of *The Truth about the Baby Murder Case* [Japanese title unknown] (January 26, 1948, in CIE file, NDL); to point out child welfare problems and the emanicipation of Japanese women in the synopsis of *The Life of a Woman* (February 15, 1948, in CIE file, NDL); to highlight women's revolt against the "master race [men]" in the script of *Five Women from Saikaku* (February 25, 1948, in CIE file, NDL); to underline the condemnation of the enslavement of a girl in payment for a debt, in the synopsis of *Sand in the Eyes* (February 25, 1948, in CIE file, NDL); and to emphasize the film's value as an "educational-entertainment film," reacting to the synopsis of *The Virgin Standing on the Hill* (February 7, 1948, in CIE file, NDL).

108. CIE stopped the project *Tipsy Boogie Woogie,* full of streetwalkers and venereal disease, on July 18, 1948 (CIE file, NDL); and CIE ordered its producer to drop the subject of abortion from *Abortion Doctor* [*Dataii*] at the synopsis stage on July 12, 1948, thus killing that project (CIE file, NDL). As for film titles, see CIE's comment on *Prostitute* [*Shumpu*], on January 31, 1948, in CIE file, NDL; Shochiku Studio reported a change of title from *A Woman in a Muddy Stream* to *Mother* [*Haha*] (1950) in CIE's comment on the script of the film, July 9, 1948, in CIE file, NDL; and *Today, I Desire* [*Kyo ware yokujosu*] was changed to *Today, I Love* [*Kyo ware ren'ai su*] at the suggestion of the censors (Makino, *Eiga tosei,* 2:238).

109. CIE files on *Sorrowful Beauty* (its script, examined on March 2, 1949), NDL; on *Mother and Son* (its script, examined on July 16, 1948), Box 331-5267, NRC.

110. CIE file on *Mother and Son* (its synopsis, examined on January 7, 1948), NRC.

111. CIE file on *The Moon Has Risen* [*Tsuki wa noborinu*] (its synopsis, examined on September 26, 1947), Box 331-5269, NRC. The script was found unobjectionable, with a few suggestions for change, on November 27, 1947. The reason why this film was not made until 1954 is not known; also see CIE file on *Sorrowful Beauty* (its script, examined on March 2, 1949), NDL.

112. CIE file on the film (its script, examined on February 14, 1950), Box 331-5296, NRC.

113. CIE file on the film (its script, examined on October 30, 1947), Box 331-5290, NRC.

114. Allyn, "Motion Picture and Theatrical Censorship in Japan," 20–21. Also see CCD's files on Obscene Films and Movie Films (Censorship) of 1948, Box 331-8579, NRC.

115. CIE comment on the newsreel clip on *Kokusai News No. 52,* March 17, 1950, in CIE file, NDL.

116. CIE file on the film, January 12, 1948, NDL.

117. CIE file on the film (its script, examined on February 24, 1948), Box 331-5290, NRC.

118. For example, in the script of *Tokyo File 212* (1951), which was directed by Darryl and Stuart MacGowan, with both Japanese and American actors, and set in Japan, in CIE file on the film, Box 331-5291, NRC. This policy is congruent with the occupation government's censorship policy of Japanese medical journals, as reported by Sey Nishimura at the Association for Asian Studies conference in Philadelphia on March 23, 1985.

119. CIE file on the film (its first script, examined on August 18, 1949, and the second script, on March 29, 1949), Box 331-5290, NRC.

120. CIE file on the film, Box 331-5267, NRC.

121. CIE record of conference between CIE and representatives of Shin-Toho Studio on March 31, 1950, in CIE file, NDL; CIE file on the film (its script, examined in April 1950), Box 331-5296, NRC.

122. CIE file on the film (its synopsis, examined on June 14, 1949), Box 331-5296, NRC.

123. CIE comments on the film on March 26 and May 15, 1951, in CIE file, NDL. On July 24, 1948, CIE's Theater Division had recommended that, although the subject was not completely objectionable, the project of a dramatization of the life of Okichi should be abandoned in favor of another play of merit.

124. CIE comment on the film, December 28, 1948, in CIE file, NDL.

125. CIE file on the film (its revised script, examined on July 24, 1948), Box 331-5267, NRC.

126. CIE file on *Battleship Island* [*Gunkan-to*], whose title was changed twice, first to *Burning Isolated Island* [*Moyuru koto*] and then to *Island with No Green* [*Midori naki shima*] (its script under the second title, examined on August 25, 1948), Box 331-5290, NRC.

127. CIE file on the film (its first script, examined on May 5, 1949), NRC.

128. Press, Pictorial and Broadcasting Division District I, News Agency Section, memorandum for record, December 26 and 28, 1947, on *Mainichi Shimbun*'s ad on December 23, 1947. A very careful reader will be able to tell the slight difference in the size of the first and second film titles in the printed ad. CCD file on British Films, Box 331-8578, NRC.

129. CIE file on the film (its script, examined on March 2, 1949), NDL.

130. CCD memorandum to CIE regarding the request by Daiei Studio to produce a film showing the function of the Civil Affairs Team in Osaka, August 2, 1949, CCD file on Movie Films, Box 331-8579, NRC. Whether or not this film was ever made is not known.

131. CIE record on "Code Interpretation," March 23, 1950, in CIE file, NDL.

132. CIE "Ethical Code for the Improvement of Japanese Feature Motion Pictures," presented July 20, 1948, at Daiei Studio in Kyoto, in CIE file, NDL; CIE record

of conference with Shochiku representatives on *Pygmy* [*Issun boshi*], June 2, 1948, in CIE file, NDL.

133. Komatsu work diary, entries for October 10 and November 13, 1946.

134. CIE comment on the script of *The Sucker,* on July 12, 1948, in CIE file, NDL.

135. CIE file on *Island with No Green* (its script, examined on August 27, 1948), Box 331-5260, NRC.

136. CIE file on the film (its script, examined on September 24, 1949), Box 331-5296, NRC.

137. CIE file on the film (its script, examined on October 30, 1947), Box 331-5290, NRC.

138. CIE comment on the script of *The Woman in the Typhoon Zone* [*Taifu-ken no onna*], July 21, 1948, in CIE file, NDL.

139. CIE file on the film (its first script, examined on August 18, 1949, and the second script, examined on November 29, 1949), Box 331-5290, NRC.

140. CIE file on the film (its script, examined on September 17, 1949, and Public Health and Welfare Section memorandum, October 10, 1949), Box 331-5296, NRC.

141. CIE file on the film (its synopsis, examined by CIE on September 20, 1949, letter from the Motion Picture Association of Japan, September 24, 1949, and its script, examined by CIE on September 26, 1949), Box 331-5290, NRC. Whether the Association volunteered its assistance, or offered it at the request of CIE is not known. The film was retitled *Sea Devil Goes on Land* [*Kaima riku o yuku*] and completed in January 1950. A documentary film researcher stated that the occupation censors liked the film very much. During the screening, they roared with laughter, exclaiming, "We heard that the Japanese do not have a sense of humor, but you do!" The American censors arranged another screening for other staff members who had missed the first one. Osamu Sugawa letter to Reader's Section in *Kinema Jumpo* (June-I, 1987), 190.

142. Boxes 331-5291 and 331-5292. All documents subsequently referred to in this section are from this source, unless otherwise noted.

143. The film was remade by Seijun Suzuki in 1964.

144. CIE note in the file on the film, date unknown, Box 331-5291, NRC.

145. Hiroyuki Soga, "Kaisetsu: Shofu-teki nikugan [An Introduction: Prostitute-like Naked Eye]," in Taijiro Tamura, *Nikutai no mon* [*The Gate of Flesh*] (Tokyo: Chikuma bunko, 1988), 240–242. This is an introductory essay on Taijiro Tamura's literature.

146. Summary of discussion between the producer and CIE officials, September 17, 1948, in the file on the film, Box 331-5292, NRC.

147. Taijiro Tamura, "Nikutai ga ningen de aru [The Flesh Is a Human Being]," (1947), in Tamura, *Nikutai no mon,* 219–221.

148. Her amazing life story did not stop there. She visited Hollywood in 1950, married artist Isamu Noguchi the following year, appeared in American films under the name Shirly Yamaguchi, divorced, and married a Japanese diplomat in 1957. She became a popular television hostess, and entered politics in 1973, when she was elected to the Japanese Diet, representing the conservative Japan Liberal Democratic Party. See Yoshiko Yamaguchi and Sakuya Fujiwara, *Ri Koran: Watakushi no hansho* [*Li Hsiang-lan: My Half Life*] (Tokyo: Shincho-sha, 1987).

149. Interview with the author on February 27, 1986, in Tokyo. Taniguchi said at that time: "When you were in a higher position [as an interrogator], you got to understand their [POWs'] English much better. When it was my turn to be interrogated after the war, I had a hard time understanding them [the interrogators]."

150. Taniguchi interview; Adachi, "Purojusa gunyu-den, no. 9," *Kinema Jumpo* (September-I, 1988), 131–132. There is no record concerning the use of the machine guns in the film in the file on it at NRC. However, an application to CIE for "borrowing and using a heavy machine-gun and blank bullets" for the shooting of the film *Listen to the Voice of the Ocean God* [*Kike wadatsumi no koe*] from May 4 to June 10, 1950, is kept in its file, in Box 331-5298, NRC. The application was examined on May 4, 1950, but it is not clear whether CIE granted the permit. Harry Slott wrote a note that "It was explained to Toyoko Co., that procurement of machine-guns was difficult at this time."

151. Taniguchi interview. Somehow, Taniguchi did not remember the making of *Desertion at Dawn* as particularly difficult. Neither did the film's producer, Tomoyuki Tanaka. According to Tanaka, the occupation government at first did not pass the script, claiming that the film would encourage militarism. Yet after Tanaka insisted that it was an antiwar film, condemning militarism, the censors passed it "unexpectedly smoothly." Adachi, "Purojusa gunya-den, no. 9," 132.

152. On January 24, 1951, the *Asahi* newspaper reported the acquisition of rights to the film by a Hong Kong distributor, and on August 19, 1951, reported its release in Hong Kong in July and the favorable response to it there.

153. Nobuyuki Okuma's review in *Eiga Shunju* (January 1950), cited in Akira Shimizu's review in *Eiga Hyoron* (April 1950), 17–21.

154. Ibid.

155. Adachi, "Purojusa gunyu-den, no. 15," *Kinema Jumpo* (December-I, 1988), 128–131.

156. Yahiro, "Jidaieiga no," 40.

157. In 1728, a young priest named Ten-ichibo claimed that he was the Shogun's illegitimate son, and, together with Iganosuke Yamanouchi, brought together a band of masterless warriors. They were executed by the government. The story soon became a popular legend and began to be used in Kabuki and other entertainment forms. It had already been filmed several times since 1925.

158. Shiro Kido, *Nippon eiga-den: Eiga seisakusha no kiroku* [*The Story of Japanese Cinema: The Record of a Film Producer*] (Tokyo: Bungei shunju-sha, 1956), 240–242.

See also Kazu Adachi, "Purojusa gunyu-den, no. 20," *Kinema Jumpo* (March-I, 1989), 118–121.

159. Masao Takeda, then working for Daiei's planning section, cited in Kusakabe, "Jitsuroku, no. 1," 193; Kisho Ogawa, *Shinema no uramado* [*The Rear Window of Cinema*] (Tokyo: Heibon-sha, 1986), 59–93. *SCAP Non-Military Activities In Japan and Korea* described this film as follows: "a costume play in which a gambling boss reforms and supports the cause of the peasants against the lord who enslaves them." Summation no. 12, September 1946, 122, Law School Library, Columbia University.

160. Joseph L. Anderson and Donald Richie, *The Japanese Film: Art and Industry* (expanded edition) (Princeton, N.J.: Princeton University Press, 1982), 162.

161. Yoshikata Yoda, *Mizoguchi Kenji no hito to geijutsu* [*Kenji Mizoguchi: The Man and His Art*] (Tokyo: Tabata shoten, 1970), 136–140.

162. Yahiro, "Jidaieiga no," 40–41.

163. Press, Pictorial and Broadcasting Division memorandum on "Trends in Japanese Motion Pictures," November 20, 1946, in CCD file on Movie Films, Box 331-8579, NRC.

164. CIE "Memorandum Concerning Old Japanese Costume Films," June 1, 1951, in CIE file, NDL; "Current Topics" column in *Kinema Jumpo* (December-III, 1951), 24. The distribution of newly produced period films during 1950 was as follows:

| Company | Month | | | | | | | | | | | | Total | Rereleases of prewar period films |
	1	2	3	4	5	6	7	8	9	10	11	12		
Shochiku	2	0	1	1	1	0	1	0	0	0	0	1	7	1
Toho	1	0	0	0	1	0	0	1	0	0	0	1	4	4
Daiei	2	0	0	0	0	1	1	1	1	2	1	1	10	0
Shin-Toho	—	—	1	0	0	1	0	1	1	1	1	2	8	1
Toei	0	1	1	2	0	1	1	1	1	1	1	1	11	1

165. Yamamoto, "Katsudo-ya," 193; anonymous studio liaisons, "Senryo-ka no," 21; Yoshinobu Ikeda, "Senryo seisaku no nisan [Two or Three Things about the Occupation Policy]," *Eiga Jiho* (November 1953), 23.

166. Robert Sklar has pointed out that this policy of the American censors seems to have some affinity with practices of the American Motion Picture Production Code. Conversation with the author on July 28, 1987, in New York.

167. Kurosawa, *Something Like*, 111–112, 117–120, 143–144.

168. Interview with the author on August 7, 1984, in Tokyo; Uekusa, *Waga seishun no Kurosawa Akira*, 95. However, a film entitled *The Beaten Lord* [*Nagurareta tonosama*] (produced by Daiei-Kyoto Studio, directed and written by Santaro Maruna, and released on March 13, 1946), has a story extremely similar to that of Uekusa's project, using the Komon Mito character. See *Kinema Jumpo* (June-I, 1946), 45–46; and Anderson and Richie, *Japanese Film*, 175.

According to the memorandum for the record on "Summary of Japanese Pictures on List Suppressed by SCAP Directive of 16 Nov. 1945," November 13, 1946, CCD felt it highly desirable to rerelease three prewar Komon Mito films—in which Lord Mito, the Vice-Shogun, traveled disguised as a commoner "in order to personally inspect and remedy conditions in society"—to promulgate the protagonist's "democratic ideas" among the Japanese people. CCD file on relationship with CIE, Box 331-8579, NRC. (Whether or not these three films were actually rereleased is not known.)

169. Yamamoto, "Katsudo-ya," 191.

170. Interview with Kaneto Shindo by the author on June 25, 1984, in Tokyo.

171. Secret intra-studio memorandum concerning CIE's guidelines, prepared by Hideo Komatsu, in Komatsu private collection.

172. Robert E. Ward, "Conclusion," in Ward and Yoshikazu Sakamoto, eds., *Democratizing Japan: The Allied Occupation* (Honolulu: University of Hawaii Press, 1987), 397.

173. Naozane Fujimoto, "Ichi purojusa no jijoden [A Producer's Autobiography]," in Hotsuki Ozaki, ed., *Purojusa jinsei: Fujimoto Naozane eiga ni kakeru [A Producer's Life: Naozane Fujimoto Challenges Film]* (Tokyo: Toho Printing, 1981), 183–186; Kaneto Shindo, *Shosetsu Tanaka Kinuyo [A Novel: Kinuyo Tanaka]* (Tokyo: Yomiuri shimbun-sha, 1982), 201–202; Yamamoto, "Katsudo-ya," 192; So Yoshiya, "Senryo seisaku to Toho sogi [The Occupation Policy and the Toho Strikes]," in *Eiga Geijutsu* (August 1976), 36.

Kokichi Takakuwa, in his book on the occupation censorship of Japanese newspapers, writes that Nisei censors often could not understand rhetorical phrases, and Japanese newspaper editors tried to paraphrase them to make them simpler. Takakuwa, *Makkaasaa no shimbun ken'etsu: Keisai kinshi sakujo ni natta shimbun kiji [MacArthur's Newpaper Censorship: Suppressed or Deleted Newspaper Articles]* (Tokyo: Yomiuri shimbun-sha, 1984), 26–27.

174. Frank Baba's comment on the author's paper on occupation film policy, delivered at a conference on "The Occupation: Its Impact on Arts and Culture," October 18–19, 1984, at the MacArthur Memorial, Norfolk, Va.

175. For example, Yahiro, "Jidaigeki no," 42; Kusakabe, "Jitsuroku, no. 1," (which is subtitled "The Film Industry Abused by Delinquent Nisei"), 196; Fujimoto, "Ichi purojusa no," 185–186.

176. Allyn, "Motion Picture and Theatrical Censorship in Japan," 19–20.

177. The day before Konno was to be sent back to the United States, he disappeared and is believed to have been living in Japan since then. Kusakabe, "Jitsuroku, no. 1," 196; Komatsu, "Sengo eiga shiriizu, no. 2," *Tokyo-eki* (n.d.), 66–67; Fujimoto, "Ichi purojusa," 186–187. Fujimoto wrote that this incident took place in March 1946, but the CCD documents prove that Konno was working until March 1947.

178. CCD Postal Station Comment Sheet, quoted in CCD memorandum, October 7, 1946, in CCD file on Relation with CIE, Box 331-8579, NRC.

179. CCD file on Relations with CIE, Box 331-8579, NRC.

180. Ibid.

181. Conde in anonymous studio liaisons, "Senryo-ka no," 17; Slott in Yahiro, "Jidaigeki no," 42; Gercke and Konno in Komatsu, "Sengo eiga shiriizu, no. 2," 66–67; Konno in Kusakabe, "Jitsuroku, no. 1," 196. We must be careful in evaluating these allegations to the extent that they may be based on gossip.

182. Iwasaki, *Senryo sareta*, 78; Shindo interview; conversation with Hajime Takizawa on July 30, 1984, in Kyoto; Kusakabe, "Jitsuroku, no. 1," 196.

183. Ibid.

184. Komatsu work diary; Kusakabe, "Jitsuroku, no. 1," 196.

185. Yamamoto, "Katsudo-ya," 193.

186. Iwasaki, *Senryo sareta*, 83.

187. Anonymous studio liasons, "Senryo-ka no," 19–20.

188. Kenji Mizoguchi in the discussion on "Seisaku kiko no shorai [The Future of the Production Structure]," *Kinema Jumpo* (November-I, 1947), 55.

189. Anonymous studio liaisons, "Senryo-ka no," 19–20; interview with Harry Slott by Kazuko Komori in *Eiga Sekai* (June 1948), 8–10. John Allyn had worked for the Press, Pictorial and Broadcasting Division of CCD in the Osaka branch from September 1945 to the end of 1948, and was then transferred to Tokyo to take charge of the theater section for all of Japan until CCD relinquished control over civil censorship in 1946. He had been a specialist in theater. Although his responsibilities included film censorship, his name has not been mentioned in the memoirs of Japanese filmmakers. See his "Motion Picture and Theatrical Censorship in Japan," 14–26.

190. The former group includes Kido, *Nippon eiga-den*, 210–211; Matsuo Kishi, *Jinbutsu Nihon Eiga-shi [Japanese Cinema History Through Personalities]* (Tokyo: Debiddo-sha, 1970), 290; anonymous studio liaisons, "Senryo-ka no," 15–16; Komatsu, "Sengo eiga shiriizu, no. 1," 21; and Yamamoto, "Katsudo-ya," 191–192. The latter group includes Kusakabe, "Jitsuroku, no. 1," 194–195; Fujimoto, "Ichi puro-jusa," 187–188; Iwasaki, *Senryo sareta*, 50–52; and Yoshiya, "Senryo seisaku to," 35–36.

191. CCD memorandum, August 20, 1946, in CCD file on "This Year 1945–1946," Box 331-8580, NRC.

192. Ogawa, *Shinema no uramado*, 72. According to Ogawa, Mihata was working as an occupation censor while operating his own film distributing business in Hawaii. This led Ogawa to suspect him of a conflict of interest.

193. Walker's employment at the censorship office appalled a few Japanese filmmakers, because he had been regarded before the war as a "delinquent associated with the fringe of the Japanese film industry" (ibid., 63–64; Yamamoto, "Katsudo-ya," 189). Ogawa stated that Walker was a Dutch national.

194. For example, Ikeda, "Senryo seisaku no," 23; and Yamamoto, "Katsudo-ya," 193.

195. CCD memorandum on "Censorship of Films by CIE," March 13, 1946, in CCD file on Relations with CIE, Box 331-8579, NRC.

196. Takakuwa, *Makkaasaa no,* 33.

CHAPTER 3

1. Interview with Eugene Dooman by Beate Gordon on the occupation, for the Oral History Research Center at Columbia University in May 1962, in Litchfield, Ct.; interview with Joseph Ballantine by Beate Gordon for the same project, on April 28, 1961, in New York.

2. Akira Iwasaki, *Senryo sareta sukuriin* [*The Occupied Screen*] (Tokyo: Shin-Nihon shuppan-sha, 1975), 86; Kiyoko Takeda, *The Dual-Image of the Japanese Emperor* (London: Macmillan Education, 1988), 8–9; Justin Williams, Sr., *Japan's Political Revolution under MacArthur: A Participant's Account* (Athens, Georgia: University of Georgia Press, 1979), 16–17; Ballantine interview. Ballantine argued that, once the occupation started, only the USSR (and not in fact China) continued to demand that the emperor be treated as a war criminal. According to Takeda (pp. 54–66), it was Australia who was most vocal regarding the abolition of the imperial system.

3. Williams, *Japan's Political Revolution,* 18; U.S. Department of State: The Acting Political Advisor in Japan [Acheson] to President Truman, November 5, 1945; U.S. Department of State, *Foreign Relations of the United States, 1945: The Far East* (Washington, D.C.: U.S. Government Printing Office, n.d.), 825–827, included in Jon Livingston, Joe Moore, and Felicia Oldfather, eds., *Postwar Japan: 1945 to the Present* (New York: Pantheon, 1973), 12–13. However, Makoto Iokibe mentions that Elmer Davis tried to separate the emperor from the militarists and announced as early as December 1942 that the emperor had nothing to do with the militarists and that to attack him would only make the Japanese indignant. Makoto Iokibe, *Beigun no Nippon senryo seisaku* [*The U.S. Army Occupation Policy for Japan*] (Tokyo: Chuo koron-sha, 1985), 1:273.

4. Ibid., vols. 1 and 2.

5. Akira Irie, *Power and Culture: The Japanese-American War 1941–1945* (Cambridge, Massachusetts: Harvard University Press, 1981), 263.

6. Masataka Kosaka, *A History of Postwar Japan* (Tokyo: Kodansha International, 1972), 40.

7. However, *Documentary Film Classics Produced by the United States Government* (Washington, D.C.: National Audio Visual Center, n.d.), 28, implies that the film was briefly released: "the abrupt cessation of the war in the Pacific resulted in the hasty withdrawal of *Know Your Enemy: Japan* and it was never widely seen."

8. Erik Barnouw, *Documentary: A History of the Non-Fiction Film* (New York: Oxford University Press, 1974), 161. Jay Leyda gives another reason for the abandonment of *Know Your Enemy: Japan*: "after more than a year under the direction of Joris Ivens, they found that the [archive] materials could not be shaped into what they wanted to say about this enemy. Perhaps the enemy films (chiefly fictional) which had been confiscated in California and Hawaii were too limited in their coverage of Japanese life, or perhaps the enemy's material resisted being turned against them; the project was not completed for release." Jay Leyda, *Films Beget Films: A Study of the Compilation Film* (New York: Hill and Wang, 1971), 59.

9. Nagisa Oshima, *Taikenteki sengo eizo-ron* [*The Theory of the Image of Postwar Cinema Based on Personal Experience*] (Tokyo: Asahi shimbun-sha, 1975), 22–23.

10. Kokichi Takakuwa, *Makkaasaa no shimbun ken'etsu: Kiesai kinshi sakujo ni natta shimbun kiji* [*MacArthur's Newspaper Censorship: Suppressed or Deleted Newspaper Articles*] (Tokyo: Yomiuri shimbun-sha, 1984), 45–47; Eiji Takemae, *GHQ* (Tokyo: Iwanami shinsho, 1983), 155.

11. It originally appeared in *Sunday Mainichi,* January 23, 1972, as cited in Iwasaki, *Senryo sareta,* 86–87; Takemae, *GHQ,* 164.

12. Kenzo Uchida mentions that only sixteen Japanese were allowed to meet General MacArthur during his administration, citing Shukan Shincho, ed., *Makkaasaa no Nippon* [*MacArthur's Japan*] (Tokyo: Shincho-sha, 1970). Uchida, "Makkaasaa to Yoshida Shigeru [MacArthur and Shigeru Yoshida]," in Rinjiro Sodei, ed., *Sekaishi no naka no Nippon senryo* [*The Occupation of Japan in World History*] (Tokyo: Nippon hyoron-sha, 1985), 166.

13. Naruhiko Higashikuni, a relative of the royal family, and Kijuro Shidehara, an aristocrat, respectively and briefly became premiers after the war until May 1946, when Yoshida became the first premier chosen in a nationwide election. In May 1947, Tetsu Katayama led the first and only Socialist government in the history of Japan, which did not last long. Hitoshi Ashida succeeded to the post the following February. In October 1948 he was again succeeded by Yoshida, who retained his office until December 1954.

14. The amazing intimacy that the Japanese people expressed in their letters to General MacArthur during his administration of the occupation (he is estimated to have received some fifty thousand) is discussed and analyzed in Rinjiro Sodei, *Haikei Makkaasaa Gensui sama* [*Dear General MacArthur*] (Tokyo: Otsuki shoten, 1985).

15. The Operation of Military and Civil Censorship file, USAFE/SWAP/AFPAC(FEC), *Documentary Appendices* no. 36, *Reporting Guide* of the CCD, Press, Pictorial and Broadcasting Division (August 15, 1949), MacArthur Memorial Archives, Norfolk, Va.

16. Telephone interview with the author on January 9, 1985, in New York.

17. Takemae, *GHQ,* 155.

18. Douglas MacArthur, *Statement on the Japanese Draft Constitution* (March 6, 1946), U.S. Department of State, *Foreign Relations of the United States 1946: The Far East* (Washington, D.C.: U.S. Government Printing Office, n.d.), 132–133, included in Jon Livingston et al., eds., *Postwar Japan*, 17–18.

19. Mark Gayn, *Japan Diary* (New York: William Sloan Associates, 1948), 125–127.

20. T. A. Bisson writes: "On November 3, 1946, when the new Constitution was promulgated, the cheers of the crowds assembled in the Imperial plaza were raised to the emperor rather than to the constitution—an omen of the future if reactionary forces should succeed in establishing control over the new regime." *Prospects for Democracy in Japan* (New York: Macmillan, 1949), 25.

21. Gayn, *Japan Diary*, 261.

22. "Fumio Kamei" in *Nihon eiga kantoku zenshu* [*The Encyclopedia of Japanese Film Directors*] (Tokyo: Kinema Jumpo-sha, 1976) 124; Fumio Kamei, *Tatakau eiga: Dokyumentarisuto no Showa-shi* [*Films at the Front: The Showa History of a Documentarist*] (Tokyo: Iwanami shinsho, 1989), 11–19; Shinkichi Noda, *Nihon dokyumentarii eiga zenshi* [*The Comprehensive History of the Japanese Documentary Film*] (Tokyo: Shakai shiso-sha, 1984), 40.

23. Ibid., 60–67.

24. Interview with the author on July 6, 1984, in Tokyo; Noda, *Nihon dokyumentarii*, 68; "Kamei Fumio no kataru hiroku: Senchu sengo eiga-shi [The Secret History Told by Fumio Kamei: The Wartime and Postwar Film History]" [a discussion by Fumio Kamei, Tetsuro Hatano, Susumu Kosaka, and Toru Ogawa], *Eiga Geijutsu* (July/August 1976), 79.

25. Fumio Kamei, "Watashi no 'Senso to heiwa' [My 'War and Peace']," *Iwanami Hall* (February 1, 1972), 11; "Kamei Fumio no kataru hiroku," 80; Shojiro Yabushita, "Nijjuseiki no koseki [The Twentieth Century Path]," no. 1594, *Asahi Shimbun*, November 20, 1985.

26. See Tadao Sato, *Kinema to hosei: Nicchu eiga zenshi* [*Cinema and Gunfire: The Prehistory of Japanese and Chinese Cinema*] (Tokyo: Livro Port, 1985); Takeshi Yamaguchi, *Maboroshi no Kinema Man-ei: Amakasu Masahiko to katsudo-ya gunzo* [*Manchurian Cinema in a Dream: Masahiko Amakasu and a Group of Movie-Makers*] (Tokyo: Heibon-sha, 1989); Yoshiko Yamaguchi, *Ri Koran: Watakushi no hansho* [*Li Hsiang-lan: My Half Life*] (Tokyo: Shincho-sha, 1987).

27. Iwasaki, *Senryo sareta*, 35, 42–45; Jun'ichiro Tanaka, *Nihon eiga hattatsushi* [*The History of the Development of Japanese Cinema*] (Tokyo: Chuo koron-sha, 1976), 392.

28. Iwasaki, *Senryo sareta*, 3:59–67, 70–71. This holiday was officially abolished by the Diet soon after, but the Japanese government revived it as the "nation's birthday" in 1969.

29. Ibid., 63–64.

30. *Asahi Shimbun,* February 9, 1946.

31. *Asahi Shimbun,* February 12, 1946.

32. Iwasaki, *Senryo sareta,* 64.

33. The treatment of this imperial national holiday matched that accorded, for example, songs about the Japanese Empire and the emperor's birthday, as well as poems by the Meiji emperor and empress that had been set to music: all were left untouched. On the other hand, songs with militaristic and imperialistic subjects were censored from the same textbook, although the deletions were quite arbitrary. Kikuji Nakamura, "Soron: Haisen to kyokasho [General Theory: The Defeat of War and Textbooks]," in *Monbusho chosaku sengo kyokasho kaisetsu* [*The Ministry of Education's Postwar Textbook Guidance*] [Tokyo: Ozora-sha, 1984], 23 and 26, cited by Yasuo Akatsuka, "Issatsu no 'suminuri' ongaku kyokasho kara [From a 'Blackened' Music Textbook]," in *Senryoshi Kenkyukai News* [*Newsletter of the Japan Association of Studies of the History of the Occupation*], 62 (June 1, 1985), 2–3.

34. This report translated the Japanese title as *Gangster Period,* but *The Dark Period* is a more accurate translation.

35. Memo from Chief, Press, Pictorial and Broadcasting Division, April 30, 1946, in "The Japanese Tragedy" file, RG-331, Box 331-8579, National Records Center, Suitland, Md. (hereafter NRC).

36. Iwasaki, *Senryo sareta,* 76; Yoshio Miyajima, his serialized memoirs, no. 32, *Kinema Jumpo* (July-I, 1985), 155.

37. Kajiro Yamamoto, "Katsudo-ya bifun-roku [The Record of the Slight Anger of a Movie-Maker]," *Bungei Shunju* (June 1952), 191–192. Naozane Fujimoto mentioned that this film led Conde to quit CIE: "Ichi purojusa no jijoden [A Producer's Autobiography]," in Hotsuki Ozaki, ed., *Purojusa jinsei: Fujimoto Naozane eiga ni kakeru* [*A Producer's Life: Naozane Fujimoto Challenges Film*] (Tokyo: Toho Printing, 1981), 187–188.

38. William Coughlin, *Conquered Press* (Palo Alto: Pacific Books, 1952), 45.

39. Letter to the author, February 27, 1986.

40. Ibid.

41. Shojiro Yabushita at a meeting with director Fumio Kamei, documentarist Yoshio Tanigawa, and the author at Kamei's office in Tokyo on January 31, 1986.

42. Kamei, ibid.

43. "The Japanese Tragedy" file, Box 331-8579, NRC.

44. Tokumitsu letter.

45. An unidentified and undated English-language newspaper article written by Peter Kalischer of United Press reports that *The Dark Age* contains a portion of the American documentary *Appointment in Tokyo* showing atrocities committed by Japanese troops in Manila. "The Japanese Tragedy" file, Box 331-8579, NRC.

46. Kamei interview; Kamei at the meeting of January 31, 1986. Conde's special attention to the Japanese army's campaign in the Philippines is evident in his

memorandum to the Chief of CIE dated May 6, 1946. He found one of the wartime Nichi-ei newsreels, *Victory Song of the Orient* [*Toyo no gaika*], particularly interesting for its "informational value." CIE Report of Conferences, May 1946, Box 331-5130, NRC.

47. Yutaka Yoshimi quoted in Yabushita, "Nijjuseiki no," no. 1506, *Asahi Shimbun* (November 23, 1985); Yabushita at the meeting of January 31, 1986.

48. Leyda, *Films Beget Films,* 38–39.

49. The description of the film is based on the script of *The Japanese Tragedy* prepared by Yoshio Tanigawa, a videocassette provided by Ned Loader, and the author's own notes. The English translation is from the script prepared by Nichi-ei and submitted to the occupation censors.

50. "The Japanese Tragedy" file, Box 331-8579, NRC; Iwasaki, *Senryo sareta,* 77–78.

51. GHQ/USAFPAC Checksheet from K.C. to R.H.K., June 13, 1946, in "The Japanese Tragedy" file, Box 331-8579, NRC. K.C. reported that "other portions of the first script were ordered deleted, but then apparently allowed to stand in the second script."

52. Ibid. The Operation of Military and Civil Censorship file, USAFE/SWAP/AFPAC(FEC), Documentary Appendices no. 36, *Reporting Guide* of the CCD, Press, Pictorial and Broadcasting Division (August 15, 1949), MacArthur Memorial Archives, Norfolk, Va.

53. GHQ/USAFPAC Checksheet from K.C. to R.H.K., June 13, 1946, in "The Japanese Tragedy" file, Box 331-8579, NRC.

54. Professor Robert M. Spaulding of Oklahoma State University, who was working at CCD during the occupation, was kind enough to identify "R.H.K." as Richard H. Kunzman and "W.B.P." as William Benjamin Putnam. However, he does not recall any censors whose initials were "K.C." and "W.S.W." in the file for *The Japanese Tragedy.* Letter to the author, November 12, 1985. The author was unsuccessful in her attempts to reach Putnam, Rufus S. Bratton, Kunzman, John J. Costello, Walter Y. Mihata, and Arthur Mori, who were all working at CCD at the time when *The Japanese Tragedy* was banned.

55. GHQ/USAPAC Checksheet from K.C. to R.H.K., June 13, 1946, in "The Japanese Tragedy" file, Box 331-8579, NRC.

56. Iwasaki, *Senryo sareta,* 78. Iwasaki mentions that Nichi-ei newsreels proved to be particularly unpopular among conservative and feudalistic spectators in local areas. Interview with Iwasaki in *Eiga Shimbun,* May 25, 1946.

57. Weekly Report of CIE, Box 331-5118, NRC. Between the week of July 12, 1946, and the week of July 19, 1946, Conde seems to have officially left CIE. From the report for the week of July 19, it is evident that William Myers, the Acting Chief of the Motion Picture and Theatrical Unit, had assumed Conde's duties.

58. Memorandum from J.J.C[ostello], Chief, Press, Pictorial and Broadcasting Division to CCD, September 2, 1946.

59. Iwasaki, *Senryo sareta*, 78–79. A Nichi-ei advertisement on the back cover of the July 1946 issue of *Eiga Seisaku* confirms that, along with a few other newsreels, *The Japanese Tragedy* was being shown.

60. Kamei interview.

61. *Tokyo Shimbun,* July 25, 1946, in "The Japanese Tragedy" file, Box 331-8579, NRC.

62. *Asahi Shimbun,* August 5, 1946.

63. Iwasaki, *Senryo sareta*, 78–79.

64. *Nikkan Mezamashi Tsushin* (July, no. 61) in "The Japanese Tragedy" file, Box 331-8579, NRC. The show at this hall seems to have been canceled, because the only Tokyo showing mentioned by Iwasaki and Kamei took place at a small theater attached to the Traffic Culture Museum in the downtown area. Iwasaki, *Senryo sareta*, 90–91, and Kamei interview.

65. Iwasaki, *Senryo sareta*, 80–84.

66. This account is questionable because, according to CIE documents and Jiro Shirasu's description of Conde, it is more likely that Conde had already left the section by the beginning of August, when the banning of *The Japanese Tragedy* occurred.

67. Tokumitsu letter.

68. Iwasaki, *Senryo sareta*, 90–92. On the other hand, Coughlin writes that the film was withdrawn "due to the poor public response." *Conquered Press,* 45.

69. Gayn, *Japan Diary,* 306–310.

70. Ibid., 304–305.

71. Ibid., 306–310.

72. Brief to Gen. W.[Willoughby] from Tait, August 2, 1946; memorandum to Col. Wood from T. P. Davis, August 2, 1946, in "The Japanese Tragedy" file, Box 331-8579, NRC.

73. Iwasaki claims that Baker was, among the occupation officials, the closest to and a protector of Ando. *Senryo sareta,* 231.

74. Davis memorandum.

75. Ibid.

76. Memorandum from J.J.C. of Press, Pictorial and Broadcasting Division to CCD, August 7, 1946, in "The Japanese Tragedy" file, Box 331-8579, NRC.

77. Memorandum from T. P. Davis to Col. Wood, August 6, 1946, in "The Japanese Tragedy" file, Box 331-8579, NRC.

78. Report from W.S.W. to Chief, Civil Intelligence Section, G-2, August 7, 1946, in "The Japanese Tragedy" file, Box 331-8579, NRC.

79. Memorandum from W.B.P. to CCD, Civil Intelligence Section, August 9, 1946, in "The Japanese Tragedy" file, Box 331-8579, NRC.

80. Brief from W.S.W. to Col. Bratton, August 10, 1946, in "The Japanese Tragedy" file, Box 331-8579, NRC.

81. Checksheet from Civil Intelligence Section to CCD, August 12, 1946, signed as W.S.W. and then crossed by a diagonal line with unidentifiable letters.

82. Iwasaki, *Senryo sareta,* 90–92.

83. Interview with Katsuro Nakamura by the author on August 15, 1989, in Tokyo.

84. Letter from Military Intelligence Section General Staff, Civil Intelligence Section, Civil Censorship Section, Press, Pictorial and Broadcasting Division, District I, to Nippon Eiga-sha, August 15, 1946, signed by Richard H. Kunzman, Censor in Charge, in "The Japanese Tragedy" file, Box 331-8579, NRC.

85. Brief from CCD to Civil Intelligence Section, G-2, August 19, 1946; Investigation Report of *The Japanese Tragedy* from Walter Y. Mihata to Head, Motion Picture Department, October 21, 1946, in "The Japanese Tragedy" file, Box 331-8579, NRC.

86. Kamei at the meeting of January 31, 1986.

87. Roger Buckley, *Occupation Diplomacy: Britain, the United States and Japan 1945–1952* (New York: Cambridge University Press, 1982), 118, 245.

88. Mihata Investigation Report, November 6, 1946, in "The Japanese Tragedy" file, Box 331-8579, NRC.

89. Ibid.

90. Tokumitsu letter; Kamei at the meeting of January 31, 1986.

91. Memorandum for Record from J.J.C. to all Press, Pictorial and Broadcasting Division Stations, August 20, 1946, in "The Japanese Tragedy" file, Box 331-8579, NRC.

92. Tokumitsu letter.

93. *Shukan Eiga Times* (second week of September 1946), 2, Prange Collection, McKeldin Library.

94. Tokumitsu letter.

95. Memorandum for Record from J.J.C. to CCD, September 2, 1946, in "The Japanese Tragedy" file, Box 331-8579, NRC.

96. Letter from C. A. Willoughy, Brigadier General, GSB, Assistant Chief of Staff, G-2, to Nippon Eiga-sha, August 22, 1946, in "The Japanese Tragedy" file, Box 331-8579, NRC.

97. *Kinema Jumpo* (September-I, 1946), 44, Prange Collection, McKeldin Library.

98. Kamei interview.

99. Fumio Kamei, "Sutaa to tenno [Stars and the Emperor]," *Eiga to Yomimono* (June 1949), 14–15.

100. "'MacArthur's Children': An Interview with Masahiro Shinoda" by the author, *Cineaste* 14(3) (February 1986), 51.

101. Sodei, *Haikei Makkaasaa Gensui,* 73.; Takeda, *Dual-Image,* 122.

102. Tokumitsu letter.

103. Interview with Professor Herbert Passin by the author on December 14, 1984, in New York (Passin was working in the Public Opinion and Sociological Research Division of CIE); Theodore Cohen [who was at the Labor Division], *Nihon senryo kakumei: GHQ kara no shogen* [*The Third Turn: MacArthur, the Americans and the Rebirth of Japan*], translated by Masaomi Omae (Tokyo: TBS Britannica, 1983), 181; Richard L. G. Deverall [who was at the Labor Education Division], *The Great Seduction: Red China's Drive to Bring Free Japan Behind the Iron Curtain* (Tokyo: International Literature Printing, 1953), 71.

104. Coughlin, *Conquered Press,* 125–126. Coughlin mentions that newsmen protested against Conde's deportation.

105. This list consists of both leftist writers (not necessarily Communist Party members) and rather nationalistic ones. Writer Yasunari Kawabata, for instance, must belong to the latter category. Documentary Appendices, Press, Pictorial and Broadcasting Division, *Reporting Guide* (August 15, 1949), MacArthur Memorial Archives, Norfolk, Va.

106. At the National Film Center in Tokyo on August 31, 1984. This screening was attended by Kamei, Yoshio Tanigawa, Keinosuke Uekusa (screenplay writer), Akira Shimizu (film critic), and others.

107. Kamei at the meeting of January 31, 1986.

108. These two films by Kamei were included in the "Japan at War" film series organized by the Japan Society, New York. In 1990, a Kamei retrospective was organized at the Hong Kong International Film Festival.

CHAPTER 4

1. Interview with Yumeji Tsukioka by Haruo Mizuno, *Kinema Jumpo* (February-I, 1985), 92.

2. Kiyohiko Ushihara, *Kiyohiko eiga-fu 50-nen* [*The Fifty-Year Film Story of Kiyohiko*] (Tokyo: Kagamiura shobo, 1968), 237–243.

3. "Eiga-kai kyutenkai no GHQ seisaku [GHQ Policy Drastically Changing the Film Industry]," *Yomiuri Shimbun,* September 20, 1982; Kazu Adachi, "Purojusa gunyu-den [The Group Portrait of Producers], no. 7," *Kinema Jumpo* (August-I, 1988), 135–136.

4. *Film Center* no. 80 (Retrospective of Tadashi Imai) (Tokyo: National Film Center, 1984), 6.

5. Flyer on *The Morning of the Osone Family* issued by the Kyoto Prefectural Film Library and reproduced in the pamphlet of the summer seminar on postwar democratic films, sponsored by the Japan Society of Image Arts and Science, Kansai Branch, July 28–30, 1984; Adachi, "Purojusa gunyu-den, no. 4," *Kinema Jumpo* (June-II, 1988), 132.

6. Kinoshita quoted ibid.

7. David Conde, Naozane Fujimoto, and Akira Iwasaki, "Watashi ga shido shita Nippon eiga to no saikai [Reencounter with Japanese Cinema That I Directed]," *Kinema Jumpo* (November-I, 1964), 27–28. Takeo Ito, "Sengo Nihon eiga no koryu to Toho sogi [The Prosperity of Postwar Japanese Film and the Toho Strikes]," in Saburo Ienaga, ed., *Showa no sengo-shi: Senryo to saisei [The Postwar History of the Showa Era: The Occupation and Revival]* (Tokyo: Yubun-sha, 1976), 228.

8. Ichiro Yuki, *Jitsuroku: Kamata koshinkyoku [Document: the Kamata March]* (Tokyo: KK Best Books, 1985), 167–176.

9. For an excellent cultural analysis of Japanese attitudes toward kissing, see "The Japanese Kiss" in Donald Richie, *Walkman, Manga and Society: Essays on Contemporary Japanese Culture,* Hisao Kanaseki and Yuichiro Takahashi, eds. (Tokyo: Kirihara shoten, 1989), 52–58.

10. *SCAP Non-Military Activities, Summation* (no. 8, May 1946, 244) describes this film as "a light comedy revolving around a father's attempt to marry his daughter to the son of his employer."

11. Hideo Komatsu, "Sengo eiga shiriizu [Postwar Film Series], no. 1," *Tokyo-eki* (n.d.), 21.

12. Heinosuke Gosho's *Girls of Izu [Izu no musumetachi]*, released on August 30, 1945, was completed around the time the war ended. Santaro Marune's *Bride's Story [Hanayome Taikoki]*, released on the same day, had been completed before August 15, and was to be added to the banned film list the following November. *Separation Is Also Pleasure [Wakare mo tanoshi]*, released on September 13, as discussed earlier in this chapter, was based on wartime planning. *Breeze* was the first postwar film based on postwar planning; see Yasushi Harada, "Senryo-ka no Nihon eiga, Ringo-en no fukko: Sasaki Yasushi ron [The Japanese Cinema under the Occupation, the Revival of the Apple Orchard: On Yasushi Sasaki]," *Eiga-shi Kenkyu* 1 (1973), 49–56; Adachi, "Purojusa gunyu-den, no. 3," *Kinema Jumpo* (June-I, 1988), 119–122.

13. Yasushi Sasaki quoted in Tamio Koike, "Geino-shi o aruku [Tracing the History of Entertainment]," *Asahi Shimbun*, January 4, 1986.

14. Toru Ogawa, "Shisetsu: Sengo Nihon eiga-shi [Private Theory: The History of Postwar Japanese Cinema]," in *Eiga Geijutsu* (February 1980), 2.

15. Jun'ichiro Tanaka, "Nihon eiga sengo-shi [Japanese Postwar Cinema History]," *Kinema Jumpo* (October-III, 1964), 49.

16. Walter Sheldon, *The Honorable Conquerors* (New York: Macmillan, 1965), 270.

17. Ogawa, "Shisetsu," 2.

18. "Michiko Ikuno," in *Nihon eiga haiyu zenshu: Joyu hen [Japanese Film Actress Encyclopedia]* (Tokyo: Kinema Jumpo-sha, 1980), 61; *Sutaa meikan [Stars Album]* (Sappro: Geibu-sha, 1949), 46.

19. "Wata to seppun [Cotton and Kiss]," *Eiga Fan* (July 1946), 33; Shin'ichi Washizu, "Eiga no kissu to rabu shiin [Kissing in Film and Love Scenes]," *Eiga Yomimono* (October 1948), 24–26.

20. This was not, however, the first Japanese film title to include the word *seppun* [kissing]. In 1935, Keisuke Sasaki had made *Kissing Crossroad* [*Seppun jujiro*] for Shochiku Studio.

21. *SCAP Non-Military Activities, Summation* (no. 8, May 1946, 244) describes this film as "a light picture with a touch of comedy about an architect, an inventor, a poet and their girls."

22. Joseph L. Anderson and Donald Richie, *The Japanese Film: Art and Industry* (expanded edition) (Princeton. N.J.: Princeton University Press, 1982), 176.

23. Kajiro Yamamoto, "Katsudo-ya bifun-roku [The Record of the Slight Anger of a Movie-Maker]," in *Bungei Shunju* (June 1952), 191.

24. *Stars and Stripes* (May 18, 1946), in CCD file on Japanese Films, Box 331-8578, National Records Center, Suitland, Md. (hereafter NRC).

25. Kyoichiro Nambu, "Genba sengo-shi: Gosshipu de tsuzuru katsudo-ya no ayumi [The Progress of Movie-Makers Written in Gossip], no. 2," *Tokyo Times*, March 13, 1972. Nambu further claims that it was actually Yuzo Kawashima's *Laughing Treasure Ship* [*Warau takarabune*] (1946, produced by Shochiku Studio) that included the first kissing scene. However, no other source supports this claim.

26. *Sutaa meikan*, 46.

27. Sheldon, *Honorable Conquerors*, 270.

28. *Stars and Stripes* (n.d.) cited in "Eiga to kisu to kankyaku to [Film, Kissing and Audience]," *Kyushu Eiga Times* (June 11, 1946), 1.

29. *Asahi Shimbun*, May 25, 1946.

30. Tadashi Iijima in *Eiga Shunju* (August 1946), quoted in his *Nihon eiga-shi* [*Japanese Cinema History*] (Tokyo: Hakusui-sha, 1955), 2:152–153.

31. Ichiro Ueno, "Shusengo no Nippon eiga o kaerimite [Reflecting on the Postwar Japanese Cinema]," *Eiga Hyoron* (February 1947), 41.

32. Iijima, *Eiga Shunju*; Seiji Togo, "Ren'ai zakko [Thoughts on Love]," *Cinema Graphic* (May 1947), 5.

33. *Eiga engeki jiten* [*Encyclopedia of Film and Theater*] (Tokyo: Jiji tsushin-sha, 1947), 50. (The author is unknown.) Similar critical opinions include Hideo Tsumura in the current cultural column in *Eiga Geijutsu* (September 1947), 20; "Aijo wa utsukushii hazuda [Love Must Be Beautiful]," *Eiga Goraku* (December 1947), 6–7; Masaya Sugano, "Eiga ni arawareta seppun no mondai [Problems of Kissings in Films]," *Daiei Journal* (1948), 16–17; Kotaro Kiwa, "Rabu shiin manwa [Funny Story of Love Scenes]," *Eiga Yomimono* (May 1948), 18–20; Shokichi Mogami, "Eiga kansho no tebiki [Guidance for Seeing Films]," *Eiga Yomimono* (September 1948), 36–38; and Kentaro Moto, "Eiga to erochishizumu [Film and Eroticism]," *Eiga Shimpo* (May 1948), 1. After a quarter century, Yasushi Harada argued that these kissing films,

imposed by the occupation forces, could not genuinely liberate Japanese thinking regarding sexual expression. See Harada, "Senryo-ka no," 54–56.

34. *Yomiuri Shimbun,* August 14, 1946.

35. Bunroku Shishi, "Seppun [Kissing]," *Asahi Shimbun,* August 1, 1948.

36. Iijima, *Nihon eiga-shi,* 153; Anderson and Richie introduce this episode as "one of the most ingenious of the postwar kisses" (*Japanese Film,* 176). *SCAP Non-Military Activities, Summation* (no. 10, July 1946, 249) describes the film as "the story of a young actress's rise to stardom in the new theater movement."

37. Terry Ramsaye, *A Million and One Nights* (New York: Simon & Schuster, 1926), 1:257–261, 273. For the responses to this film, see also Charles Musser, *Before the Nickelodeon: Edwin S. Porter and the Edison Manufacturing Company* (Berkeley and Los Angeles: University of California Press, 1991), 65, 80–84, 89.

38. Richie, "The Japanese Kiss," 54.

39. *Asahi Shimbun,* March 24, 1946.

40. In the reader letters section in *Eiga* (November 1946), 26, Prange Collection, McKeldin Library.

41. Jun Izawa, review of the film in *Asahi Shimbun,* December 14, 1947.

42. Akira Shimizu, review of the film in *Eiga Hyoron* (February 1948), 23–24; similar praises include Washizu, "Eiga no kissu to," 26, and *Sutaa meikan.*

43. "Uwasa no shinso-bako [The Truth of Rumors]," *Eiga Bunko* (October 1947), 24–26; *Sutaa meikan,* 46.

44. Setsuko Hara interviewed by *Stars and Stripes* (n.d.), quoted in *Eiga Fan* (January 1947), 3.

45. Yoshiko Yamaguchi, *Ri Koran: Watashi no hansho* [*Li Hsiang-lan: My Half Life*] (Tokyo: Shincho-sha, 1987), 346.

46. Yoshiko Yamaguchi, "Eiga to seppun [Film and Kissing]," *Eiga Sekai* (August 1948), 22–23.

47. See Akira Yamamoto, "Kasutori Zasshi," in Ienaga, *Showa no sengo-shi,* 241–252; and Jay Rubin, "From Wholesomeness to Decadence: The Censorship of Literature under the Allied Occupation," *Journal of Japanese Studies,* 2(1) (Winter 1985), 71–103.

48. Yamamoto, "Kasutori Zasshi," 248–249.

49. Hotsuki Ozaki, "Sei-fuzoku no kaiho [The Liberation of Sexual Customs]," in Ienaga, *Showa no sengo-shi,* 259–261. The film *The Gate of Flesh* has been remade three times: by Seijun Suzuki in 1964, by Shogoro Nishimura in 1977, and by Hideo Gosha in 1989.

50. "Beigun yori homerareta 'Yoru no onna-tachi' ['Women of the Night' Praised by the American Forces]," *Screen Times* (March 2, 1948), 1.

51. The negative reviews include Hiroshi Seko, "Yami no onna, Aku no hana [Women in the Dark, Flowers of Evil]," *Screen Pic* 2 (April 5, 1948), 3; and Hajime Takizawa, "Kenji Mizoguchi," in *Nihon eiga kantoku zenshu* [*Encyclopedia of Japanese*

Directors] (Tokyo: Kinema Jumpo-sha, 1976), 390. The positive reviews include the introduction of the film in *Film Center* 16 (Tokyo: National Film Center, 1973), 32; and the article on the film in *Nihon eiga sakuhin zenshu* [*Encyclopedia of Japanese Films*] (Tokyo: Kinema Jumpo-sha, 1971), 201.

52. Anderson and Richie, *Japanese Film,* 194.

53. The negative reviews include Jusanro Futaba and Ichiro Ueno, "1950-nen sakuhin gaikan [General Views on the Films of 1950]," *Kinema Jumpo* 5 (December-III, 1950), 18–19. The positive reviews include the article on the film in *Nihon eiga sakuhin zenshu,* 198.

54. Toshimi Aoyama, "Eiga ken'etsu no omoide [Memoirs of Film Censorship]," *Eiga-shi Kenkyu* 21 (1986), 2–3.

55. Kaneto Shindo, *Shosetsu: Tanaka Kinuyo* [*A Novel: Kinuyo Tanaka*] (Tokyo: Yomiuri shimbun-sha, 1983), 202–218.

56. Yoshikata Yoda, "'Joyu Sumako no koi' o hansei su [Reflecting on 'The Love of Actress Sumako']," in *Nihon Eiga e no Iyoku to Hansei* [*Ambition for and Reflection on Japanese Cinema*] (n.p., 1947), 68–70; *Mizoguchi Kenji no hito to geijutsu* [*The Personality and Art of Kenji Mizoguchi*] (Tokyo: Tabata shoten, 1970), 142–175.

57. Interview with Yoshikata Yoda by Kaneto Shindo in his documentary film on the life of Mizoguchi, *Aru eiga kantoku no shogai* [*The Life of a Film Director*] (1975), published script (Tokyo: Eijin-sha, 1975), 36.

58. Isuzu Yamada, *Eiga to tomoni* [*Together with Cinema*] (Tokyo: San'ichi shobo, 1953), 115–128. Kinugasa was also active in the Toho labor union's strikes. Kato was also married when they began to live together. Yamada's marriage to Kato lasted from 1950 to 1954.

59. Excerpt from Jap[anese] Press Sum[mation], Government Section, August 8, 1946, in "Japan, Political Situation," in *Political, Economic, Social Situation,* 2, RG-4 USAFPAC Intelligence file, MacArthur Memorial, Norfolk, Va.

60. Hitoshi Ashida, Hideo Shibusawa, and Masaichi Nagata, "Minshu kakumei e no hitoyaku: Shin kenpo happu kinen eiga o meguru zadankai [One Role for Democratic Revolution: Discussion on the Films Commemorating the Proclamation of the New Constitution]," *Kinema Jumpo* (April 1947), 8–11; Adachi, "Purojusa gunyu-den, no. 10," *Kinema Jumpo* (September-II, 1988), 130–131.

61. Ito, "Sengo Nihon eiga," 233.

62. CCD memo, May 7, 1947, in CCD file on *Senso to heiwa,* Box 331-8579, NRC.

63. Ito, "Sengo Nihon eiga," 233; Adachi, "Purojusa gunyu-den, no. 10," 132–133.

64. Ito, "Sengo Nihon eiga," 233.

65. CCD Memorandum for Record, May 22, 1947, in CCD file on the film, Box 331-8579, NRC.

66. Memorandum for Record of Press, Pictorial and Broadcasting Division, CCD, May 26, 1947, in CCD file on the film, Box 331-8579, NRC.

67. Press, Pictorial and Broadcasting Division Routing Slip, June 10, 1947, reported to [John] Costello of Press, Pictorial and Broadcasting Division, June 11, 1947, in CCD file on the film, Box 331-8579, NRC.

68. See Nagasaki City's *Eiga Shuho* (July 6, 1947), 2, Prange Collection, McKeldin Library.

69. Press, Pictorial and Broadcasting Division Routing Slip (presumably), June 5, 1947, in CCD file on the film, Box 331-8579, NRC.

70. G-2, GHQ Inter-Office Memorandum from CCD to Deputy Chief, Civil Intelligence Section, June 12, 1947, in CCD file on the film, Box 331-8579, NRC.

71. Interview with Takeo Ito by Shigehiko Hasumi, *Lumière* (Summer 1986), 84.

72. Akira Shimizu in *Kinema Jumpo* (October 1947), 29–30; Toru Takagi in *Eiga to Spotsu* (July 18, 1947), 4; Ryo Shirasawa in *Kinema News* (February 10, 1948), 2; K.I. in *Eiga Bunka* (October 1947), 18–19; and the current film criticism section in *Eiga Kansho* (October 1947), 66.

73. Adachi cites research showing that, among 4,500 questioned, 721 liked *Between War and Peace,* while 495 liked *Political Theater,* and 229 liked *Flames of Passion.* "Purojusa gunyu-den, no. 10," 133.

74. Masahiro Makino, *Eiga tosei [Film Life]* (Tokyo: Heibon-sha, 1977), 2:188–189.

75. *Eiga Gorakugai* (March 1949), 3.

76. CIE memorandum on the synopsis of the film, January 13, 1948, CIE file, National Diet Library, Tokyo (hereafter NDL).

77. CIE memorandum on the script of the film, CIE file, NDL.

78. CIE record of conference at Toyoko's Kyoto Studio, July 21, 1948, CIE file, NDL.

79. *Eiga Shimpo* (August 23, 1947), 1.

80. Kirio Urayama, "Sengo kenbunroku: Yottari sametari [The Postwar Record of Hearing and Seeing: Getting Drunk and Awakening], no. 2," *Cine Front* (July 1985), 55.

81. Ushihara, *Kiyohiko eiga-fu,* 243.

82. Setsuo Noto quoted in Kyushiro Kusakabe, "Jitsuroku: Sengo Nippon eigashi hito to jiken to [Document: The History of Postwar Japanese Cinema with Personalities and Events], no. 1," *Hoseki* (1982), 191.

83. Yamamoto, "Katsudo-ya," 192.

84. Komatsu, "Sengo eiga shiriizu [Postwar Cinema Series], no. 2," *Tokyo-eki* (n.d.), 66.

CHAPTER 5

1. The literal translation of the title is "No Regret in My Youth."

2. A number of people have commented on the impact the film had on them when they first saw it in the fall of 1946. For example, see Hayato Akasegawa's *Eiga-kan o deruto yakeato datta [Outside the Movie Theater, There Was a Burnt Field]*

(Tokyo: Soshi-sha, 1982), whose front cover includes a photo of Setsuko Hara from the film.

3. Yoshishige Yoshida, "Jiden to jisaku o kataru [Talking on My Life and Films]" [interview with Yoshio Shirai], in *Sekai no eiga sakka* [*Film Directors of the World*], no. 10 (Tokyo: Kinema Jumpo-sha, 1971), 181.

4. Kei Kumai quoted in Kazu Adachi, "Purojusa gunyu-den [The Group Portrait of Producers], no. 5," *Kinema Jumpo* (July-I, 1988), 128.

5. Kazuo Kuroki quoted in ibid., 128.

6. Civil Affairs Division files on film 062.2 (June 22, 1946), Modern Military History Division, National Archives, Washington, D.C.

7. Because this affair related to the USSR, Maj. Gen. Charles Willoughby of the Intelligence Section of the occupation government paid special attention to the collecting of information on the Sorge-Ozaki case. See his *Shanghai Conspiracy: The Sorge Spy Ring* (New York: Dutton, 1952); Chalmers Johnson, *An Instance of Treason: Ozaki Hotsumi and the Sorge Spy Ring* (Palo Alto: Stanford University Press, 1962); and Gordon W. Prange, with Donald M. Goldstein and Katherine V. Dillon, *Target Tokyo: The Story of the Sorge Spy Ring* (New York: McGraw-Hill, 1985).

8. Article 14 of the Constitution of Japan of 1947 proclaims: "All people are equal under the law and there shall be no discrimination in political, economic, or social relations because of race, creed, sex, social status, or family origin." As for the situation in the United States, the required minimum of 38 states had not approved the Equal Rights Amendment as of 1992.

9. Eiji Takemae, *GHQ* (Tokyo: Iwanami shinsho, 1983), 156.

10. Akira Kurosawa in "Kurosawa Akira zensakuhin o kataru [Talking about My Filmography]" [interview with Masahiro Ogi], in *Sekai no eiga sakka,* no. 3 (Tokyo: Kinema Jumpo-sha, 1970), 116.

11. Tadao Uriu, *Eigateki seishin no keifu* [*The Lineage of the Film Spirit*] (Tokyo: Getsuyo shobo, 1947), cited in Nagisa Oshima, *Taikenteki sengo eizo-ron* [*A Theory of the Postwar Film Image Based on Personal Experience*] (Tokyo: Asahi shimbun-sha, 1975), 48.

12. *The New Earth* was originally to be a true German-Japanese co-production, with Fanck and Mansaku Itami as co-directors. When the two directors could not agree on a number of issues, two separate films were made, with Fanck directing the German version and Itami the Japanese. *Les Misérables* was adapted by Mansaku Itami as *Kyojin-den* [*Portrait of a Giant*] (1938); *The Pastoral Symphony* [*Den'en kokyogaku*] was adapted by Satsuo Yamamoto as the film of the same title in 1938; and *Stella Dallas* was adapted by Yamamoto as *Mother's Song* [*Haha no kyoku*] (1937). Setsuko Hara in *Nihon eiga haiyu zenshu: Joyu hen* [*Japanese Film Actress Encyclopedia*] (Tokyo: Kinema Jumpo-sha, 1980), 536–541.

13. Tadashi Iijima's review of the film in *Nishi Nippon Shimbun,* October 10, 1943, and his note on the film in his *Senchu eiga-shi shiki* [*Private History of Wartime Film*] (Tokyo: MG Shuppan, 1984), 201, 271–272.

14. Hara appeared in one other Kurosawa film, *The Idiot.*

15. Eijiro Hisaita in the epilogue to the published scenario, *Waga seishun ni kui nashi* (Tokyo: Chuo-sha, 1947).

16. Fuyuhiko Kitagawa in "Hisaita Eijiro ron [On Eijiro Hisaita]," *Eiga Shunju* (February 1947), cited in Oshima, *Taikenteki*, 48, 51.

17. Keiji Matsuzaki, "'Waga seishun ni kui nashi': Seisaku oboegaki ['No Regrets for Our Youth': Notes on the Production]," *Eiga Seisaku* (January 1947), 34–35.

18. Interview with the author on September 27, 1985, in New York.

19. Matsuzaki, "Waga seishun," 34.

20. Akira Kurosawa, *Something Like an Autobiograpy*, translated by Audie Bock (New York: Alfred A. Knopf, 1982), 78.

21. Ibid., 77–79.

22. Ibid., 77–78.

23. Burton Crane, who was then working as a *New York Times* reporter in Japan and had lived there before the war, stated that, in 1925, it seemed that every other book in a Tokyo bookstore was *Das Kapital* in Japanese, German, or English. Interview with Crane by Beate Gordon on the occupation, for the Oral History Research Center at Columbia University in March 1961 in New York.

24. The original scenario of *Waga seishun ni kui nashi* by Hisaita published by Chuo-sha; its script in *Eiga Seisaku* (January 1947), 36–65; also cited in Oshima, *Taikenteki*, 49–50.

25. Oshima, *Taikenteki*, 50–51.

26. SCAPIN-919, May 3, 1946, "Removal and Exclusion from Public Office of Diet Member." U.S. Public Document Section, Law School Library, Columbia University.

27. Oshima, *Taikenteki*, 50–51.

28. Telephone interview with Arthur Behrstock by the author on January 9, 1985. Behrstock passed away in October 1985.

29. Crane interview.

30. Interview with Beate Gordon on the occupation for the Oral History Research Center at Columbia University on November 9, 1961, in New York.

31. Ichiro Hatoyama, *Watashi no jijoden* [*My Autobiography*] (Tokyo: Kaizo-sha, 1951), 333–334.

32. Akira Iwasaki, *Senryo sareta sukuriin* [*The Occupied Screen*] (Tokyo: Shin-Nihon shuppan-sha), 1975, 106.

33. Interview with Beate Gordon on the occupation for the Oral History Research Center at Columbia University on October 2, 1960, in New York.

34. In the script of the film prepared by Yoshio Tanigawa; also on the videocassette provided by Ned Loader.

35. Kurosawa interview.

36. Oshima, *Taikenteki*, 45–47.

37. Kurosawa, *Something Like*, 150.

38. According to Hisaita's original scenario, Itokawa's mother's house is described as "a modest house that formerly contained a store that went out of business," whereas in the completed film, her house looks quite comfortable, although not luxurious.

39. Kurosawa's association of the kimono with traditional values and Western dress with progressive ideas was also used by Kenji Mizoguchi in his women's liberation film *My Love Has Been Burning*. In that film, actress Kinuyo Tanaka portrays Eiko Kageyama, an early Meiji Era political activist. During every crucial moment of the film, such as her first love scene and the last scene of her departure, she wears Western dress.

40. Oshima, *Taikenteki*, 49.

41. Kitagawa, "Hisaita Eijiro ron," quoted in Oshima, *Taikenteki*, 48.

42. Uriu, *Eigateki*, quoted in ibid., 48.

43. Tadashi Iijima, "Eiga Jihyo [Current Film Reviews]," *Eiga Shunju* (January 1947), 18–19.

44. "A Short Review" section in *Eiga Times* (November 1, 1946), 3.

45. Naoki Togawa, "Waga seishun ni kuinashi [No Regrets for Our Youth]," *Eiga Hyoron* (February 1947), 33.

46. Akira Kurosawa, *Eiga Junkan* (Special issue, 1956), cited in Oshima, *Taikenteki*, 48; Tadao Sato, *Currents in Japanese Cinema*, translated by Gregory Barrett (Tokyo: Kodansha International, 1982), 121–122.

47. Kurosawa interview.

48. Adachi, "Purojusa gunyu-den," 127.

49. Kurosawa, *Something Like*, 149. Hideo Komatsu provided a photo of this party at the house of a censor, Clifford Konno, which was attended by George Gercke and George Ishikawa from CIE, as well as Kurosawa, Matsuzaki, and Hisaita, in addition to the stars, Hara, Okochi, Fujita, Akitake Kono, and Chieko Nakakita. This photo accompanies Komatsu's essay on postwar film in *Tokyo-eki* (n.d.).

50. *SCAP Non-Military Activities, Summation* (no. 10, July 1946, 249) reports that, among seven Japanese features reviewed in the previous month, this film is "the story of an anti-war journalist who carried on underground activities at the cost of his life."

51. Kurosawa, "Kurosawa Akira zensakuhin o kataru," 116; Sato, *Currents*, 122; Kurosawa, *Something Like*, 148–150.

52. Kurosawa interview.

53. Donald Richie, *Ozu* (Berkeley and Los Angeles: University of California Press, 1974), 230, concerning Yasujiro Ozu's help for Kurosawa, as told by Kurosawa. See also Kurosawa's remarks on the wartime censors in chapter 2, page 99.

54. According to Yoshio Miyajima, Kurosawa was furious about this decision. Miyajima, "Kaiso-roku [Memoirs], no. 36," *Kinema Jumpo* (September-I, 1985), 114–115.

55. Iijima's review in *Eiga Shunju*, 18–19.

56. Oshima, *Taikentenki*, 54.

57. Ibid., 55–56.

58. Kurosawa, *Something Like*, 145.

59. Ibid., 150.

60. Donald Richie, *The Films of Akira Kurosawa* (Berkeley and Los Angeles: University of California Press, 1984), 36.

61. Matsuzaki, "Waga seishun," 34.

62. Kurosawa cited in Togawa, "Waga seishun," 33.

63. Tadao Sato, speaking at the symposium on "Japan at War," held March 28, 1987, at the Japan Society, New York.

64. Mansaku Itami, "Senso sekininsha no mondai [The Problem of Those Responsible for the War]," in Kenzaburo Oe, ed., *Itami Mansaku Essei-shu* [*Essays of Mansaku Itami*] (Tokyo: Chikuma shobo, 1971), 75–85. Itami is the father of Juzo Itami, a director who in the late 1980s became extremely popular in the United States for his comedies, including *The Funeral* [*Ososhiki*] (1985), *Tampopo* (1987), *A Taxing Woman* [*Marusa no onna*] (1988), and *The Return of a Taxing Woman* [*Marusa no onna II*] (1989).

65. Ozaki's letters to his wife from prison were first published in a magazine in February 1946, and, in September 1946, the first book comprised of these letters was published, entitled *Love Is Like a Falling Star* [*Aijo wa furu hoshi no gotoku*]. It soon became a best-seller and several editions were published over the next seventeen years. In addition to Kusuda's 1946 film modeled on the Ozaki case, in 1956 Nikkatsu made a film based on this book, entitled *Ai wa furu hoshi no kanatani* (literally, "Love Is Beyond a Falling Star," but rendered in English as *The Man Who Came from Shanghai*).

66. Susumu Fujita, "Boku mo kankyaku [I Am Also a Spectator]," *Eiga Fan* (July 1946), 8, Prange Collection, McKeldin Library. When Fujita mentioned his wartime characters, such as the military gods, in his essay, the section was deleted.

67. Hideo Nishiwaki, "Fujita Susumu," in *Nihon eiga haiyu zenshu: Danyu-hen* [*Japan Film Actor Encyclopedia*] (Tokyo: Kinema Jumpo-sha, 1979), 504.

68. Interview with the author on May 30, 1984, in Tokyo.

69. Interview with Haruo Mizuno, *Kinema Jumpo* (April-II, 1982), 115.

CHAPTER 6

1. Tadao Sato, "Toho eiga 50-nen no ayumi [The History of the 50 Years of Toho], no. 1," *Film Center* 74 (Tokyo: National Film Center, 1982), 2.

2. *Toho 50-nen-shi* [*50-Year History of Toho*] (Tokyo: Toho Printing, 1982), 155–169; "Ichizo Kobayashi," in *Engeki daijiten* [*Great Encyclopedia of Theater*] (Tokyo: Heibon-sha, 1983), 503; Joseph L. Anderson and Donald Richie, *The Japanese Film: Art and Industry* (expanded edition) (Princeton, N.J.: Princeton University Press, 1982), 81–83.

3. The traditionalism and feudalism of the Japanese film industry are discussed by David Bordwell in "Our Dream-Cinema: Western Historiography and the Japanese Film," *Film Reader* 4 (1979), 45–62.

4. *Toho 50-nen-shi*, 164, 179.

5. When PCL Studio recruited assistant directors for the first time in 1936, five were chosen out of five hundred who applied: the first four were university graduates. The last one, who had not gone to college and had been a painter, was chosen because interviewers Kajiro Yamamoto and Iwao Mori found special talent in him despite his apparent lack of qualifications. His name was Akira Kurosawa. All the others chosen at the same time disappeared from Japanese film history. Tadao Sato, "Tokii jidai [The Period of the Talkie]," in *Tokii no jidai* [*The Period of the Talkie*] (Tokyo: Iwanami shoten, 1986), 6–8.

6. Naoki Togawa, "Waga kuni no purojusa seido [The Producer System of Our Country]," *Eiga Hyoron* (September 1950), 9–10.

7. Hasegawa remained a big star for the next four and a half decades, until his death in 1983. Concerning the attack on Hasegawa, see the account by Naozane Fujimoto (a Toho producer), "Ichi purojusa no jijoden [A Producer's Autobiography]," in Hotsuki Ozaki, ed., *Fujimoto Naozane eiga ni kakeru* [*Naozane Fujimoto Challenges Film*] (Tokyo: Toho Printing, 1981), 160–163.

8. Masahiro Makino, *Eiga tosei* [*Film Life*] (Tokyo: Heibon-sha, 1977), 1:393, 398–404.

9. Togawa, "Waga kuni no," 12.

10. Jun'ichiro Tanaka, *Nihon eiga hattatsu-shi* [*The History of the Development of Japanese Cinema*] (Tokyo: Chuo koron-sha, 1984), 3:98–100.

11. OSS Research and Analysis Branch Report no. 1307, "Japanese Films: A Phase of Psychological Warfare" (March 30, 1944), Modern Military Section, National Archives, Washington, D.C.; Anderson and Richie, *Japanese Film*, 154–155.

12. Interview with Takeo Ito by Shigehiko Hasumi, *Lumière* (Summer 1986), 83.

13. Tanaka, *Nihon eiga hattatsu-shi*, 220–221.

14. Ibid., 233–234; *Toho 50-nen-shi*, 194.

15. Kumagai, a brother-in-law of film star Setsuko Hara, was active in war film production until 1941, when he established an ultrarightist political organization, with which he was associated during the war. He did not direct films again until 1953.

16. Tanaka, *Nihon eiga hattatsu-shi*, 223; *Eiga engeki jiten* [*Encyclopedia of Film and Theater*] (Tokyo: Jiji tsushin-sha, 1947), 42, 56–57.

17. Tanaka, *Nihon eiga hattatsu-shi*, 222–223; *Eiga engeki jiten*, 56.

18. Tanaka, *Nihon eiga hattatsu-shi*, 232–233; *Toho 50-nen-shi*, 19–191.

19. Kazu Adachi, "Purojusa gunyu-den [The Group Portrait of Producers], no. 8," *Kinema Jumpo* (August-II, 1988), 121.

20. Fujimoto, "Ichi projusa no," 185. *SCAP Non-Military Activities, Summation* (no. 8, May 1946, 243) mentions this film as showing "how individual members of a Japanese family react to the growth of the union movement."

21. Interview with Shigemi Hijikata by Masako Ishikawa on June 2, 1976, in *Konakatta no wa gunkan dake: Toho sogi kenkyu shiryo-shu* [*Everything Came but the*

Battleships: The Record of the Toho Strikes] (Tokyo: Masako Ishikawa, November 1976), 1:11.

22. Matsuo Kishi, *Jinbutsu Nihon eiga-shi* [*Japanese Film History of Personalities*] (Tokyo: Dabbido-sha, 1970), 290. Kishi agreed with Tokuda's opinion.

23. Akira Kurosawa, "Kurosawa Akira zensakuhin o kataru [Talking about My Filmography]" [interview with Masahiro Ogi], in *Sekai no eiga sakka* [*Film Directors of the World*], no. 3 (Tokyo: Kinema Jumpo-sha, 1970), 115–116. Also in Donald Richie, "Kurosawa on Kurosawa" *Sight and Sound* (Summer 1964), 109.

24. Tanaka, *Nihon eiga hattatsu-shi*, 234–235; *Toho eiga 50-nen-shi*, 194.

25. An interview with Takeo Ito by the author on May 30, 1984, in Tokyo; Ito interview by Hasumi, 82–83; Akira Iwasaki, "Toho sogi [Toho Strike]," in Masaji Shimoda, ed., *Dokyumento: Showa 50-nen-shi* [*Document: 50-Year History of the Showa Era*] (Tokyo: Heibon-sha, 1974), 5:145; Yoshio Miyajima, "Miyajima Yoshio Kaiso-roku [Yoshio Miyajima's Memoir] [interviewed and edited by Takeshi Yamaguchi], no. 26," *Kinema Jumpo* (April-I, 1985), 111.

26. Denjiro Okochi, quoted in Masaichi Ito, *Kiri to toride: Toho daisogi no kiroku* [*Fog and Fortress: The Record of the Great Toho Strike*] (Tokyo: Rengo tsushin-sha, n.d.), cited in Iwasaki, "Toho sogi," 5:154–156.

27. Tanaka, *Nihon eiga hattatsu-shi*, 236. Iwasaki (ibid., 5:158) states that 438 employees quit the first union, and that Kon Ichikawa (who would become a director at Shin-Toho) wrote the announcement of the group's separation. The second and the third unions joined Zen-ei-en on May 7, 1948.

28. Ito interview by Hasumi, 82.

29. Ibid., 82–83.

30. Tanaka, *Nihon eiga hattatsu-shi*, 235–236; *Toho 50-nen-shi*, 194–195.

31. *Toho 50-nen-shi*, 196.

32. Akira Kurosawa, *Something Like an Autobiography*, translated by Audie Bock (New York: Alfred A. Knopf, 1982), 160–162. Kurosawa criticized the policy that gave equal weight in the selection process to the opinions of labor union members— who he felt were incapable of judging the potential of interviewees—and the observations of "movie-industry professionals," i.e., directors, cinematographers, producers, and actors.

33. An example of the latter is Keinosuke Uekusa, interviewed by the author on August 7, 1984, in Tokyo.

34. Tanaka, *Nihon eiga no hattatsu-shi*, 244; *Toho 50-nen-shi*, 196–197.

35. Yoshio Miyajima, "Miyajima Yoshio Kaiso-roku, no. 59," *Kinema Jumpo* (September-II, 1986), 107.

36. *Toho 50-nen-shi*, 196.

37. OSS file, Intelligence Report of Office of Chief of Naval Operations, no. 1408–45 (August 24, 1945), Modern Military section, National Archives, Washington, D.C.

38. Shunsuke Tsurumi et al., *Nippon no hyaku-nen* [*100 Years of Japan*], vol. 2 (Tokyo: Chikuma shobo, n.d.), cited in Nagisa Oshima, *Taikenteki sengo eizo-ron* [*A Theory of the Postwar Film Image Based on Personal Experience*] (Tokyo: Asahi shimbun-sha, 1975), 75–76.

39. Iwasaki, "Toho sogi," 5:162; Ito interview by Hasumi, 85.

40. Interview with Tetsuzo Watanabe, *Kinema Jumpo* (March-III, 1948), 20.

41. Iwasaki, *Senryo sareta*, 162; "Current People" section in *Screen Digest* (April 13, 1948), 4; Tetsuzo Watanabe, *Hansen hankyo 40-nen* [*40 Years against War and against Communism*] (n.p., n.d.), cited in Oshima, *Taikenteki*, 75.

42. Kurosawa, *Something Like*, 164–165, 166–167.

43. Press, Pictorial and Broadcasting Division, District I, Motion Picture Section Memorandum for Record, April 18, 1948, in CCD File on Press, Pictorial and Broadcasting Division Memo for Record, no. 2, Motion Picture Section, Box 331-8580, National Records Center, Suitland, Md. (hereafter NRC). This report states that the severance pay Toho offered averaged about ¥40,000 plus one month's salary, and that cameraman Miyajima was supposedly offered close to ¥200,000 because of his long employment at the company.

44. Tanaka, *Nihon eiga hattatsu-shi*, 245–247.

45. Interview with Tetsuzo Watanabe, *Kinema Jumpo* (May-III, 1948), 26, cited by Tanaka, *Nihon eiga hattatsu-shi*, 247.

46. Takeo Ito, *Kinema Jumpo* (May-III, 1948), 26–28; cited by Tanaka.

47. Letter from an anonymous female unionist, *Konakatta no wa* 4 (October 1979), 33–34, 37–38.

48. Iwasaki, "Toho sogi," 5:165.

49. Miyajima, "Miyajima Yoshio Kaiso-roku, no. 57," *Kinema Jumpo* (August-II, 1986), 113–114.

50. A CCD Index Sheet of July 26, 1948, stated that the "Toho Studio Reconstruction League" was composed of only ten intensely anticommunist studio employees. CCD File on Movie Films (Censorship) 1948, Box 331-8579, NRC.

51. *Toho 50-nen-shi*, 199–200.

52. Takeo Ito, "Sengo nippon eiga no koryu to Toho sogi [The Development of Postwar Japanese Cinema and the Toho Strikes]," in Saburo Ienaga, ed., *Showa no sengo-shi* [*Postwar History of the Showa Era*] (Tokyo: Yubun-sha, 1976), 1:237.

53. Keinosuke Uekusa, *Waga seishun no Kurosawa Akira* [*Akira Kurosawa of My Youth*] (Tokyo: Bungei shunju-sha, 1985), 238.

54. Interview with Seiji Tsuchiya by Masako Ishikawa, *Konakatta no wa* 3 (October 1978), 45.

55. The promise was not kept: So Yoshiya, "Senryo seisaku to Toho sogi [Occupation Policy and Toho Strikes]," *Eiga Geijutsu* (August-September 1976), 38. A CCD, Press, Pictorial and Broadcasting Division District I memorandum of August 19, 1948, mentioned this actor's "one-man demonstration, . . . equipped with a

shelter half and food. . . . [He] stated, 'this will be my grave, unless this studio is again made a pleasant place to work in.'" CCD File on Movie Films (Censorship) 1948, Box 331-8579, NRC.

56. Interview with Shigeo Kume by Masako Ishikawa, *Konakatta no wa* 2 (October 1979), 40. Kume was a light technician who was working in the building where the fire started.

57. Incoming Message from CG IX Corps to CINCFE [Commander in Chief, Far East] (Attn G-2), on August 19, 1948. Willoughby Collection, MacArthur Memorial, Norfolk, Va.; CCD File on Movie Films (Censorship) 1948, Box 331-8579, NRC.

58. Tanaka, *Nihon eiga hattatsu-shi,* 252.

59. The Spot Intelligence report of GHQ/SCAP G-II at 0930 on August 19, 1948, stated that "In order to protect occupation personnel and property, at 0800, 19 Aug 48, 302nd Recon Troop of 1st Cav Div had six armored cars, five tanks, two jeeps and one platoon of dismounted cavalry at scene. One squadron at Camp Drake will be on one-hour alert." Willoughby Collection, MacArthur Memorial, Norfolk, Va.

60. Iwasaki, "Toho sogi," 5:167.

61. *Toho 50-nen-shi* (200), Iwasaki ("Toho sogi," 5:166), and Ito (interview by Hasumi, 237) cite this number, whereas Tanaka (*Nihon eiga hattatsu-shi,* 252) cites the number 2,500. The American occupation forces reports cite the following numbers: "Approximately 1,500" (CIC Spot Report, "Toho Dispute," August 19, 1948, cited in Intelligence Review of G-2 GHQ, FEC, dis. no. 2188 in "World Situation Summary: Military, Political, Economic, Social Situation, Press Review, Civil Intelligence, Miscellaneous," Selected Items for the Information of Commanders and Staffs of the Far East Command); 1,300 (Spot Intelligence, General Headquarters Supreme Commander for the Allied Powers Military Intelligence Section, General Staff, 0930, August 19, 1948); 1,000 (Incoming Message); and "several hundred" (Intelligence Review of G-2 GHQ, FEC, dis. no. 2187, August 19, 1948, in "World Situation Summary"). All sources in Willoughby Collection, MacArthur Memorial, Norfolk, Va.

62. Uekusa, *Waga seishun,* 251–252; interview with Fumio Kamei by Masako Ishikawa, *Konakatta no wa* 3 (October 1978), 14.

63. Kurosawa, *Something Like,* 165–166.

64. Kamei interview by Ishikawa, 14; Shinkichi Noda, "Toho sogi no shiteki kaiso oboegaki (My Private Notes on the Toho Strikes)," *Konakatta no wa* 5 (October 1980), 98–99.

65. CIC Spot Report, "Toho Dispute," August 19, 1948, cited in "World Situation Summary" no. 2188, Willoughby Collection, MacArthur Memorial, Norfolk, Va.

66. Kume interview, 43.

67. GHQ/SCAP G-II Spot Intelligence report, 12:20, August 19, 1948, Willoughby Collection, MacArthur Memorial, Norfolk, Va. The "World Situation Summary" puts the number of strikers as 1,200 from G-2 GHQ, FEC dis. no. 2187 (August 19, 1948).

68. *Asahi Shimbun,* August 20, 1948; Tanaka, *Nihon eiga hattatsu-shi,* 253; "Toho satsueijo reporutaju: Satsueijo sodatsu kara karishobun made (Toho Studio Reportage: From the Takeover of the Studio to the Provisional Execution)," *Kinema Jumpo* (August-II, 1948), 20; Shinkichi Noda, "Toho sogi no," 100–101. Noda states that in twenty minutes he persuaded a group of approximately forty Korean Association supporters to surrender, and that, around 11:00, the union conveyed its decision, which was followed by some ten minutes of negotiation about the conditions that the union had demanded.

69. Tetsuzo Watanabe probably exaggerated in saying that it was only when the American tanks and bulldozers threatened the strikers at five minutes to noon that the union decided to leave the studio, while inside the studio, two actresses and the Korean Association insisted on fighting until the end. Cited by Oshima, *Taikenteki,* 75.

Shin Watarai, a union member and sound technician, remembered that it took thirty to forty minutes to reach the decision, and the Korean Association insisted that the unionists should not give up until forced to do so. Interview with Masako Ishikawa, *Konakatta no wa* 3 (October 1978), 57.

The American occupation Counter Intelligence Corps reported that an agreement was reached at 11:30 A.M., under which all the strikers would vacate the studio within two hours, with negotiations to continue after that time. Spot Intelligence, 1220, August 19, 1948, Willoughby Collection, MacArthur Memorial, Norfolk, Va.

70. In *The Japanese Film,* 170, Anderson and Richie, in describing the incident, remark that "the only thing that didn't come was a battleship." As for Japanese sources, Hajima Nagasaki, in *Sekai eiga jiken jimbutsu jiten* [*Encyclopedia of World Film Events and Personalities*] (Tokyo: Kinema Jumpo-sha, 1970), 183, discusses this incident with the headline "Konakatta wa gunkan dake [Everything Came but the Battleship]." See also Masako Ishikawa, *Konakatta no wa gunkan dake: Toho sogi kenkyu shiryo-shu* [*Everything Came but the Battleships: The Record of the Toho Strikes*], vols. 1–5 (Tokyo: Masako Ishikawa, 1976–1980).

71. Ito interview by Hasumi, 86; Tanaka, *Nihon eiga hattasu-shi,* 256. Yamagata stated that all twenty belonged to the Communist Party. Interview with Masako Ishikawa, *Konakatta no wa* 5 (October 1980), 62.

72. Ito interview by Hasumi, 85–86; Tanaka, *Nihon eiga hittasu-shi,* 255–256.

73. Kurosawa, *Something Like,* 167.

74. Iwasaki, "Toho sogi," 5:168–169.

75. Kurosawa, *Something Like,* 167–168. Kurosawa avoided mentioning Mabuchi's name in his book, perhaps because Mabuchi has continued as a Toho executive.

76. Ibid., 166–167.

77. Yoshiya, "Senryo seisaku," 37; "Kubikiri ninjo ron [Theory on Firing and Humanity]," *Kinema Jumpo* (July-I, 1947), 31.

78. CCD, Press, Pictorial and Broadcasting Division District I, Pictorial Section Memorandum, June 23, 1948, in CCD File on Film Export, Box 331-8580, NRC.

79. Hideko Takamine, *Watashi no tosei nikki* [*My Life Diary*] (Tokyo: Asahi shimbun-sha, 1980), 2:33–39.

80. Isuzu Yamada, *Eiga to tomoni* [*Together with Film*] (Tokyo: San'ichi shobo, 1953), 110–115, 125–150.

81. Ibid., 110–111.

82. Interview with Takako Shirota by Masako Ishikawa, *Konakatta no wa* 1 (November 1976), 4.

83. Yoshikata Yoda, *Mizoguchi Kenji no hito to geijutsu* [*Kenji Mizoguchi: The Man and His Art*] (Tokyo: Tabata shoten, 1970), 131.

84. Interview in *Eiga Hyoron* (September 1948), 4–8.

85. Interview with Kaneto Shindo in Shindo, *Aru eiga kantoku no shogai: Mizoguchi Kenji no kiroku* [*The Life of a Director: The Record of Kenji Mizoguchi*] (Tokyo: Eijin-sha, 1980), 36. Fuji Yahiro cites examples of the above in "Jidaieiga no ki jusan-nen [The Record of Period Films for Thirteen Years]," *Kinema Jumpo* (March-I, 1964), 43.

86. Makino, *Eiga tosei,* 2:190.

87. Interview with an anonymous female unionist by Masako Ishikawa, *Konakatta no wa* 4 (October 1979), 37.

88. *Toho 50-nen-shi,* 200–201.

89. Tanaka, *Nihon eiga hattatsu-shi,* 258.

90. *Toho 50-nen-shi,* 201–202; Tanaka, *Nihon eiga hattatsu-shi,* 290–293, 295–296.

91. Ibid., 294–295; Shohei Tokizane's current film industry review in *Eiga Hyoron* (September 1949, 11) further stated that Mabuchi, supported by former Toho president Tanabe, defeated Watanabe as well.

92. Interview with Hirobumi Iwama by Koji Tanabe, *Konakatta no wa* 3 (October 1978), 42–43.

93. Interview with Sin'ichi Takahashi by Masako Ishikawa, *Konakatta no wa* 1 (November 1976), 18–19; interview with Kyozo Niinuma by Masako Ishikawa, *Konakatta no wa* 2 (October 1977), 22–23.

94. Interview with Shiro Amikura by Masako Ishikawa, *Konakatta no wa* 3 (October 1978), 23–24.

95. *Asahi Shimbun,* August 20, 1948.

96. *Kinema Jumpo* (August-II, 1948), 22.

97. CCD, Press, Pictorial and Broadcasting Division Memorandum on "Newsreels on Eviction of Toho Strikers," August 29, 1948. The screenings of the newsreels produced by three Japanese companies were attended by the First Cavalry Division public information officer, Maj. R. C. Buckles, First Cavalry Division, G-2 Section, and Maj. H.H. Grannis, First Cavalry Division, G-2 Section, in addition to Press,

Pictorial and Broadcasting Division censors. All three newsreels were passed in their entirety. CCD File on Movie Films (Censorship) 1948, Box 331-8579, NRC.

98. *Stars and Stripes,* August 19, 1948, cited in SCAP Outgoing Message from SCAP to "CG Eighth Army . . . Priority," August 20, 1948, Willoughby Collection, MacArthur Memorial, Norfolk, Va.

99. *New York Times,* August 19, 1948.

100. Watarai interview, 57.

101. The Intelligence Review of the "World Situation Summary" (1) evaluates this studio as having "been doing much work for the occupation." Willoughby Collection, MacArthur Memorial, Norfolk, Va.

102. Spot Intelligence reports at 0930, 1110, 1220, 1250, 1600, and 1830 on August 19, 1948, to Chief of Staff, notified to ADC, Deputy Chiefs of Staff SCAP and FEC [Far Eastern Commission], ESS [Economic and Science Section, of which Labor Division was a part], GS, CIE, and G-3. Willoughby Collection, MacArthur Memorial, Norfolk, Va.

103. G-2 GHQ, FEC, dis. no. 2187, August 19, 1948, cited in the Intelligence Review of the World Situation Summary and GHQ/SCAP G-II Spot Intelligence at 1110 on August 19, 1948. Willoughby Collection, MacArthur Memorial, Norfolk, Va.

104. Yoshiki Shimazaki, "Tabata Seiko chan no koto [About Seiko Tabata]," *Konakatta no wa* 3 (October 1978), 63. Seiji Tsuchiya stated that a Japanese policeman took notes on his speech and reported the incident to the American censors. Interview in *Konakatta no wa* 4 (October 1979), 46.

105. Ibid.

106. Conversation with Kin'ichi Matsumaru by Masako Ishikawa, *Konakatta no wa* 1 (November 1976), 32.

107. Interview with Hiroshi Komatsu by Masako Ishikawa, *Konakatta no wa* 3(October 1978), 35–36; Noda, "Toho sogi no," 100; Tsuchiya interview, 42.

108. Matsumaru conversation with Ishikawa, 35–36.

109. Miriam Farley, "SCAP Policy Toward Labor Unions," in Jon Livingston, Joe Moore, and Felicia Oldfather, eds. *Postwar Japan: 1945 to Present* (New York: Pantheon, 1973), 153.

110. Miriam Farley, "SCAP and Government Employees, 1948" in Livinston et al., *Postwar Japan,* 168–170.

111. Eiji Takemae, *GHQ* (Tokyo: Iwanami shinsho, 1983), 198.

112. Tadashi Hanami, *Labor Relations in Japan Today* (Tokyo: Kodansha International, 1981), 171. CIE's conference report of August 5, 1946, stated that Yomiuri Company representatives visited CIE officers (Col. Nugent and Col. Summers) and complained about the unionists. CIE Conference Reports, CIE Section, NRC. For the Yomiuri dispute, see Mark Gayn, "Yomiuri Strike," in Livingston et al., *Postwar Japan,* 153–161; and Satoshi Kamata, *Hankotsu: Susuki Tomin no shogai [Rebellious: The Life*

of Tomin Suzuki] (Tokyo: Kodansha, 1989), a biography of Suzuki, the chairman of Yomiuri's labor union.

113. Robert Sklar, *Movie-Made America: A Cultural History of American Movies* (New York: Vintage Books, 1975), 258–260. For the Hollywood labor force and its relation to the mode of production, see Janet Staiger's chapter on "The Labor-Force, Financing and the Mode of Production," in David Bordwell, Janet Staiger, and Kristin Thompson, *The Classic Hollywood Cinema: Film Style & Mode of Production to 1960* (New York: Columbia University Press, 1985).

114. For instance, Atsushi Senoo's series of articles on Hollywood and HUAC in *Kinema Jumpo*, nos. 20 (December-III, 1947), 26 (February-II, 1948), and 27 (February-III, 1948).

115. Ito's interview by Hasumi, 84.

CHAPTER 7

1. CIE, Motion Picture Office memo written by Harry Slott on "Motion Picture Critics' Role in the Democratization of Japanese Motion Pictures," July 9, 1948, answering a question from leftist critic Jun Izawa on the Toho Strike. CIE file, National Diet Library, Tokyo (hereafter NDL).

2. CIE comment on a reference to labor disputes in *Man of Talk* [*Uwasa no otoko*], January 3, 1948; CIE comment on an argument about Marxism in *The Wise Wife* [*Kenjo Katagi*], February 20, 1948; CIE comment on a discussion about "capital vs. labor" in *Together with Passsion,* May 26, 1948, all in CIE file, NDL.

3. CCD, Press, Pictorial and Broadcasting Division, Pictorial Section, memorandum concerning Nippon Newsreel no. 195, October 1, 1949, in CCD File on Violation (Pictorial) Movies 1949, Box 331-8580, National Records Center, Suitland, Md. (hereafter NRC).

4. CIE comments on Nichi-ei's Nippon News no. 215 and Riken's Cultural News no. 156, February 18, 1950, in CIE file, NDL.

5. CCD, Press, Pictorial and Broadcasting Division District I memorandum, August 15, 1946, in CCD file, Box 331-8580, NRC.

6. CIE comment on the film, July 2, 1948, in CIE file, NDL.

7. CCD, Press, Pictorial and Broadcasting Division, Pictorial Section, memorandum, July 8, 1949, in CCD File on Violation (Pictorial) Movies 1949, Box 331-8580, NRC.

8. CIE comment on the film, February 7, 1948, in CIE file, NDL.

9. CIE comment on the film, July 19, 1949, in CIE file, NDL.

10. Heinosuke Gosho quoted in Tadao Sato, *Obake entotsu no sekai: Eiga kantoku Gosho Heinosuke no hito to shigoto* [*The World of Strange Chimneys: The*

Personality and Work of Film Director Heinosuke Gosho] (Tokyo: Noberu shobo, 1977), 204.

11. CIE comment on Nichi-ei News no. 241, August 19, 1950, in CIE file, NDL.

12. CIE comments on Nichi-ei News no. 244 and Riken's Cultural News no. 185, September 8, 1950, in CIE file, NDL.

13. CIE comments on Yomiuri Kokusai News no. 77, September 8, 1950, in CIE file, NDL.

14. CIE comment on the film, February 13, 1948, in CIE file, NDL.

15. CIE memorandum, June 23, 1947, in CIE file, NDL; Jun'ichiro Tanaka, *Nihon eiga no hattatsu-shi* [*The History of the Development of Japanese Cinema*] (Tokyo: Chuo koron-sha, 1976), 3:273-274.

16. *Gorakugai* (September 17, 1946), 1.

17. Seventy-seven prints were distributed and exhibited in some 1,708 theaters in Japan weekly. CCD, Press, Pictorial and Broadcasting Division District I memorandum, October 12, 1948, in CCD file on American Films, Box 331-8578, NRC.

18. Memorandum from Central Motion Picture Exchange, Tokyo, to Col. D. R. Nugent of CIE, April 5, 1949, and memorandum from Col. John H. Allen, Chief of New York Field Office of Civil Affairs Department, to Col. Nugent of CIE, June 16, 1949, in CIE file, NDL.

19. Memorandum from Charles Mayer, Central Motion Picture Exchange, Tokyo, to Lt. Col. Nugent of CIE, June 28, 1949, and memorandum from Lt. Col. D. R. Nugent of CIE to Central Motion Picture Exchange, July 7, 1949, in CIE file, NDL.

20. Memorandum from Chief, CIE, Office for Occupied Areas, to Chief, CIE, SCAP, March 3, 1952, in CIE file, NDL.

21. CIE comment on the film, June 2, 1948, in CIE file, NDL.

22. CIE comment on an Italian film, May 23, 1950, in CIE file, NDL. In this statement, CIE nonetheless recognized the high quality of the film, calling it "an outstanding example of postwar Italian film making."

23. Memorandum from DS (Diplomatic Section) to CIE, February 24, 1951, and memorandum from CIE to DS, March 21, 1951, in CIE file, NDL.

24. CCD, Press, Pictorial and Broadcasting Division District I memorandum (by R.H.K.), August 15, 1946, in CCD file on American Films, Box 331-8578, NRC.

25. CIE comment on the film, April 26, 1950, in CIE file, NDL.

26. CIE comment on the film in Intra-Section Memorandum to Chief of Information Division, May 8, 1950, in CIE file, NDL.

27. CCD memorandum, March 3, 1947, in CCD file on American Films, Box 331-8578, NRC.

28. Ibid.

29. CIE comment on the film, May 20, 1950, in CIE file, NDL.

30. CIE comment on Tokyo News Edition no. 8, August 28-29-30, 1950, in CIE file, NDL.

31. CIE comment on United Newsreel no. 47, October 6, 1950, in CIE file, NDL.

32. Script of Nichi-ei's Nippon News no. 240, released on August 15, 1950, censored by CIE, Box 331-5288, NRC.

33. Script of Nichi-ei's Nippon News no. 235, censored by CIE, Box 331-5288, NRC.

34. SCAP Civil Information Division, Civil Affairs Section memorandum, September 30, 1950, and CIE memorandum, October 13, 1950, in CIE file, NDL.

35. Memorandum from the Soviet representative to the Allied Council in Japan to SCAP, August 15, 1949, in CIE file, NDL.

36. Digest of letter from Matsusada Okada, Tokyo, to General MacArthur, October 4, 1949, in CIE Information Section file, NDL.

37. *Eiga Hyoron* (September 1949), 16–17.

38. CIE memorandum to Central Motion Picture Exchange, September 25, 1951, in CIE file, NDL.

39. Memorandum from the Soviet representative to the Allied Council in Japan to SCAP, September 7, 1949; protest from the Soviet Repatriate Livelihood Welfare Union to SCAP, September 21, 1949; checksheet from CIE's Lt. Col. Nugent to Don Brown, September 7, 1949; checksheet from Nugent to Special Service Section, November 14, 1949; checksheet from Special Service Section to CIE, November 25, 1949, CCD file on *Damoi*, Box 331-8579, NRC. CCD also reported on the film and the Shin-Toho Studio, claiming that CIE had suggested the deletion of one scene from the depiction of the wife's suicide in the last episode, a scene that seemingly remained in the completed film. CCD's memorandum to Operation Officers concerning *Damoi*, n.d., in CCD file on *Damoi;* the film's introduction in *Kinema Jumpo* (November-III, 1949), 8–9.

40. *Eiga engeki jiten* [*Encyclopedia of Cinema and Theater*] (Tokyo: Jiji tsushin-sha, 1947), 92.

41. Tanaka, *Nihon eiga hattatsu-shi*, 278; *Eiga engeki jiten*, 92.

42. Tanaka, *Nihon eiga hattatsu-shi*, 282–285.

43. *Eiga nenkan* [*Film Almanac*] (Tokyo: n.p., 1951) lists the number of foreign films released in Japan, according to their country of origin, as follows:

Country	1946	1947	1948	1949	1950	Total
United States	39	70	72	91	85	357
France	0	0	15	34	11	60
Great Britain	0	1	18	24	14	57
Italy	0	0	0	2	3	5
Russia	0	2	9	2	2	15
Argentina	0	0	0	0	2	2
Total	39	73	114	153	117	496

In contrast to these figures, a letter from the Russian representative to the Allied Council for Japan states that four Russian films were passed by the occupation censors in 1949 and three in 1950, as against the 135 American, 22 French, 19 British, and 5 Italian films released in Japan in 1950. Letter from the Soviet representative to the Allied Council for Japan to GHQ/SCAP, April 27, 1951, CIE file, NDL.

Tanaka's *Nihon eiga hattatsu-shi* (372–373) cites figures that are closer to those cited in this letter. According to this source, the 1950 releases were as follows: 135 American, 22 French, 18 British, 5 Italian, and 3 Russian films. Its tally of American films released in Japan is 38 in 1946, 55 in 1947, 62 in 1948, 86 in 1949.

44. Paragraph 2, Enclosure 3, Circular 12, GHQ/SCAP, May 9, 1948. The occupation government reserved the right to impose other limits, and to allow exceptions to limits, if circumstances warranted. This may have been a subterfuge to allow in more American films, while minimizing the number of Russian imports. Cited in CIE memorandum concerning Importation of Soviet Films, October 13, 1948, in CIE file, NDL.

45. Ibid.; letter from the Soviet representative to the Allied Council for Japan to GHQ/SCAP, November 17, 1948, in CIE file, NDL.

46. CIE memorandum concerning "Soviet Grumbling," February 3, 1949, in CIE file, NDL.

47. Cited in CIE report of conference with the representative of Hokusei eiga-sha, handling the importation of Russian films into Japan, February 17, 1950, in CIE file, NDL.

48. For instance, CIE's conference report of February 17, 1950, cited the delay in the clearance of two Soviet films, and CIE's memorandum of October 17, 1950, mentioned a similar instance. Both in CIE file, NDL.

49. CIE comment on the film, May 16, 1950, in CIE file, NDL.

50. These included *Michurin* (1947), *Bogdan Khmelnitsky* (1941), *Story of a Real Man* (1948), and *White Gold* in 1949, and *Young Guards* (1947), *Battle of Stalingrad* (1950), *Meeting on the Elbe* (1949), *Konstantin Zalonov, Sons, Miklukho Maklay, Academician Ivan Pavlov* (1949), *Brave People,* and *The Judgement of Honor* in 1950. Letter from the Soviet representative to the Allied Council for Japan to GHQ/SCAP, April 27, 1951, CIE file, NDL.

51. CIE comments on the color films *Far Away from Moscow* ("seeking to convince the people that the communist spirit can overcome any obstacle and that work in Siberia is both noble and stimulating"), *Bountiful Summer* ("idealizing the setting of higher quotas for crop deliveries and combating opposition to the policy of forcing collective farms into mergers"), and *Mussorgsky* ("trying to strengthen Russian nationalism by distorting facts and disparaging what is good in other cultures") in CIE checksheet to DCS/SCAP, August 3, 1951, in CIE file, NDL.

52. CIE memorandum to G-II, March 4, 1949, in CIE file, NDL.

53. Report of G-II, GHQ Far East Command, July 12, 1951, in CIE file, NDL; checksheet from G-II to CIE, February 15, 1952, in CIE file, NDL.

54. Kaneto Shindo, *Tsuihosha-tachi: Eiga no reddo paaji* [*The Expelled: The Red Purge of Film*] (Tokyo: Iwanami shoten, 1983), 32–33; Tanaka, *Nihon eiga hattatsu-shi*, 3:360–362.

55. Shindo, *Tsuihosha-tachi*, 8–10.

56. Tanaka, *Nihon eiga hattatsu-shi*, 3:361–362; Shindo, *Tsuihosha-tachi*, 7–8.

57. Ibid., 119, 131, 144–145, 156, 193–203.

58. Ibid., 71–293.

59. Tanaka (*Nihon eiga hattatsu-shi*, 3:345) lists the number of the Japanese films produced each year as follows:

Year	Shochiku	Toho	Daiei	Shin-Toho	Toei	Independent	Total
1946	21	18	25	—	—	3	67
1947	33	14	33	—	—	17	97
1948	42	6	37	—	—	38	123
1949	44	6	39	—	—	67	156
1950	42	16	43	20	—	94	215
1951	53	27	49	35	18	26	208

CHAPTER 8

1. Because of differences in methods of calculation of military budgets, precise international comparison is difficult. For example, the NATO countries include military pension plans and coast guards in their military expenditures. If Japan follows their method, Japan's military expenditure becomes the second highest in the world, after the United States.

2. *Asahi Shimbun*, February 22, 1983.

BIBLIOGRAPHY

I. PRIMARY SOURCES

A. *Interviews Conducted by the Author*

Oshima, Nagisa (director), October 9, 1983, New York.
Yamamoto, Kikuo (film historian), May 16, 1984, Tokyo.
Komatsu, Hideo (former Shochiku Studio liaison), May 28, 1984, Tokyo.
Ito, Takeo (producer and unionist), May 30 and July 3, 1984, Tokyo.
Ogawa, Toru (film writer and magazine editor), May 31, 1984, Tokyo.
Miyagawa, Kazuo (cinematographer), June 3, 1984, Kyoto.
Yoda, Yoshikata (screenplay writer), June 3, 1984, Kyoto.
Noto, Setsuo (producer and former Toho Studio liaison), June 4, 1984, Tokyo.
Yoshida, Yoshishige (director), June 22 and July 5, 1984, Tokyo.
Ogawa, Shinsuke (director), June 23, 1984, Tokyo.
Shindo, Kaneto (director and screenplay writer), June 25, 1984, Tokyo.

Kamei, Fumio (director), July 6, 1984, Tokyo; July 12, 1984, telephone interview, Tokyo; January 31, 1986, Tokyo.

Kubota, Kinuko (law professor), July 9, 1984, Tokyo.

Koschmann, J. Victor (intellectual historian), July 10, 1984, Tokyo.

Ga, Hatsuhiko (mass communication scholar), July 10, 1984, Tokyo.

Nakamura, Tomoko (journalist), July 13, 1984, Tokyo.

Shimizu, Akira (film critic), July 20, 1984, Tokyo.

Aoyama, Toshimi (foreign film specialist), July 23, 1984, Tokyo.

Shinoda, Masahiro (director), July 23, 1984, Tokyo; April 29, 1985, New York; April 22, 1986, New York.

Togawa, Naoki (film critic), July 24, 1984, Tokyo.

Richie, Donald (film critic), July 25, 1984, Tokyo.

Horikawa, Hiromichi (director), August 5, 1984, Tokyo.

Uekusa, Keinosuke (screenplay writer), August 7, 1984, Tokyo; February 28, 1986, Tokyo.

Mishima, Yoshiji (producer), August 9, 1984, Tokyo.

Buckley, Roger (historian), August 25, 1984, Tokyo.

Daniels, Gordon (historian), September 1, 1984, Tokyo.

Toba, Yukinobu (former Japanese government official), September 4, 1984, Tokyo.

Atsuta, Yuharu (cinematographer), September 5, 1984, Tokyo.

Yamauchi, Shizuo (producer), September 5, 1984, Tokyo.

Kuroda, Toyoji (film export specialist), September 10, 1984, Tokyo.

Ishikawa, Masako (former unionist and editor of the Toho strike records), September 13, 1984, Tokyo.

Kawamoto, Kihachiro (director), October 30, 1984, telephone interview, New York.

Passin, Herbert (former CIE official), December 14, 1984, New York.

Behrstock, Arthur (former CIE official), January 7 and 9, 1985, telephone interview, New York.

Palestin, Seymour (former CCD official), January 10, 1985, New York.

Yamaguchi, Kazunobu (former magazine editor), January 23, 1985, New York.

Kurosawa, Akira (director), September 27, 1985, New York.

Anderson, Joseph L. (film scholar), October 18, 1985, New York.

Baba, Frank Shozo (former CIE official), November 11, 1985, Washington, D.C.

Taniguchi, Senkichi (director), February 27, 1986, Tokyo.

Sato, Tadao (film critic), October 1, 1986, New York.

Nakamura, Katsuro (President, Wadatsumi-kai Society), August 15, 1989, Tokyo.

B. Correspondence

Watanabe, Dai (former film importer), August 1984.

Ooka, Shohei (novelist), October 2, 1985.

Spaulding, Robert (former CCD official), November 12, 1985.
Tokumitsu, Hisao (former producer), February 27, 1986.
Anderson, Joseph L., December 1986.

C. Bibliography

1. Unpublished Official Documents Concerning the Wartime and Occupation Media Policy

Japanese Films: A Phase of Psychological Warfare: An Analysis of the Themes, Psychological Content, Technical Quality, and Propaganda Value of Twenty Recent Japanese Films, Office of Strategic Services, Research and Analysis Branch Report no. 1307, March 30, 1944, National Archives, Washington, D.C.

The Japanese Press as an Instrument for Control, Office of Strategic Services, Research and Analysis Branch Report no. 3162S, June 29, 1945, National Archives, Washington, D.C.

Radio Broadcasting in Japan, (Office of Strategic Services, Research and Analysis Branch Report no. 3355S, August 31, 1945, National Archives, Washington, D.C.

Motion Pictures of Japanese Origin, United States of America, Department of Justice, Office of Alien Property, August 1, 1953,

Intelligence report, Intelligence Division, Office of Chief of Naval Operations, Navy Department, Series 1408-45, August 24, 1945, National Archives, Washington, D.C.

U.S. Nisei in Japan, Military Intelligence Division, WDGS, military attache report, Report no. 1884, September 23, 1944, National Archives, Washington, D.C.

War Department, Civil Affairs Division, papers, August 1945 to December 1946, National Archives, Washington, D.C.

Japanese Radio Themes, State Department papers, February 22, 1943, National Archives, Washington, D.C.

SCAP Non-Military Activities in Japan and Korea Summation nos. 1 (September/October 1945) to 15 (December 1946), Columbia University Law Library.

SCAP Non-Military Activities in Japan Summation nos. 16 (January 1947) to 35 (August 1948), Columbia University Law Library.

Declassified Reports of the Office of Intelligence Research as of July 1, 1950, Bibliography no. 53, July 7, 1950, National Archives, Washington, D.C.

CIE documents, National Records Center, Suitland, Md., and National Diet Library, Tokyo.

CCD documents, National Records Center, Suitland, Md.

General Charles A. Willoughby Collection (military intelligence documents), MacArthur Memorial, Norfolk, Va.

Gordon W. Prange Collection (censored printed materials and printed materials from the occupation period), McKeldin Library, University of Maryland.

2. Published Private Papers Concerning the Occupation Media Policy

The Occupation of Japan: Interviews, conducted with seventeen people, including
Roger Baldwin, Faubion Bowers, Burton Crane, and Eugene Doorman by Beate
Gordon in 1960–1961, and transcribed by the Oral History Center, Columbia
University. 1,488 pages.
Hideo Komatsu [Shochiku Studio's liaison with the occupation government, September
1946 to April 1947]. *Renraku Nisshi* [*Liaison Diary*], Komatsu private collection.
————. *CIE eiga-ka Ishikawa George shi no eiga-ka no ninmu ni kansuru ippanteki
kaisetsu narabini saikin no seisaku jokyo ni taisuru shoken narabi ni kibo kankoku*
[*Mr. George Ishikawa of the Motion Picture Unit of CIE: General Explanation of
His Role and the Opinions, Desires and Advice Concerning the Recent Production
Situation*]. n.d., Komatsu private collection.
————. *Saikin no keiko ni tsuite* [*On Recent Tendencies*]. n.d., Komatsu private collection.

3. Published Official Documents

Supreme Commander, for Allied Powers, Directives to the Japanese Government
(nos. 1–2204):
SCAPIN no. 33 (September 18, 1945), "Press Code for Japan."
SCAPIN no. 66 (September 27, 1945), "Further Step Toward Freedom of Press
and Speech."
SCAPIN no. 93 (October 4, 1945), "Removal of Restrictions on Political, Civil
and Religious Liberties."
SCAPIN no. 146 (October 16, 1945), "Elimination of Japanese Government Con-
trol of the Motion Picture Industry."
SCAPIN no. 287 (November 16, 1945), "Elimination of Undemocratic Motion
Pictures."
SCAPIN no. 658 (May 3, 1946), "Removal and Exclusion from Public Office of
Diet Member."

II. SECONDARY SOURCES

A. *Bibliography in English*

1. Books on the Occupation Policy and Period

Benedict, Ruth. *The Chrysanthemum and the Sword* (New York: Houghton Mifflin,
1946).
Bisson, T. A. *Prospects for Democracy in Japan* (New York: Macmillan, 1949).
Brins, Russell. *MacArthur's Japan* (Philadelphia: J. B. Lippincott, 1948).

Buckley, Roger. *Occupation Diplomacy: Britain, the United States and Japan 1945–1952* (New York: Cambridge University Press, 1982).

Busche, Noel F. *Fallen Sun: A Report on Japan* (New York and London: D. Appleton Century, 1948).

Cary, Otis, ed. *From a Ruined Empire: Letters—Japan, China, Korea 1945–46* (Tokyo: Kodansha International, 1975).

Chira, Susan Deborah. *Cautious Revolutionaries: Occupation Planners and Japan's Postwar Land Reform* (Tokyo: Agricultural Policy Research Center, 1982).

Deverall, Richard L. G. *The Great Seduction: Red China's Drive to Bring Free Japan Behind the Iron Curtain* (Tokyo: International Literature Printing, 1953).

Dower, John W. *Empire and Aftermath: Yoshida Shigeru and the Japanese Experience, 1878–1954* (Cambridge, Mass.: Harvard University Press, 1979).

———. *War Without Mercy: Race and Power in the Pacific War* (New York: Pantheon, 1986).

Duus, Masayo. *Tokyo Rose: Orphan of the Pacific* (Tokyo: Kodansha International, 1979).

Fearey, R. A. *The Occupation of Japan: Second Phase* (Westport, Ct.: Greenwood Press, 1950).

Feis, Herbert. *Contest Over Japan* (New York: Norton, 1967).

Fukutake, Tadayoshi. *The Japanese Social Structure: Its Evolution in the Modern Century,* translated by Ronald P. Dore (Tokyo: University of Tokyo Press, 1981).

Gayn, Mark. *Japan Diary* (New York: William Sloan Associates, 1948).

Goodman, Grant K. *The American Occupation of Japan: A Retrospective View* (Lawrence: Center for East Asian Studies, University of Kansas, 1968).

Hanami, Tadashi. *Labor Relations in Japan Today* (Tokyo: Kodansha International, 1979).

Hedges, Frank H. *What Do Americans Think About Japan?* (Tokyo: Senshin-sha, 1932).

Horing, Douglas G., ed. *Japan's Prospect* (Cambridge, Mass.: Harvard University Press, 1946).

Ienaga, Saburo. *The Pacific War, 1931–1945,* translated by Frank Baldwin (New York: Pantheon, 1978).

Irie, Akira. *Power and Culture: The Japanese-American War, 1941–1945* (Cambridge, Mass.: Harvard University Press, 1981).

James, D. Clayton. *Aristocrat in Uniform: The Years of MacArthur,* vols. 1–3 (New York: Houghton Mifflin, 1985).

Johnson, Chalmers. *An Instance of Treason: Ozaki Hotsumi and the Sorge Spy Ring* (Stanford, Calif.: Stanford University Press, 1964).

Kawai, Kazuo. *Japan's American Interlude* (Chicago: University of Chicago Press, 1960).

Koppes, Clayton R., and Gregory D. Black. *Hollywood Goes To War: How Politics, Profits and Propaganda Shaped World War II Movies* (Berkeley and Los Angeles: University of California Press, 1990).

Kosaka, Masataka. *A History of Postwar Japan* (Tokyo: Kodansha International, 1972).

Livingston, Jon, Joe Moore, and Felicia Oldfather, eds. *Postwar Japan: 1945 to the Present* (New York: Pantheon, 1973).

Martin, Edwin M. *The Allied Occupation of Japan* (Westport, Ct.: Greenwood Press, 1972).

Maruyama, Masao. *Nationalism in Post-War Japan* (Tokyo: Japan Institute of Pacific Relations, 1950).

Murakami, Hyoe. *Japan: The Years of Trial, 1919–1952* (Tokyo: Kodansha International, 1983).

Nishi, Toshio. *Unconditional Democracy: Education and Politics in Occupied Japan, 1945–1952* (Stanford: Hoover Institute Press, 1982).

Noble, Harold J. *What It Takes to Rule Japan* (New York: U.S. Camera Publishing, 1946).

Pacific War Research Society. *Japan's Longest Day* (Tokyo: Kodansha International, 1968).

Passin, Herbert. *Encounter with Japan* (New York: Kodansha International, 1982).

———. *Society and Education in Japan* (Tokyo: Kodansha International, 1982).

Perry, John Curtis. *Beneath the Eagle's Wings: Americans in Occupied Japan* (New York: Dodd, Mead, 1980).

Reischauer, Edwin O. *The United States and Japan* (Cambridge, Mass.: Harvard University Press, 1970).

Richie, Donald. *Where Are the Victors? A Novel of the Occupation of Japan* (Tokyo: Tuttle, 1956).

Sakamoto, Yoshikazu, and Robert E. Ward. *Democratizing Japan: Allied Occupation* (Honolulu: University of Hawaii Press, 1987).

Schaller, Michael. *The American Occupation of Japan: The Origin of the Cold War in Asia* (New York: Oxford University Press, 1985).

Sebalt, William J., and C. Nelson Spinks. *Japan: Prospects, Options and Opportunities* (Washington, D.C.: American Enterprise Institute for Public Policy Research, 1967).

Sheldon, Walter. *The Honorable Conquerors* (New York: Macmillan, 1965).

Shiroyama, Saburo. *War Criminal: The Life and Death of Hirota Koki,* translated by John Bester (Tokyo: Kodansha International, 1977).

Sigel, Frederick F. *Troubled Journey: From Pearl Harbor to Ronald Reagan* (New York: Hill & Wang, 1984).

Storry, Richard. *A History of Modern Japan* (Harmondsworth, U.K.: Penguin Books, 1983).

Takeda, Kiyoro. *The Dual Image of the Japanese Emperor* (London: Macmillan Education, 1988).

Terasaki, Gwen. *Bridge to the Sun* (Chapel Hill: University of North Carolina Press, 1957).

Textor, Robert B. *Failure in Japan: With Keystones for a Positive Policy* (New York: John Day, 1951).

Terkel, Studs. *The Good War: An Oral History of World War Two* (New York: Pantheon, 1984).

Wakefield, Harold. *New Path for Japan* (New York: Oxford University Press, 1948).

Ward, Robert E., and Yoshikazu Sakamoto, eds. *Democratizing Japan: The Allied Occupation* (Honolulu: University of Hawaii Press, 1987).

Welfield, John. *An Empire in Eclipse: Japan in the Postwar American Alliance System* (Atlantic Highlands, N.J.: Athlon Press, 1988).

Wilde, Harry Emerson. *Typhoon in Tokyo* (New York: Macmillan, 1954).

Williams, Justin, Sr. *Japan's Political Revolution Under MacArthur: A Participant's Account* (Atlanta: University of Georgia Press, 1979).

Willoughby, Charles A. *Shanghai Conspiracy: The Sorge Spy Ring* (New York: Dutton, 1952).

Yoshida, Shigeru. *The Yoshida Memoir,* translated by Kenichi Yoshida (Westport, Conn.: Greenwood Press, 1973).

2. Books on Media Propaganda

Brown, James A. C. *Techniques of Persuasion: From Propaganda to Brainwashing* (Baltimore, Md.: Penguin Books, 1963).

Coughlin, William. *Conquered Press* (Palo Alto, Calif.: Pacific Books, 1952).

Daugherty, William E., and Morris Janowitz. *Psychological Warfare Casebook* (Baltimore, Md.: Johns Hopkins University Press, 1958).

Furhammer, Leif, and Folke Isaksson. *Politics and Film,* translated by Kersti French (New York: Praeger, 1971).

Harley, Eugene. *World-Wide Influence of the Cinema: A Study of Official Censorship and the International Cultural Aspects of Motion Pictures* (Berkeley and Los Angeles: University of California Press, 1940).

Hovland, Carl, Arthur Lumbdaine, and Fred Sheffield. *Experiments on Mass Communication* (Princeton, N.J.: Princeton Unviersity Press, 1949).

Klapper, Joseph L. *Effects of Mass Communication,* edited by Paul F. Lazarsfeld and Bernard Berelson (Glencoe, Ill.: Free Press, 1960).

Leyda, Jay. *Films Beget Films: A Story of the Compilation Film* (New York: Hill & Wang, 1971).

Leynse, Humphrey W. *Selected Short Subjects: Studies in Cinema* (Dubuque, Ia.: Kendall/Hunt, 1974).

Short, K. R. M., ed. *Films and Radio Propaganda in World War II* (Knoxville: University of Tennessee Press, 1983).

3. Books on Japanese Cinema

Anderson, Joseph L., and Donald Richie. *The Japanese Film: Art and Industry* (expanded edition) (Princeton, N.J.: Princeton University Press, 1982).

Barrett, Gregory. *Archetypes in Japanese Film: The Sociopolitical and Religious Significance of the Principal Heroes and Heroines* (London and Toronto, Ont.: Associated University Presses, 1989).

Bock, Audie. *Japanese Film Directors* (Tokyo: Kodansha International, 1978).

Bordwell, David. *Ozu and the Poetics of Cinema* (Princeton, N.J.: Princeton University Press, 1988).

Burch, Noel. *To the Distant Observer: Form and Meaning in the Japanese Cinema*
(Berkeley and Los Angeles: University of California Press, 1979).

Burma, Ian. *Behind the Mask: On Sexual Demons, Sacred Mothers, Transvestites,
Gangsters, Drifters and Other Japanese Cultural Heroes* (New York: Pantheon,
1984).

Desser, David. *The Samurai Films of Akira Kurosawa* (Ann Arbor, Mich.: UMI Research Press, 1983).

———. *Eros Plus Massacre: The Japanese New Wave Cinema* (Bloomington: University of Indiana Press, 1987).

Kurosawa, Akira. *Something Like an Autobiography,* translated by Audie Bock (New
York: Alfred A. Knopf, 1982).

McDonald, Keiko I. *Cinema East: A Critical Study of Major Japanese Films* (London
and Toronto, Ont.: Associated University Presses, 1983).

Mellen, Joan. *Voices from Japanese Cinema* (New York: Liveright, 1975).

———. *The Waves at Genji's Door: Japan Through Its Cinema* (New York: Pantheon, 1976).

Richie, Donald. *The Japanese Movie: An Illustrated History* (Tokyo: Kodansha International, 1982).

———. *The Films of Akira Kurosawa* (Berkeley and Los Angeles: University of California Press, 1965).

———. *The Japanese Cinema: Film Style and National Character* (New York: Dou-
bleday, 1971).

———. *Ozu: His Life and Films* (Berkeley and Los Angeles: University of California
Press, 1974).

———. *Walkman, Manga and Society: Essays on Contemporary Japanese Culture*
(Tokyo: Kurihara Shoten, 1989).

———. *Japanese Cinema: An Introduction* (Hong Kong: Oxford University Press,
1990).

Sato, Tadao. *Currents in Japanese Cinema,* translated by Gregory Barrett (Tokyo:
Kodansha International, 1982).

Schrader, Paul. *Transcendental Style in Film: Ozu, Bresson and Dryer* (Berkeley and
Los Angeles: University of California Press, 1972).

Silver, Alain. *The Samurai Film* (New York: A. S. Barnes, 1977).

Svensson, Arn. *Japan* (New York: A. S. Barnes, 1971).

Tucker, Richard N. *Japan: Film Image* (London: Studio Vista, 1973).

4. Proceedings

The Occupation of Japan (proceedings of symposia on the Occupation of Japan held
at the MacArthur Memorial, Norfolk, Va):
    The Occupation of Japan and Its Legacy to the Postwar World (November 1975;
    publication date unlisted).
    The Occupation of Japan: Impact of Legal Reform (April 1977; publication date un-
    listed).
    The Occupation of Japan: Economic Policy and Reform (April 1978; publication
    date unlisted).
    The Occupation of Japan: Educational and Social Reform (October 1980; pub-
    lished in 1982).
    The Occupation of Japan: The International Context (October 1982; published in
    1984).
    The Occupation of Japan: Arts and Culture (October 1984; published in 1988).

5. Monographs and Film Series Program Catalogues

Kurosawa: A Retrospective (October–December 1981, Japan Society, New York).
A Tribute to Toshiro Mifune (March–April 1984, Japan Society, New York).
Mikio Naruse: A Master of the Japanese Cinema (September 1984, The Film Center,
    Art Institute of Chicago).
Japan At War (February–April 1987, Japan Society, New York). *Documentary Film
    Classics Produced by the United States Government* (Washington, D.C.: National
    Audiovisual Center, n.d.).

6. Articles on Occupation Policy

Allyn, John. "Motion Picture and Theatrical Censorship in Japan." *Waseda Journal
    of Asian Studies* 7 (1985), 14–31.
Barnet, Richard J. "Annals of Diplomacy: Alliance—I." *New Yorker* (October 10,
    1983), 53–105.
Boruff, John. "Under New Management: The Japanese Theater—The American
    Military Government Helps Stage a Reform." *Town and Country* (September
    1946), 161–163, 275–278, 280.
Daniels, Gordon. "Japanese Domestic Radio and Cinema Propaganda, 1937–1945:
    An Overview." *Historical Journal of Film, Radio and Television* 2(2) (1982), 115–
    132.
Dower, John. "Japanese Cinema Goes to War." *Japan Society Newsletter* 34(10)
    (June 1987), 2–9.
———. "Occupied Japan and the American Lake, 1945–1950," in Edward Fried-
    man and Mark Selden, eds., *America's Asia: Dissenting Essays on Asian-American
    Relations* (New York: Pantheon, 1971), 146–206.

Eto, Jun. "The American Occupation and Post-War Japanese Literature." *Studies of Comparative Literature* 38 (September 1980), 1–18.

Frost, Peter. "General MacArthur's Vision of Reform." *Journal of Japanese Studies* 10(2) (Summer 1984), 539–540.

Gluck, Carol. "Entangling Illusions: Japanese and American Views of the Occupation," in Warren I. Cohen, ed., *New Frontiers in American-East Asian Relations* (New York: Columbia University Press, 1983), 169–236.

Hirano, Kyoko. "The Banning of Japanese Period Films by the American Occupation." *Iconics* 1 (1987), 193–208.

———. "Film Policy," in Thomas W. Burkman, ed., *The Occupation of Japan: Arts and Culture* (Norfolk, Va.: MacArthur Memorial, 1988), 140–153.

———. "Japan," in William Luhr, ed., *World Cinema Since 1945* (New York: Ungar, 1987), 380–423.

———. "The Japanese Tragedy: Film Censorship and the American Occupation." *Radical History Review* 41 (May 1988), 67–92.

———. "The Japanese Tragedy: Film Censorship and the American Occupation," in Robert Sklar and Charles Musser, eds., *Resisting Images: Essays on Cinema and History* (Philadelphia: Temple University Press, 1990), 200–224.

Hopewell, Jim. "Press Censorship: A Case Study." *Argus* 6(6) (May 1971), 19–20, 58–64.

Kawakita, Toshio. "A Crisis of Kabuki and Its Revival Right After the World War II." *Waseda Journal of Asian Studies* 5 (1983), 32–42.

Mayo, Merlene. "Psychological Disarmament: American Wartime Planning for the Education and Re-education of Defeated Japan, 1943–1945," in Thomas W. Burkman, ed., *The Occupation of Japan: Educational and Social Reform* (Norfolk, Va.: MacArthur Memorial, 1982), 21–128.

———. "Americans in Occupied Japan: Some Reflectives on Economic Transformation." *Japan Society Newsletter* 30(9) (March 1983), 6–9.

Moore, Ray A. "The Occupation of Japan from British and Japanese Perspectives." *Journal of Japanese Studies* 10(1) (Winter 1984), 240–255.

Rubin, Jay. "From Wholesomeness to Decadence: The Censorship of Literature under the Allied Occupation." *Journal of Japanese Studies* 11(1) (Winter 1985), 71–103.

Squires, Vernon C. "Landing at Tokyo Bay: Two Letters from a Navy Lieutenant to His Wife Tell the Story of the Last Hours of WWII." *American Heritage* (August/September 1985), 24–33.

7. Unpublished Theses

Ewing, Charles Burgess. *An Analysis of Frank Capra's War Rhetoric in the "Why We Fight" Films* (Ph.D. thesis, Department of Speech, Washington State University, 1983).

Wilson, John Gaddis. *Public Information in Japan Under American Occupation: A Study of Democratization Effects through a Genesis of Public Expression* (thesis, University of Geneva, 1950).

Woodward, H. Mark. *The Formulation and Implementation of U.S. Feature Film Policy in Occupied Germany, 1945–1948*. (Ph.D. thesis, The University of Texas at Dallas, 1987).

8. Unpublished Bibliographies

Shulman, Frank Joseph. *Bibliography on the Allied Occupation of Japan: A Bibliography of Western-Language Publications from the Years 1970–1980* (preliminary edition) (University Park, Md.: East Asian Collection, McKeldin Library, University of Maryland, 1980).

Shulman, Frank Joseph. *Selected Listing of Books Published About the Allied Occupation of Japan Between 1982 and 1988* (University Park, Md.: East Asian Collection, McKeldin Library, University of Maryland, 1988).

9. Newspapers

New York Times
Japan Times
Stars and Stripes

B. Selected Bibliography in Japanese

1. Books on the Occupation Cultural Policy

Cohen, Theodore. *Nihon senryo kakumei* [*MacArthur, the Americans and the Rebirth of Japan*], vols. 1 and 2, translated by Masaomi Omae (Tokyo: TBS Britannica, 1983).

Eto, Jun. *Tozasareta gengo kukan: Senryo-gun no ken'etsu to Sengo no Nippon* [*Closed Space: The Occupation Forces' Censorship and Postwar Japan*] (Tokyo: Bengei shunju-sha, 1989).

Fukushima, Juro, ed. *1946 nen 9 gatsu GHQ no soshiki to jinji* [*GHQ's Organization and Personnel in September 1946*] (Tokyo: Gannan-do, 1984).

Goodman, Grant K. *Amerika no Nihon-Gannen, 1945–46* [*America's Japan: The First Year, 1945–46*] (Tokyo: Otsuki shoten, 1986).

Hatoyama, Ichiro. *Watashi no jijoden* [*My Autobiography*] (Tokyo: Kaizo-sha, 1951).

Iokibe, Makoto. *Beikoku no Nihon senryo seisaku* [*American Occupation Policy in Japan*], vols. 1 and 2 (Tokyo: Chuo koron-sha, 1985).

Kamata, Satoshi. *Hankotsu: Suzuki Tomin no shogai* [*Rebellious: The Life of Tomin Suzuki*] (Tokyo: Kodansha, 1989).

Moore, Ray A., ed. *Tenno ga baiburu o yonda hi* [*The Day the Emperor Read the Bible*] (Tokyo: Kodansha, 1982).

Nakazono, Eisuke. *Orinposu no hashira no kageni: Aru gaiko kan no tatakai* [*Behind the Pillars of Olympus: The Struggle of a Diplomat*], vols. 1 and 2 (Tokyo: Mainichi shimbun-sha, 1985).

NHK Hoso Bunka Chosa Kenkyu-jo. *GHQ bunsho ni yoru senryo-ki hoso-shi nenpyo* [*Chronicle of the Broadcast History under the Occuption According to GHQ Documents*] (Tokyo: NHK, 1987).

Sodei, Rinjiro. *Haikei Makkasaa gensui: Senryo-ka no Nipponjin no tegami* [*Dear General MacArthur: The Letters of Japanese under the Occupation*] (Tokyo: Otsuki shoten, 1985).

———, ed. *Sekai-shi no naka no Nihon senryo* [*The Occupation of Japan in World History*] (Tokyo: Nippon hyoron-sha, 1985).

———. *Senryo shita mono sareta mono* [*The Occupier and the Occupied*] (Tokyo: Simul Press, 1986).

Takakuwa, Kokichi. *Makkasaa no shinbun ken'etsu: Keisai kinshi sakujo ni natta shinbun kiji* [*MacArthur's Newspaper Censorship: Banned or Suppressed Newspaper Articles*] (Tokyo: Yomiuri shimbun-sha, 1979).

Takemae, Eiji. *GHQ* (Tokyo: Iwanami shinsho, 1983).

Torio, Tae. *Watashi no ashioto ga kikoeru: Madamu Torio no kaiso* [*I Hear My Own Steps: The Memoirs of Madame Torio*] (Tokyo: Bungei shunju-sha, 1985).

Woodard, William P. *Tenno to Shinto* [*The Allied Occupation of Japan 1945–1952 and Japanese Religions*], translated by Yoshiya Abe (Tokyo: Simul Press, 1988).

2. Books on Cinema Covering the Occupation Period

Akasegawa, Hayato. *Eiga-kan o deruto yakeato datta* [*Outside the Movie Theater, There Was a Burnt Field*] (Tokyo: Soshi-sha, 1982).

Atsuta, Yuharu, and Shigehiko Hasumi. *Ozu Yasujiro monogatari* [*The Story of Yasujiro Ozu*] (Tokyo: Chikuma shobo, 1989).

Fujita, Motoharu. *Nihon eiga gendai-shi* [*Modern History of Japanese Cinema*] (Tokyo: Kashin-sha, 1977).

———. *Eiga sakka Itami Mansaku* [*Film Artist Mansaku Itami*] (Tokyo: Chikuma shobo, 1985).

Furuya, Tsunamasa. *Watashi dake no eiga-shi* [*My Own Film History*] (Tokyo: Kurashi no techo-sha, 1978).

Iijima, Tadashi. *Nihon eiga-shi* [*Japanese Cinema History*], vol. 2 (Tokyo: Hakusui-sha, 1955).

———. *Senchu eiga shi: Shiki* [*Wartime Film History: Personal Note*] (Tokyo: MG shuppan, 1984).

Inomata, Katsuhito. *Nihon eiga meisaku zenshi: Senzen-hen* [*Comprehensive History of Japanese Classic Film: Prewar Period*] (Tokyo: Shakai shiso-sha, 1974).

Ito, Masaichi. *Kiri to toride: Toho daisogi no kiroku* [*Fog and Fortress: The Record of the Great Toho Strike*] (Tokyo: Rengo tsushin-sha, n.d.).

Iwasaki, Akira. *Senryo sareta sukuriin* [*The Occupied Screen*] (Tokyo: Shin Nihon shuppan-sha, 1975).

Kamei, Fumio. *Tatakau eiga: Dokyumentarisuto no Showa-shi* [*Films at the Front: The Showa History of a Documentarist*] (Tokyo: Iwanami shinsho, 1989).

Kamei, Shunsuke. *Saakasu ga kita: Amerika taishu bunka oboegaki* [*Here Comes the Circus: A Note on American Popular Culture*] (Tokyo: Tokyo Daigaku shuppan, 1976).

Kido, Shiro. *Nihon eiga den: Eiga seisakusha no kiroku* [*The Story of Japanese Film: A Movie Producer's Record*] (Tokyo: Bungei shunju-sha, 1956).

Kimura, Takeo. *Waga honseki-chi wa eiga-kan* [*My Address Was a Movie Theater*] (Tokyo: Shunju-sha, 1986).

Kishi, Matsuo. *Jinbutsu: Nihon eiga-shi* [*Personalities: Japanese Film History*] (Tokyo: Dabiddo-sha, 1970).

Kitagawa, Tetsuya, ed. *Nippon no dokuritsu puro* [*Japanese Independent Productions*] (Tokyo: Eiga "Wakamono tachi" zenkoku joen iinkai, 1970).

Kokusai Bunka Kaikan, ed. *Nichibei kankei no kenkyu* [*The Study of the Japan-America Relationship*], vols. 1 and 2 (Tokyo: Tokyo Daigaku shuppan, 1968, 1970).

Kurosawa, Akira. *Gama no abura: Jiden no yo na mono* [*The Oil of the Toad: Something Like an Autobiography*] (Tokyo: Iwanami shoten, 1984).

Makino, Masahiro. *Eiga tosei* [*Film Life*], vols. 1 and 2 (Tokyo: Heibon-sha, 1977).

Nagata, Masaichi. *Eiga jigakyo* [*Film's Personal Scroll*] (Tokyo: Heibon shuppan, 1957).

Noda, Shinkichi. *Nihon dokyumentarii eiga zenshi* [*Comprehensive History of Japanese Documentary Film*] (Tokyo: Shakai shiso-sha, 1984).

Oe, Kenzaburo, ed. *Itami Mansaku essei-shu* [*Essays of Mansaku Itami*] (Tokyo: Chikuma shobo, 1971).

Oshima, Nagisa. *Taikenteki sengo eizo-ron* [*A Theory of the Postwar Film Image Based on Personal Experience*] (Tokyo: Asahi shimbun-sha, 1975).

Oshima, Nagisa, Kozaburo Yoshimura, Katsumi Nishikawa, Toshiyuki Yamane, Masanori Kakei, Kazuo Inoue, and Kazuo Kuroki. *Nihon eiga o yomu: Paionia tachi no isan* [*Reading Japanese Cinema: Heritage of the Pioneers*] (Tokyo: Dagguereo Press, 1984).

Ozaki, Hotsuki, ed. *Purojusaa jinsei: Fujimoto Naozane eiga ni kakeru* [*A Producer's Life: Naozane Fujimoto Challenges Film*] (Tokyo: Toho shuppan, 1981).

Saeki, Shoichi. *Uchinaru Amerika sotonaru Amerika* [*America Inside and Outside*] (Tokyo: Shincho-sha, 1971).

Sato, Tadao. *Nippon kiroku eizo-shi* [*History of Japanese Documentary Film Image*] (Tokyo: Hyoron-sha, 1977).

———. *Obake entotsu no sekai: Eiga kantoku Gosho Heinosuke no hito to shigoto* [*The World of Strange Chimneys: The Personality and Work of Film Director Heinosuke Gosho*] (Tokyo: Noberu shobo, 1977).

———. *Kinoshita Keisuke no eiga* [*The Films of Keisuke Kinoshita*] (Tokyo: Haga shoten, 1984).

———. *Kinema to hosei: Nicchu eiga zenshi* [*Cinema and Bombardment: Prehistory of Japanese and Chinese Cinema*] (Tokyo: Libro Port, 1985).

———. *Tokii no jidai* [*The Period of the Talkie*] (Tokyo: Iwanami shoten, 1986).

Shindo, Kaneto. *Aru eiga kantoku no shogai: Mizoguchi Kenji no kiroku* [*The Life of a Director: The Record of Kenji Mizoguchi*] (Tokyo: Eijin-sha, 1975).

———. *Shosetsu Tanaka Kinuyo* [*A Novel: Kinuyo Tanaka*] (Tokyo: Yomiuri shimbun-sha, 1983).

———. *Tsuihosha-tachi: Eiga no reddo paaji* [*The Expelled: The Red Purge in Film*] (Tokyo: Iwanami shoten, 1983).

Shinoda, Masahiro. *Yami no naka no ansoku* [*A Rest in the Darkness*] (Tokyo: Film Art-sha, 1979).

Takahashi, Osamu. *Kenrantaru kagee: Ozu Yasujiro* [*Brilliant Shadow Painting: Yasujiro Ozu*] (Tokyo: Bungei shunju-sha, 1982).

Takamine, Hideko. *Watashi no tosei nikki* [*My Professional Diary*], vols. 1 and 2 (Tokyo: Asahi shimbun-sha, 1980).

Tanaka, Junichiro. *Nihon eiga hattatsu-shi* [*The History of the Development of Japanese Cinema*], vol. 3 (Tokyo: Chuo koron-sha, 1976).

Tayama, Rikiya. *Waga taikenteki Nihon goraku eiga shi: Senzen-hen* [*Japanese Entertainment Film History Based on Personal Experience*] (Tokyo: Shakai shiso-sha, 1980).

Uekusa, Keinosuke. *Waga seishun no Kurosawa Akira* [*Akira Kurosawa of My Youth*] (Tokyo: Bungei shunju-sha, 1985).

Uriu, Tadao. *Eigateki seishin no keifu* [*The Lineage of the Film Spirit*] (Tokyo: Getsuyo shobo, 1947).

———. *Sengo Nihon eiga shoshi* [*A Short History of Postwar Japanese Cinema*] (Tokyo: Hosei Daigaku shuppan-kyoku, 1981).

Ushihara, Kiyohiko. *Kiyohiko eiga-fu 50-nen* [*50 Years of Kiyohiko's Film Record*] (Tokyo: Kagamiura shobo, 1968).

Yamada, Izuzu. *Eiga to tomoni* [*Together with Film*] (Tokyo: Sanichi shobo, 1953).

Yamada, Kazuo. *Nihon eiga no gendai-shi* [*The Modern History of Japanese Cinema*] (Tokyo: Shin Nihon shuppan-sha, 1970).

———. *Nihon eiga no 80-nen* [*80 Years of Japanese Cinema*] (Tokyo: Issei-sha, 1976).

Yamaguchi, Yoshiko, and Sakuya Fujiwara. *Ri Koran: Watakushi no hansho* [*Li Hsiang-lan: My Half Life*] (Tokyo: Shincho-sha, 1987).

Yamamoto, Kikuo. *Nihon eiga ni okeru gaikoku eiga no eikyo* [*The Influence of Foreign Films on Japanese Cinema*] (Tokyo: Waseda Daigaku shuppan, 1983).

Yoda, Yoshikata. *Mizoguchi Kenji no hito to geijutsu* [*Kenji Mizoguchi: The Man and His Art*] (Tokyo: Tabata shoten, 1970).

Yoshida, Chieo. *Mo hitotsu no eiga-shi: Katsuben no jidai* [*Another Film History: The Age of Katsuben*] (Tokyo: Jiji tsushin-sha, 1978).

Yuki, Ichiro. *Jitsuroku: Kamata koshinkyoku* [*Document: The Kamata March*] (Tokyo: KK Book, 1985).

3. Monographs and Newsletters

Film Center (Tokyo: National Film Center):
   (# unknown) Japanese Films Under the Occupation (1973)
   #16 Kenji Mizoguchi (1973)
   #17 Choko Iida (1973)
   #21 Heinosuke Gosho (1974)
   #32 Yasujiro Ozu (1976)
   #35 Teinosuke Kinugasa (1976)
   #40 Daisuke Ito (1977)
   #42 1930s–1940s (1977)
   #49 Shozo Makino (1978)
   #52 Tomotaka Tasaka (1979)
   #53 Kazuo Hasegawa (1979)
   #62 Kozaburo Yoshimura and Kaneto Shindo (1980)
   #74 Fifty Years of Toho Film (1982)
   #80 Tadashi Imai (1983)
   #82 Kazuo Miyakawa (1984)

Ishikawa, Masako. *Konakatta no wa gunkan dake: Toho sogi kenkyu shiryo-shu* [*Everything Came but the Battleships: The Record of the Toho Strikes*], vols. 1–5 (Tokyo: Masako Ishikawa, 1976–1980).

Sekai no eiga sakka [*Film Directors of the World*] (Tokyo: Kinema Jumpo-sha):
   #3 Akira Kurosawa (1970)
   #6 Nagisa Oshima (1970)
   #10 Masahiro Shinoda/Yoshishige Yoshida (1971)

Senryo-shi kenkyu-kai News [*Newsletter of the Japan Association for the Study of the History of the Occupation*]

Toei eiga 30-nen [*30 Years of Toei Film*] (Tokyo: Toei, 1981).

Toho 30-nen-shi [*30 Years of Toho*] (Tokyo: Toho shuppan, 1962).

Toho 50-nen-shi [*50 Years of Toho*] (Tokyo: Toho shuppan, 1982).

Towa eiga no ayumi [*The History of Towa Film*] (Tokyo: Towa Film, 1955).

4. Film Encyclopedias

Eiga engeki jiten [*Encyclopedia of Film and Theater*] (Tokyo: Jiji tsushin-sha, 1947).

Eiga no jiten [*Encyclopedia of Film*] (Tokyo: Godo shuppan, 1978).

Gendai eiga jiten [*Modern Film Encyclopedia*] (Tokyo: Bijutsu shuppan-sha, 1973).

Nihon eiga haiyu zenshu: Danyu-hen [*Encyclopedia of Japanese Actors*] (Tokyo: Kinema Jumpo-sha, 1979).

Nihon eiga kantoku zenshu [*Encyclopedia of Japanese Directors*] (Tokyo: Kinema Jumpo-sha, 1976).

Nihon eiga sakuhin zenshu [*Encyclopedia of Japanese Films*] (Tokyo: Kinema Jumpo-sha, 1971).

Nihon eiga haiyu zenshu: Joyu-hen [*Encyclopedia of Japanese Actresses*] (Tokyo: Kinema Jumpo-sha, 1980).

Sekai eiga jiken jimbutsu jiten [*Encyclopedia of World Film Events and Personalities*] (Tokyo: Kinema Jumpo-sha, 1970).

Sekai eiga kiroku zenshu [*Encyclopedia of World Films*] (Tokyo: Kinema Jumpo-sha, 1973).

5. Journals

Film magazines (published monthly, semimonthly, or bimonthly):

Cinema Jidai	*Eiga-jin*	*Eiga Sokuho*
Cinemagraphic	*Eiga Junkan*	*Eiga Star*
Cine-Front	*Eiga Kageki*	*Eiga Tenbo*
Eiga	*Eiga Kansho*	*Eiga Times*
Eiga and Eiga	*Eiga Kikan*	*Eiga to Bungaku*
Eiga Bijutsu	*Eiga Kurabu*	*Eiga to Yomimono*
Eiga Bunka	*Eiga Kyoiku Shiryo*	*Eiga Yomimono*
Eiga Bunko	*Eiga Kyoshitsu*	*Ernie Pyle Theater*
Eiga Circle	*Eiga Monogatari*	*Eiga-shi Kenkyu*
Eiga Digest	*Eiga News*	*Image Forum*
Eiga Engeki Shimpo	*Eiga no Tomo*	*Iwanami Hall*
Eiga Fan	*Eiga Note*	*Kinema Gaho*
Eiga Gakko Tomo no Kai	*Eiga Romance*	*Kinema Gurafu*
	Eiga Sakka	*Kinema Gurupu*
Eiga Geijutsu	*Eiga Seisaku*	*Kinema Jumpo*
Eiga Gijutsu	*Eiga Sekai*	*Lumière*
Eiga Goraku	*Eiga Shonen*	*Movie*
Eiga Gurafu	*Eiga Shudan*	*Movie Text*
Eiga Hyoron	*Eiga Shunju*	*Shin Eiga*
Eiga Jiho	*Eiga Snapp*	

Film periodicals (published weekly or semiweekly):

Cinema Guide
Cinema Herald
Cinema MTM
    Shinpo
Cinema News
Cinema Shimbun
Cinema Times
Eiga
Eiga ABC
Eiga-gai
Eiga Geijutsu News
Eiga Geino Times
Eiga Gorakuban
Eiga Hochi
Eiga Joho
Eiga Jumpo
Eiga Kantoku
Eiga Kenkyu Geppo
Eiga Magazine
Eiga News

Eiga Shimpo
Eiga Shuho
Eiga Stage
Eiga Star
Eiga Times
Eiga to Bunka
Eiga to Butai
Eiga to Engeki
Eiga to Spotsu
Eiga Tsushin
Eiga Weekly
Eigyo Shashin
    Shimbun
Eiken Geppo
Eiken Tsushin
Eikyo
Eiren Kaiho
Eiren Times
Eisha
Eiso

Goraku-gai
Hachioji Eiga Weekly
Hokuei Cinema
    Guide
Kinema News
Movie Fan
Movie Text
Movie Times
MPEA Weekly
Screen Digest
Screen Guide
Screen Himeji
Screen News
Screen Pic
Screen Review
Screen Shinsekai
Screen Sports
Screen Stage
Screen Times
Screen Vinus

Academic periodical:
Eizo-gaku

General magazines:
Bungei Shunju
Hoseki
Sekai

6. Newspapers

Asahi Shimbun
Mainichi Shimbun

Nikkan Mezamashi
    Tsushin

Tokyo Times
Yomiuri Shimbun

7. Articles

Adachi, Kazu. "Nihon Eizo-shi: Purojusa gunyu-den [The History of Japanese Film Images: The Group Portrait of Producers]" series. *Kinema Jumpo* (May-I, 1988–December-I, 1989).

Akatsuka, Yasuo. "Issatsu no 'suminuri' ongaka kyokasha kara" [From a "Blackened" Textbook], *Senryoshi Kenkyukai News* 62 (June 1985), 2–3.

Anonymous. "Eiga-kai kyutenkai no GHQ seisaku [The Drastic Change in GHQ Policy Toward the Film Industry]." *Yomiuri Shimbun,* September 20, 1982.

Aoyama, Toshimi. "Eiga ken'etsu no omoide [Memoirs of Film Censorship], no. 1." *Eiga-shi Kenkyu* 21 (1986), 1–12.

Arase, Yutaka. "Senryo-ki ni okeru hodo hyogen no henyo [Changes in the Expression of News under the Occupation]." *Shimbun Kenkyujo Kiyo* 31 (1983), 145–158.

Chiba, Yasuki. "Boku no sakuhin ni okeru 'ie' ni tsuite [On the "Family" in My Films]." *Kinema Jumpo* 34 (May-II, 1948), 16–17.

Conde, David. "Nihon eiga no senryo-shi [The History of Japanese Cinema under the Occupation]." *Sekai* (August 1965), 248–255.

Gayn, Mark. "Horibata no don to daigashi tachi [The Don Beside the Imperial Palace and His Followers]," translated by Toyoo Kuga. *Bungei Shunju* (January 1978), 198–214.

Harada, Yasushi. "Senryo-ka no Nihon eiga ringo-en no fukko: Sasaki Yasushi den [The Japanese Cinema under the Occupation and the Revival of the Apple Orchard: On Yasushi Sasaki]." *Eiga-shi Kenkyu* 1 (1973), 49–56.

Ikeda, Yoshinobu. "Senryo seisaku no nisan [A Few Things about the Occupation Policy]." *Eiga Jiho* (November 1953), 22–23.

Itami, Mansaku. "Seiji ni kansuru zuiso [An Essay on Politics]." *Kinema Jumpo* (June 1946), 24–25.

———. "Senso sekininsha no mondai [The Problem of Those Responsible for the War]." *Eiga Shunju* (August 1946), reprinted in Kenzaburo Oe, ed., *Itami Mansaku Essei-shu* [*Essays of Mansaku Itami*] (Tokyo: Chikuma shubo, 1971), 75–85.

Ito, Takeo. "Sengo Nippon eiga no koryu to Toho sogi [Prosperity of Postwar Japanese Film and the Toho Strikes]," in Saburo Ienaga, ed., *Showa no sengo-shi: Senryo to saisei* [*Postwar History of the Showa Era: Occupation and Revival*] (Tokyo: Yubun-sha, 1976), 223–239.

———. "Toho sogi te nanda? [What Are the Toho Strikes?]," in Chiba University Humanities Department, ed., *Sengo Nippon no shakai to rodo: Shuyo rodo sogi (1945–1960) o chushin ni* [*Postwar Japanese Society and Labor: Around the Major Labor Strikes (1945–1960)*] (Chiba: Chiba Daigaku, 1983), 12–13.

———. "Nippon eiga no ogon jidai o maneita hitobito [People Who Invited the Golden Age of Japanese Cinema]." *Waseda Gakuho* (May 1984), 26–29.

Iwasaki, Akira. "Toho Sogi [The Toho Strikes]," in Masaji Shimoda, ed., *Dokyumento: Showa 50-nen-shi: Senryo-ka no Nippon* [*Document: The 50-Year History of the Showa Era: Japan under the Occupation*] (Tokyo: Heibon-sha, 1974), 141–171.

Kamei, Fumio. "Botsu ni natta 'Tatakau heitai' [The Suppressed 'Soldiers at the Front']," in *Ichioku-nin no Showa-shi* [*The History of the Showa Era of Ten Million*] (Mainichi shimbun-sha, n.d.), 120–123.

————. "Mushoku tomei eiga-ron: Eiga to seiji ni tsuite [Transparent Film Theory: On Film and Politics]." *Kinema Jumpo* 67 (October-I, 1946), 20–21.

————. "Tomato to eiga: Aru eiga enshutsuka o shibou suru seinen e no tegami [Tomato and Film: A Letter to a Young Man Aspiring to Become a Film Director]." *Kinema Jumpo* (April-I, 1948).

————. "Watashi no 'Senso to heiwa' [My 'War and Peace']." *Iwanami Hall* (February 1972), 10–11.

Kitagawa, Fuyuhiko. "Hisaita Eijiro ron [On Eijiro Hisaita]." *Eiga Shunju* (February 1947).

Komatsu, Hideo. "Sengo eiga shiriizu [Postwar Film Series]," nos. 1 and 2. *Tokyo-eki* (n.d.), 20–21, 66–67.

Kumanomido, Sadamu. "Genka no Nihon eiga-kai ni atou [Giving to the Present Japanese Film Industry]." *Eiga Hyoron* 1(2) (January–February 1944), 3.

Kusakabe, Kyushiro. "Jitsuroku sengo Nihon eiga-shi: Hito to jiken to [The Documents of the Postwar Japanese Film History: People and Events]," nos. 1–10. *Hoseki* (1982).

Matsuura, Sozo. "Senryo-ka no genron dan'atsu [Media Oppression under the Occupation]," in Ryusuke Sagara, ed., *Dokyumento: Showa-shi [Document: Showa Era History]* (Tokyo: Heibon-sha, 1975), 258–266.

————. "Ken'etsu seido to sogo zasshi no fukkatsu [The Censorship System and Revival of General Magazines]," in Saburo Ienaga, ed., *Showa no sengo-shi: Senryo to saisei [Postwar History of the Showa Era: Occupation and Revival]* (Tokyo: Yubun-sha, 1976), 265–279.

Miyajima, Yoshio. "Miyajima Yoshio Kaiso-roku: Satsuei kantoku 50-nen [Yoshio Miyajima's Memoirs: 50 Years of a Cinematographer]" series. *Kinema Jumpo* (December-II, 1983–October-I, 1987).

Nambu, Kyoichiro. "Genba sengo-shi: Goshippu de tsuzuru katsudoya no ayumi [Postwar History on the Spot: The Movement of Movie-makers Written with Gossip]," nos. 1–6. *Tokyo Times* (March 12–16, 1972), 15 (all parts).

Nishimura, Sey. "Senryo-ka no Nippon [Japan under the Occupation]." *Nihon Iji Shimpo* 3128 (April 1984), 59–68.

Ogawa, Toru. "Shisetsu: Sengo Nihon eiga-shi [Private Theory: The History of Postwar Japanese Cinema]." *Eiga Geijutsu* 332 (February 1980), 1–8.

Oshima, Nagisa. "Eiga ni totte senso towa nanika [What Is War For Cinema?]," in *Nihon eiga o yomu [Reading Japanese Cinema]* (Tokyo: Daguerreo Press, 1984), 13–38.

Ozaki, Hotsuki. "Sei-fuzoku no kaiho [The Liberation of Sexual Customs]," in Saburo Ienaga, ed., *Showa no sengo-shi: Senryo to saisei [Postwar History of the Showa Era: Occupation and Revival]* (Tokyo: Yubun-sha, 1976).

Sakaguchi, Ango. "Nichi-ei no omoide [My Memories of Nichi-ei]." *Kinema Jumpo* 10 (February-I, 1947), 25.

Sawamura, Tsutomu. "Shinario zuiso: Eiga no hyogen ni kansuru hansei [Essay on Scenario: Reflection Concerning Filmic Expression]." *Eiga Hyoron* 2(1) (January–February 1944), 3–11.

Shimizu, Akira. "20.9.22 kara 23.8.19 made: Senryo-ka no eiga-kai no kiroku [From September 22, 1945, to August 19, 1948: The Record of the Film Industry under the Occupation]." *Film Center* (1973), 9–11.

Shishi, Bunroku. "Seppun [Kissing]." *Asahi Shimbun* (August 1, 1948), 4.

Tada, Michitaro. "Kurosawa Akira [Akira Kurosawa]," in Ryusuke Sagara, ed., *Dokyumento: Showa-shi* [*Document: Showa Era History*] (Tokyo: Heibon-sha, 1975).

Tanaka, Jun'ichiro. "Nihon eiga sengo-shi [Japanese Postwar Cinema History]." *Kinema Jumpo* (October-III, 1964), 48–57.

Togawa, Naoki (a.k.a. Naosa). "Waga seishun ni kuinashi [No Regrets for Our Youth]." *Eiga Hyoron* 64(1) (February 1947), 29–33.

———. "Waga kuni no projusaa seido [The Producer System of Our Country]." *Eiga Hyoron* 25 (September 1950), 8–15.

Ueno, Ichiro. "Meijin Aoyama Toshimi san [Master Toshimi Aoyama]," in *Towa eiga no ayumi* [*The History of Towa Film*] (Tokyo: Towa Film, 1955), 244–245.

Yahiro, Fuji. "Jidaieiga no ki jusan-nen [The Record of Period Films for Thirteen Years]." *Kinema Jumpo* (March-I, 1964), 40–43.

Yamamoto, Akira. "Kasutori zasshi [Kasutori Magazines]," in Saburo Ienaga, ed., *Showa no sengo-shi: Senryo to saisei* [*Postwar History of the Showa Era: Occupation and Revival*] (Tokyo: Yubun-sha, 1976), 241–264.

Yamamoto, Kajiro. "Katsudo-ya bifun-roku [The Record of the Slight Anger of a Movie-Maker]." *Bungei Shunju* (June 1952), 188–193.

Yamane, Sadao. "Sengo taishu eiga no nagare [Tendencies of the Postwar Popular Films]." *Bijutsu Techo* (December 1975), 218–219.

Yoshiya, So. "Senryo seisaku to Toho sogi [The Occupation Policy and Toho Strikes]." *Eiga Geijutsu* 312 (August–September 1976), 35–38.

8. Interviews

Fujita, Susumu. Interviewed by Hauro Mizuno. *Kinema Jumpo* 906 and 908 (March-II and April-II, 1982), 115–120, 112–118.

Ito, Takeo. Interviewed by Shigehiko Hasumi. *Lumière* 4 (Summer 1986), 82–91.

Makino, Masahiro. Interviewed by Kenji Iwamoto, Tomonori Saeki, and Atsuko Saito. *Image Forum* 46 (July 1984) 39–60.

Miyajima, Yoshio. Interviewed by Takeshi Yamaguchi. *Kinema Jumpo* (December-II, 1983), 113–115.

Shibata, Masaru. Interviewed by Kenji Iwamoto and Tomonori Saeki. *Image Forum* 42 (March 1984), 124–134.

Tsukioka, Yumeji. Interviewed by Haruo Mizuno. *Kinema Jumpo* 903 (February-I, 1985), 89–96.

Watanabe, Tetsuzo. Interviewed by the editors. *Kinema Jumpo* 30 (March-III, 1948), 20.

9. Discussions

Anonymous discussion, "Senryo-ka no eiga gyosei no uchimaku [The Inside Story of the Film Administration under the Occupation]." *Eiga Jiho* (November 1953), 15–21.

Aoyagi, Nobuo, Naozane Fujimoto, Sojuro Futaba, Tsuneo Hazumi, Shiro Kaga, Shogoro Motoki, and Chiyota Shimizu. "Purojusaa wa nani o kangaete iruka [What Are Producers Thinking?]." *Kinema Jumpo* 41 (December-I, 1950), 18–23.

Ashida, Hitoshi, Masaichi Nagata, and Hideo Shibusawa. "Minshu kakumei e no hitoyaku: Shin kenpo happu kinen eiga o meguru zadankai [One Role for Democratic Revolution: Discussion on the Films Commemorating the Proclamation of the New Constitution]." *Kinema Jumpo* 121 (April 1947), 8–11.

Conde, David, Naozane Fujimoto, and Akira Iwasaki. "Shidoshita Nihon eiga to no saikai: GHQ shodai eiga engeki hancho Debiddo Konde shi to kataru [The Reunion with Japanese Cinema That I Led: Discussion with Mr. Conde, the First Chief of the Motion Picture and Theatrical Branch of GHQ]." *Kinema Jumpo* (November-III, 1964), 26–30.

Imamura, Miyoo, Kozo Kubo, Keiji Matsuzaki, and Itsuo Oi. "Kongo no purojusaa mondai o kento suru zadankai [The Discussion of the Problem of the Producers from Now On]." *Eiga Hyoron* 4(1) (February 1947), 8–14.

Kamei, Fumio, Tetsuro Hatano, Sumumu Kosaka, and Toru Ogawa. "Kamei Fumio no kataru hiroku: Senchu sengo eiga-shi [Secret History Told by Fumio Kamei: Wartime and Postwar Film History]." *Eiga Geijutsu* 24(3) (July–August 1976), 78–89.

Kikuchi, Hiroshi, and Yusuke Tsurumi. "Eiga hodan [Free Discussion on Cinema]." *Eiga Hyoron* (October–November 1944), 10–13.

Kurosawa, Akira, Toru Takemitsu, and Nagaharu Yodokawa. "Kurosawa Akira no sekai [The World of Akira Kurosawa]." *Sekai* (January 1984), 269–295.

Naruse, Mikio, Shin Saburi, Minoru Shibuya, and Kozaburo Yoshimura. "Gendai Nihon fuzoku o kataru [Talking about Modern Japanese Customs]." *Kinema Jumpo* 29 (December-I, 1951), 32–38.

GLOSSARY OF JAPANESE WORDS

aite opponent
benshi narrator for silent films
bunka eiga culture films
bushido the code of samurai rules
dai-sangokujin third-nationality people
Eiga Haikyu Kosha Film Distribution Corporation
Eiga-ho Film Law
Eiga Kosha Film Corporation
Eirin Film Ethics Regulation Control Committee
ero-gro erotic-grotesque
geta wooden sandals

go unit of measure equal to about 0.18 liter; magazine issue
gunbatsu military clique
gunshin "military gods"; heroic military figures
harakiri ritual suicide by disembowelment
jiji eiga current films
Joho-kyoku Information Bureau
kairan-ban circulation board
kamikaze literally "divine wind": name applied to military suicide missions
kasutori zasshi "dregs magazines": sensationalistic pulp magazines,

named after a cheap beverage made
from sake dregs

katsuben narrator for silent films

keiko eiga tendency films

kumi group

miai arranged meetings for
prospective marriage partners

Monbu-sho Ministry of Education

Naimu-sho Ministry of Interior Affairs

Nichi-ei-en Japan Movie and Theater
Workers Union

Nikutai-ha The so-called Flesh School
literary movement

Nisei second-generation
Japanese-American

oyabun-kobun boss-follower
(relationship)

pan-pan streetwalker

samurai warrior

seisan kanri union takeover of
management administration

tachimawari swordplay

teki enemy

tonari-gumi neighborhood groups

yakuza traditional gangsters

zaibatsu family-owned conglomerate

INDEX OF FILMS

INDEX OF NAMES